Globalization and Language in the Spanish-Speaking World

Language and Globalization

Series Editors: **Sue Wright**, University of Portsmouth, UK; and **Helen Kelly-Holmes**, University of Limerick, Ireland.

In the context of current political and social developments, where the national group is not so clearly defined and delineated, the state language not so clearly dominant in every domain, and cross-border flows and transfers affect more than a small elite, new patterns of language use will develop. The series aims to provide a framework for reporting on and analysing the linguistic outcomes of globalization and localization.

Titles include:

David Block
MULTILINGUAL IDENTITIES IN A GLOBAL CITY
London Stories

Julian Edge (*editor*)
(RE)LOCATING TESOL IN AN AGE OF EMPIRE

Clare Mar-Molinero and Patrick Stevenson (*editors*)
LANGUAGE IDEOLOGIES, POLICIES AND PRACTICES
Language and the Future of Europe

Clare Mar-Molinero and Miranda Stewart (*editors*)
GLOBALIZATION AND LANGUAGE IN THE SPANISH-SPEAKING WORLD
Macro and Micro Perspectives

Ulrike Hanna Meinhof and Dariusz Galasinski
THE LANGUAGE OF BELONGING

Forthcoming titles:

Roxy Harris
NEW ETHNICITIES AND LANGUAGE USE

Leigh Oakes and Jane Warren
LANGUAGE, CITIZENSHIP AND IDENTITY IN QUEBEC

Colin Williams
LINGUISTIC MINORITIES IN DEMOCRATIC CONTEXT

Language and Globalization
Series Standing Order ISBN 1–4039–9731–4
(outside North America only)

You can receive future titles in this series as they are published by placing a standing order. Please contact your bookseller or, in case of difficulty, write to us at the address below with your name and address, the title of the series and the ISBN quoted above.

Customer Services Department, Macmillan Distribution Ltd, Houndmills, Basingstoke, Hampshire RG21 6XS, England

Globalization and Language in the Spanish-Speaking World

Macro and Micro Perspectives

Edited by

Clare Mar-Molinero
University of Southampton

and

Miranda Stewart
University of Strathclyde

First published 2006 by
PALGRAVE MACMILLAN
Houndmills, Basingstoke, Hampshire RG21 6XS and
175 Fifth Avenue, New York, N.Y. 10010
Companies and representatives throughout the world.

PALGRAVE MACMILLAN is the global academic imprint of the Palgrave Macmillan division of St. Martin's Press, LLC and of Palgrave Macmillan Ltd. Macmillan® is a registered trademark in the United States, United Kingdom and other countries. Palgrave is a registered trademark in the European Union and other countries.

ISBN-13: 978–0–230–00018–6

This book is printed on paper suitable for recycling and made from fully managed and sustained forest sources.

A catalogue record for this book is available from the British Library.

Library of Congress Cataloging-in-Publication Data

Globalization and language in the Spanish-speaking world : macro and micro perspectives / edited by Clare Mar-Molinero & Miranda Stewart.
  p. cm.—(Language and globalization)
Includes bibliographical references and index.

I. Mar-Molinero, Clare, 1948– II. Stewart, Miranda, 1954– III. Series.

PC4074.7.G66 2006
460.9—dc22   2006041638

10 9 8 7 6 5 4 3
15 14 13 12 11 10 09 08

Transferred To Digital Printing 2011

Contents

List of Tables, Figures and Maps   vii

Acknowledgements   ix

Notes on the Contributors   x

1   Introduction   1
    Clare Mar-Molinero and Miranda Stewart

2   Forces of Globalization in the Spanish-Speaking World:
    Linguistic Imperialism or Grassroots Adaptation   8
    Clare Mar-Molinero

3   US Latinos, *la hispanofonía* and the Language Ideologies
    of High Modernity   27
    José del Valle

4   Language Conflict and the Micro–Macro Link in the
    Spanish-Speaking World   47
    Rainer Enrique Hamel

5   Spanish/English Interaction in US Hispanic Heritage
    Learners' Writing   76
    Marta Fairclough

6   Andean Spanish and the Spanish of Lima: Linguistic
    Variation and Change in a Contact Situation   94
    Carol A. Klee and Rocío Caravedo

7   Spanish as L2 on the Dominican/Haitian Border
    and Universal Processes of Acquisition   114
    Luis A. Ortiz López

8   Whose Story Is It Anyway? Representing Oral Testimony
    in a Multilingual 'Contact Zone'   137
    Jane Freeland

9   Spanish-Speaking Latin Americans in Catalonia:
    Reflexivity and Knowledgeability in Constructions
    of Catalan   158
    Steve Marshall

10 Language Contact between Galician and Spanish:
Conflict or Harmony? Young People's Linguistic
Attitudes in Contemporary Galicia   178
Bernadette O'Rourke

11 Linguistic Shift and Community Language: The Effect of
Demographic Factors in the Valencian Region,
Balearic Islands and Catalonia   197
*Raquel Casesnoves Ferrer, David Sankoff and
M. Teresa Turell*

References   220

Name Index   243

Subject Index   247

List of Tables, Figures and Maps

Tables

5.1	Distribution per level based on country of origin	87
5.2	Distribution of code-switching per total number of words produced by level	88
5.3	Average number of tokens produced in each category by level	89
6.1	Characteristics of speakers	98
6.2	The use of the palatal lateral vs the non-palatal lateral by first-generation Andean migrants	100
6.3	Linguistic factors and /r/ assibilation	101
6.4	Social factors and assibilation of /r/	102
6.5	/s/ elision according to position and number of syllables	103
6.6	/s/elision vs /s/ aspiration according to social variables	104
6.7	*Leísmo*	106
6.8	*Leísmo* and animacy	107
6.9	Archmorpheme *lo*	109
7.1	Informants, according to social variables	123
7.2	Corpus of verbs, according to ethnicity	128
7.3	Use of the infinitive, the third person of the verb and the gerund, according to ethnic group	129
7.4	Non-standard uses, according to verb type	130
7.5	Class of verb, according to presence/absence of pronouns or subject NPs in Haitians, Dominican-Haitians, Arayanos and Dominicans	132
8.1	Demography of Nicaragua's Caribbean Coast Region	142

Figures

4.1	Discourse levels of language conflict	56
4.2	Modalities of language shift	57
4.3	Community assembly: handing over the judge's office	66
5.1	Model of linguistic interaction: English/Spanish code-switching in the USA	81
5.2	Pilot study: summary of the methodology	85

5.3	Students born in the USA or in other Spanish-speaking countries per level	88
8.1	Contact zones between oral testimony and data	140
11.1	Evolution of foreign migration during the 1990s	203
11.2	Evolution of foreign population by continent of origin in Catalonia, the Valencian Region and the Balearic Islands (1996–2003)	204
11.3	Knowledge of Catalan in Catalonia, the Valencian Region and the Balearic Islands	207
11.4	Change in the knowledge of Catalan between 1991 and 2001	207
11.5	Changes in the abilities to understand and speak Catalan according to age	208
11.6	Changes in the abilities to read and write Catalan according to age	209
11.7	Gender differences in changing abilities to understand and speak Catalan	210
11.8	Gender differences in changing abilities to read and write Catalan	211
11.9	Knowledge of Catalan in the Valencian Region, Catalonia and the Balearic Islands, according to birthplace	212
11.10	Change in the knowledge of Catalan in the Valencian Region, Catalonia and the Balearic Islands, according to birthplace	213
11.11	Ability to understand and speak Catalan according to counties in the Valencian Region, Catalonia and the Balearic Islands	214
11.12	Changes in the ability to speak Catalan according to counties in the Valencian Region, Catalonia and the Balearic Islands and birthplace	216

Maps

| 7.1 | The border area between the Dominican Republic and Haiti | 123 |
| 11.1 | Autonomous communities with historic and official languages | 198 |

Acknowledgements

We would like to thank the many people who have helped in the preparation and production of this book. Its conception owes much to the stimulating conference, *UK Hispanic Linguistics Symposium II*, held at the University of Southampton in April 2004. Versions of many of the chapters included here were first aired as papers at that conference, and discussions and feedback that we received have helped shape the ensuing volume. We would also like to thank the anonymous reviewer of the book for helpful and insightful comments which we hope that we have been able to address. Thanks are also due to Sue Wright and Helen Kelly-Holmes, the editors of this series, and especially to Jill Lake of Palgrave Macmillan for her support and guidance in the development of the project. We are very grateful to Vanessa Mar-Molinero for the many hours she spent amalgamating stubborn individual bibliographies. Above all we wish to thank our fellow contributors for their enthusiasm, patience, hard work and stimulating chapters.

University of Southampton   CLARE MAR-MOLINERO

University of Strathclyde   MIRANDA STEWART

Notes on the Contributors

Rocío Caravedo is Associate Professor of Hispanic Linguistics in the Department of Romance Languages and Literatures and in the Graduate School of Linguistics at the University of Pisa, Italy. Her research interests include linguistic variation and change, linguistic ideology, sociolinguistics, corpus linguistics, language contact and perception. She is author of *Estudios sobre el español de Lima; El español de Lima. Materiales para su estudio; La competencia lingüística; Sociolingüística del español de Lima; La lingüística del corpus; Léxico del habla culta de Lima*, and has published articles on sociolinguistic theory and methods, Spanish phonology, discourse analysis, Latin American Spanish, Peruvian varieties in contact, linguistic evaluation and attitudes towards Spanish American varieties. As a collaborator on the *Atlas of Latin American Spanish*, she has conducted sociolinguistic fieldwork in the Coastal, Andean and Amazonean regions of Peru.

Raquel Casesnoves Ferrer is a Visiting Scholar at the Institut Universitari de Lingüística Aplicada of the Universitat Pompeu Fabra in Barcelona, Spain. She studied Hispanic philology at the Universitat de València and received her PhD in anthropology, specializing in ethno-linguistics, from the Université de Montréal (2001). She has published extensively on the relationships among attitudes, identity and linguistic performance in Valencia. During postdoctoral studies at the University of Ottawa, she has been studying linguistic normalization, educational patterns and demographic change, and their effects on speakers of the historic languages in the traditionally Catalan-, Basque- and Galician-speaking Autonomous Communities in Spain.

José del Valle teaches Hispanic Linguistics at the Graduate Center of the City University of New York. He is the author of *El trueque s/x en español antiguo: aproximaciones teóricas*, and co-editor of *The Battle over Spanish between 1800 and 2000: Language Ideologies and Hispanic Intellectuals* and its Spanish edition *La batalla del idioma: la intelectualidad hispánica ante la lengua*. His research interests are in language policy and language ideologies in the recent linguistic history of Spain and Latin America.

Marta Fairclough is Assistant Professor of Spanish Linguistics and Director of Heritage Language Education at the University of Houston,

USA. She specializes in heritage language education, language acquisition, and sociolinguistics with an emphasis on US Spanish. Her research focuses on the acquisition of Standard Spanish by Hispanic heritage learners. Her most recent publications include *Spanish and Heritage Language Education in the United States: Struggling with Hypothetics*.

Jane Freeland is a Visiting Research Fellow in the School of Humanities at the University of Southampton, UK, before which she was a Senior Lecturer in Language at the University of Portsmouth. Her research has centred on language rights and language survival in the plurilingual and interethnic Caribbean Coast region of Nicaragua. Latterly, her chief concern has been the interaction between the discourse of minority language rights and popular ideologies of language, and its impact on the implementation of language rights policies in such plurilingual areas. She is currently directing a research project, financed by the British Academy, into popular language ideology and its relation to language loss among the Sumu-Mayangna Indians of this region. Recent publications include (co-edited with Donna Patrick), *Language Rights and Language Survival*, and *Lengua*, one of a series of texts for trainee teachers in Nicaragua's intercultural-bilingual programmes.

Rainer Enrique Hamel is Professor of Linguistics in the Department of Anthropology, Universidad Autónoma Metropolitana, Mexico City, Mexico. He has been a visiting researcher and professor in many countries, including Brazil (Campino), the USA (Stanford, UC Santa Barbara), and Germany (Frankfurt, Mannheim). He is an editorial or advisory board member for many international journals, and he has published extensively in various languages over a wide range of fields and topics.

Carol A. Klee is Associate Professor of Hispanic Linguistics in the Department of Spanish and Portuguese Studies at the University of Minnesota, USA. Her research interests include Spanish sociolinguistics, language contact, and second-language acquisition. She is co-author of *Lingüística aplicada: la adquisición del español como segunda lengua* and has published articles on Spanish-Quechua language contact, Spanish in the USA, and second-language acquisition. She has edited and co-edited several collections of research including *Sociolinguistics of the Spanish-Speaking World; Faces in a Crowd: The Individual Learner in Multisection Courses;* and *The Interaction of Social and Cognitive Factors in Second Language Acquisition*. She has conducted sociolinguistic fieldwork in the Rio Grande Valley of Texas and in the Andean region of Peru, as well as in Lima.

Clare Mar-Molinero is Professor of Spanish and Head of Modern Languages at the University of Southampton. She teaches and has published widely on language policies and on global Spanish. Her publications include *The Politics of Language in the Spanish-Speaking World*; *The Spanish-Speaking World*; *Introduction to Sociolinguistic Issues*; *Nationalism and the Nation in the Iberian Peninsula*, co-edited with Angel Smith; and *Language Ideologies, Policies and Practices: Language and the Future of Europe*, co-edited with Patrick Stevenson. She is chair of the recently formed International Association for the Study of Spanish in Society (SiS).

Steve Marshall is a Lecturer at Simon Fraser University, Canada, in the Centre for Writing-Intensive Learning. Previously he was a lecturer in English for Academic Purposes at the Language Centre, University College London for twelve years. He has also spent three years teaching English in Colombia and Venezuela, and has both TESOL qualifications and a PhD on 'Spanish-speaking Latin Americans in Catalonia: Constructions of Catalan'.

Bernadette O'Rourke is Lecturer in the School of Applied Languages and Intercultural Studies at Dublin City University, Ireland. Her main research interests, on which she has published various articles, are in sociolinguistics and the sociology of language, with a particular focus on minority language issues. In her doctoral thesis she looked comparatively at the survival prospects of Irish and Galician.

Luis A. Ortiz López is Professor at the Department of Hispanic Studies and contributes to the Graduate Program in Linguistics at the University of Puerto Rico. His areas of research broadly include sociolinguistics, language contact and language variation. He has published extensively in national and international journals and in edited volumes. Recent work includes *Huellas etno-sociolingüísticas bozales y afrocubanas*; *El Caribe hispánico: perspectivas lingüísticas actuales* (editor) and (co-edited with Manel Lacorte) *Contacto y contextos lingüísticos: el español en los Estados Unidos y en contacto con otras lenguas*. He is currently preparing a volume on language contact and language change on the border between the Dominican Republic and Haiti, focusing on Haitianized Spanish.

David Sankoff holds the Canada Research Chair in Mathematical Genomics at the University of Ottawa and is a member of the Centre de recherches mathématiques at the Université de Montréal. His research involves the formulation of mathematical models and the development of analytical methods in the sciences and humanities. This includes the design of algorithms and probability models for problems in computational biology, and statistical methodology for studying grammatical variation and change in speech communities. He is a Fellow of the Royal Society of Canada and of the Canadian Institute for Advanced Research, and has received the Médaille Vincent from the Association Canadienne-Française pour l'Avancement des Sciences, the Senior Scientist Accomplishment Award from the International Society for Computational Biology and the Weldon Memorial Prize from Oxford University.

Miranda Stewart is Senior Lecturer in Spanish and Latin American Studies at the University of Strathclyde, Glasgow. Her teaching and research interests include sociolinguistics, spoken interaction, discourse analysis, interactional pragmatics and translation studies. Her publications include *The Spanish Language Today*, and (co-edited with Leo Hickey), *Politeness in Europe*; as well as articles for journals such as *the Journal of Pragmatics* and *Multilingua* where she explores issues such as the pragmatics of personal reference. She is a member of the Executive Committee of the recently formed International Association for the Study of Spanish in Society (SiS).

M. Teresa Turell is Professor of English Linguistics at Universitat Pompeu Fabra (Barcelona), and Director of the Institut Universitari de Lingüística Aplicada (IULA) at the same university. She has conducted extensive research on Catalan and English sociolinguistic variation, and more recently on qualitative and quantitative studies of language contact. She is the author of *No One-to-One in Grammar; Elements per a la Recerca Sociolingüística a Catalunya; Nuevas Corrientes Lingüísticas; La Sociolingüística de la Variació*; and *Multilingualism in Spain*. She has carried out and supervised extensive research on the interplay between internal and external factors in the bilingual speech modes of linguistic minority groups in Spain and on the variable nature of second and foreign language acquisition and learning. Her recent research interests include the analysis of language variation in real time and demolinguistic projections to evaluate language planning in a bilingual context, and, more recently, forensic linguistics in Spain.

1
Introduction

Clare Mar-Molinero and Miranda Stewart

The themes and threads underpinning the chapters of this book arise from considering the spread of Spanish today and particularly its role in the face of processes of globalization. However, it is also our belief that discussions of the global – the macro level – must be informed by detailed observations of how the impacting outcomes of globalization play out at local or micro level.

All the contributions analyse linguistic situations in the Spanish-speaking world, very many of them from the perspective of language contact. In the majority of cases Spanish is the dominant language in this contact situation, but we will see that this is not always so. Some of the chapters focus on the languages with which Spanish is in contact in order to examine how these are prospering in a world where it is generally thought that a few strong, global languages are, or will be, taking over the linguistic domains of many other weaker, minoritized languages. Generally the view to emerge is that Spanish is a dominant, hegemonic language with a steadily increasing number of speakers and whose value, symbolic and actual, is being exploited and promoted by certain agents of language spread. However, the authors in this volume also question how homogeneous this profile of Spanish is; to what extent its hegemony is contested or alternatively promoted; and how far contact with it does indeed threaten other languages. How porous are the boundaries around Spanish? How unified or fragmented are its forms? What is the nature of its influence and its dominance? Who are those who are determining its influence? These are all questions variously addressed in the chapters of this book.

The authority of Spanish can usefully be analysed by adopting the approach proposed by Gal and Woolard (2001) and developed by Woolard (2005) in the specific context of Spanish and Catalan, in which they argue that '[t]wo distinct ideologies underpin linguistic authority in modern societies ... *authenticity* and *anonymity*' (Woolard, 2005: 1). Gal and Woolard describe dominant, hegemonic languages as resting their authority on anonymity because this corresponds to the de-personalized, generalized context of public languages and public spaces. Woolard writes:

> The citizen-speaker is supposed to *sound* like an Everyman, using a common, unmarked standard public language. In that public standard, we are not expected to hear the interests and experiences of a historically specific social group. Rather, the language is idealized as a transparent window on a disinterested rational mind and thus on truth itself (Silverstein 1987; Woolard 1989). By this reasoning, public languages can represent and be used equally by everyone precisely because they belong to no-one-in-particular. (2005: 2, italics in original)

Global Spanish could well be expected to be presented as just such a language, and has been by certain commentators (see, López García, 1985; Lodares, 2001; Salvador, 1987, 1992). Discussions particularly about the Instituto Cervantes (for example Mar-Molinero, and Del Valle, this volume) resonate with this description. However, many of the case studies examined in this volume explore the use of Spanish or of other languages in contact with it at a more local and marginalized level. In these cases Gal and Woolard's concept of the ideology of authenticity seems more appropriate:

> Within the logic of authenticity, a speech variety must be deeply rooted to social and geographic territory in speakers' consciousness, or it has no value ... Often, speech that is heard as authentic is taken as not just an indexical sign associated with a particular group, but even as iconic, as a natural image of the essence of a particular kind of person. (Woolard, 2005: 1)

Woolard specifically refers to the notion of '*lengua propia*' (best translated into English as 'own language') which is used to refer to the minority languages in Spain, as an example of the concept of authenticity. However, we will see in some of the following chapters that authenticity is not necessarily a label exclusive to minority languages and that this description may well fit certain speakers of Spanish. This raises the interesting question of whether in fact such groups or communities are, through the authority they acquire from their authentic relationship with Spanish, influencing global Spanish from a grassroots impact from below. An important aspect of this book is to focus on the impact of globalization on the local and on the minoritized, to foreground the micro albeit framed by the macro. In a recent collection of papers edited by Camagarajah (2005) which specifically sets out to address a perceived absence of the local when discussing language policies, he writes,

> ... we talk of globalization as ushering in a new life of border-free, unrestricted, fluid relationships between communities, but knowledge itself is narrowly constructed, splintering along different communities, devoid of effective attempts at developing an intercultural understanding of a fair exchange of ideas. (Camagarajah, 2005: xiv)

Camagarajah (and other contributors in his volume) argue the need to 'point to ways in which the negotiation of the global can be conducted by taking greater account of the local and respecting its value and validity' (*ibid.*); this is a concern mirrored in many of the following chapters.

In order to establish an overarching framework for the chapters of the volume, Mar-Molinero's chapter discusses some of the characteristics and processes of globalization that are commonly suggested as relevant to the study of current macro sociolinguistics. She also specifically applies these to the spread of Spanish, giving a brief historical context to its spread, and then focusing on two salient features of Spanish today: the policies of the Spanish government in promoting the global spread of Spanish, and the role of the US Latino Spanish-speaking population in its promotion. The former, and in particular, as she highlights, those of the Instituto Cervantes, are clear examples of the top-down impact of linguistic globalization (and imperialistic) forces, whereas, the situation of Spanish and the Spanish-speaking community in the USA is in diametrical contrast, as we have mentioned above.

José del Valle's chapter continues the theme of interrogating the language policies of contemporary Spanish governments, and in particular their desire to promote Spanish in the USA and to be a counterweight to the spread of US Spanish. He explores the language ideologies that he sees surrounding the complex sociolinguistic situation of the US Latinos, and he discusses the debates about Spanglish and standard Spanish. As Del Valle writes, 'in the negations of Spanglish, the aggressive promotion of monoglossia operates at times by excessively conspicuous erasures' (pp. 75–6). Moreover, we would argue, that when speaking of Spanglish, detractors are not comparing like with like. They set it against standard, written, formal Spanish when maybe it should be located within a style-shifting paradigm with speakers drawing on the resources of two languages to create a colloquial, in-group, conversational style which then may migrate to other areas (for example literature, song) for a countercultural effect.

Using a conflict-imperialist framework, Rainer Enrique Hamel also explores the spread of global Spanish whilst making a strong plea that such discussion must adopt a micro perspective too. He argues that

> we must explore the concrete, practical and multiple ways in which different ethnolinguistic groups interact on a local and a global level, how they communicate successfully and to what extent they fall prey to cultural misunderstandings ... how conflicts emerge, explode or are settled in negotiated ways. (pp. 1–2)

Hamel's micro case study investigates the Hñähñú (formerly known as the Otomi) peoples of central Mexico, their relationship to Spanish, and the processes of language shift which he observes are defined 'by clashes between cultural models, competing discourse strategies and discourse styles'. He also suggests, following the methodology he has developed for his micro case study on Hñähñú, that a more sensitive model for investigating language shift, of a micro-macro nature, can help us understand the US Latino sociolinugistic situation.

Marta Fairclough also offers a micro perspective on the wider implications of globalization processes, again taking a US Spanish example. She examines language-mixing phenomena in the writing of heritage learners of Spanish in the United States. The description and quantification of the different types of Spanish/English interaction show the degree of grammaticalization or lexicalization of the code-mixing and the possible emergence of a new mixed code. As such it demonstrates a fascinating example of Gal and Woolard's concept of authenticity that suggests, as does so-called Spanglish generally, different and innovative influences on global Spanish.

The possible emergence of a new form of Spanish is also explored with the detailed micro observations carried out in Chapter 6 by Carol Klee and Rocío Caravedo. They, too, focus on the language changes brought about by forces of globalization, in this instance the linguistic shifts produced by the mass migration of Peruvians from their Andean homelands to the capital Lima. Many of these migrants are themselves native Quechua speakers and bring with them their second language, Andean

Spanish. Klee and Caravedo study the outcomes of the contact of Andean Spanish, a largely stigmatized variety in Lima, with Coastal Spanish of the *limeños*. They conclude that

> in Lima while the forces of globalization combined with negative attitudes toward indigenous languages are bringing about an end to Quechua within the city, at the same time the contact of Andean and coastal Spanish may result in the creation of a new variety of Spanish – different from the traditional coastal model – by the descendants of Andean migrants. (p. 173)

The informants that Klee and Caravedo interviewed were, by the nature of their migrant status or the fact that, in the case of the *limeños*, they interacted with the migrants, all from lower social classes. They share this characteristic with the informants of Luis Ortiz López's study of Haitians and Dominicans living on the border between the two countries. This is the third of our three micro-intensive studies of linguistic shift in contexts which are the direct result of globalizing processes. In this case Ortiz López observes the particular features that are displayed by various groups of Haitians or descendants of Haitians living in the Dominican Republic. He notes processes of reduced inflection in their Spanish and argues that they are determined as much by extra-linguistic factors as by linguistic variables. Extra-linguistic factors include, firstly, degree of contact, ranging from that of the *'viejo'* (long-established immigrants) or *'congó'* (new arrivals) Haitian, on one side of the linguistic cline, who has poor access to the target language, and, at the opposite extreme, the *arayano* (of mixed Haitian-Dominican ancestry) who is always bilingual to some degree. Secondly, there are the ethno-linguistic attitudes which arise from a contact situation which is rarely amicable and which frequently occasions linguistic stress, due to the rejection on grounds of ethnicity, culture and language, to which Haitians and their descendents are always subjected.

The role of borders is important in very many of the case studies in this volume, and much of the linguistic contact and conflict is a result of the need or desire to cross them. A useful frame for conceiving the role of borders and the barriers and obstacles they present is that of 'contact zones' as proposed by Mary Louise Pratt (1987, 1992). She describes these as 'the space of colonial encounters, the space where peoples geographically and historically separated come into contact with each other and establish ongoing relations, usually involving conditions of coercion, racial inequality, and intractable conflict

(1992: 6). This reminds us of the comments of Camagarajah quoted earlier in which he emphasized the fact that encounters such as those that Pratt describes are rarely equal, symmetrical and unproblematic, but rather are conflictual and painful to the less powerful. This is certainly the case for the Haitians.

Jane Freeland takes up the concept of 'contact zones' centrally to frame her study, which besides examining the linguistic practices of bi/multilingual speakers on the Atlantic Coast of Nicaragua and the impact once more that typical forces of globalization have had and are having on language in this community, is also an interesting reflexive examination of the processes involved in translation and of the outsider's role in multilingual communities. Freeland offers an innovative and important critique of the concept of *lingua franca*, showing how the use of Spanish in this way is not neutral and unattached, but instead laden with ideological overtones of the dominant linguistic community, conveyed through the education system. Far from the 'anonymous' language of 'no-one' that we have normally considered a *lingua franca* to be, she demonstrates that Spanish belongs, and is seen to belong, very clearly to those in power. As global languages spread across the world, above all but not exclusively English, and perform the role of *lingua franca*, this is a timely reminder.

The final three chapters concentrate on linguistic situations in the minority language communities of Spain, where Spanish is in contact with those historic languages which have recently received considerable support and protection from the post-Franco constitution and political organization (the 'autonomous regions'). The first of these by Steve Marshall reminds us also that a further interesting outcome of globalization is that the language contact and conflict that we have already observed with migrant languages and dominant national languages is further complicated by the presence of other autochthonous languages. The recent arrival of hundreds of thousands of allochthonous new migrants in Catalonia has altered the sociolinguistic situation during a key stage of linguistic 'normalization' of the Catalan language. This not only presents new problems to policy-makers, it also challenges many of the existing analytic paradigms that have been employed recently to analyse the sociolinguistic situation in Catalonia (Woolard 1989; Pujolar 2001; Turell 2001a). Marshall explores the experiences of Spanish-speaking Latin American immigrants as they encounter the '*lengua propia*' of their new home, Catalan.

Whilst the sociolingustic situation in Catalonia is complex and significantly affected by immigration, both from Spanish speakers and others, another of Spain's minority linguistic communities, Galicia, provides a sharp contrast. Here, the autochthonous language, Galician, is still the majority mother tongue in its community, a region which has not experienced globalization in the sense of movement of peoples into Galicia, although many have emigrated to other parts. O'Rourke discusses the impact that modernization, urbanization and the recent Spanish language 'normalization' policies have had in this region and on the use of Galician. She analyses the attitudes of a key group of informants, university students, to gauge likely trends for the future of Galician amongst a group of people who can be expected to be role models in their society. Her findings suggest that despite the recent positive political and legal changes towards Spain's minority languages, Spanish is seen increasingly as the hegemonic – necessary – language.

Finally, continuing with the analysis of Spain's minority languages, Casesnoves, Sankoff and Turell present some interesting data on the demographic trends noted in recent census figures in the Catalan speaking regions of Catalonia, Valencia and the Balearic Islands. They present and analyse the comparative data from 1991 and 2001 in order to discover what factors are influencing language shift. The picture varies across these regions, due in large part to the very different political support and resources Catalan receives in them, as well as the diverse historical context for its use. However, the authors observe some 'de-regionalization', admittedly least strong in Catalonia, but present in both other communities. They suggest that

> the trend we have sketched towards a degree of de-regionalization in all areas where traditionally Catalan was strongest, and despite strenuous efforts, particularly in the case of Catalonia, to revitalize the language, could be seen as evidence of the globalizing power of Spanish, and this within its traditional homeland. (p. 326)

This collection of studies demonstrates a wide range of geographical case studies, many different methodological approaches and a variation in the emphasis on the macro and the micro. However, all the chapters recognize the impact of globalization on Spanish and the languages with which it comes into contact in the current era, and whilst acknowledging the significance and the status of global Spanish, we are given insights into interesting and innovative discussions which raise questions about the nature and totality of its all-embracing dominance.

2
Forces of Globalization in the Spanish-Speaking World: Linguistic Imperialism or Grassroots Adaptation

Clare Mar-Molinero

Introduction

There has recently been – arguably somewhat belatedly – a growing interest in the relationship between language and globalization. There is work which explores the impact of globalization on language issues, as well as studies of how language in turn affects globalization (see, for example, the themed issue of *Journal of Sociolinguistics*, 2003; Fairclough, 2001; Gardt and Hüppauf, 2004; Maurais and Morris, 2003; Wright, 2004). Moreover, other analyses of language spread, contact and change and of the phenomenon of so-called 'world' languages, particularly the situation of English, also examine developments and outcomes created or influenced by global geopolitical processes (for example, Brutt-Griffler, 2002; Crystal, 1997; 2000; Graddol, 1997; Pennycook, 1998; Phillipson, 1992, 2003; Ricento, 2000).

In this chapter I will briefly trace some of these debates and discussions surrounding language issues in a global era, attempting to identify those aspects of globalization of particular interest when it comes to explaining language behaviour. I will seek to identify some of the key agents acting as the forces of globalization on language processes and will discuss the nature of this relationship. This will raise issues concerning the definition and role of world language(s), especially the place of English in the global linguistic theatre. To date, and probably inevitably, most of this work on languages and global contexts has concentrated on examining the case of English and its impact on other languages or, on the other hand, focusing on endangered languages and language death, with only a very few studies looking at other major international languages.

The aim of this chapter is to explore how far any discussion and analysis of globalization and world languages are of any particular and specific relevance to an understanding of the case of Spanish and the languages of what is commonly referred to as the Spanish-speaking world. Relatively little has been published as regards Spanish as a world language or its spread in a time of globalization (see, however, Hamel, 2003b; Mar-Molinero, 2000, 2004; Sánchez and Dueñas, 2002; Tamarón, 1995; as well as the regular *Anuarios* published by the Instituto Cervantes). This chapter seeks, as does the book as a whole, to contribute to filling this gap.

Language ideology and globalization

In their ground-breaking work on language ideologies, Woolard and Schieffelin (1994) and Woolard (1998) discuss many different definitions of ideology. Particularly useful for the study of language spread is that which sees ideology as 'ideas, discourse or signifying practices in the service of the struggle to acquire or maintain power' (Woolard, 1998: 7). This power may be striven for by those dominated, or, more normally, exercised by those who dominate and intend to continue to dominate. Whilst Woolard and Schieffelin suggest that there are at least three areas of debate where language ideology is central,[1] I shall concentrate my analysis within the area of what they call 'language contact, competition and politics' as this is the most relevant to a discussion of language spread and globalization. In line with Blommaert's (2003: 612) view that 'language ideologies affect language change', the contributors to this book examine what language ideologies might underpin the decisions, policies, planning and processes that have led to the world-wide spread of Spanish in recent years and to the fates of those languages which come into contact with it.

An explicit application of language ideology is found in both overt and covert language planning where such ideology underpins laws and regulations that guide a society's language use. The use and variety of language to be employed in public administration, the legal system, the media and, particularly, the education system is the product of a particular set of ideas and beliefs about that community's language repertoire. Frequently this is based on nationalistic, and especially Western, views that equate one language to one nation and strive to maintain this.[2] It is therefore the case that often when examining the relationship between language and globalization we discover that the ideologies underpinning language contact and language spread are still fundamentally rooted in the nation-state paradigm. Global processes today inevitably do affect language use and spread, and provide us with interesting situations to analyse. Coupland (2003) suggests that there are four key processes to take into account when analysing language in a global era. These are: *interdependence, the compression of time and space, disembedding,* and *commodification.* 'Interdependence' is indeed a hallmark of globalization, whether seen in economic, political or cultural terms. As Coupland notes:

> under globalization, communities interface with, and impact upon one another, and ... language is both a medium and a marker of new forms of *interdependence.* (2003: 467, italics in original)

These transnational and global interconnections create the phenomenon that Coupland calls a 'compression of time and space'. Various commentators have given as an example of this the role of the 'virtual' call centre in communications across the English- or French-speaking worlds (for example Cameron, 2000; Heller, 2003). As a result of these global interconnections created by multinational businesses, by tourism, by global media, and so on, Coupland claims 'new, restructured interdependencies give varieties new values as marketable commodities' (*ibid.*). The packaging of 'international' Spanish will be examined later as just such a 'marketable commodity' on the world stage.

Coupland considers disembedding (followed by re-embedding) as a especially rich sociolinguistic term of particular relevance as regards global languages where culturally-linked language is removed from its place of origin and reinterpreted in entirely different social and geographical sites. The words of popular music, advertisements by multinational companies, or the language of international tourism are examples of this practice. All of these have their resonance in the Spanish-speaking world.

Coupland's four key processes are closely related to issues of dominance and imposition as will be discussed in this context later in relation to Spanish. As Maurais and Morris (2003: 9) write:

> A globalising world poses a challenge of rising interdependence for all languages, since no linguistic sphere is protected or assured and a more tightly integrated world generally favours the spread of English. Language shift is not new, but the contemporary global scope of linguistic competition is.

The concept of globalization today frames our understanding of world systems and our social, political and cultural interconnections. Amongst the growing volume of literature on globalization there are clear differences and disputes as to the nature and outcomes of the phenomenon (Wright, 2004). For the purposes of discussion here, and in particular its relationship with language, I understand globalization to mean 'an increasing inter-connectivity on all levels' (Hamel, 2003b: 6) across geographical, political, cultural and linguistic borders. It is especially associated with the economic impact 'whereby financial capital is taking the lead over productive capital' (*ibid.*). What is not disputed is that modern electronic technology has enhanced dramatically the communications that underpin these relationships. However, Blommaert (2003: 612) stresses that the fact that we are envisaging interactions on such a wide geographical level should not lead us to believe there is total uniformity about globalization processes. As these processes cross boundaries and connect at transnational levels, there are tensions between both the national and the transnational reactions to global trends. Blommaert argues that

the system is marked by both the existence of separate spaces (e.g. states) and deep inter-connectiveness of the different spaces, often, precisely, through the existence of worldwide elites. (*Ibid.*)

Indeed those who argue about the benefits of globalization usually point to how it is, above all, in the developed world where these are felt. As Wright states:

Globalization is thus far an affair that touches elites far more than other groups, and having access to technology divides the world into the haves and have-nots. (2004: 157–8)

Similarly and more strongly, Pratt argues that

The economic polarisation produced by neoliberalism means that the world is now full of people, places, whole regions and countries which, far from being integrated into a planetary Walmart, are and know themselves to be, entirely dispensable with respect to what is seen as the global economic and political order, to be nonparticipants in any of the futures that order invites people to imagine for themselves. (2005: 284)

Fairclough (2001: 204) agrees that 'this is a new economic order but it is not just economic: there is also a more general process of globalization, including, for instance, politics and culture'. He goes on to insist that in any analysis of the new world order 'the question of language and power is absolutely central' (*ibid.*). He claims:

> Struggles to impose or resist the new world order are partly struggles over language, both over new ways of using language, and over linguistic repercussions of change. (*Ibid.*)

These twin struggles will be examined below in the case of Spanish today. These struggles are inevitably between those in power and those below them. As Blommaert states:

> Globalization implies that developments at the 'top' or the core of the world system have a wide variety of effects at the 'bottom' or the periphery of that system. (2003: 612)

Once again, commentators disagree as to the nature of these effects, with many, however, concluding that this is a further example of power domination, hegemonic imposition and imperialism.

In his pioneering and polemic book on linguistic imperialism, Phillipson argues that the concept is a 'subset of linguicism' which in turn he defines as

> ideologies, structures and practices which are used to legitimate, effectuate and reproduce an unequal division of power and resources (both material and im material) between groups which are defined on the basis of language. (Phillipson 1992: 47)

Whilst Phillipson is criticized for explaining the spread and creation of 'world' English as being *solely* the product of linguistic imperialism and linguicism (for example Brutt-Griffler 2002; Spolsky, 2004), his contribution to a theory of language spread and language hierarchies is useful and frequently applicable.

Phillipson's and others' characterization of language spread as linguistic imperialism is important in terms of defining who the agents of such spread might be. It is particularly over this that Phillipson has been taken to task by various commentators, notably Brutt-Griffler, who writes that in linguistic imperialism theory

> Agency is invested in various representations of institutionalised power. In contrast, the speech communities acquiring the language

figure as passive recipients of language policy ... It is assumed that to have *political* control is to have *linguistic* control. (2002: viii, italics in original)

She describes such an interpretation of language spread in the case of English:

The centre-driven narrative of English language spread writes people residing outside the West out of their central role in the spread of English and their place in the making of the language we call English. (*Ibid.*)

This debate about the dominance of institutionalized power or the influence of grassroots communities in determining linguistic configurations is taken up in many of the chapters of this book in the context of Spanish and the Spanish-speaking world (for example, Hamel, Freeland, Marshall and Del Valle, this volume).

Hamel (2003b) in particular has argued strongly that the important need to identify the agent of language change and language spread is often lost when analysing such political, cultural and linguistic processes from the globalization perspective. He argues that theories of globalization tend to lose sight of the actor or agent in the process. He writes that with globalization

new impersonalised tertiary bonds, mediated by technologies and corporations, increasingly determine our lives ... New de-territorialised 'third cultures' such as fashion or the new international management culture, are emerging with their own discourses and language usages. (Hamel, 2003b: 7)

He refers to

the increasing dominance, restrictions and global control over a growing number of domains in our lives, while at the same time the actors and sources behind the scenes appear more and more diluted. (*Ibid.*)

Pratt, in considering the 'preferred metaphor' of 'the metropolitan discourse of globalisation' is that of 'flows' (2005: 276), believes that this has allowed for an uncritical interpretation of globalization as symmetrical relationships and exchange, when in fact, she argues, these flows are very much asymmetrical and to the disadvantage of the poor and dominated parts of the world. In particular, Pratt criticizes the concept of 'flow' on various counts including the following which chimes with Hamel's argument:

> 'Flow' obliterates human agency and intentionality – it is an intransitive verb. This is very handy ... People who 'flow' are people who have *decided* to go or return who have been *sent* or *sent for* by others, as part of a considered strategy. By eliminating agency, flow takes the existential dimensions of human movement off the table, from excruciating choices forced upon people to the emancipatory possibilities to which mobility gives rise. (2005: 277, italics in original)

We could add that decisions about which language to speak and to whom and how are also decided by *someone* for their purposes.

Hamel urges a reinterpretation of current global linguistic change from the linguistic imperialism perspective in order to identify the actors and agents of language spread and to understand the power dominance within this. I believe that in fact a linguistic imperialism framework or the more currently prominent one of globalization are not opposing theoretical perspectives, but complementary ones. One plausible interpretation of globalization and all its effects is indeed that it is a form of dominance brought about by a kind of imperialism – albeit a different kind of postmodern imperialism, no longer characterized only by military victory or nation-state political power. The agents of imperialism, and therefore many globalization processes, are no longer only armies and national governments, but multinational companies, transnational cultural and leisure organisations, global media corporations, or international political elites. This may entail a different, more subtle, form of imposition and dominance, but nonetheless seems to me to be a kind of imperialism in a postcolonial world, a twenty-first century form of hegemony.

In the discussion below (and in the following chapters) of the spread of Spanish and of language change in the Spanish-speaking world, key processes of globalization will be examined, ranging from political and economic imposition; technological and cultural inter-connectivitiy; demographic and cultural cross-border flows; to grassroots adaptation and appropriation of such processes.

Language in the 'Spanish-speaking world': contact, shift, competition

In this section I will start by briefly tracing the historical background to the emergence of this large and growing global population of Spanish-speakers[3] before analysing the current situation and how it is shaped by and responds to globalization forces. It is estimated that across the world there are over 400 million speakers of Spanish (SIL, 15th edn, 2005).[4] The vast majority of these are mother-tongue speakers, or highly proficient second-language users, but increasingly the numbers are being strengthened by a growing population of competent speakers of Spanish as a Foreign Language (*español como lengua extranjera*, or ELE), demonstrating the popularity of Spanish as a language learnt by business people, cultural and artistic trend-setters, politicians and tourists. There are, of course, also groups of second-language speakers of Spanish who are not so proficient or confident in the use of the language – or are led to believe that they are not in the face of particular attitudes of first-language users with whom they interact (see Freeland, this volume).

The history of the development and domination of first a distinct variety called 'Castilian'; and its emergence as 'Spanish', the national language, mirrors very closely the emergence and consolidation of the Spanish nation-state. Throughout the nation-building process national identity was clearly linked with linguistic identity.[5] The nature of the spread of the Spanish language was underpinned by the process of rapid colonization in Latin America. Language played a significant role in the consolidation of Spain's American Empire. Not only did Castilian quickly dominate over the thousands of existing indigenous languages as the language of power, of administration and public life, and, especially, of the Church, but it was a particularly suitable medium over such enormous geographical distances because of its highly developed literacy. This spread of a print community, albeit of the ruling elites, created the 'imagined' community (Anderson, 1983) of a Spanish-speaking world in the Americas. The idea of 'pan-Hispanism', '*Hispanidad*' or a 'Spanish-speaking world' can be said to date back to these beginnings.[6]

In the same way that Spanish had been the great unifier of a vast Empire during the colonial days, its total integration and permanence in Latin American society was also assured from the period of independence on. The presence in Latin America of a ruling elite who were made up exclusively of those of European descent – unlike in many other ex-colonial situations – ensured the maintenance of Spanish as the language of power. However, the link of Spanish to national identity was very different from that found in Spain.

Significantly, Spanish was not the unique national language in any of the new independent republics; it was not their 'own', as they *all* used Spanish. Nor was Spanish the original indigenous language of the region. It was, on the contrary, the imposed, imperialist language of the very enemy that the wars of independence had just defeated. And yet despite this, Spanish did indeed serve a nation-forming role in Latin America as it had done previously in Spain, thereby reinforcing its dramatic spread across the world. Within the new and highly-constructed independent republics there was an urgent need to create a sense of national identity – a uniqueness that distinguished Ecuadorians from Peruvians, Argentineans from Uruguayans, Mexicans from Guatemalans, and so on. Indeed, these were artificial units containing many different ethnic groups, cultures and histories. Most also contained many different linguistic groups. For this reason the role of the Spanish language was seen as one of unifying these disparate groups under the banner of their new national identity. In some of the republics even a particular form of Spanish was emphasized: Mexican Spanish, Argentinean Spanish, and others (Sánchez and Dueñas, 2002). Spanish was taught in schools and used for all forms of written communication, notably in constitutions, laws and the Church. Furthermore, Spanish was the official and often also the 'national' language recognized in the republics' new constitutions. In fact, only later, in the twentieth century, did some of these states begin to recognize the existence of other non-Spanish languages as national or even co-official (see Alvar, 1986; Hamel,1994).

In the twentieth century, urbanization, industrialization and techno-logical advances led to the rapid decrease or even death of indigenous languages in Latin America, and the consolidation of Spanish in all the independent republics. Education systems and greater access to literacy generally also helped promote the learning and use of Spanish, to the detriment of the indigenous languages which until recently have scarcely been taught and do not have a tradition of literacy[7] (Morales-González and Torres, 1992).

Not only has internal migration from rural areas where local indigenous languages are spoken to large Latin American cities where the use of Spanish prevails had a significant impact (see Klee and Caravedo, this volume), but so too has the immigration out of Spanish-speaking Latin America into the United States, producing an ever-growing Spanish-speaking population there. This US Hispanic community has very different features from the earlier Spanish colonization phenomenon. The language spread process outlined so far was characterized by dominance and elite imposition. In contrast, US Hispanic communities are frequently characterized by marginalization and discrimination, being the underdogs in an Anglophone-dominant society. It is significant, nonetheless, that, despite this, Spanish has maintained and reinforced a firm footing in the USA ever since the twentieth century, when large groups of Spanish speakers have started immigrating there, legally and illegally.[8]

The contemporary spread of Spanish in a globalized world

The significance of the Spanish-speaking community in the USA, despite its minority status, highlights the changing nature of language spread in the late twentieth century as a direct consequence of the forces of globalization discussed above. What has changed, above all, is the greater proximity and accessibility to their homelands offered to immigrant groups by advances in transportation and high-tech communications. The existence of trains, motorways, aeroplanes, telephones, televisions and email, some or all of which are now available to even the poorest immigrants, has changed the relationship of the immigrant with their host country and consequently their sense of identity. In particular, we have seen a change in the nature of language spread in contexts such as the USA from that of imposed 'top-down' colonizing processes only to 'bottom-up' infiltrating phenomena in many cases, as will be discussed further later in this chapter.

The spread of Spanish has been affected by many of the forces of globalization, both in terms of how immigrants do, or do not, integrate into host societies, and even how permanent they perceive their settlement to be. Moreover, globalization has brought with it a role for languages, such as Spanish, of wide global communication crossing borders and taking over in domains where previously local languages were used. The former phenomenon, (temporary) migration, can be seen as an example of the grassroots or bottom-up impact of globalization processes on language use and spread, whereas, on the other hand, the latter (global dominance) is a clear indication of the continuing imposition by the powerful of linguistic norms and discourse. There are examples of both of these types of responses to globalization forces in the Spanish-speaking world. The situation of the Latino or Hispanic population in the USA serves to illustrate the impact of grassroots agents of language change on society, whereas the language policies of the Spanish government, and particularly of its major agent, the Instituto Cervantes, reinforce the claims that linguistic imperialism by European political powers in global language spread is at work.

If we return to Coupland's (2003) four characteristics of language in relation to globalization introduced earlier, we can see that the contemporary spread of Spanish means that the global *interdependence* of these communities to one another and to other parts of the world system has a significant impact on the language itself. The Spanish-speaking world shares media and cultural production, in particular those available through fast technological forms of communication such as television, film, recorded music and the internet. Collectively this language community responds to new linguistic needs and creates or borrows new words and terms. The second marker identified by Coupland, the *compression across time and space*, experienced by this large population of Spanish speakers is part of the same phenomenon as electronic communication makes geographical distance much less important.

There is no doubt, too, that the Spanish language is increasingly treated as a '*commodity*' seen, for example, in the Instituto Cervantes' packaging of it on behalf of the Spanish government, as will be expanded on below. Hüppauf argues, in a discussion about the success of English and the perceived decline in popularity of German, that

> the global language [i.e. English] is highly attractive and successful in seducing people the world over ... It is the idiom of hopes and promises ... of consumption and unrestricted movement. (2004: 17)

This kind of popularity and 'seduction' is increasingly recognized by the guardians and promoters of Spanish who are currently selling their product to a world-wide public whose attraction to Spanish is characterized, for instance, by a craze for Hispanic music, dance and fashion, by mass tourism to Spanish-speaking destinations, as well as by the recognition of the existence of growing Spanish-speaking economic markets.

The concept of '*disembedding*' referred to by Coupland is apparent in the transfer of culturally-specific speech items originated in one Spanish speech community to another and their consequent adaptation or re-embedding. Coupland (2003: 468) cites Giddens (1991: 18) in explaining this concept as 'the "lifting out" of social relations from their local contexts and their rearticulation across indefinite tracts of time-space'. In the case of Spanish, the twin effects of this are hybridity, on the one hand, and homogeneity, on the other. That is to say that Spanish created to address international or global audiences (for example in films, the media, the Internet) is characterized both by a tendency to bring together various regional or national varieties (often those considered 'non-standard', and frequently also containing numerous anglicisms) or the opposite effect of aspiring to an exaggerated neutral, form of the language bereft of any regional or national traces. Neither form is 'owned' by their speech communities and lead to alarm and defensive action from those who set themselves up to guard the 'pure' standard form of

Spanish; above all those who support Castilian Spanish from central Spain as the model for the language.

Such *agents* of language spread – the self-appointed guardians of the Spanish language – fit the label given by Brutt-Griffler (2002), in the earlier quotation, as 'representations of institutionalised power'. In their attempts to respond to the threat of such *features* of globalization affecting Spanish (of hybridity or of homogeneity), certain language 'purists', like the Spanish government, the Spanish Royal Language Academy (*La Real Academia de la Lengua Española*, the RAE), Spanish media outlets, academics and educationalists, seek to promote and extend the role and status of (standard) Spanish and to define the nature of the language. Insofar as the relationship between language and national identity has always been a significant and often contentious one throughout the history of Spanish nation-building (Mar-Molinero, 2000), this defence is also to some extent a rearguard action against the forces of globalization in a world where the nation-state is losing its centrality.

Globalization has, thus, been seen by members of the Spanish elites as the cause of a perceived threat to the loss of dominance and control by the former imperialist power (see, for example, Del Valle, this volume). Expression of such concerns has routinely been heard at the various meetings of the *Congreso Internacional de la Lengua Española*, held in Zacatecas (1997), Valladolid (1998) and Rosario (2004) which, more than just an international gathering of academics and experts engaged in the study of the Spanish language, tends to be a political forum consisting of particular agents in the promotion of international Spanish and sponsored by the Spanish government (as well as certain prominent invited academics). However, these same self-appointed guardians of Spanish are also increasingly aware of how globalization processes can at the same time serve to further and to retain cultural dominance, leading too to their push for economic and political leadership. In the following section I will highlight one particularly influential agent of the current planned spread of Spanish, the Instituto Cervantes.[9]

Creating a global language: ELE and the role of the Instituto Cervantes

The Spanish government is engaged in a deliberate attempt to promote the global spread of Spanish (see Del Valle, this volume) by, amongst other things, focusing on the teaching of Spanish as an international language (and through that the transmission of Spanish language culture). This raises interesting questions about the concept of 'Standard

Language', both as a way of policing and controlling language spread and as a method of hegemonic imposition in an age of globalization. Lippi-Green (amongst others) has identified the link between language standardization and culturally dominant groups as Standard Language Ideology which she defines as

> a bias towards an abstract, idealized, homogeneous spoken language which is imposed and maintained by dominant bloc institutions and which names as its model the written language, but which is drawn primarily from the spoken language of the upper middle class. (1997: 54)

In the case of the international Spanish promoted by the Spanish government across the world, this is drawn above all from the educated variety of Castilian Spanish from central Spain.

The popularity currently observed for learning Spanish is created by a series of motivations including those overtly promoted by the Spanish government as part of its aim to strengthen and enhance a pan-Hispanic community across the world. This is in part a desire to strengthen Spain's sense of its own national identity in a world of increasing supranational identities and lessening national sovereign importance, but it is also a desire to consolidate a power bloc with some claim to counter the overwhelming march of global English. The Spanish language learning/teaching industry is a flourishing and expanding one. Whilst smaller in scale, it is modelled on and similar to the enormous EFL/ELT industry.[10] A major agent in this delivery of Spanish language learning is the Instituto Cervantes.

Since its beginnings in 1991, when it was set up by the Spanish government of the day, the Instituto Cervantes has expanded the number of its centres across the world dramatically. Besides those in existence in Spain, there are now centres in Europe, North America, Brazil, Africa, the Middle East and Asia. Today there are some 40 Instituto Cervantes centres around the world situated in over 25 countries. The Instituto's website describes its purpose as the following:

> The Instituto Cervantes is the public institution created by Spain in 1991 for the promotion and teaching of the Spanish language and for the diffusion of Spanish and Hispano-american culture. (www. cervantes.es; my translation)

The teaching of Spanish is considered the Instituto's most important role and activity. Since its creation the Instituto has translated this priority into the provision of language classes, teacher development and examinations venues throughout its many centres. It has developed its own second-language teaching/learning methodology and set up an on-line Spanish course (AVE, *Aula Virtual de Español*). It has also worked with Spain's national radio and television to deliver Spanish language courses. With its publications, on-line bibliographies, library holdings, and the hosting of major conferences on the state of the Spanish language, the Instituto aims to provide vast coverage of the needs of learners of Spanish as a Foreign Language.

The mission of the Instituto to promote 'widespread cultural activities', albeit in collaboration with 'Spanish and Hispanoamerican organiza-tions', has meant that its centres across the world are hugely proactive in introducing cultural events, lectures, film showings, book launch-ing, and so on, all of which celebrate a particular Hispanic world-view, one which whilst not necessarily only Spanish (from Spain) nonethe-less occupies the privileged position of Eurocentric/Western Hispanism. Globalization encourages the prominence of this particular cultural and linguistic elite through economic and technological dominance by the highly successful and active post-Franco Spanish state.

We have seen that both during the colonial period and with the independence of the new Spanish American republics in Latin America linguistic imperialism dominated the continent's language tapestry with Spanish required in all public spheres. If the efforts of such lan-guage policy agents as the Instituto Cervantes are successful, we would expect such domination by Spanish to continue today in a globalized world where Spanish comes into contact with other languages. This contact and competition is, therefore, examined in many of the chapters of this book with mixed results reported. Some confirm the trend towards the loss of non-standard varieties or indigenous lan-guages to (standard or prestige varieties of) Spanish (Hamel; Klee and Caravedo, this volume) whilst others give evidence of some gains in sta-tus by minority languages in, at least, post-Franco Spain (Casesnoves *et al.*, and, to a lesser extent with the case of Galician, O'Rourke, this volume).

Freeland's chapter highlights a different relationship altogether for global Spanish, as she characterizes its role as a *lingua franca* in her case study of Nicaragua's Atlantic Coast. This apparently neutral and 'disem-bodied' Spanish, supposedly removed from its role as identity marker, is in fact yet another example of institutionalized power, this time repre-senting the governing elites of the national (Nicaraguan) government through the education system. Moreover, as Freeland recounts, it is not in fact some neutral 'standard' form of Spanish that emerges as the shared code for the speakers in this context. This ambiguous relationship, encountered when a major language becomes the *lingua franca* for various second-language (or even foreign language) speaking groups, is a phenomenon observed also with international English across the globe. The Nicaraguan example suggests that in the Spanish-speaking world this global-language-as-*lingua-franca* is not unproblematic. When it remains an idealized, standardized form of the language (based presumably on the written form) it can be seen as neutral, but in any other communication role the characteristics of its masters have a bearing on the attitudes towards it, and the sociolinguistic context of its speakers dictate its form.

We have seen, therefore, in this section that increasingly there is a presence of something that we might call global Spanish. Often this manifests itself in the re-embedded sense characterized by Coupland, as a form of mass communication removed from its speech community of origin and even performing a role of *lingua franca*. Whilst the enormous attraction of the marketability of such a commodity is grasped by such powerful agents of language planning as the Spanish government, a disembodied 'neutral' and hybrid Spanish is not welcomed by them if it threatens the strong link with national identity and the leadership role of 'Standard' Spanish in the Spanish-speaking world. To this end the Instituto Cervantes, the RAE, the *Congreso Internacional de la Lengua Española*, and the Spanish Ministry of Education and Culture promote 'their' form of Standard Spanish across the globe, imposing an ideology of 'correctness', of social and culture status, and of historical validity and legitimacy. However, not all parts of the Spanish-speaking world adopt this attitude to the spread of Spanish and nor is the variety of Spanish promoted by the Spanish government always the form supported by the forces of globalization. Nor, as we will see in the following section, do the language policies and planning of powerful governments and international pressure groups always shape the trends in language use and choice.

Globalization from below: the US Latinos

To conclude this chapter I will briefly comment on the situation of the US Latino community. This community is a good example of modern migration, as described earlier in this chapter. The community is able, through modern technology, to keep in close contact with its countries of origin, and in many cases resides only on a semi-permanent basis in the new host society, physically and emotionally. As Mary Louise Pratt writes about Mexican immigrants to the USA:

> The myth of the immigrant eager to leave origins behind still exists, but it coexists alongside [the] other immigrant story whose project is sustaining the place of origin, often through processes of self-duplication ... Working abroad to sustain home often implies dual citizenship in both the literal sense (more and more countries are allowing it) and the existential sense of a kind of doubling of the self into parallel identities in one place and the other. (2005: 284–5)

As noted already, despite being a minority, and often marginalized, community, one of its most important identity markers, the Spanish language, is increasingly emerging as a potent and serious force, affecting policies and economic and cultural decision-making within mainstream US society. Whilst this is a significant example of pressure from below influencing societal linguistic practices, created by various typical characteristics of globalization – mass movement of peoples, interconnecting technological communications, global culture, and so on – it also nonetheless demonstrates that it is groups or individuals in positions of power who have advanced this process, such as TV and press networks, advertising companies or the international music industry. Writing about the way that Latino ethnicity (including linguistic elements) are marketed by the tourist industry in the USA (and particularly in the city of San Antonio), Miguel de Oliver argues:

> it is evident that the consequential economic benefits of marketing Latinos for a local underprivileged population is entirely secondary, if not extraneous, to the commercial imperatives of members of a more privileged, and usually external, population. Thus, marketing Latino culture is clearly another expression of the long-standing process of displacement of socio-economically marginal populations, and such displacement intensifies with the commercial potential of the landscape that hosts it. (2004: 416)

This supports Hamel's observations mentioned above that the identification of the agents of linguistic globalization simply confirms the fact that it is those in positions of power, who are able to dominate, impose and ultimately achieve change. The changes that they can bring about are achieved because they are the holders of purse strings, the politicians in power and the articulate elites.

The number of Latinos in the USA is estimated as around 35 million (US Bureau of Census. 2000)[11] although this is a much-contested census and the numbers of illegal immigrants make such estimates unreliable. These are not all mother tongue speakers of Spanish, nor necessarily Spanish speakers at all, as the inter-generational transmission of Spanish in the States has been weak. As a marginalized and stigmatized group the Latinos have tended to move towards the dominant culture and language, notwithstanding the earlier comment that contact with their former homelands and cultures is stronger than with previous immigrant groups. Nonetheless the sheer size of the community has led US companies and entrepreneurs to see them as a potentially important market (Carreira, 2002; Villa, 2000). Carreira (2002) also shows how the recent marked increase in Spanish-language radio, television and print outlets (with their advertising possibilities) in the USA, along with the growing recognition of the professional usefulness of some bilingual competence to strengthen businesses, have all made the use of Spanish economically and commercially attractive and potentially lucrative (Casilda Béjar, 2001). The growing importance of Spanish in a country as influential economically and politically as the USA has not been lost on business and commercial interests in Spain (and, to a lesser extent, other major Spanish-speaking countries) who, as we have seen, realize the potential of their language as a marketable and economically-rewarding commodity. This is a further example of a form of linguistic globalization whereby a poor, underprivileged Spanish-speaking community may ultimately affect economic and cultural policies and priorities across the Spanish-speaking world.

It is not only the use of Spanish in the USA but also its forms that are the subject of debate and global influences. The varieties of Spanish spoken in the USA, significantly influenced as many of them are inevitably by English, have been and are extensively discussed by academics and media commentators within the USA and in the Spanish-speaking world generally. The argument between those who view US Spanish as a single variety, heavily influenced by the contact variety of English and which they term, often derogatively, as 'Spanglish', versus those who believe US Spanish(es) is simply evolving its own characteristics as in any other Spanish-speaking community outside Spain over time, is not a new one, and aspects of this debate are explored in the chapters in this book by Fairclough and Del Valle. Once more this raises the important and controversial discussion over language standards that are increasingly challenged in a globalized Spanish-speaking world. With the 'standard' varieties of Spanish normally reflecting the elite norm found in the capitals of the various Spanish-speaking nations, and above all in the Spanish of central Spain and Madrid, it is significant that US Spanish does not have a national 'capital'. The Spanish spoken by US Latinos is ignored and stigmatized by many commentators (and particularly those from Spain, see Del Valle, this volume) as rural or inadequate, evidence of its speakers' undereducated origins or their linguistic incompetence in learning either Spanish or English. Others, however, argue for the appropriateness of US Spanish(es) as the legitimate forms of the language living and developing in the US Spanish-speaking communities. What is indisputable is that forces of globalization have raised the importance of Spanish in the USA as well as influencing the way the particular varieties develop.

As I have argued elsewhere (Mar-Molinero, 2004: 16):

> The desire for a standard or norm has historically been so embedded in the concept of national identity and autonomy that only sovereign national status has been considered acceptable for determining such norms. Standard language has been promoted and protected and regulated by national governments (through, for example, their education systems and such organisations as language academies). This is clearly evident in the Spanish-speaking world. Where this national government direction is absent and the link with national identity ambiguous, as in the case of US Spanish speakers, the debate over standard forms of Spanish has been caught up in the still persisting constraints of mapping the world by the nation-state paradigm.

Indeed, we see in the example of US Spanish many of the challenges posed by the processes of globalization to traditionally accepted understandings of linguistic behaviour and use. As responses to the issues raised by language debates over Spanish in the USA unfold, alongside an evaluation of the effectiveness of the Spanish government's language-spread policies, it will become clearer what the impact of globalization processes is on the languages of the Spanish-speaking world. Some of these processes too are discussed and analysed in the following chapters of this book.

Notes

1 Woolard and Schieffelin observe 'At least three scholarly discussions ... implicitly invoke language or linguistic ideology, often in seeming mutual unawareness. One such group of studies concerns contact between languages or language varieties ... The recently burgeoning historiography of linguistics

and public discourses on language has produced a second explicit focus on language ideologies, including scientific ideologies ... Finally, there is a significant theoretically coherent body of work on linguistic ideology concentrating on its relation to linguistic structures' (1994: 56).

2 Amongst the vast literature on the relationship between language and nationalism, see, for example, Barbour and Carmichael (2000); Mar-Molinero (2000); May (2001); Wright (2004).

3 For a detailed discussion of language spread and the creation of the Spanish-speaking world, see Sánchez and Dueñas (2002).

4 In commenting on this earlier, I have written (Mar-Molinero, 2004: 8–9) 'Estimates as to how many people speak Spanish inevitably vary, reflecting the unreliability of many language censuses. It is essential to treat statistics reporting numbers of speakers of languages with enormous care given the potential ambiguities that such censuses may contain, arising from the nature of the questions asked. Self-reporting can hide very different attitudes and behaviour, from the desire to hide ethnic origins to a wish to exaggerate linguistic competence. Categories such as 'mother tongue', 'language' and even 'speaking a language' can contain a wide variation resulting in significant differences in the totals produced. The Summer Institute of Linguists' *Ethnologue* publication is a generally respected source for linguistic data, where the number of 417 million speakers of Spanish across the world is currently reported (SIL, 2002), placing it amongst the most widely spoken languages, after English and Chinese. Significantly, too, with the exception of Spain (as well as Equatorial Guinea and the Philippines where speakers of Spanish are now very reduced) all the principal Spanish-speaking states border other Spanish-speaking states. This has been important in terms of language spread and in maintaining the presence of the language'.

5 For a fuller discussion of the relationship between the Castilian language and Spanish nation-state building see Del Valle and Gabriel-Stheeman (2002); Lodares (2001); Mar-Molinero (2000); Siguan (1992).

6 See Del Valle, this volume, for further discussion of these terms.

7 Quechua and Nahuatl (the languages of the Inca and the Aztec empires respectively) both of which served imperial purposes of their own, and did develop forms of writing. Indeed, because Quechua was developed as a *lingua general* it began to be written in Roman script and taught in the universities.

8 We should also note that this immigration in fact was not the first to bring Spanish-speakers to the USA; a small community of Spanish-speakers has existed in parts of the Southwest from when these territories were Mexican-governed.

9 For a more detailed discussion of the Instituto's role in the promotion of international Spanish see Mar-Molinero (2006).

10 See Sánchez and Dueñas (2002).

11 For a detailed breakdown of the Hispanic population in the USA according to this census, see Therrien and Ramírez (2000).

3
US Latinos, *la hispanofonía*, and the Language Ideologies of High Modernity

José del Valle

'Muere el spanglish y surge el español globalizado'
(Spanglish dies; global Spanish is born)

(El País, 27 July 2004)

Latinos and language ideologies: local, national and global

This chapter studies how Spain's language policy (LP) agents view US Latinos and their linguistic practices, and examines the connection between these beliefs and recent efforts to promote the status of Spanish as a global language.[1] The concept of language ideologies (Gal and Woolard, 2001) and the tensions produced by the co-existence of modern and high modern views of language (Heller, 1999) will offer the theoretical backdrop against which the analysis will be displayed.

The historical spread of Spanish beyond the Iberian Peninsula is, of course, a product of the conquest and colonization of the Americas and of the homogenizing nation-building efforts of the independent republics in the nineteenth century (Cifuentes and Pellicer, 1989; Heath, 1972; Lodares, 2001). However, in recent decades, coinciding with the advent of globalization as a central theme in the humanities and the social sciences, the extension and status of Spanish internationally has reached an unprecedented level. This development was mainly due to two factors: first, the aggressive pursuit of policies of language promotion led by Spanish governments and the private sector (del Valle, 2005; Mar-Molinero, this volume; Sánchez and Dueñas, 2002), and second, the emergence of the Latino population of the USA as the largest ethnic minority in the country.

Public discussion of the demographic growth, upward social mobility and cultural prominence of Latinos abounds, and in such discussion, almost invariably, the language question figures prominently. The histories and linguistic profiles of Latinos and the appropriate policies for 'dealing with' multilingual individuals and sociolinguistically complex situations have indeed received much attention from both experts and non-experts (Fairclough, 2003; González, 2001; González Echevarría, 1997; Morales, 2002; Stavans, 2003; Silva-Corvalán, 1994; Urciuoli, 1996; Zentella, 1997). In most cases, the frame of reference – the legal, linguistic, political and social context in which Latinos and their linguistic practices are analysed – is either the local contact space or the US State institutions that have traditionally provided political legitimacy to social actions and beliefs.

While local and national territories and institutional frameworks are indeed central to the full understanding of the sociolinguistic situations of Latinos, the global or transnational context must necessarily be brought into the analysis (Mar-Molinero, this volume; Villa, 2000). Latinos are active participants in multiple and complex networks of interaction: the neighbourhood, the local community, the nation-state, the heritage country, the Spanish-speaking world, and global markets. Their linguistic practices, therefore, influence and are influenced by these diverse environments; and, similarly, their linguistic beliefs are produced, reproduced, and transformed in multiple ideological settings.

This chapter focuses specifically on language ideologies: 'cultural conceptions of the nature, form and purpose of language, and communicative behaviour as an enactment of a collective order' (Gal and Woolard, 2001: 1). Our understanding of this concept and its usefulness for the theoretical development of sociolinguistics has grown in the past decades as a result of efforts made by scholars from different fields to converge around a common view of language that focuses on its non-referential functions, on the linguistic 'awareness' of speakers (Kroskrity, 2000: 4–23), and on its cultural and historical specificity (Gal and Woolard, 2001; Joseph and Taylor, 1990; Kroskrity, 2000; Schieffelin, Woolard and Kroskrity, 1998).

Looking at educational institutions as sites where multiple language ideologies converge, Heller (1999: 344) has called attention to the fact that Franco-Ontarian schools, while conceived with an essentially modernist orientation, face high modern conditions of existence. Following Giddens (1990), she identifies high modernity with economic shifts that favour the service and information sectors; and through observation of the deployment of practices and beliefs in the school, she explores 'the ways in which ideologies of language and national identity are changing as part of current processes of globalization' (Heller, 1999: 336). The new paradigm has triggered 'the breakdown of modern ideologies of language and nation-state' and rearranged the distribution of value to different types of linguistic competence (*ibid.*). While linguistic nationalism has not vanished, it now coexists with properly high modern ideologies that construct language as a commodity, call for standardized international languages, and value local linguistic commodities that carry a mark of distinction (*ibid.*).

These shifts in the world's linguistic ecology (Haugen, 1972: 325–39; Spolsky, 2004: 7–8) and the tensions that characterize the coexistence of modernist and high modern language ideologies are also apparent in discussions of the history and prospects of the Spanish-speaking world and of Spanish as a valuable, standardized global language. Interestingly, Latinos and their linguistic practices are often central themes in such discussions. As we will see, even a superficial look at their speech and the beliefs held about them, both by themselves and others, yields an intricate scenario where multiple language ideologies converge, often in mutual contradiction. This is hardly surprising, since, as Kroskrity has indicated,

> language ideologies are profitably conceived as multiple because of the multiplicity of meaningful social divisions (class, gender, clan, elites, generations and so on) within sociocultural groups that have the potential to produce divergent perspectives expressed as indices of group membership. (Kroskrity, 2000: 12)

We can therefore expect to find evidence of language ideologies in a wide variety of sources: the narratives of Latinos themselves (González, 2001), the testimonials of Latino intellectuals (Anzaldúa, 1999), the analyses of non-Latino and Latino academics (Huntington, 2004; Zentella, 1997), the statements of politicians and advocates of language legislation (for example the US English Foundation). As anticipated earlier, the LP agents in charge of the contemporary imagining of *hispanofonía* have also contributed significantly to the discussion of Spanglish and the linguistic practices of Latinos and provided us with yet another valuable source of data.[2]

La hispanofonía

The interest in constructing a modern, postcolonial hispanophone community is almost as old as the fall of the Spanish empire (Mar-Molinero, this volume). The *hispanismo* movement (Pike, 1971), which started to emerge in the second half of the nineteenth century, hoped to spread the idea of a pan-Hispanic brotherhood and was based on the belief that, in spite of the political independence of the former colonies, a Spanish culture embodied in the Spanish language remained as an inalienable link among all Spanish-speaking nations. However, the consolidation of this community as a true *hispanofonía*, as a culturally, economically, and politically operative entity (cf. the notion of a unified linguistic market in Bourdieu, 1991: 45–6), has faced serious challenges: the development of national identities in the new republics, subsequent regional rivalries, the dismissal of Spain as a cultural beacon, or the multilingual nature of most national territories within the imagined hispanophone community (starting with Spain and its yet unsolved 'national problem') have all conspired against the project of *hispanismo* (del Valle and Gabriel-Stheeman, 2002, 2004). But, in spite of these hurdles, or probably because of them, the efforts have persisted and even gained renewed strength, especially beginning in the 1990s, a decade that bore witness to Spain's economic take-off and to its enthusiastic incorporation into the highways of late capitalism and globalization. A few Spanish companies became transnational corporations and zoomed in on Latin America, which they perceived as a territory where their intervention would be not only legitimate but natural (del Valle, 2005):

> Iberoamérica es un área de expansión natural para las entidades y empresas españolas, porque las raíces culturales y el idioma común facilitan el acceso a los mercados y la clientela. (Casilda Béjar, 2001) (Iberoamérica is a region where the expansion of Spanish organizations and corporations is natural, because the common cultural roots and language facilitate access to markets and customers.)

Several labels circulate in public discussions of Spanish to refer to the group of nations where the language is spoken or to the community of human beings who have it as their native tongue: *Hispanoamérica, el mundo hispánico, la comunidad hispanohablante*. Lately, *Iberoamérica* has gained ground in formal contexts, especially in Spain, but it often includes – just like *Latinoamérica* or *América Latina* – Portugal and Brazil. Each of these terms has its own linguistic, cultural and, of course, ideological history (a complex and fascinating topic in its own right). With due apologies, I would like to further complicate this already tricky semantic field by advancing the term *hispanofonía*. As I see it, *hispanofonía* is not simply an objective fact, a group of nations, a network of interaction threaded by a shared communicative code. It is rather an imagined community (Anderson, 1982) grounded in a common language, itself imagined, and which ties together in an emotional bond those who feel they possess it and those who have a sense of loyalty to it. *Hispanofonía* is a language ideology, a historically situated conception of Spanish as an enactment of a collective order in which Spain performs a central role (cf. above, Gal and Woolard's definition). Víctor García de la Concha, Professor of Spanish at the University of Salamanca, Spain, and Director of the Spanish Royal Academy (henceforth RAE), expressed the essence of this ideology with succinct eloquence:

Es realmente emocionante cómo la lengua está sirviendo de lugar de encuentro y no sólo como canal de comunicación. La lengua nos hace patria común en una concordia superior. (Cited in *El País*, 9 July 2000) (It is truly moving to see how the language is being used as a place of encounter and not only as a mode of communication. The language provides us with a common fatherland in superior harmony.)

Hispanofonía has been promoted as a post-colonial order, as a post-national order. Yet the problem remains as to whether we should focus on the chronological 'post' or the relational hyphen: does *hispanofonía* place us in a new social reality beyond the injustices of colonialism and the fanatical loyalties of nationalism, or does it rely on those very historical processes to build an allegedly new global order? (del Valle, 2005; Mar-Molinero, this volume).

Spain's contemporary LP should be understood in this context. Two principal goals have been pursued: securing the unity of the Spanish language and promoting its international spread. The consolidation of the Spanish-speaking world into a true *hispanofonía* was entrusted to the RAE, which embarked on the modernization of its public image and on the improvement of its relationship with Latin America by strengthening the Association of Academies of the Spanish Language. For the international promotion of the language, the Spanish government (a socialist government) created in 1991 the Cervantes Institute. The main strategy followed by these institutions has been to provide Spanish with a positive public image that would facilitate its acceptance, on one hand, as the common language of Spain and the basis of *la hispanofonía*, and on the other, as a valuable international language of culture and business.[3] As suggested in del Valle (2005), this image has been created around four notions: first, Spanish is a language that promotes the encounter of diverse peoples, it is used as a means of expression in multiple cultures, and therefore functions as a symbol of democratic harmony; second, Spanish is a prestigious and expanding language; third, its acceptance as a pan-Hispanic, multinational language renders it a symbol of internationalism against the dangerous traditional loyalties of ethnicism and nationalism; and fourth, Spanish is a useful and profitable language, knowledge of which may constitute a valuable economic resource for those who possess it:

> La apuesta por la lengua española como lengua de futuro, como vehículo para el progreso y el bienestar de las sociedades en el tiempo que viene, no sólo obedece a planteamientos culturales: tiene también sólida base económica. (García Delgado, 2001)
> (A commitment to Spanish as a language for the future, as a vehicle for the progress and well-being of societies in the years to come, is not simply the result of cultural arguments: it has a strong economic base too.)

As anticipated above, the presence of a Spanish-speaking population in the USA and the popularity of Spanish as a foreign language in its schools and universities has been frequently discussed by Spain's LP agents and strategically used, first, in the conceptual elaboration of *la hispanofonía*, and second, in the promotion of Spanish as a valuable language. Let us now turn to a few texts that illustrate the nature of this interest.

Spain and 'the vigour of everything Hispanic'

In 2003, the US Census Bureau released figures confirming that Hispanics had officially become the largest minority group in the nation. This demographic milestone offered an excellent opportunity for Spain's press to examine and in some cases celebrate the emergent social prominence of Latinos. In a lengthy article entitled '¿PRESIDENT LÓPEZ?' the Madrid daily *El País* discussed the phenomenon:

> Los hispanos, además de estar ya por encima de la minoría negra, son más jóvenes, tienen más hijos y empiezan a salir del pozo de la pobreza para atisbar su propia manera de realizar el sueño americano. Aún no son una clase media poderosa, pero sus posibilidades de

crecimiento resultan cada vez más atractivas para los mercados y para los cazadores de votos. (*El País*, 20 July 2003)
(Hispanics, in addition to outnumbering the black minority, are younger, have more children, and are beginning to overcome poverty and get a glimpse of their own way of fulfilling the American dream. They are not a powerful middle class yet, but their potential for growth is becoming more and more attractive for markets and vote-chasers.)

In addition to the increasing strategic (political and economic) value of Latinos, the spread of Spanish to new domains in the North American nation and the growing interest in its study as a foreign language also caught the attention of the Spanish media:

40 MILLONES DE HISPANOS FORZARÁN A EEUU A APOYAR LA EDUCACIÓN BILINGÜE. (*El País*, 12 February 1997)
(40 million Hispanics will force the USA to support bilingual education.)

EL CASTELLANO ENTRA EN POLÍTICA. Por primera vez en la historia dos candidatos a gobernadores en EEUU debaten en español. (*El País*, 2 March 2002)
(Spanish penetrates politics. For the first time in history two candidates for governor in the USA hold a debate in Spanish.)

LOS CONGRESISTAS DE EE.UU. ESTUDIAN ESPAÑOL EN CURSOS INTENSIVOS DE VERANO.
(US Congressmen study Spanish in intensive summer courses.) (*ABC*, 22 August 2003)

All this attention to the 'Latino phenomenon' coincided with parallel interest by Spanish institutions that were attempting to establish a presence in the United States:

DON FELIPE CELEBRA LA PUJANZA DE LO HISPANO EN LA APERTURA DEL INSTITUTO CERVANTES DE NUEVA YORK. Acompañaron al Príncipe el secretario de Estado de Cooperación Internacional, Miguel Ángel Cortés, y el Director del Instituto Cervantes, Jon Juaristi. (*ABC*, 12 October 2003)
(Don Felipe [heir to Spain's throne] celebrates the vigour of everything Hispanic at the inauguration of the Cervantes Institute in New York. The Prince was escorted by State Secretary for International

Cooperation, Miguel Ángel Cortés, and by the Director of the Cervantes, Jon Juaristi.)

Foreign policy, language policy

This project, of course, is not unrelated to Spain's foreign policy – the Instituto Cervantes was in fact created under the umbrella of the Ministry of Foreign Affairs. Perhaps the most forthright statements of Spain's interest in the USA were made by José María Aznar, Prime Minister between 1996 and 2004, during his 2003 visit. The following headlines from the coverage of Aznar's trip will help us understand the terms in which the relationship between Spain, the USA and its Latino population was being conceived:

AZNAR TRATA DE AFIANZAR EN ESTADOS UNIDOS UN LIDERAZGO ENTRE LA POBLACIÓN HISPANA. (*El País*, 8 July 2003)
(Aznar tries to secure a role of leadership among the Hispanic population in the United States.)

AZNAR ANIMA A LOS HISPANOS PARA QUE ACERQUEN EEUU A IBEROAMÉRICA Y EUROPA. (*El País* 14 July 2003)
(Aznar encourages Hispanics to bring the US closer to Iberoamérica and Europe.)

La pujanza económica y demográfica configura estas comunidades como un mercado en alza y una fuerza social en auge. (*El País*, 8 July 2003)
(Their demographic and economic vigour turns these communities into a rising market and an emergent social force.)

The Wall Street Journal, reporting on the same trip, put it even more bluntly. In an article entitled 'As His Tenure Winds Down, Aznar Stresses Spain's Ties to Americas' the Prime Minister was quoted as saying 'I want Hispanics in the US to know that they have common European roots and a heritage that can be as solid as the Anglo-Saxon one' (*The Wall Street Journal*, 16 September 2003). The reporters writing the piece then commented: 'For good reason. In just over a decade, Spanish companies have invested more than $90 million to expand in Latin America, and have increasingly spoken about using Mexico as a platform to enter the US market' (*ibid.*). Prime Minister Aznar was in fact advocating the spread of *hispanofonía* in order to create a 'natural' bond between Spain and US Latinos that would facilitate access to their market.

In 2001, during the II International Conference on the Spanish Language – organized by the Instituto Cervantes and the RAE in

Valladolid – Enrique V. Iglesias, President at the time of the Interamerican Development Bank, stated in his plenary address the importance of Latinos as a market:

> La población hispana de los Estados Unidos constituye la tercera entidad económica del mundo latino ... el español tiene una importante y creciente impronta en la cultura, las comunicaciones y en el volumen del consumo de los Estados Unidos. (Iglesias, 2001)
> (The Hispanic population of the United States is the third largest economic bloc in the Latin world ... Spanish is making an important and growing mark on the culture, communications and volume of consumption in the United States.)

Most important for our purposes is the role that Spanish is given in the configuration of that market. Óscar Berdugo, President of the *Asociación para el Progreso del Español como Recurso Económico* (Association for the Development of Spanish as an Economic Asset), stated during his presentation at the same conference:

> Si España se consigue colocar como referente de identidad o como proveedor de señas de identidad culturales con respecto a la comunidad hispanohablante de Estados Unidos, estaremos en una inmejorable situación para mejorar nuestras posiciones en aqu país. (Berdugo, 2001)
> (If Spain manages to become a point of reference or a signpost for cultural identity for the Spanish-speaking community of the United States, we will be in an unbeatable situation to improve our positions in that country.)

It is important to highlight one aspect of Spain's LP evident in the following statements: 'AZNAR TRATA DE AFIANZAR EN ESTADOS UNIDOS UN LIDERAZGO'; 'AZNAR ANIMA A LOS HISPANOS'; 'I want Hispanics in the US to know'; 'Si España se consigue colocar como referente de identidad' (Aznar tries to secure a role of leadership; Aznar encourages Hispanics; ... ; If Spain manages to become a point of reference for identity). These expressions reveal a strategic desire by Spanish officials to have an active role in the configuration of Latinos' language ideologies: Latinos must be persuaded not only that Spanish is a valuable language but also that it is the central pillar of an *hispanofonía* to which they belong, and in which Spain is a benevolent *primus inter pares*.

Spanglish: a no man's 'land-gauge'?

Questions of language and identity have always been a part of public life in the history of the USA (Baron, 1990). While English is the dominant language of the nation, there has always been some concern over internal variation or over the presence of other languages: some of these were spoken in a given territory before it was taken over by the USA, and others were brought in by immigrant groups. Concern over linguistic and therefore national integrity continues today, as demonstrated by institutions such as the US English Foundation:

> U.S. ENGLISH, Inc. is the nation's oldest, largest citizens' action group dedicated to preserving the unifying role of the English language in the United States. (http://www.us-english.org/inc/)

Some contemporary expressions of concern about the collapse of the USA's national identity have referred to multilingualism and, in particular, to the presence of Spanish as factors supporting this process. In one of the most widely publicized and controversial discussions of the matter, Samuel Huntington foresees the Hispanization of the United States mentioning the persistence of Spanish among Mexican immigrants as a possible hurdle to their assimilation into the national project and as an agent of the transformation of America (2004: 221–56).

One of the themes that appears with relative frequency in public discussions of US Latinos, their linguistic practices, and their cultural and national loyalties – to the USA, to their ancestral country or to *hispanofonía* – is Spanglish. In spite of the strength of purist ideas about language among Latinos (De Genova and Ramos-Zayas, 2003: 151–5), there is little doubt that the linguistic practices that result from contact between Spanish and English have become, at least for some Latinos, more than just useful strategies of verbal interaction. They have in fact developed into an important sign of group membership that iconically reflects their multiple worlds and loyalties (Urciuoli, 1996; Zentella, 1997). One of the most emblematic statements of this connection between Spanglish and Latino identities was made by Gloria Anzaldúa in her classic work, *Borderlands*/La Frontera:

> For a people who are neither Spanish nor live in a country in which Spanish is the first language; for a people who live in a country in which English is the reigning tongue but who are not Anglo; for a people who cannot entirely identify with either standard (formal,

Castilian) Spanish nor standard English, what recourse is left to them but to create their own language? A language which they can connect their identity to, one capable of communicating the realities and values true to themselves – a language with terms that are neither *español ni inglés*, but both. We speak a patois, a forked tongue, a variation of two languages. (Anzaldúa, 1999: 77)

This view of language and Latino identity clashes with the image of the USA as a monolingual nation that institutions such as the US English Foundation or scholars like Huntington seem to embrace. And it also clashes with the ideology of *hispanofonía*. In fact, agents of Spain's contemporary LP have striven to discredit Spanglish. In their condemnation, they have tended to bypass the linguistic arguments of American nationalism and have focused instead on describing Spanglish as the artificial fabrication of eccentric intellectuals with an agenda and an axe to grind, as a source of marginality, and as a sign of mental deprivation.

Among the strategies we find in attempts to question the legitimacy of Spanglish are the denial of its existence and the attribution of artificiality:

Víctor García de la Concha, Presidente de la Real Academia de la Lengua expresó que el spanglish no puede considerarse 'idioma, ni dialecto, ni siquiera jerga. Es un invento de laboratorio'. (*HOY*, 8 June 2001)
(Víctor García de la Concha, President of the RAE said that Spanglish cannot be considered 'a language or a dialect, not even a jargon. It is something created in a laboratory'.)

[Según García de la Concha] en esta sección [del II Congreso de la Lengua Española] se discutirá sobre la norma hispánica, el español de América y de Estados Unidos – 'se aclarará para siempre que el *spanglish* sólo existe en el marketing o, mejor dicho, mercadotecnia'. (*El País*, 20 June 2001)
([According to García de la Concha] in this section [of the II Conference on the Spanish Language] there will be a discussion of the pan-Hispanic norm, American and US Spanish – 'we will make it clear once and forever that *Spanglish* only exists as a product of marketing'.)

Pointing to its lack of value, Humberto López Morales, a well-known sociolinguist and Secretary of the Association of Academies of the Spanish Language, predicted a ruinous future for speakers of Spanglish:

> [López Morales] dice que el *spanglish* es una ruina y un fracaso. 'Hoy lo que la gente quiere es hablar bien español y hablar bien inglés, los dos idiomas'. (*El País*, 23 July 2004)
> (He says that Spanglish is a wreck and a failure. 'Today what people want is to speak Spanish well and English well, both languages'.)

A similar denial of legitimacy was evident in an academic event that took place in November of 2000 at Dartmouth College in New Hampshire. According to *El País*, during the meeting, Professor Beatriz Pastor (from Dartmouth) stated:

> [E]l spanglish no es ni una aberración ni una catástrofe, sino algo que fuerza la transformación del monolingüismo del poder. (*El País*, 23 November 2000)
> (Spanglish is neither an aberration nor a catastrophe, but something that forces the transformation of the monolingualism of power.)

To this, Antonio Garrido, Professor of Spanish Language and Literature at the University of Málaga, Spain, who at the time was Director of the New York branch of the Cervantes, replied:

> Dígase lo que se diga, el Spanglish no es una lengua canónica ni intelectual, y ningún documento serio de investigación será escrito jamás en Spanglish ... O se escribe en español o se escribe en inglés. (*Ibid.*)
> (You may say whatever you want, but Spanglish is neither a canonical nor an intellectual language, and no serious research document will ever be written in Spanglish ... Either you write in Spanish or in English.)

The late Fernando Lázaro Carreter, Professor of Linguistics at the *Complutense* University of Madrid who after presiding over the RAE for several years became one of Spain's most prominent language mavens (Cameron 1995: vii) and representatives of a complaint tradition (Milroy and Milroy, 1999), began one of his famous columns on language in *El País* reproducing a classified ad published in a car magazine in Oregon, USA:

> No Credito Mal o buen Credito todos reciviran el buen trato que se meresen Aquí en Broadway Toyota Fabor de hablar para su cita al

... Pregunte Por el Señor NoeENriquez Que estara a sus ordenes acistiendo ala comunida Hispana. Se habla español. (*El País*, 7 April 2002)
(No Credit Bad or good Credit everyone will recieve the polite attention they decerve Here in Broadway Toyota Pleaze for an appointment talk to # ... Ask For Mr. NoeENriquez Who will be at your service helping the Hispanic community. We speak Spanish.)

After quoting the ad, Lázaro added:

Un paisano que ha estado en semejante lugar me envía una página con ese aborto de final tan patético, para no tener que creerlo a pura fe. ¿Quién está interesado en mantener a muchos hispanos en tanta indigencia mental? (*El País*, 7 April 2002)
(A fellow countryman who's been to such a place sends me one page with that pathetic abortion of an ending, so that I don't have to take his word for it. Who is interested in keeping so many Hispanics in such mental indigence?)

Lázaro Carreter frequently affirmed the connection between intellectual competence and correct usage. In a 2001 interview, he stated that 'si se empobrece la lengua, se empobrece el pensamiento' (if language becomes impoverished, then thought becomes impoverished too). When asked whether *Spanglish* would threaten the unity of Spanish, he answered:

Tampoco es mayor peligro. No alcanza los medios de comunicación hispanos. Es, eso sí, un fenómeno muy duradero que se renueva continuamente. Hay, por otro lado, muchos hispanos con conciencia clara de que el español, aunque sea para rechazarlo, pertenece a aquello que quieren dejar atrás. Lo importante es que exista esa conciencia, aunque sea para hablar un buen inglés, porque eso es también bueno para el español. Evita la contaminación entre los dos idiomas. El *spanglish* es un gesto de afirmación personal sin conciencia. A alguien que dice *lookear* por mirar y *rentar* por alquilar le da lo mismo la lengua. Sólo quiere hacerse entender. (*El País*, 13 October 2001)
(No, it is not a big threat. It does not reach the Hispanic media. It is a long-lasting phenomenon, though, constantly renewed. On the other hand, there are many Hispanics clearly aware – even if it is to reject it – that Spanish is part of that which they want to leave behind. It is this awareness that is important, even if it is to learn

English well, because that is also good for Spanish. It avoids contamination between the two languages. Spanglish is an unreflexive act of individual affirmation. Someone who says *lookear* instead of *mirar* or *rentar* instead of *alquilar* does not care for the language. He just wants to make himself understood.)

Some of Spain's language guardians, such as Gregorio Salvador, Professor of Spanish at the *Autónoma* University of Madrid and Associate Director of the RAE, have gone so far in their concern with linguistic contamination that they have even warned against the dangers of bilingualism:

GREGORIO SALVADOR ALERTA SOBRE LOS DAÑOS QUE CAUSA EL BILINGÜISMO ... El académico dijo que en las comunidades autónomas bilingües hay personas que 'hablan una lengua mezclada o contaminan la suya', lo que 'acaba estropeando las dos' ... Quitó importancia al fenómeno del *spanglish* que, en su opinión, no pasa de ser 'lo que hablan los inmigrantes que no acaban de hablar inglés'. (*El País*, 7 September 2004)
(GREGORIO SALVADOR WARNS AGAINST THE DAMAGE CAUSED BY BILINGUALISM ... The academician said that in [Spain's] bilingual autonomous communities there are people who 'speak a mixed language or contaminate their own', which 'ends up ruining both' ... He minimized the importance of the *Spanglish* phenomenon which, in his opinion, is nothing but 'what immigrants who don't quite learn English speak'.)

We must of course ask ourselves the extent to which these views of Spanglish reach Latinos. The opinions thus far presented were after all voiced by prominent representatives of Spain's LP institutions, and most of the extracts reproduced above were taken from Spanish newspapers. While more research is indeed needed on the circulation of language ideologies it seems clear that Spain's cultural institutions are not alone in policing the borders of Spanish. The most salient public display of anti-Spanglish views in the USA in recent years was produced by Yale Professor of Hispanic and Comparative Literature Roberto González Echevarría and staged in one of the most distinguished venues for ideological spread: the Op-Ed section of *The New York Times*. In an article entitled 'Kay possa! Is "Spanglish" a language?' (28 March 1998) González Echevarría laid out his position. His views did not differ in essence from those expressed by the Spanish academicians: Spanglish is the result of deficient knowledge of the standard varieties of both languages and constitutes a threat to the linguistic, cultural, and economic health of the community:

> The sad reality is that Spanglish is primarily the language of poor Hispanics, many barely literate in either language. They incorporate English words and constructions into their daily speech because they lack the vocabulary and education in Spanish to adapt to the changing culture around them. (*TNYT*, 28 March 1998)

He admits, of course, that Spanglish is also used by highly educated people who have an excellent command of both languages. For them he offers a different explanation:

> Educated Hispanics who do likewise have a different motivation: Some are embarrassed by their background and feel empowered by using English words and directly translated English idioms. Doing so, they think, is to claim membership in the mainstream. Politically, however, Spanglish is a capitulation; it indicates marginalization, not enfranchisement. (*Ibid.*)

In expressing his fears, González Echevarría was even more explicit than the Spanish professors, and warned against the threat posed by Spanglish to the unity of the Spanish language:

> The last thing we need is to have each group carve out its own Spanglish, creating a Babel of hybrid tongues. Spanish is our strongest bond, and it is vital that we preserve it. (*Ibid.*)

Spanglish and language ideologies

Thus, views of Latinos, their linguistic practices, and their status *vis-à-vis* societal structures and cultural institutions reveal the presence of multiple language ideologies. We saw, for example, how the prominence of Latinos in American society tends to be portrayed by the Spanish press and by agents of Spain's LP in triumphal terms that equate demographic growth with the increasing power of language. As a result, Spanish is presented as making significant inroads into one of the bastions of the Anglophone world and thus increasing its value in the USA and in the international linguistic markets: the fact that a significant portion of the population speaks Spanish, for example, has made politicians want to learn it in order to appeal to Latinos; it has also become coveted linguistic capital by non-Spanish-speaking Americans who hope to land more lucrative jobs or somehow gain access to the Latino market; moreover, such popularity in the USA will help promote internationally an image of Spanish as a truly global language (cf. note 1). This approach to Latinos and US Spanish is obviously mediated by the commodification of language, an ideology to which I will refer, following Ángel López García's suggestion, as the *emolinguistic ideology* (from Lat. *emo* = 'to buy').[4]

We also saw that the demographic growth of Latinos has been perceived by Spanish governments and entrepreneurs from Spanish-speaking countries (mainly Spain) as an opening through which to enter the US market. Viewing Spanish through the lens of *hispanismo* and emolinguism, former Prime Minister Aznar or language 'impresarios' such as Óscar Berdugo bluntly state their desire to secure the loyalty of Latinos encouraging them to perceive their Spanish-speaking roots as a link to a transnational cultural community to which they owe some sort of allegiance.

In a study of the operation of language ideologies, Irvine and Gal (2000) identified three semiotic processes involved in locating, interpreting and rationalizing sociolinguistic complexity (Irvine and Gal, 2000: 36). These processes are *erasure, iconization* and *fractal recursivity*, and at least the first two can be identified in the texts reviewed. Firstly, Latinos are presented as a totality: the assumption is made that all Latinos speak Spanish and that they constitute a culturally and linguistically homogeneous entity. Such assumption erases the diverse character of this demographic group and ignores the complexity of the relations among Latinos of different origins (De Genova and Ramos-Zayas, 2003). Similarly, the unqualified equation of population growth with sociopolitical power and the iconic linking of demographic weight with linguistic prestige erase the conditions of existence of a vast number of Latinos as a racialized minority (De Genova and Ramos-Zayas, 2003; Urciuoli, 1996).

The public representations of Spanglish display an even more complex net of interacting language ideologies. The harsh condemnation of linguistic practices that fall outside the conceptual constraints of a standard grammar is deeply grounded in the ideology of *monoglossia*, which consists of two principles: *focused grammar*, or the assumption that what linguistically characterizes an individual as well as a community is possession of a well-defined and relatively stable grammar: speaking is always speaking a language; and its diachronic counterpart, the *principle of convergence*, or the assumption that people's linguistic behaviour tends to become homogeneous over time through pressure from the dominant norm of the community (del Valle, 1999).[5] Monoglossic beliefs obstruct the perception of diffused linguistic practices as legitimate means of verbal interaction and encourage the iconic association of such practices with intellectual deprivation and social marginality. There is tolerance of multilingualism in monoglossia, but, as in Milroy and Milroy's description of standardization (Milroy, 2001; Milroy and Milroy, 1999), the grammars involved must remain uncontaminated and performance in each case must comply or tend to converge with the ideal standard form.

As we saw above, in the negations of Spanglish, the aggressive promotion of monoglossia operates at times by excessively conspicuous erasures. This is a common feature of the authoritative discourses through which the spread of ideologies may be encouraged (Tsitsikis, 2004). Authoritative discourse demands to be acknowledged and adopted ('we will make it clear once and forever ...'), derives its power from an independent source (for example a prestigious Professorship), and rejects dialogic relations to other ideologies ('Spanglish is a wreck and a failure') (Bakhtin, 1981: 342 and 1986: 163; Tsitsikis, 2004: 570–1). Aggressive erasure is a dangerous strategy, though, since its hyperbolic tendencies may end up revealing precisely that which they are trying to hide.

Such a strong-handed approach is in fact quite revealing of the objectives of these policies. Through these diatribes, all Spanish-speakers, not just Latinos, are being warned against the dangers of mixing and the careless adoption of anglicisms. Monoglossia and verbal hygiene (Cameron, 1995) are undoubtedly at work in the expression of these views. However, in staging such severe condemnation of language mixing, LP agents engage in policing the boundaries of Spanish, protecting the linguistic oilfield, asserting their control of the resource, and unifying the linguistic market, thus claiming legitimacy as the principal source of credentialization of linguistic competence. Strong public warnings from representatives of the institutions of linguistic power have a double effect: linguistic insecurity is kept alive, and, under threat of giving away their intellectual poverty, speakers are encouraged to remain loyal to the legitimate form of the language and to its guardians.

The rhetorical excesses and harsh disapproval of Spanglish may also be reactive to challenges (direct or indirect) to Spain's language policies and desired hegemony. As we saw above, favourable views of Spanglish and Latino identities have been advanced and publicly defended by individuals endowed with some level of cultural and social legitimacy in the eyes of Latinos (symbolic power in Bourdieu's terminology). The position represented by Anzaldúa, for example, endorses a Latino culture that commits not to one language but to a multiplicity of norms that reflect the group's heterogeneity. Such views are mediated by the ideology of *heteroglossia* which constructs diffused speech (Le Page and Tabouret-Keller, 1985) as the realization of multiple coexisting norms and as the product of diverse types of linguistic competence. An individual's heteroglot language is therefore better described as a dot in a three-dimensional space moving in the direction of multiple vectors that point to the different norms available to them (del Valle, 1999). The ideology of heteroglossia is more likely to surface in linguistic contexts that James Milroy (2001: 539–43) has described as 'language in an unstandardized universe'. Like all ideologies, heteroglossia may rise to a high level of consciousness, and heteroglot practices may become reified and used as a political instrument or an economic asset. Ilan Stavans, Professor of Spanish and Latinamerican and Latino Culture at Amherst College, has attempted to legitimize Spanglish precisely by performing this type of reification: he has set out to elaborate a dictionary of Spanglish and a Spanglish rendition of the first chapter of *Don Quixote* (Stavans, 2003). His efforts certainly caught the attention of the media, including, in Spain, frequent references in *El País* and, in the USA, a television interview in PBS's *The Newshour with Jim Lehrer*. Daniel Villa, Professor of Hispanic Linguistics at New Mexico State University, used Spanglish to deliver the Presidential Address at the 2001 Conference of the Linguistic Association of the Southwest in Puebla, Mexico, making a political statement that challenged academic conventions that reproduce monoglossic ideologies (Villa, 2001).

Finally, the popularity and worldwide success of reggaeton – the hybrid musical style combining diverse rhythms and mixing Spanish and English in its lyrics that emerged in Puerto Rico, caught on among US Latinos of all origins, and is now spreading internationally – offers another case in point: the commodification of forms of cultural expression not just close to Spanglish but closely interlocked with it. DJ Nelson, one of its original creators, described the process quite bluntly: 'Ten years ago, reggaeton was music. Now it is a business' (cited in *The New York Times*, 17 July 2005).[6]

In modern times, Spanish may have been a language: a system of communication and sign of identity; but, like reggaeton, in high modernity '[l]o que puede ser el español, o lo que es de hecho ya, es un negocio' (what Spanish may become, or rather what it has already become, is a business) (*El País*, 9 February 2005). Spanish is indeed defined as a commodity that Spain's LP agencies are determined to control and commercialize, and, as we have seen, the US is a strategic market in this enterprise. Juan Ramón Lodares, Professor until his recent death at the *Autónoma* University of Madrid and staunch and brilliant supporter of emolinguism, stated during the presentation of one of his books: 'En Estados Unidos [el español] es un idioma que hace ganar dinero' (In the United States you can make money with Spanish) (*El País*, 9 February 2005). For Spain's LP agencies and for those whose interests they represent, this requires preserving the unity of the market and holding on to the *skeptron* (Bourdieu, 1991: 113) that signals their linguistic power and authorizes them to grant the linguistic credentials that have been defined as most valuable. The linguistic practices of Latinos, their instrumentalization as signs of hybrid identities, and the current political climate of the USA (highly resistant to official bilingualism and generally unfriendly to institutional support for mother tongue retention among immigrants) pose serious challenges to that project.

While some see the international spread of English as a historical chance for worldwide communication, others perceive its hegemony as a sign of the USA's domination of international cultural markets. Just like *la francophonie*, the Spanish-speaking world offers the possibility of creating an alternative system of production and circulation of forms of cultural expression. However, as our analysis has shown, the question remains as to whether Spain's *hispanofonía* will become a true alternative or whether it will be nothing but a competitor who, using the threat of hegemonic English as an alibi, ends up promoting the very same ideologies for the very same purposes.

Notes

1 I use 'global language', following Crystal, as one that 'develops a special role that is recognized in every country ... To achieve such a status, a language has to be taken up by other countries around the world' (2003: 3–4). I do not subscribe, though, to Crystal's the-right-place-at-the-right-time views on the emergence of global English. Spanish language agencies in claiming Spanish's global status perpetrate a similar type of erasure (see below).

2 Throughout this chapter I will use the term 'Spanglish' as shorthand for the linguistic practices that reflect the complex multilingual and multidialectal repertoire of Latinos, which includes varieties of both English and Spanish (Zentella, 1997). In general usage, depending on its discursive position, 'Spanglish' may or may not have pejorative connotations. The same occurs with alternative terms such as 'Tex-Mex' or 'Pocho'.

3 On *acceptance* as a component of language planning see Haugen (1972): 252.

4   His paper '¿Ideas o ideologías de la lengua española?' was presented on 1 April 2005 at a colloquium at New York University's King Juan Carlos I of Spain Center under the title 'El español como ideología en la era de la globalización'. A volume of the colloquium's papers is in preparation and being edited by José del Valle.

5   In my 1999 article I referred to monoglossia as a linguistic 'culture', following Schiffman (1996). The shift in terminology is due to the perspective of the present study, from which I try to unveil how culture is interlocked with power (cf. Philips 1998: 213).

6   Cf. Stroud (2004): 204–6, on the appropriation and commodification of the Swedish known as Rinkeby Swedish.

4
Language Conflict and the Micro–Macro Link in the Spanish-Speaking World

Rainer Enrique Hamel

'Language has always been the loyal companion of the empire' – Antonio de Nebrija's classic prophecy is frequently quoted as an early visionary perspective of what was to become the main ideological foundation[1] of the unity between nation, empire and the Spanish language. Not only did this vision accompany the Spanish Empire throughout its time of glory but it managed to survive its decline with the loss of the main Spanish colonies in America. Indeed, as a vision, it has regularly arisen whenever Spain has felt in need of reaffirming its hegemony over the Spanish-speaking world and its positioning *vis-à-vis* other world languages (see Cifuentes, 1998; Cifuentes and Ros Romero, 1993; Mar-Molinero, 2000, 2004; Del Valle, 2002; Del Valle and Gabriel-Stheeman, 2002, 2004). Since Nebrija's times, it has constituted the basis for the foundational myth of *Hispanidad* ('Hispanity'), a singularly robust ideological construct that stresses the admirable homogeneity and unity of the Spanish language compared to other international rivals, a language which can stake its claim to play a significant role in the globalized world.

Some enthusiastic Hispanists, for example the Venezuelan Leáñez Astimuño (2002), feel that Spanish is in a commanding position, for not only can it assert its role as a leading international language, but it can even defy English in its position of the sole hyper-language of the world today. They even envisage the future fusion of the Spanish-speaking countries into one polity, the 'Hispanic nation', united by the centripetal force of the common language.

Any substantive analysis of globalization, however, places Spanish far behind English – it is no rival for the global language, since mere numbers of native speakers and homogeneity will certainly not suffice to determine the power of a language community in the international arena. Its economic and military weight, together with its vitality in key areas of future growth such as international relations, science and technology and, particularly, the composition and dynamics of its third, expanding circle will certainly play a decisive role (see Kachru's rather Anglo-centric model, 1986; Kachru and Nelson, 1996). There is little doubt that Spanish will still count among the dozen super central languages[2] in a hundred years or more (Graddol, 1997; Fisher, 2000).

This political science view of linguistic globalization on the macro level considers languages as large sociological and demographic aggregates and places them in the field of language policy (for example de Swaan, 2001). If we are to achieve a differentiated comprehension of multilingualism in our present world we also need further, complementary perspectives. In what follows I will examine the Hispanic world and Hispanic sociolinguistics, which I feel play a crucial role in modern sociolinguistics.

Cultural boundaries, language conflicts and shared territories

Over the past two decades, we have seen a groundswell of overt local and regional confrontations in many parts of the world. Some of them display global implications such as the present conflict triggered by the Western invasion of Iraq led by the two main English-speaking countries (USA, UK) in 2003. From an ethnolinguistic communities' perspective, such confrontations may appear, at least at first sight, to be cultural conflicts. Such radically differing US theorists as Samuel Huntington (1996) and Immanuel Wallerstein (1983) have coincidentally formulated the prognosis (correctly, it would seem) that the twenty-first century, in contrast to the twentieth century with its systemic opposition between East and West, is to become a century of cultural conflicts, conflicts that tend to be religious, ethnic and linguistic in nature or a combination of them all. This new and old focus of polarization posits, as a central challenge for the twenty-first century, the question of how some six thousand ethnolinguistic groups and peoples in the world, representing different religions and world views, will be able to coexist more or less peacefully in nearly two hundred nation-states some of which are sited within regional blocks of supra-national integration. In times of massive migration, the nineteenth-century nationalist ideal of the monolingual and monocultural nation-state looks more utopian than ever. The historical nationalist proposal of providing a territorial base for linguistic and other ethnic rights claims, as successfully fought for by Catalans and Basques in Spain or Francophones in Canada, and less successfully by indigenous peoples in Latin America, seems to offer no appropriate solution for language conflict situations today. New approaches are called for, such as the concepts of cultural (Rosaldo, 1994) or ethnic (de la Peña, 1995, 1999) citizenship in anthropology, where intercultural spaces of a territorial, virtual or discursive nature need to be developed both theoretically and empirically from the perspective of pluriculturalism[3] and additive bilingualism. I shall return to this later.

A salient aspect of globalization seems to be, then, the resurgence of ethnic, linguistic, religious and other cultural claims issued by minorities in the context of worldwide economic and political homogenization. The effects of globalization, which means first and foremost an increased connectivity on all levels, are not only to produce worldwide economic and political homogenization and weaken most nation-states[4] as autonomous entities, but also to stimulate the upsurge of certain minorities believed to have been integrated successfully into existing nation-states during the era of modernity. Over recent years, however, the increasing multicultural diversity of old and new minorities has been 'ethnicised' to a large extent in the USA and elsewhere, a process which, according to critical voices in Europe (Bourdieu, 2001) and Latin America (García Canclini, 1999, 2004), contributes to the fragmentation of culture and stimulates ethnic fundamentalism. Current testimonies of such tendencies may be found in so-called 'White Nativism' or in Samuel Huntington's 'clash of civilizations' (1996), and in his more recent alarm that America's model of integration was at risk because Hispanics are unwilling to assimilate anymore into mainstream society (Huntington, 2004). Thus we can see a growing polarization of US society which, given its cultural globalization, influences other nations in many parts of the world. Considering recent confrontations and increasing migration as a result of globalization, we need more than ever to study and develop experiences and models of pluriculturalism, that is an enrichment perspective of multicultural coexistence in common spaces (Hamel, 2000, 2003).

To achieve this we must explore the concrete, practical and multiple ways in which different ethnolinguistic groups interact on a local and a global level, how they communicate successfully and to what extent they fall prey to cultural misunderstandings (see Gumperz, 1982), how conflicts emerge, explode or are settled in negotiated ways.

Two complementary anthropological and sociolinguistic metaphors play a significant role in this context: Cultural boundaries and cultural conflicts. Ever since Barth's (1969) provocative essay on the conceptual relevance of boundaries as constructs for ethnic identities, the metaphors of borders, frontiers and boundaries have permeated anthropological and sociolinguistic debate. Massive migration, a centrepiece of globalization, has highlighted and at the same time diversified their role. Globalization does not simply erase existing frontiers; rather, as García Canclini (1999) points out, it rearticulates the foundational differences they divide and it accepts old and new discontinuities. Traditional walls that brutally separate nations or cut through existing communities live alongside with new invisible, blurred or extended boundaries that reach far into alien territory. Language contact and conflict reflect and at the same time constitute rich examples of old and modern borderlines of all kinds. If we analyse both language policies with their macro narratives and ideologies, and micro interactional encounters from this perspective, we may reach an understanding of how these tokens of social language practice participate in the construction of often conflicting and contradictory identities – whether they be local, class, ethnic, national and transnational.

The Hispanic world, a pluricentric language area par excellence for some (Clyne, 1992; Oesterreicher, 2002), and of contested nature for others, with its wealth of diverse contact and conflict situations, constitutes a privileged realm for the development of specific models and ways of thinking; in particular, this kind of research allows us to relate macro and micro analysis within one and the same study from a political and critical perspective. At the same time, it opens up the possibility of a significant role for Hispanic sociolinguistics and discourse analysis in the international academic arena.

Although probably a majority of native speakers of Spanish live today as monolinguals within their vast territories, Spanish has been a border language right from its first consolidation as a language of both a nascent state and an empire (see, for example, Ortiz López, this volume).

At least four boundaries characterizing different aspects of Spanish in relation to other linguistic communities emerge as relevant. Spanish is a dominant language in most of its contact situations, namely in central Spain and in Hispanic America *vis-à-vis* the indigenous and immigrant languages. Only since the mid-nineteenth century has it also experienced becoming a widely-spoken dominated language in the USA. It is a significant border language in South and North America, with complex state-internal and external frontiers in Spain.[5] Moreover, Spanish plays a role as an important international language of the second level – a super central language in numerous international organizations, with a dynamically expanding circle in many areas of the world.

The concept of language conflict, as framed by Catalan sociolinguists in the 1970s, represents a typical border from within Spain. The Catalans, in light of their struggle against what they clearly saw as Castilian oppression, substituted this more militant term for Weinreich's (1953) (socio)linguistic metonymy of 'language contact'. They argued that a structuralist view of 'languages in contact' presented an image of false harmony. In the real world more cases of conflict prevailed than of peaceful contact (for example Vallverdú, 1980). Their provocative redefinition of 'diglossia as language conflict' certainly sharpened a critical awareness of certain ideological implications unrevealed hitherto. They redefined the term as a dynamic conflict relationship between a dominant and a dominated language, which is unlikely to remain stable over a long period of time. Rather it will result in processes of either shift and displacement of the subordinate language, or in its revitalization, expansion into the high domains from which it had been previously excluded, thus achieving a 'normalization' of its status and corpus. Clearly, activists and later Catalan governments fought for the latter. After thirty years, Catalan language policies are known worldwide to be an instance of the successful normalization of a formerly oppressed, almost endemic language. Unsurprisingly, the 'conflict' concept has faded away over time with former rebels sitting in government.

Catalan sociolinguistics has been instrumental in introducing a historical perspective of language dynamics and change, developing conceptual frameworks and methodologies for its study. A distinct approach with its own academic and political orientation, it converged with a central area of Anglo-American mainstream sociolinguistics,[6] namely the study of language shift, maintenance, and revitalization, so admirably developed by Joshua A. Fishman (1964, 1991) and others over four decades.[7]

The Catalan conflict approach represents a rich historical process of theoretical debate, political activity and empirical research accumulated in Spain and in other parts of the world that should not fall into oblivion. It is, in my view, of high topicality, especially since theorists of globalization from other disciplines converge in affirming the centrality of a cultural conflict approach (Huntington, 1996; Wallerstein, 1983; Díaz-Polanco, 2000). With its wealth of theoretical models, methodologies and research experience, sociolinguistics can certainly contribute considerably to the more general debate. In the remainder of this chapter I will examine examples of this contribution observed in Hispanic sociolinguistic situations.

The analysis of language conflict and shift in a Mexican context

The micro–macro link in sociolinguistics

Given that most approaches to language conflict, shift and maintenance, as well as to language policy belong by and large to the field of macro social sciences, they possess very few tools to support their macro hypothesis with substantial analysis on the micro level.[8] For some the micro level is simply irrelevant for theoretical modelling or abstract systemic debate.[9] Others do not have the tools to build bridges between the micro and macro and lack arguments when they are asked for concrete empirical evidence for their abstract postulates. Conversely, some current strands of micro analysis in the fields of pragmatics, discourse, conversation, and interaction analysis do not transcend the immediateness of the single ethnographic situation or discursive pattern to develop interpretations and generalizations on a sociological macro level.

In such cases the lack of integration weakens the possible power of conclusions of both sides. More than ever in times of globalization (which also implies glocalization), topics are interconnected to others in multiple ways. Therefore, general macro hypotheses need detailed data analyses which are, in part, of micro nature. Conversely, fine-grained interaction and variation analyses require global parameters derived from disciplines other than (socio) linguistics or discourse analysis in order to interpret their descriptive results.

By means of example, I shall explore a piece of Latin American research that pulls together various strings. My own research into language conflict, maintenance and shift between Spanish and Mexican Indian languages focuses on the markers of shift that can be traced in verbal interaction. It belongs to the field of language loss studies which investigate shifts in usage and do not consider attrition or other changes in competence of individual skills (cf. Hakuta *et al.*, 1992). Individual speakers are not taken into account as such as in sociolinguistic network analysis (cf. Milroy, 1980), but only as participants in specific speech events. The focus is on the collective bilingual repertoire and the ways an indigenous community mobilizes its communicative resources and develops discourse strategies to solve transactional tasks within specific speech events.

After formulating basic sociolinguistic questions and hypotheses on the macro level, ethnographic analysis of the speech community identifies key speech events and yields a general scheme of language use and distribution (mezzo level). It sets the ground for generating hypotheses about specific fields of language conflict and change. In a third step, a multi-layer discourse analysis of selected speech events describes the discursive resources actually exploited to address specific communicative needs. It reveals how different components of discourse structure including language distribution build up specific discourse strategies. In a fourth step, different discourse strategies, speech events, and types of speech events are compared to identify indicators of processes of language maintenance and loss to show how language change can be observed *in situ* and *in actu*, that is in the process of interaction itself. Next, a framework based on the distinction between language structure, discourse structure, and cultural models helps to identify two basic modalities of language shift in progress in the case under study.

Thus the analytic procedure as a whole focuses not only on language surface and structural phenomena, but also on the underlying discourse strategies and structures, as well as cultural models (patterns and procedures), all considered central components of language. Finally, the results from triangulation and contrastive analyses will be interpreted in terms of the macro questions posited.

Socio-cultural change and the communicative repertoire

In the central highlands of Mexico, the Valle del Mezquital hosts some 80,000 members of the Hñähñú (or Otomí[10]) people who live predominantly in communities between 400 and 1,500 inhabitants. Over 90 per cent of the population in the higher, arid areas of the valley is indigenous; 70 per cent is considered to be bilingual, some 25 per cent of the rest is monolingual in the native language.

Over the past 30 years native communities in this area have undergone a radical process of socioeconomic change. Under outside pressure, a growing number of households have given up their traditional settlement patterns based on scattered hamlets, and have built villages of brick houses centred on a plaza where a new primary school with its basketball field has by and large replaced the church as community centre. Only thus was it possible to connect the villages with a new infrastructure of dirt roads, electricity and water supplies. Precarious subsistence farming forced a growing number of young men and women to seek employment as migrant workers in the regional centres, in Mexico City or in the USA. Since these people generally maintain close network ties with their communities and fulfill their obligations as village citizens, a constant flow of money, new patterns of consumption and other cultural practices find their way into the villages along with the Spanish language. Radio broadcasting and incipient television reception may also play a significant role in cultural change. The primary school has definitively found its place as an institution of prestige which nourishes the expectations of social mobility and integration through the transmission of Spanish and other skills of mainstream society.

From a macro sociolinguistic perspective the language situation in the Mezquital Valley can be described as the relationship between two conflicting historical tendencies of language change. The presently dominant tendency is characterized by substitutive diglossia (in the sense of Catalan sociolinguistics, see Vallverdù, 1973; Boyer, 1991), that is a conflictual, non-stable relationship between Spanish as the dominant and Hñähñú as the subordinate language. Spanish is making inroads into the vernacular's geographical extension, its functional domains, and its lexical and grammatical structure. On the other hand, our ethnographic observation reveals a significant potential for cultural and linguistic resistance located in the close network structures of traditional kinship and farming, everyday communication, and in part in the traditional cargo system of local organization, elements of language maintenance which tend to co-occur.

Significant macro-societal factors of displacement coincide with elements such as these in other well-researched cases where language shift has actually taken place (see Gal, 1979; Fasold, 1984; Fishman, 1991, 2001; Kulick, 1992, and others). As I had argued before, however, there are good reasons not to establish a direct, causal relationship between macro societal factors and linguistic data to predict the communities' sociolinguistic behaviour in the future. Before the why-question of language shift can be addressed from an integrative, broader perspective, we still have to explore in more detail and depth the how-question, the process and mechanisms through which language shift actually takes place. My assumption is that a fine-grained multi-layer discourse analysis of language in interaction, that is the place where shift is in fact anticipated, enacted, and consolidated, can shed light on the interlinking constituents that relate socio-economic factors with linguistic data.

Ethnographic observation suggests that the recent changes in settlement patterns, migrant work, and political organization described above have led to a significant increase and a qualitative transformation of certain kinds of speech event. More everyday communication takes place due to people living closer together. More and more governmental and private institutions interfere with community life. Whereas in the past a single traditional authority or 'cacique' used to take many decisions individually, today almost all important resolutions are established collectively. Thus new and different types of committees, cooperatives, *cargos* (posts), and electoral procedures have emerged over time which have transformed many kinds of meetings into key ethnographic events for community organization. New literacy needs have thus emerged within the local societies' predominantly oral, vernacular culture that affect the communities' communicative repertoire.[11] An initial schema of speech events emerges from this ethnography, based on a general pattern of language distribution over key speech situations.

At this point we reach the limits of traditional ethnographic analysis. The scrutiny of a schema of speech events can only yield language surface descriptions as in domain analysis, that is it assesses the presence, coexistence, or absence of the languages involved. It is not able, however, to interpret the functions and effects of language choice and alternations. Nor can it describe and interpret the complex modalities of language conflict and shift, since many of their components do not appear on the language surface.

To unravel the concrete, interactive functioning of these kinds of language processes, we used a multi-layer approach of discourse analysis which deals separately with various aspects of discourse constitution. It includes the formal organization of interaction (conversation analysis), action structure (frames or action schemas, speech acts, cf. pragmatics), and communicative schemas such as argumentation and narrative. Language choice and switching phenomena are analysed as a further level of discourse organization. Further aspects of discourse constitution can be included as distinct levels of analysis if needed (Hamel, 1982, 1988a).

Modalities of language shift: ruptures and phase shift between cultural models, discourse structure and language use

Our corpus comprises speech events in various settings; analysis focuses on key events including the organization of collective farm work, local administration (Hamel, 1988a; Sierra, 1992), the legal system (Hamel, 1996; Sierra, 1990, 1995), and bilingual education (Hamel, 1988b; Francis and Hamel, 1992). It has revealed that the processes of language conflict and shift occur on at least three levels of cognitive and discourse organization that can be distinguished analytically (Figure 4.1).

Cultural models and procedures (CM)

Components: concepts and definitions of speech events, procedures (such as procedures of politeness, of problem solving, etc.), conflict or conciliation management (e.g. discourse styles of bureaucratic procedure vs. ethnic styles in intercultural communication), overreaching discourse styles, habitus, and their underlying world views

---

Discourse structures (DS)

Techniques for the organization of interaction (turn-taking, sequencing, etc.), pragmatic categories such as verbal action schemes, techniques for argumentation, narration, etc., discourse strategies

---

Linguistic codes and structures (LC)

Units on all levels of systemic linguistic analysis: phonology, morphology, syntax, semantics.

Figure 4.1   Discourse levels of language conflict

The first level of cultural models takes elements from a range of fields. Starting with the ethnographic tradition of 'ways of doing things' and Goffman's (1974) frame analysis, it draws on Bourdieu's habitus concept (1979, 1980) and encompasses developments in cognitive anthropology and related fields (Holland and Quinn, 1987; D'Andrade and Strauss, 1992). It refers to overreaching, endurable categories that cannot be reduced to discourse structures, although in many cases there are corresponding discourse units on level 2.

In the case of Hñähñú, level 1 includes procedures and models of farming and other problem-solving devices, or conflict and conciliation management. They may materialize in social and ethnic styles that are commonly related to a specific habitus and may activate a certain range of discourse strategies. Two problems arise here: how to operationalize this level without recurrence to discourse categories; and how to distinguish it in each case from the level of discourse structures. It was necessary to introduce this level beyond the more traditional dual framework of discourse vs linguistic structure (for example Gumperz, 1982) for two reasons: (a) because of its enduring, habitus-type characteristics which go beyond specific discourse structures; and (b) because there were cases where a rupture between these cultural models and given discourse structures occurs and in which this divergence is relevant (see the following examples). Levels 2 and 3 are more or less self-explanatory. Many relevant phenomena like code-switching and borrowings may be analysed on level 2 (function) and level 3 (form).

Traditionally, language shift or loss is investigated only on the third level of analysis, the object of mainstream descriptive linguistics. As we shall see, however, changes on the linguistic surface can very often only be explained if levels of discourse and cultural organization that underlie surface structure are taken into account. Among the most revealing findings was the discovery that language shift regularly operates through ruptures and phase shifts between the different levels of discourse organization mentioned above. Such dislocations transform the cultural basis of interpretation for the ethnolinguistic group, that is they interfere with their cultural models and lead to breaches between the language in use and the historical experience the group has accumulated over time (Lang, 1980).

In the Mezquital Valley, at least two different modalities of language can be distinguished, both of which operate through three phases of language dislocation and ruptures between levels of discourse organization as shown in an idealized form in Figure 4.2.

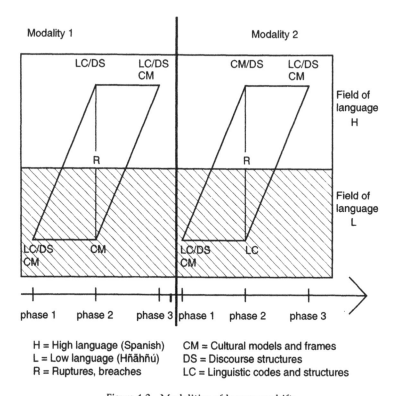

H = High language (Spanish) CM = Cultural models and frames
L = Low language (Hñähñú)   DS = Discourse structures
R = Ruptures, breaches   LC = Linguistic codes and structures

Figure 4.2 Modalities of language shift

Modality 1

- *Phase 1*: Before the national language and culture break into a certain domain at a given point in history, the three levels coincide within the indigenous universe.

- *Phase 2*: In some cases changing conditions will at first force the speakers to adopt new linguistic codes and discourse structures from the dominant language. This typically happens in domains of central relevance for social organization and language conflict: in bilingual education, local and regional administration, and in a series of contact situations between the communities and external agents (bureaucracy, service institutions, banks, and so on). The new linguistic codes and discourse structures remain inherently incomprehensible in the first instance, because the Indian speakers cannot establish a relationship between them and their own historical and biographical experience.

- *Phase 3*: It is only in the third phase that the breach is overcome, reunifying cultural patterns, discourse structures, and linguistic codes in the realm of the dominant language and mainstream culture. Language and discourse phenomena that used to be incomprehensible now become accessible, since at this stage indigenous speakers have acquired the modes of appropriation of social experience from the dominant society, that is the cultural base of interpretation for their linguistic codes and discourse patterns. In sum, the Indian language, its discourse structures and cultural models are gradually excluded in a complex process consisting of three phases in which one or two discourse levels are replaced at the time. In the long run this process leads to a situation where the indigenous language is abandoned and, according to Mexican ethnicity ideology, a given community is no longer considered indigenous, but rural ('campesina') in generic terms.

The third phase is no doubt the most idealized in this framework. Very often it is never reached as a homogeneous cultural model belonging to the mainstream society on a large scale. Frequently new syncretic models emerge and stabilize over time in a hybrid area somewhere in between the two language fields, as is sustained by researchers in sociolinguistics (cf. Hill and Hill, 1986) and anthropology (cf. Bonfil Batalla, 1990). Nevertheless, in many cases it can be shown that the cycle of language shift is completed when a new coherence is established between cultural models, discourse structure, and linguistic surface structure in the realm of the dominant language.[12]

Let us consider a contact situation where usually the indigenous language prevails (internal meeting), but where the presence of an external agent imposes Spanish as the main but not exclusive language of the meeting.

Case 1: Settlement of damages in the cooperative

Participants: RB = employee of the agricultural bank; A, B, C, ... = indigenous peasants, members of the ejido; K = indigenous peasant and primary school teacher.

Setting: A bank employee is participating in a meeting of the peasant council in Pozuelos which takes place in the inner court of a peasant house used as a regular meeting place in the village.

Topic: Procedural questions regarding the settlement of damages for a lost harvest are discussed with the bank employee.

Background: The last harvest was lost due to the lack of rain. Since the harvest was insured, a damage settlement was claimed. One of the conditions for settlement is that the peasants must have sown between two pre-established dates (15–25 July, and in this case 1–8 July). Harvest insurance is a new procedure for the indigenous peasants in Pozuelos. The previous year they lost indemnities because they did not know how to present their claims. This year the agricultural bank granted a loan for the seeds, which can only be recovered if the insurance company settles damages. The bank employee, whose bank is interested in a damage settlement, calls this meeting to help the peasants prepare the damage claim, just a week before an insurance agent is to visit the village to investigate the situation. In sum, a potential conflict of interests between two institutions (the insurance company and the bank) is at stake, a setting which is altogether alien to the peasants' experience.

Transcription (the text in Hñähñú is underlined).

1st segment

1 RB   entonces usted don Vidal, así son dos hectáreas, no se, no se reportaron..
       well then, don Vidal, it's two hectares, you didn't report them..

2   no sé si ya sembró..   o sembraron
       I don't know whether you sowed already..   or did you sow

3 B   sí ya sembré ahorita
                                yes I've sown just now

4 RB   pero después del 15 de julio.. entonces va a decir usted cualquier día
       but after July 15.. then you will tell them any day

5 después del 15 de Julio del 15 al 25 de julio, pero cualquier día
  after July 15 July 15 to 25, just any day

6 B haha
  yes

7 RB presenta usted para que le reconozcan (IC),
  you [tell them] to make them accept it (IC),

8 B haha.haha.haha
  yes, yes, yes

9 RB porque si no no le van a reconocer nada ... ¡Ventura Mendieta
  Sánchez!
  'cause otherwise they won't acknowledge anything ... (NAME)

2nd segment

10 RB por ahí ¡Teotonio Angeles Hernández! son dos
  there now, (NAME) there are

11 C ¡presente!
  here!

12 RB hectáreas, nos reportó una una no está sembrada
  2 hectares, you reported one one hasn't been sowed

13 C haha
  yes

14 RB si está sembrada es despúes del 15
  if it has been sowed it was after the 15th

15 C sí..el 15
  yes..the 15th

16 RB así es.. y sembró del primero al ocho de julio
  very well..and you sowed between July 1st and 8

17 C sí
  yes

18 RB ¿se acuerda? del primero al ocho de julio, no la
  remember? from July 1st to 8th, just don't

19 C sí
  yes

20 RB vayan a regar, cuando la rieguen, todo esto se va abajo, eh?
  mess it up, if you do, [it'll all come down on you], ok?

21 C sí
  yes

22 K oxqui punfri nu ra fecha porque nu b-u ya con con que-a hinda recibi
  don't forget the date, 'cause otherwise with. With.. they won't accept it

23 C
    <u>haha</u>   yes
24 RB ¡Absalón Pérez B.!
      (NAME)

Analysis[13]

The analysis follows standard procedures for multi-layer analysis in the following order:

1 The formal organization of the sequential structure: turn-taking, conditional relevance, etc.
2 Action structure analysis (verbal action pattern or frame, speech acts, strategies).
3 Social relations.
4 Language distribution.
5 Traces of language shift in process.

Point 5 integrates the analysis by describing general strategies of minorization, the establishment of hegemony, and the rupture between experience and discourse structure.

1. Sequential structure The bank employee calls on one peasant after the other to analyse each case. All other peasants are present. Segment 1 represents the standard procedure. Segment 2 contains two expansions.

In terms of the local management of the sequential structure RB controls the distribution of turns throughout the session. By calling on each peasant he selects the next speaker (lines 9, 10, 24) and principal interlocutor for this segment. No self-selection takes place except by K, the teacher (22), who intervenes as a cultural broker and translates the instruction into Hñähñú. RB maintains institutional control over the initiation of each pair sequence (summons – reply). He establishes conditional relevance very directly through the list (number of reported hectares, sowing dates). His organizational control is marked by a loud, official voice, and a fast, 'executive type' speed and voice modulation; names are shouted out in accordance with custom in such (and bigger) meetings.

2. Action structure Here we identify verbal interaction patterns or frames, speech acts and strategies. From a pragmatic perspective we explore how turns and utterances are constituted as actions and how they enact interaction patterns.

RB establishes the action structure of the event based on a general pattern of business meetings with a fixed agenda and a chairperson (institutional role). The verbal interaction pattern (VIP) contains the following underlying structural units or steps:

1 Opening and establishment of the agenda.
2 Participants' roll.
3 Discussion of business.
4 Conclusions, resolutions.
5 Formal closings.

Within step 3 a small VIP is enacted and repeated with each peasant (P), altogether 11 times.

Steps:

1 Calling a name (RB) and verifying presence (RB + P).
2 Stating reported information (RB).
3 Verifying, clarifying information (RB + P).
4 Instructing future action concerning report (RB).
5 Dismissal through initiation of next VIP (calling new name) (RB).

In the first segment the standard model develops. RB utters direct instructions for the peasant's future action in the form of directive speech acts (orders, instructions) (lines 4, 5, 7). Indeed, he instructs the peasant (B) very bluntly how to act at the meeting with the insurance agent. Then he adds a justification (7) with the illocutionary force of a warning (9).

The second segment contains two expansions. First we find an exhortation in the form of a pattern expansion intended to develop a shared perspective of the issue (18–21). RB defines the situation as a counselling event with this utterance. From the point of view of social relations, the turn (18, 20) also contains a proposal to establish a relationship of complicity which is accomplished through its uttering and ratification by the peasant (21, 23).

The second expansion consists of a pattern reinforcement uttered by the peasant teacher (K) who acts as a cultural broker and repeats the instructions in Hñähñú (22). He focuses on the decisive question of the sowing date.

3. Social relations   Social relations are in general terms asymmetrical: RB is a member of the dominant society; he is the expert, and he controls the session resorting to series of discursive resources (list, and so on). Unlike many other interethnic encounters in these communities, however, all participants are making an obvious effort to build up a working relationship of cooperation and to keep the objective and subjective tension (Bourdieu, 1980) as low as possible. Although the bank employee maintains control during the whole session, no conversational sanctions against the indigenous speakers can be observed. RB makes a significant effort to establish a relationship of complicity which is more evident in segment 2 than in segment 1 and consolidates over time. K acts as cultural broker.

4. Language distribution Language choice and distribution fit neatly into the picture of cooperation. Spanish dominates throughout the event, but Hñähñú is never excluded. Participant-oriented language choice obliges the Indians to use Spanish in their interactions with the monolingual bank employee. In spite of their obviously limited competence there are no signs of stigmatization *vis-à-vis* their ethnic dialect of Spanish or the use of Hñähñú among themselves. The competent bilingual teacher intervenes as an interpreter when communication is at risk.

5. Traces of language shift in process Our discourse analysis reveals some basic mechanisms of language shift *in actu* as part of an overall process of language minoritization. It is precisely the kind of hegemonic constellation (in a Gramscian sense) described above that sets the stage for language minoritization and displacement. Given the overall power relations, limited competence in Spanish and task-related deficiencies in the indigenous discourse repertoire are exhibited as 'objective' shortcomings, without the need to resort to stigmatization or meta-discursive discrimination. Such interethnic conditions create a favourable climate for the adoption of frames, discourse techniques and pragmatic conventions from the dominant society, as can be observed in this example.

Frequently the peasants' general insecurity becomes evident, as is manifested by hesitation phenomena and other conversational cues; they obviously find it extremely difficult to interpret the technical relations between sowing dates and damage claims, and to decipher the underlying discourse patterns (DS) they have to rehearse in Spanish (LC), since they do not correspond to their cultural models (CM) of farming experience (see schema 3). According to their own cultural base, sowing and harvesting are determined by a different time logic related to the climate, to rain and drought, not to fixed calendar dates. The breach between language and discourse structures on the one hand, and historically accumulated experience (the cultural model), on the other, is clearly demonstrated in this instance of adopting new discourse techniques needed for a successful damage claim.

The new convergence of the three discourse levels in the dominant universe (phase 3) is virtually foreshadowed in the teacher's and other cultural brokers' behaviour, since they have at least in part acquired the cultural models crystallized in the discourse and language structures which make them comprehensible.

Modality 2

A second modality that can be reconstructed from the data concerns a shift in cultural models:

- *Phase 1*: Here too, the three discourse levels coincide within the realm of the indigenous culture before Spanish makes its inroads.
- *Phase 2*: In this phase the cultural models (CM) and in part the discourse structures (DS) from the national society are introduced first, whereas the indigenous language (LC) remains present on the surface. Examples of this modality can be found in intra-ethnic institutional (or semi-institutional) speech events on the community level such as dispute settlements (conciliations), committee meetings, or general assemblies where certain obligatory rules of native language use apply predominantly (field A, in part B, of schema 1). Members of the new leadership (teachers, migrant workers) typically introduce new procedures for political and social organization such as agendas and participant roles for meetings, the nomination of chairpersons or steering committees, written reports, summaries, elections, among others.
- *Phase 3*: Once the cultural models and discourse patterns are well-established and a conceptual, that is a cognitive reorientation has taken place, the loss of the native language on the surface level (LC) can occur more easily, given the asymmetric power relations that obtain between the two language groups. At this point Spanish seems much more appropriate than the Indian language to satisfy new communicative needs. Thus, also through this modality the production and appropriation of social experience may ultimately converge within the dominant culture and language, unless a process of language awareness and resistance emerges at this point as sometimes occurs in language shift situations (cf. Hill and Hill, 1986).

Case 2: Community assembly – passing over the judge's office

This case corresponds to phase 2 of the second modality. The indigenous language (LC) is maintained as the legitimate means of communication, although Spanish breaks in through side sequences and in specific episodes (report, and so on) (field B of schema 1). The assembly as a whole is a fairly new event (CM), which contains some traditional ethnic discourse units; in the decisive episodes, however, new discourse structures (DS) (chair, participant roles, oral report based on written text, and others) dominate the course of action.

Participants: OJ = outgoing judge, a teacher; S = secretary; NJ = new judge, a peasant; CH = chairperson; C1-X = some 100 citizens (family heads), mainly peasants.

Setting: At this general assembly all citizens of the village Decá are summoned to participate in the annual ritual event of handing over the judge's office to the new office bearer elected in a previous assembly.

Topic: The main point on the agenda is the handing over of the judge's office. The judge is at the same time the mayor, that is the highest authority in the community. Prior to the act itself the outgoing judge renders an activity report which has to be discussed and approved. Then the judge's office is handed over.

Background: The annual election and installation of the judge in two subsequent assemblies constitute a highlight in the community's political life, since the nomination of candidates, the election itself and the report of activities presented by the outgoing judge open a space for sometimes controversial debates on local politics, value systems and community norms.[14] In former times the selection of the new office bearer was performed through a much less public procedure in the Hñähñú villages, such as the nomination by the predecessor or the council of the elderly. At the time of our data collection in the early eighties, however, a more democratic schema had been adopted, without all procedural details already having been defined, as we shall see.

The analysed speech event is a general assembly convened to hand over the judge's office; it comprises three key episodes: the debate about the nomination of a chair for the meeting (for the first time in this village), the report of activities presented by the outgoing judge, and the handing over of office.

A first segmentation of the transcript reveals a number of noteworthy phenomena. First, the main active participants (mostly school teachers and other cultural brokers) engage in extended and complex conversational activities to establish, open, carry through and close the assembly. Second, a number of very explicit focusing accomplishments occur which function to establish and re-establish order according to the overall verbal interaction pattern of the meeting. Some of the obstacles that hamper the orderly development of the meeting show up very clearly in the complex interlinking of the sequential structure on the surface and the underlying verbal action structure (Figure 4.3).

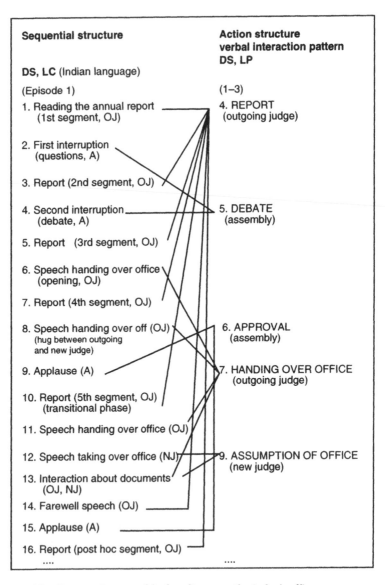

Figure 4.3 Community assembly: handing over the judge's office
(OJ = outgoing judge, NJ = new judge, A = assembly)

Analysis[15]

The assembly is based on a verbal interaction pattern which contains, in a simplified version, the following steps: (1) establishment of opening conditions; (2) formal opening; (3) agreement on the agenda, election of a chairperson, and beginning; (4) activity report (OJ); (5) debate; (6) approval (or disapproval); (7) handing over the office (OJ); (8) assumption of office (NJ); (9) handing over other offices (secretary, treasurer, etc.); (10) formal resolutions and closing (Figure 4.3 only shows steps 4 to 8).

Striking intersections occur between certain steps in the action (structure, report, debate, approval, handing over the office) and the sequential structure. The report is interrupted several times by activities belonging to other steps of the action structure which violate the sequential logic. Indeed, the report continues even after (segment 16) the official transfer of office has happened, at a time when the outgoing judge is no longer in office.[16]

A complex pattern of post-diglossic language distribution can be observed, where domain boundaries are weakened through the leakage of functions and mixing of forms. Although Hñähñú still acts as the legitimate language of communication in the assembly, Spanish is already making its inroads into the event. In many side sequences among the leading figures of the assembly, as well as through code-shifting into Spanish in the report and other formal episodes, the dominant language is present.

All these phenomena characterize the assembly as an event undergoing a fundamental process of change. Many of its constituent parts and procedures are not yet well established. Public elections and taking up office are derived from new cultural models imported from the wider national society. Detailed discourse analysis reveals how difficult it is to establish the corresponding discourse structures such as verbal interaction patterns as general frames of orientation. Here again we encounter the breach between levels of discourse organization typical for processes of language shift. In this case, the process starts with the introduction of cultural models and, in part, discourse structures from the national society, whereas the indigenous language is maintained on the surface level in phase 2. Once more, the perspective of total shift is prefigured in the behaviour of the cultural brokers who demonstrate a sustained language preference for Spanish in this kind of event through numerous code-switches and transfers.

In both modalities of language shift, the typical breach and phase shift between language codes, discourse structure, and cultural models leads to a rupture between socio-historical production and the discursive appropriation of experience. Such a procedure of cultural and linguistic fragmentation has proven to be an effective language policy strategy that tends to minoritize subordinate ethnolinguistic cultures.

Sociolinguistic theory and method: the role of cultural models, discourse and language structure

At the beginning I had argued that a deeper understanding of language shift would imply a change in focus from the analysis of large-scale outcomes of language shift to the processes themselves. Three related issues surface from my analysis which call for debate and further research: (1) the sociolinguistics of societal bi- and multilingualism; (2) the phases, dynamics, and mechanisms of language shift; and (3) the relation between societal macro factors and linguistic behaviour.

The social relationship between hegemonic and subordinate languages

In order to comprehend more fully the mechanisms of language shift it seems to me that we will have to reconceptualize first of all the relationship between 'high' and 'low' languages and the corresponding frameworks of interpretation. In the sociology of language this relationship relates to the structural and functional attributes of the languages themselves as reflected in the classic concept of diglossia (Ferguson, 1959; Fishman, 1967, 1980). Languages or dialect varieties possess high or low status, they are labelled as having ± morphological complexity, ± prestige, ± literacy, and so forth. Languages appear thus isolated from discourse, culture, and from their speakers. The underlying concept of languages in contact or conflict constitutes a metonymic metaphor, a reduction which excludes the speakers. Of course, it is not languages which are in contact but speakers, users, language communities for whom the languages may be the object and sometimes the instrument of a social relationship of conflict and struggle. And very rarely do the frontiers and conflict lines coincide neatly with the language boundaries involved. Therefore, a framework is called for which (re)incorporates the pragmatic dimension of discourse and the actors, and differentiates between various dimensions of language structure, discourse, and culture.

The findings of my research – as well as those of other studies (for example Gal, 1979; Kulick, 1992) – lead to the conclusion that the mechanisms underlying language conflict, shift, or maintenance processes are less defined by patterns of language distribution over domains than by clashes between cultural models, competing discourse strategies and discourse styles. These phenomena are based on communicative repertoires and speakers' resources, among which language choice and code-switching are a central but not exclusive component. Hence the dividing lines of conflict and shift do not necessarily coincide with language boundaries on the surface. Social relations of domination which refer directly to cultural conflict are produced, in my research, both in Spanish and in the indigenous language. A member of parliament of Hñähñú heritage from the state party PRI may well develop a 'dominant' discourse in the Indian language. And many acts of protest and resistance may be presented in Spanish, but based on ethnic cultural patterns.[17]

Thus a theoretically appropriate model should not start with the languages as abstract entities, but with the social relations of power and dominance between communities and their members, relationships which are often implemented under the modalities of hegemony and subalternity. Although the two languages in question proto-typically appear as central foci in such a framework,[18] the relations of power are constituted and reproduced with variable discursive resources. It is only on the basis of a great number of repetitive procedures in the (re)production of discourse patterns and strategies that overreaching, more stable discourse styles (cultural models) emerge and consolidate as general forms of habitus. In this perspective, the old debate about 'languages in contact' vs 'languages in conflict' loses much of its relevance since it only refers to surface phenomena that do not necessarily reflect the underlying relations of power. In our case, as in many others, the construction of hegemony and the mechanisms of language displacement work most efficiently when no open conflict is in sight.

Mechanisms of language shift

The structural provisions for language shift are rooted in the remarkable synchronic heterogeneity of the indigenous communicative system. Its broad repertoire of coexisting resources serves as a starting point for a gradual redistribution of coexisting variants based on a reassessment of values and meaning potentials (status, efficiency, ethnic loyalty) attached to each of the languages concerned. A systematic comparison of different speakers' verbal behaviour in each speech event, of discourse strategies across events, of types of speech events and of different communities allow us to construct an 'apparent time' axis of the historical process of change in language choice patterns, discourse patterns and cultural models. As a typical procedure we encounter relatively long-lasting processes of negotiation which start with the first occurrence of a new pattern in a few speakers' repertoire and culminate with its general acceptance and use by the local speech community. Sometimes participants explicitly discuss a new procedure or refer to novel terms or patterns in stretches of metadiscursive speech.[19] In most cases, however, the degree of innovation of a given item, its evaluation and its relative acceptance will have to be reconstructed through the procedures and levels of discourse analysis shown above.

The examples analysed in this paper highlight the great complexity typical in many language conflict and shift situations. Indeed, it proved impossible to restrict the analysis to the linguistic codes and structures on the surface as is usually the case in traditional sociolinguistics, since decisive shift phenomena occurred at the levels of discourse structures and cultural models. As we have seen, a typical process of language shift is often triggered by new discourse patterns and cultural models which are introduced while the minority language is still preserved on the surface during a certain phase.

In both modalities of language shift the ruptures and phase disloca-tions between the three levels (culture, discourse, language) in the Hñähñús' communicative universe led to a contradiction between the historical production of experience (e.g. farm work, political organization) and its linguistic-discursive appropriation. This first step of cultural frag-mentation belongs to the typical repertoire of language policy strategies that promote the minoritization of a subordinate ethnolinguistic group; the process occurs largely behind the backs of the speakers. It operates even more efficiently because it works as a strategy without a 'strategic calculus', a process which is not planned consciously and in which the minority group members participate actively. The most significant and probably most enduring effect of language displacement is achieved when a given discourse in the dominant language, which initially remained incomprehensible for the minority language speakers, becomes comprehensible because they have by and large adopted the forms of appropriation of the social experience inherent in the discourse.

Macro societal factors and language shift

At the beginning I discussed the central issues concerning the relationship between macro societal factors and linguistic behaviour, and the resulting explanatory and predictive power of models for language shift. Perhaps these questions could now be reformulated in a more precise way.

Rather than interpret language shift as a direct, causal effect of socioeconomic change, it has to be seen as the outcome of intervening cognitive and pragmatic instances such as the reorientation of the minority speakers towards new languages, their cultural models, and pragmatic conventions. In the long run such a reorientation may lead to a change in their ethnic status. This approach focuses on the markers and traces of language shift *in actu* and *in situ*; that is, in the process of verbal interaction itself. It seeks to argue theoretically and demonstrate empirically the ways in which language (surface) structure, discourse structure, and cultural models form constitutive components of language shift. It seems that processes of language change (shift or revitalization) function, perhaps typically, through ruptures and phase dislocations between the three levels of analysis.

The Hispanic community in the USA: cultural models, discourse structures, language use

No doubt this approach and methodological procedure could yield interesting results in the many other contexts of language contact, including in the Hispanic world. The sociolinguistics of Spanish in the USA is a case in point. From the point of view of the Spanish language community, a new member has emerged with its own characteristics that plays a key role in the relationship between Spanish and English. For some (Mar-Molinero, 2004), even the future of Spanish as a global language is at stake in the USA.

The question of whether immigrants eventually assimilate and give up their languages has been a key issue for the sociology of language (Fishman, 1964). Given the enormous growth of the Hispanic community to over 30 million in the USA, this controversial question is discussed increasingly often in relation to Spanish. Whereas some researchers document ongoing language shift (Veltman, 1983, 1990; Hudson, Hernández Chávez and Bills, 1995; Bills, Hernández Chávez and Hudson, 1995), others (Huntington, 2004) sustain that the Hispanics are no longer assimilating in the same way as other immigrants in the past, thus apparently violating a foundational contract of the American nation and provoking a crisis of its national identity.

A micro–macro approach certainly has the potential to draw a much more differentiated picture of the language situation in the USA than did Huntington's recent rather crude statistical review. It could shed light on the hybrid nature of multiple contact and conflict aspects which connect language, discourse, and culture in complex ways. No doubt ruptures between these components occur on a massive scale. Many Hispanics experience such cultural and communicative fragmentation upon their arrival. They then adopt new cultural and discourse patterns while still speaking Spanish in a given context. Conversely, they often act on the basis of their traditional patterns and encounter conflict and cultural misunderstandings when using English in domains where it is mandatory. Language shift in terms of interrupted intergenerational transmission no doubt continues. By the time many immigrants understand what were to them initially incomprehensible types of US discourse, even in Spanish, they will have adopted the social experience inherent in those discourse patterns. At the same time, Hispanic (Mexican) culture is experiencing a period of vigorous renaissance, either reshaped as US Latino culture, or reinforcing traditional heritage patterns in the US-Mexican community. Spanish in its multiple varieties is consolidating in some domains and moving forcefully into others (Suárez, 2002).[20] From a perspective of individual and societal enrichment and additive bilingualism, this process shows dynamic signs of a new hybrid bilingual repertoire. A simple analysis of the surface phenomena – the presence or absence of Spanish in a given domain – will certainly not suffice to explain the complex landscape of language dynamics in the USA.

Back to the macro: findings on the micro level as a basis for language policy

There can be little doubt that the findings from integrated micro–macro research in sociolinguistics and discourse analysis are essential if we are to draw a more differentiated picture of language contact situations and shift processes as a basis for language policy and planning decisions. Such an enterprise will work successfully if the initial hypotheses that guide the research design and data collection include central macro issues from the perspective of sociolinguistics and language policy. In my own research on language conflict and shift, bilingual education, institutional interaction and other topics, I usually start with macro questions (conflict, shift, identity, power) that orient a step-by-step procedure which moves from macro to mezzo levels (ethnography, speech events), then to the micro (interactional discourse analysis) in order to return to a macro level of interpretation.

Research on language policy in Latin America has not yet fully explored the richness of the diverse and multiple language situations in its territory, despite significant explorations on many topics (for example Heath, 1972; Cerrón-Palomino, 1993; Cifuentes and Rosmeso, 1993; Hornberger, 1997; López and Jung, 1998; Hamel, 1993, 2001, to quote but a few). Present indigenous movements that increasingly challenge the homogeneous nation-state voice demands relating to linguistic rights such as the use of their languages in education and other public domains of political relevance. There are calls to move away from a traditional assimilationist education and strive for a new pluricultural and plurilingual perspective of integration without assimilation. Since its rebellion in 1994, the principal demands of the indigenous Zapatista movement in Mexico have clustered around the central concept of autonomy, as have those of other, less well-known movements in Colombia, Panama, Bolivia and elsewhere. It is difficult to imagine that any language policy – or the study of it – could be relevant and successful if it reduces its scope languages to objectified structural entities, without taking into account the discursive repertoires, dynamic systems of action, language ideologies and cultural models sustained by their collective subjects/protagonists. All these topics call for detailed analysis on the mezzo and micro level.

Similarly, Spain's present quest to reconstruct its linguistic and cultural hegemony in the Spanish-speaking world based on the ideology of grandeur, cohesion and unity of the Spanish language (see Del Valle and Gabriel-Stheeman, 2004, chapter 10), will probably fail as long as it is sustained by a reductionist and idealized concept of the 'langue' that excludes foundational components such as diverse communicative repertoires and cultural models. As discourse patterns and cultural models usually vary more than the structure of the language itself within a language community, any attempt to reestablish a common Hispanic identity will encounter significant difficulties as long as it does not take into account differentiated discourse traditions, cultural models and local communities which serve as the prime referents for identity planning and construction. These points of reference central to diverse Spanish communicative systems are to a large extent responsible for the vitality and strength of the Spanish language.

In the Hispanic world Spanish operates together with its communicative and ideological repertoires in multiple functions and contexts, as a dominant and subordinate language, as border and conflict language as well as the principal focus of identity for millions of speakers, a pluricentric language (Clyne, 1992; Oesterreicher, 2002) at home in more than 21 countries. Given this richness of scope and field, Hispanic sociolinguistics may well contribute significantly to both Hispanic language debates and general sociolinguistics if it takes up the challenge and seeks to develop models of micro–macro relations able to cope with the richness and diversity of its realm.

Notes

1 Whether Nebrija's expression, which accompanied the presentation of his famous early grammar of Spanish, really meant what it is normally quoted as saying has been questioned by detailed historical analysis (Bierbach, 1989). Issued several months before the 'discovery' of America, it was oriented more towards the normalization of Spanish than conceived of as the basis for an imperial language policy. In any case, the discursive effect is evident and has been reinforced by its multiple uses and possible abuses from colonial times to the present day.

2 In his well-known typology of languages, De Swaan (1993, 2001) reserves the term 'hyper-central' language to English, whereas the second-layer international languages such as Spanish, French, Portuguese, Russian, German and a few others are called 'super-central' (see also Calvet, 1999, 2002 who adopts this terminology in his ecological model).

3 A significant differentiation between divergent ideological orientations related to factual diversity needs to be established here. In my own work (Hamel, 1997, 2000, 2003) I distinguish between 'multiculturalism' and 'pluriculturalism'. The first frames diversity as a problem which includes a certain tolerance of minority rights as an inevitable, but uncomfortable necessity. This is a typical mainstream orientation in the US and most Latin American states that recognize indigenous minorities and their rights, but regard them as a barrier to national unity and promote subtractive bilingualism. 'Pluriculturalism' in turn represents an enrichment orientation which considers diversity as an asset and potential cultural capital for a nation. It is usually related to additive bilingualism. The term 'pluriculturalism', although it is less used in English, recovers UN and UNESCO terminology and retrieves positive connotations *vis-à-vis* the more neutral 'multiculturalism'.

4 Except the USA and, to a lesser extent, a handful of other central imperial states, as Chomsky (2003) so brilliantly points out.

5 The borders of Spanish establish a dynamic relationship with national frontiers. Whereas they are blurring in South America between Brazil and its Hispanic neighbours given increasing regional integration, the 'hard' border in North America between the USA and Mexico does no longer exist as a true linguistic borderline. In Spain, on the contrary, the regional autonomies of Catalonia and the Basque country are reinforcing their linguistic boundaries against Spanish.

6 I use the term 'sociolinguistics' here as the broadest term to encompass all different approaches that relate language and society, including the sociology of language (see Fishman's foreword to Glyn Williams' (1992) sociological critique of sociolinguistics).

7 Fishman himself has radicalized his own process of taking sides in favour of the oppressed language groups of the world, in a countermovement to the general trend of increasingly depoliticized sociolinguistics elsewhere.

8 An pioneering exception is Gal (1979). Throughout the 1980s and 90s, more integrated approaches emerged (for example Heller, 1994, 1999),

including in the field of Hispanic sociolinguistics (Woolard, 1989; Hamel, 1988a), despite the general tendency of fragmentation I refer to later on.

9 The critique of 'grand theories' in sociology and their impossibility of falsification in Glaser and Strauss' (1967) first chapter of *Grounded Theory* is still today a jewel of theoretical debate well worth reading.

10 The Hñähñú are better known as 'Otomí', meaning 'bird arrow' or 'bird hunter', a Nahuatl name imposed during Aztec domination before Spanish colonization. Today the group is recovering its name 'Hñähñú' in its own language, meaning 'sons of the people hñú'. Hñähñú has now become the official name of the sixth largest indigenous people in Mexico with some 280,000 members according to the 1990 census.

11 On the development of literacy practices in this area, see Hamel (1996).

12 In no way does this framework claim to be deterministic in the sense that it predicts a *necessary* outcome of the process. Its aim is to reconstruct a process as can be shown retrospectively in empirical data.

13 This is a summary of what is a much more detailed analysis.

14 Within our research project, see Sierra (1992) for a detailed analysis of this kind of speech event.

15 In this case analysis will be restricted to a structural comparison between the sequential (level 1) and the action structure (level 2).

16 A methodological objection could be raised in the sense that this case might represent a variant of the pattern which is specific for the Hñähñú culture. Detailed analysis reveals, however, that the chairperson's interventions are not ratified and typically occur when the report gets stuck. Furthermore, all active participants engage in conspicuous focussing activities which reveal the 'inappropriate' embedding of the sequences in question (see Hamel, 1988a).

17 This appears very clearly in the discourse developed in Mexico by the indigenous EZLN (Zapatista Army of National Liberation) in their negotiations with the federal government during 1994 and 1995 and in their public interventions since.

18 This occurs mainly at the level of diglossic ideologies, cf. Gardy and Lafont (1981), see also Woolard (1998) and Silverstein (1998).

19 These comments are relatively easy to obtain in interviews and other elicitation procedures (Hill and Hill, 1986; Muñoz Cruz, 1987). While useful to generate hypothesis or to confirm other analyses, it is only when they happen in naturally occurring speech events that they acquire their full significance for the discourse approach applied here.

20 I will not address here the debate on convergence or preservation of different varieties of Spanish as markers of national identity (see Silva-Corvalán, 1994; Mar-Molinero, 2004).

5
Spanish/English Interaction in US Hispanic Heritage Learners' Writing

Marta Fairclough

Introduction

The 2000 US Census indicated that the Hispanic or Latino population in the United States was 35.3 million or 12.5 per cent of the total population. This figure shows a 60 per cent increase in US Hispanics since the 1990 Census (22.4 million). Today, 'Latinos are this country's largest minority, with the United States the fifth most populous Spanish-speaking country in the world, after Mexico, Spain, Colombia, and Argentina' (Carreira, 2002: 39). The number of Hispanics in the US is increasing almost four times as fast as the rest of the population and it is anticipated that nearly one of every four Americans will be Hispanic by the year 2050 (Robinson, 1998). While today more than one-third of US Hispanics were born in other Spanish-speaking countries, demographic projections estimate that by the year 2100, more than 90 percent of Hispanics in the United States will have been born in this country (*Hispanic Market Weekly*, 2000: 38).

Although, typically, heritage languages die out within three generations (Brecht and Ingold, 1998), Hispanics in the United States have been relatively successful in maintaining the Spanish language, and they have done so mostly on account of the large number of new immigrants and their spatial concentration (Hudson, Hernández-Chávez and Bills, 1995; Valdés, 2000). However, at the individual level, the language skills in the heritage language continue to diminish due to the contact with English, the dominant language. Abundant evidence points towards a dramatic loss of the Spanish language, often after one or two generations (Fishman, 1991; Hernández-Chávez, 1993; Veltman, 2000). New generations often acquire an incomplete and frequently simplified variety of the language, and they repeatedly resort to code-switching.

76

Many cross-generational studies have focused on this progressive decrease of proficiency in the Spanish language – a decrease that Silva-Corvalán (1994) captures with the term 'bilingual continuum'. Within this continuum, the first generation of speakers usually produces a native-like variety of the language, although in some cases it is often a rural and/or stigmatized variety. As we move towards the other end of the continuum, proficiency in the heritage language diminishes with the second, third and successive generations that tend to produce a more creolized variety, characteristic of language contact situations. This gradual loss of language skills produces a large number of what Lipski (1993: 157–8) labels 'transitional bilinguals', vestigial speakers and semi-speakers of Spanish who possess limited knowledge of the Spanish language due to rapid linguistic assimilation to the majority language.

Due to the increase in the Hispanic population in the United States and a growing interest in the Spanish language, more and more colleges and universities are offering courses especially designed for heritage learners. A 'heritage language learner' is 'a student who is raised in a home where a non-English language is spoken, who speaks or merely understands the heritage language, and who is to some degree bilingual in English and the heritage language' (Valdés, 2000: 1). Despite the diversity of heritage learner backgrounds and the different levels of language ability in the standard minority language, the speech and writing of most heritage speakers show considerable influence from the majority language. Many sociolinguistic studies (Fairclough, 2000; Gutiérrez, 1994, 1996, 1997, 2001; Silva-Corvalán, 1986, 1994; to cite a few) have provided evidence of the influence of the English language on the Spanish grammatical system of bilingual Hispanics in the United States. In most cases, the linguistic changes attested in the bilingual setting are present in monolingual contexts, but the processes are usually acceler-ated due to the contact situation. However, the characteristic that most distinguishes the US Spanish variety from other Spanish varieties is evidenced at the lexical level.

Mixing or alternating the two languages appear as options that bilin-guals have within certain constraints that researchers have identified. Pfaff (1982: 292), for example, asserts that '[i]t is unnecessary to posit the existence of a third grammars to account for the utterances in which the languages are mixed; rather, the grammars of Spanish and English are meshed according to a number of constraints [functional, structural, semantic, discourse, etc. constraints]'. Maschler (1998: 125), on the other hand, proposes that there may be '[t]wo types of language alternation phenomena in bilingual conversation ... code-switching ... [and] a mixed code – using two languages such that a third, new code emerges, in which elements from the two languages are incorporated into a structurally definable pattern'. According to Auer (1998: 20), this mixed code

> is the emergence of a new structural division of linguistic labour between the elements originally taken from language A and those from language B ... the elements take on a new grammatical function [grammaticalization] or lexical meaning [lexicalization] which is *not* based any longer on the interferences which are triggered by their other-languageness; rather, it is defined in structural terms, by paradigmatic oppositions and syntagmatic links.

Oesch Serra (1998) offers a clear example of a case of grammaticalization of certain elements in a contact situation between Italian and French. Her study shows that bilingual (Italian/French) migrant speakers have developed an argumentative system on the basis of two monolingual systems, which is not identical to either of them. In such a system there are three adversary connectives, rather than two as in monolingual Italian or one as in monolingual French. From this point of view the system constitutes a case of an *emerging mixed code*, which has no equivalent in the source languages. The system uses the Italian adversative connectives *ma* and *però* and the French *mais* with their own rules for application in order to organize argumentative patterns (1998: 118–19).

Several contact situations are claimed to have led to the emergence of mixed codes: the grammatical convergence exhibited by four languages in contact in Kupwar (India), two Dravidian languages (Kannada and Telugu), and two Indo-Aryan languages (Urdu and Marathi) (Gumperz and Wilson, 1977). Additional examples include linguistic contact between French and African languages (for example Kikongo, Swahili, and others) in Zaire (Meeuwis and Blommaert, 1998), Italian and French in Switzerland (Oesch Serra, 1998), and the case of American immigrants in Israel studied by Maschler (1998).

So is a new code emerging as the result of linguistic interaction between Spanish and English in the United States? First, we should clarify what is meant by 'grammaticalization' and 'lexicalization' in the specific context of linguistic contact. Then, we need to be able to assert that the samples of language mixing are not merely functional switches. 'Grammaticalization' or 'grammaticization' (henceforth, grammatic(al)ization) and 'lexicalization') are terms that have been used in different and often confusing ways (Himmelmann, 2004: 21). Grammatic(al)ization is usually defined as a process by which items with lexical meaning evolve into grammatical markers, and grammatical elements take on new grammatical functions. The development of grammatical morphemes out of lexical ones is generally the product of semantic changes, often involving the loss of specific features of meaning. This has been labelled 'semantic reduction' (Bybee *et al.*, 1994: 6), 'bleaching' (Givón, 1975), and 'desemanticization' (Heine, 1993; Lehmann, 1982). A synchronic result of grammatic(al)ization is 'layering' (Hopper, 1991: 22), in which 'new layers emerge without necessarily replacing older layers in the same domain, so the same grammatical function may be carried out by different forms'. For example, there is variation between expressions of future temporal reference *will* and *be going to* in English (Poplack and Tagliamonte, 1999) or in expressions of progressive aspect *estar* 'be (located)' / *andar* 'go around' + gerund in Spanish (Torres Cacoullos, 2001). However, Himmelmann (2004: 35) adds that usually 'there is a tendency in the literature to use grammaticization as a cover term for all kinds of grammatical change, including simple reanalyses, analogical leveling and contact-induced changes'.

Hopper and Traugott (1993: 49) explain that '[t]he process whereby a non-lexical form such as *up* becomes a fully referential lexical item is called "lexicalization". It is relatively uncommon, but instances can be found in most languages'. On the other hand, the term 'lexicalization,' from a broad perspective, 'covers all the processes which lead to the emergence of a new lexical item' (Lehmann, 1989, in Himmelmann, 2004: 22). For the purpose of this study, we are using the terms 'lexicalization' and 'grammatic(al)ization' in their broad sense, as synonyms of grammatical change (or, the creation of new grammatical resources) and emergence of new lexical items, as used by Auer (1998).

Auer (1998: 16) posits that '[Functional] code-switching and usage of a mixed code often co-occur in a given conversation so that it is analytically difficult to disentangle the two phenomena'. One of the difficulties in analysing CS in speech (or in some informal written contexts such as electronic mail or journal entries) resides in the fact that mixing two languages is an option that a person has in some contexts for expressing certain semantic, pragmatic and/or discursive functions, such as solidarity with his or her audience, emphasis, clarification, and so on. Therefore, it becomes a very complex task to try to measure up to what point the mixture of the two languages is not intentional. Evidence of both phenomena in contexts where code-switching is not optional, that is, where one code (Spanish, in this case) would be expected, would signal the emergence of a new mixed-code.

According to Maschler (1998: 137), there are two issues that determine if a case of code-switching has been grammaticized into part of a new, mixed code: 'The first is statistical: if the *ad hoc* switch repeats itself in a statistically significant way, we are concerned with a recurring pattern. The second issue concerns the nature of the switch: it must result in some *structural* pattern which can be discerned in the new code'. A third issue proposed by Maschler involves the functions of the switched elements in the mixed code: '[they] have to have exclusive functions that do not belong in the data ... with no equivalents in the other language' (1998: 144–5).

The purpose of this research is to describe and quantify the different types of language-mixing phenomena found in an entrance examination completed by bilingual Hispanic students upon entering a Spanish programme at a major urban university in the United States. The results of this study are intended to show the degree of grammatic(al)ization and of lexicalization of the code-mixing into a *new mixed code*; that is, the emergence of a new code (not two languages mixed but an independent language that can be acquired directly) (Auer, 1998).

The linguistic variable

Definitions

Language change is a natural process. Extended linguistic contact often causes changes in languages that coexist due to mutual transfer. According to Silva-Corvalán (2001: 281), this transfer can affect all the subsystems of a language: phonological, morphological, syntactic, lexical, semantic and pragmatic. Transfer from English is often present in the Spanish spoken in the United States (Otheguy *et al.*, 1989; Silva-Corvalán, 1994; Zentella, 1997; among many others). Usually, the alternating use of two languages in the discourse of bilingual individuals is labelled 'code-switching' (CS). However, in many cases, researchers use different labels and subcategories to organize the phenomena caused by this type of language interaction. Among the most recent typologies, we find Poplack and Meechan's (1998) method in which the following five elements are operationalized for analysing bilingual discourse: (1) unmixed L1; (2) unmixed L2; (3) multiword alternations or code-switches; (4) attested loanwords; and (5) ambiguous lone items (in Sankoff, 2002: 651). Muysken (2000: 1), on the other hand, uses the term 'code-mixing' to refer to 'cases where lexical items and grammatical features from two languages appear in one sentence' while the term 'code-switching' is used only for a subset of 'code-mixing'. Within code-mixing, Muysken's typology (2000: 32) includes three types of mixing strategies: 'insertion [into a matrix or base language], alternation [of the two codes] and congruent lexicalization [of single or multiple lexical or functional items]'.[1]

For simplification purposes, throughout this study we will follow the label used by Zentella (1997), Bernal-Enríquez and Hernández-Chávez (2003) and Fairclough (2003) which group together all the phenomena of English/Spanish interaction under the term 'code-switching' (CS). CS, then, includes not only single- and multiple-word transfers that preserve English phonology, but also borrowing (loan and single-word calques) and the different types of multiple-word calques, all adapted to Spanish

---

Single-word transfers

Switches: preserve English phonology
Ellas son más <u>educated</u>

Borrowings: adapted to Spanish phonology
    Loan (transfer of form + meaning)
        <u>Troca</u> (= 'truck' → camioneta)

    Calque (transfer of meaning only)
        <u>Aplicación</u> (= 'application' → solicitud)

Multiple-word transfers

Switches: preserve English phonology
    Intersentential switches
        El no sabe hacerlo. <u>I'll do it</u>.
    Intrasentential switches
        Y luego <u>during the war</u>, él se fue al Valle.

Calques: adapted to Spanish phonology
    Conceptual/cultural calques
        <u>Estampillas de comida</u> (= 'food stamps')
    Calques of bound collocations, idioms and proverbs
        So él sabrá si <u>se cambia su mente</u> (= '…if (he) changes his mind' →… si cambia de opinión/de idea)
    Lexico-syntactic calques
        <u>Tuvimos un buen tiempo</u> (= 'We had a good time'/ → Lo pasamos bien)

Figure 5.1 Model of linguistic interaction: English/Spanish code-switching in the USA

Sources: Based on Silva-Corvalán (1994), Otheguy *et al.* (1989) and Otheguy (1993).

phonology. Taking into account previous studies of English/Spanish interaction in the USA (Otheguy, 1993; Otheguy *et al.*, 1989; and Silva-Corvalán, 1994), the model of transfer depicted in Figure 5.1 will be followed in this project, for it includes all the categories that maybe encountered in this specific language contact situation.

Previous studies

Most of the studies of CS (English/Spanish in the USA) are based on oral data. On the one hand, we find research that attempts to explain the syntactic constraints that govern this phenomenon (Lipski, 1982; Pfaff, 1982; Poplack, 1982; and others); on the other, we find a number of studies that analyse the socio-pragmatic function(s) of individual production (Gumperz, 1982; McClure, 1981; Otheguy, 1993; Torres, 1997; Zentella, 1990; Valdés-Fallis, 1976; among others). Several studies have examined the production of CS in the Spanish spoken by bilinguals in different areas of the United States (Puerto Ricans and Cuban-Americans in New York: Álvarez (1991), Otheguy (2001), Otheguy *et al.* (1989), Poplack (1982), Torres (1997); Mexican-Americans in the Southwest and in Los Angeles: Pfaff (1982), Silva-Corvalán (1994); and others). The results of most of the studies show that the percentage of Spanish/English interaction is relatively low when compared to the total number of words produced.[2]

A few studies have analysed CS in written texts, but they have mostly focused on the analysis of these phenomena in the speech of the characters in literary works. Callahan (2001) for example, studied CS in 30 texts published in the USA between 1970 and the year 2000. Montes-Alcalá (2000, 2001) examined the socio-pragmatic functions of CS in a variety of bilingual texts including literature, narratives, magazines and personal manuscripts (such as letters, electronic mail and journal entries), and looked for parallelisms with oral CS. However, although these studies examined written texts, the type of contexts where the CS was measured still offered the writer the choice to use one language or the other, or a mixture of both.

To the best of my knowledge, there are no studies that examine the types and degree of language interaction between English and Spanish in the United States when CS is not expected, such as in Spanish placement exams. Grosjean (1997) reminds us that when we examine bilingual competence and performance, we must take into account language mode; that is, whether the individual is in (a) a monolingual mode in language A; (b) a monolingual mode in language B; or (c) a bilingual mode. In the bilingual mode, both languages are active, thus transfer between them and the tendency to code-switch will be more pronounced. In placement exams, a monolingual Spanish mode would be expected. The presence of English in this type of data would not be considered an 'option', but possibly part of an emerging new code, provided the corpus offers enough evidence of new and recurring lexical items and structural patterns.

Methodology

The corpus consists of 450+ placement/credit written exams completed by heritage speakers of Spanish between 1996 and 1998 upon entering the Spanish programme at a major urban university. The exam is used to place students at the appropriate level and to grant credit for previous knowledge of Spanish. The placement / credit exam for heritage speakers of Spanish offered by this institution is a local testing instrument given several times a year. The exam consists of about fifty grammatical items (use of prepositions, articles, verb forms, conjunctions, and so on), which according to sociolinguistic research of US Spanish were found to be challenging to these heritage learners. Some of these challenges include the simplification of tense, mood and aspect (Gutiérrez, 1996, 1997; Ocampo, 1990; Silva-Corvalán, 1994; to cite a few), incorrect use of articles and prepositions, errors in number and gender agreement, and so on (Lipski, 1993). Short essays eliciting all the basic types of discourse (descriptive, narrative, argumentative and hypothetical) are also part of the exam, and they make up the corpus of this study. The following are the topics for the essays:

1 Descriptive: *La casa en que vivo* ('The house I live in').
2 Narrative: *Mis últimas vacaciones* ('My last vacation').
3 Argumentative: *Los derechos de los hispanos en los Estados Unidos* ('The rights of Hispanics in the United States').
4 Hypothetical: *Si yo pudiera cambiar algunas cosas de mi país ...* ('If I could change some things in my country ...').

The reason for including a variety of topics in the exam was to try and obtain samples of different types of discourse in which students had to use a broad range of structures and lexical items. Some of the topics were 'easier' since the students only had to produce information that they already knew; others were more complex since they required students to transform the knowledge they possessed (following Bereiter and

Scardamalia's (1987) model of dual writing – *knowledge-telling* and *knowledge-transformation*). In general, students who are placed in level 1 have a broad passive knowledge of Spanish, but their lexicon is limited and their morphosyntactic system appears rather simplified. In addition, their reading and writing abilities are very basic, since most of them never studied Spanish in a formal context. On the other hand, students who are placed in levels 4 and 5 (the advanced levels) are usually those born and educated in monolingual Spanish-speaking countries.

Over 200 students take the test every academic year and are placed in five different levels:

1 SPAN 1505 – Intensive Elementary Spanish (Beginner level).
2 SPAN 2307 – Spanish for Hispanic Heritage Learners I (Intermediate level A).
3 SPAN 2308 – Spanish for Hispanic Heritage Learners II (Intermediate level B).
4 SPAN 3308 – Written Communication for Hispanic Heritage Learners (Advanced level A).
5 AL (All levels – Advanced level B).

Students who place in levels 3 and above receive credit for the previous courses. Those who are placed in level 5 receive credit for all levels, and they can take any classes at the advanced level (literature, linguistics and culture).

For this pilot study we only analysed 150 exams. The corpus was organized according to the level into which the students were placed (1 to 5); we chose the first 30 students for each level. All the cases of CS in each sample were identified first by the researcher, and then by a group of 12 graduate students born and raised in different Spanish-speaking countries (Venezuela, Argentina, Spain, Mexico, Honduras, Peru and the United States). The results were compared, those cases that were not transparent were discussed and additional help was sought whenever it was deemed necessary. Then, following the abovementioned model (Figure 5.1), the items were coded according to one of the following five categories:

1 Single-word switches.
2 Single-word loans.
3 Single-word calques.
4 Multiple-word code-switching.
5 Multiple-word calques.

Subsequently, the items were quantified according to category and level. Each item was counted as one, whether it was a single word or a phrase. Orthographic transfer, although frequent, was not analysed. Many instances of English influence in the spelling were found, including duplication of letters (*classe* instead of *clase* 'class'), 'h' instead of 'j' or 'g' (in words such as *trabahar* or *hente* instead of *trabajar* 'to work' or *gente* 'people', for example). The use of upper case where it was not necessary was also very common (*Mexicano* 'Mexican', *Inglés* 'English'), but it was not considered either. We also left out all the proper nouns (Sea World, for example) unless the Spanish form is regularly used (for example, *Estados Unidos* 'United States'). Foreign words that have been incorporated in official Spanish dictionaries were also excluded (*hobby*, *chance*, *posters*, for example). Finally, dialectal differences were taken into account to the best of our abilities. A summary of the methodology is presented in Figure 5.2.

The following are examples of each category of CS. The codification after the examples indicates: student number, sex (F/M) and level (1, 2, 3, 4, 5).

A. Participants

Level placed	Participants (= *n*)
Beginner	30
Intermediate A	30
Intermediate B	30
Advanced A	30
Advanced B	30
Total	**150**

B. Instrument: four short essays
- a. Descriptive
- b. Narrative
- c. Argumentative
- d. Hypothetical

C. Linguistic variable

(1) Single-word switches
(2) Single-word borrowings
(3) Single-word calques
(4) Multiple-word switches
(5) Multiple-word calques

Figure 5.2 Pilot study: summary of the methodology

Examples

1 Single-word switches

(a) *Fuimos a visitar a una amiga que esta en el* **Navy**. (65F/3)[3]

(b) *Si yo pudiera cambiar algunas cosas de mi pais yo cambiara los* **injustices** *de unos a otros*. (3F/1)

(c) *Yo he visto que los trabajos del* **freeway** *y de las calles siempre se los dan a los mejicanos ...* (67M/2)

(d) *En Cozumel fuimos* **scubadiving**. (21M-2)

2 Single-word loans

(a) *Si yo pudiera cambiar algunas cosas de mi país cambiaría la forma de pagar* **taxas**. (87F/3)

(b) *No se mortifican por* **billes** *de agua y luz*. (353F/1)

(c) *Este* **espano** *[span] de tiempo es una temporada de vacaciones que nos dan a todos los estudiantes de la Universidad ...* (90M/4)

3 Single-word calques

(a) *El piso de la casa es* **carpeta**. (119M/1)

(b) *También, recuerdas que hay muchas películas, radio y* **papeles** *en español para los hispanos que no saben comunicar en inglés*. (27F/2)

(c) *La* **yarda** *de atrás es muy grande. Mis niños le gustan jugar afuera en la* **yarda**. (173F/3)

(d) *Ahora para hacer valer los derechos de los hispanos, éstos deben de* **aplicar** *a la ciudadanía Americana*. (125F/5)

4 Multiple-word switches

(a) *Los Puertorriqaños se estan* **increasing in education and social status**. (3F/1)

(b) *En esto pais los mas ricos* **own** *mas de 1/2 half del dinero y* **most of the power**. (7F/1)

5 Multiple-word calques

(a) *Yo me levantaría todas las mañanas para poder* **ver el sol salir**. (156F/3)

(b) *Los derechos de los hispanos en Los Estados Unidos* **son extraños a mí**. (168M/3)

(c) *Yo se mis derechos y nada o nadie* **me va tener para atrás**. (26F/4)

(d) *No entre en el río a nadar porque* **no sé cómo nadar**. *Pero si* **entré la alberca de tres pies**. (87F/3)

(e) *Un gran número de hispanos que* **hacen la jornada** ['make the journey'] *a este país se encuentra frecuentemente atrapados por un sistema legal que es lento e injusto*. (19M/4)

Once all the cases of CS were identified and categorized, an attempt was made (a) to verify the emergence of new lexical items that would offer proof of lexicalization, and (b) to recognize new and recurring structural patterns that would suggest some type of grammatic(al)ization.

Results

Table 5.1 shows the distribution of the participants based on country of origin. More than half of the students were born in the USA (n = 87/150; 58%). The rest were from different Central and South American countries (Argentina, Colombia, Costa Rica, Ecuador, El Salvador, Guatemala, Honduras, Mexico (n = 29; almost 50% of the foreign born), Peru and Venezuela.[4]

Figure 5.3 shows how the number of students born in the USA decreases as the level increases. while the number of students from other Spanish-speaking countries increases with the level. At this point in the study it would seem that the number of students from other Spanish-speaking countries increases with the level; however, a larger number of subjects are needed in order to make this determination. There were 96 female (64%) and 54 male participants (36%).

The minimum number of words produced by the students was 28 and the maximum reached was 588 words (mean = 308.29; SD 79.96). The distribution of CS per total number of words produced by each level appears in Table 5.2.

Despite the wide range of writing abilities, the average number of words per level was not so different. The mean for the total number of words produced by level 1 was almost 250 words, while students placed at level 5 wrote an average of 328 words. A statistical analysis (Pearson, 2-tailed)

Table 5.1   Distribution per level based on country of origin

Country of origin	Level					Total
	1	2	3	4	5	
Argentina		2	1	1		4
Colombia					3	3
Costa Rica	1		2			3
Cuba		1			2	3
Ecuador				1	1	2
El Salvador			1	2		3
Guatemala			1			1
Honduras				1		1
Mexico	2	4	6	8	9	29
Peru				1	1	2
USA	28	25	18	11	5	87
Unknown			1	2	5	8
Venezuela				1	3	4
Total	**30**	**30**	**30**	**30**	**30**	**150**

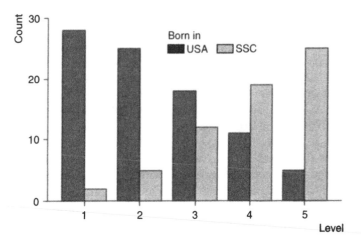

Figure 5.3   Students born in the USA or in other Spanish-speaking countries per level

Table 5.2   Distribution of code-switching per total number of words produced by level

		Level					
		1	*2*	*3*	*4*	*5*	*Total*
Mean	Total number of CS	11.77	10.90	4.97	4.10	4.03	7.15
	Total number of words produced	249.33	301.43	329.23	333.10	328.37	308.29
Std. deviation	total number of CS	6.78	7.58	3.66	4.82	3.22	6.42
	Total number of words produced	92.16	71.13	65.29	75.33	64.85	79.96
% of total sum	Total number of CS	32.9%	30.5%	13.9%	11.5%	11.3	100.0%
	Total number of words produced	16.2%	19.6%	21.4%	21.6%	21.3%	100.0%

found significant correlations between level and total number of CS ($-.492 < 0.01$), between origin (USA vs other Spanish-speaking countries) and total number of CS ($-.367 < 0.01$), and between total number of words produced and total number of CS ($.193 < 0.05$).

Table 5.3 Average number of tokens produced in each category by level

Level	Single-word switches	Single-word loans	Single-word calques	Multiple-word code-switching	Multiple-word calques	Total number of CS
1	1.47	.63	2.13	.20	7.33	11.77
2	.60	.30	1.70	.10	8.20	10.90
3	.23	.43	1.03	.00	3.27	4.97
4	.07	.20	.53	.00	3.30	4.10
5	.17	.03	.90	.00	2.93	4.03
Total	.51	.32	1.26	.06	5.01	7.15

Table 5.3 shows the means for each category by level. For example, the total number of CS for students in level 1 was 11.77. This total included: 1.47 cases of single-word switches, .63 single-word loans, and 2.13 single-word calques. Multiple-word CS was almost non-existent in level 1 (.20) while the category that reached the highest number was multiple-word calques (7.33). The average number of tokens produced by the other levels decreased most of the time as the level increased.

The following points summarize the main findings of the data analysis:

(a) In general terms, we found low percentages of the total number of CS in the analysed written samples (7.15 words per average sample of 308 words). As expected, the influence of English appears to decrease as competence in Spanish increases.
(b) The results show a very low number of single- and multiple-word switches to English across the levels (means of .51 and .06 words respectively in the writing samples with an average of 308 words). Most of the cases were found at the lower levels, and it seems they were caused by lexical gaps. The following examples (1–10) include some single- and multiple-word switches found in the essays:

(1) *Nosortros manija San Antonio y* **(stayed)** *a proximo de la Market Square.* (3F/1).
(2) *En esto pais los mas ricos* **own** *mas de 1/2* **half** *del dinero y* **most of the power.** (7F/1)
(3) *Por eso quieren terminan* **'affirmative'** *acíon.* (54M/1)
(4) *Y también tienen los* **lobsters** *muy baratos.* (161M/1)
(5) *Cuando llegamos al hotel femos caminando en los calles y comiendo* **'hot dogs'.** (211F/1)
(6) *Pero yo creo también que es bueno que los hispanos necesitan ser* **citizens** *de los Estados Unidos primero antes los derechos son* **granted.**
(7) *Yo cambiara los* **'jails.'** *A mucha gente mala.* (336M-1)
(8) *Entonces, ponemos un* **plaster** *en la parides.* (342M/1)

(9)   ¿*Que paso con el **ozone layer***? (27F/2)

(10)   *Tiene antigüedades de la epoca de Carlos Quinto y ademas tiene muebles de **majogani**.* (50F/3)

The usage of Spanish in the USA is usually restricted to informal contexts with family and friends, so most of the switches that appear in the examples above are words that heritage speakers would not normally hear in their daily exchanges in Spanish ('lobsters', *'majogani', 'ozone layer', 'citizens', 'granted', and 'plaster'). In some of the other examples, there is no doubt that the writer did not know the Spanish word since the English equivalent appears in quotation marks or in parenthesis (examples 1, 2 3, 5 and 7).

(c)   Loans and single-word calques were also very sporadic. We found an average of .32 loans and 1.26 single-word calques per writing sample. There were a few instances of unusual words such as *espano* 'span' in example 2c, but in most cases (see examples 2a, 2b, 3a, 3b, 3c and 3d) these words have been incorporated into the Spanish of the USA to such degree that many times the writer was not aware that they were not part of a more general Spanish.[5]

Some of the most frequent single-word calques were found in the essays that described the students' homes. The word *carpeta* 'carpet', for example, appeared 67% of the times (6/9) while the more general Spanish term *alfombra*, appeared 33% of the times (3/9) (examples 11–13):

(11)   *Mi cuarto es el más grande. La **carpeta** en mi cuarto es de color violeta.* (87F/3)

(12)   *Hemos puesto todas las puertas nuevas, pintamos las paderes, y también sacamos la **carpeta**.* (38F/2)

(13)   *Mi casa es pequeñia pero bonita. Cuando mi mama la compre no erra bonita. Tenia muchas manchadas en la **enformbras** y todos los vientanas estavan quebrados.* (211F/1)

Another high-frequency calque was the word *yarda* 'yard'. It appeared in 16% of the contexts (8/51), while other forms (*jardín*: 22/51, *patio*: 18/51, *solar*: 2/51, *el terreno de atrás*: 1/51) were the preferred choices in most cases (43/51, 84%). Examples 14–17 illustrate the usage of this specific calque and its alternatives:

(14)   *La **yarda** de atrás esta muy grande y la de enfrente esta chiquita.* (375F/1)

(15) *El patio o la 'yarda' es muy amplia.* (56M/4)
(16) *Tenemos un **patio** muy grande, bueno para jugar diferentes deportes. Mi mama y papa tienen muchas flores y arboles de fruta.* (79 F/2)
(17) *Ademas, mi casa tiene un **jardin** muy amplio en el cual mi hermano menor y yo jugamos nuestras pequeñas copas del mundo de fultbol.* (138M/4)

(d) Of all the analysed phenomena, multiple-word calques were the most frequent across the levels, yet the means were still very low when compared to the total number of words (total number of words produced: 46,244; total number of CS: 1,073; total number of multiple-word calques: 751). The highest numbers were found in levels 1 and 2: approximately 8 calques per student. The higher levels (3, 4 and 5) averaged 3 calques per writing sample. In some of these cases, there was evidence of items with new grammatical functions. For example in (18) the intransitive verb *caminar* 'to walk' becomes transitive, whereas in (19) the opposite takes place: the transitive Spanish verb *visitar* 'to visit', which may be used intransitively in English, becomes intransitive also in Spanish.

(18) *Antes de regresar a los Estados Unidos, **pasé tres días mas cami-nando las calles de París.*** (139M/4)
(19) *Estuve la mayor parte **visitando con amigos** y familiares que no había visto durante mucho tiempo.* (23M/5)
(20) *Lo que pasa es que una de mis hermanas no pudo visitarnos. Así la familia no estaba completa y bien que nos hacía falta ella y su familia. Aunque sin ella **tuvimos un buen tiempo**, pero no cómo los de antes.* (76F/3)

However, while a few multiple-word calques appeared several times in the examined data such as *tener un buen tiempo* 'to have a good time' (instead of *divertirse o pasarla bien*), illustrated in example (20), most of the instances of this phenomenon were isolated cases of transfer. Yet, it merits mentioning that even students who were born and educated in monolingual Spanish-speaking countries produced several multiple-word calques in a context where they were expected to write exclusively in Spanish.

Conclusions

Although the percentages of Spanish/English interaction were very low in the analysed samples across all levels of proficiency when compared to the total number of words produced (1,073/46,244 words), CS was present across the levels, especially in the form of multiple-word calques. Since we are only at the initial phase of this research project, it is too soon to reach any definite conclusions, but we could suggest that there are some single-word calques and loans that are undergoing a lexicalization process and are being adopted by a large number of speakers of the US Spanish variety. Established borrowings such as 'carpeta' and 'yarda' are slowly replacing more general Spanish terms.

Regarding grammatic(al)ization, although we cannot ignore the presence of multiple-word calques in the writing of these bilingual students, in general there is too much individual variation to categorize any of these phenomena as grammatic(al)ized item/s. We were unable to identify statistically significant recurring patterns in our data. All the examples classified as multiple-word calques could easily fit into one of the following three categories identified by Silva-Corvalán (1994) in her study of Los Angeles Spanish. She suggests that

> [g]iven a primary language A and a secondary language B, the permeability [of the grammar] of B will not be evident in the incorporation of new syntactic structures on the model of A, but first and foremost in the following: (a) the extension of the discourse-pragmatic functions of a structure in B according to the model of the functions of the parallel structure in A ... (b) the preferential use or increase in the frequency of use in B of an existing structure parallel to one in A to the detriment of variants in B ... ; and (c) the loss of semantic-pragmatic constraints governing the use of the variants of a syntactic variable in B when the corresponding structure in A is not sensitive to such constraints. (1994: 135)

It is possible that given enough time, and if the influx of Hispanics is dramatically reduced and at the same time the number of Hispanics born in the United States increases as predicted by demographic projections (see the Introduction), the presence of some of these multiple-word calques will become statistically significant so that they can be considered grammatic(al)ized items.

There are many limitations in using open production activities such as composition writing and a limited number of samples. Our data are also restricted to college or college-bound students. A follow-up study with a larger number of samples as well as quantitative studies of specific CS items, especially multiple-word calques, may be able to offer more insights into this matter. However, so far we have been unable to find evidence of a new mixed-code when analysing Spanish/English interaction in the writing of Hispanic heritage learners in the USA. The analysis of the data seems to indicate that US Spanish is not a mixed code, but another variety of Spanish with a few lexicalized elements incorporated as result of the prolonged contact with English and some random individual cases of transfer at the discourse-pragmatic levels attested at all levels of proficiency in Spanish.

Notes

I would like to thank Alejandra Balestra and Rena Torres Cacoullos for their helpful comments on earlier versions of this chapter. I am also very grateful to the reviewers and the editors of this volume for their valuable observations and detailed revisions and editorial suggestions.

1 See Montes-Alcalá (2001: 12–14) for a detailed explanation of the terminology used by different researchers.
2 For example, Otheguy's (2001) study of US Spanish in New York City identified only 535 neologisms in a corpus of approximately 33 hours of recorded interviews. A previous study by Silva-Corvalán (1994) found an average of 0.9 and 1.3 cases of multiple-word calques per 10 minutes of recorded interviews with second and third-generation Mexican-Americans in Los Angeles. For a comprehensive summary of these and some additional studies, see Fairclough (2003).
3 Students' original spelling was maintained throughout the examples.
4 The country of origin of eight of the participants could not be identified.
5 Other examples include: 'facto' (instead of 'hecho'), 'resulto' (for 'resultado'), 'blokes' (for 'cuadras'), 'minoridades' (for 'minorías'), and others.

6
Andean Spanish and the Spanish of Lima: Linguistic Variation and Change in a Contact Situation

Carol A. Klee and Rocío Caravedo

Introduction

One of the frequently mentioned results of globalization has been its detrimental effects on the maintenance of minority languages. It has been estimated that of the roughly 6,000 languages spoken across the globe in 2000, between 50 per cent and 90 per cent will not survive the twenty-first century. For the Quechua-speaking masses in Peru, who lived in relative isolation in the Andean region following the Spanish invasion in the sixteenth century, the twentieth century brought increased opportunities for contact with Spanish speakers as a result of the modernization of the economy, the development of communication networks and the initiation of massive migration from the Andean region to the coast. These changes have brought about a rather rapid language shift from Quechua to Spanish, as is apparent in census data. In 1940 over half the population of Peru spoke an indigenous language. However, by the 1980s only one-quarter of the population claimed some proficiency in one of these languages. According to census data, approximately 60 per cent of those who speak an indigenous language in Peru also speak Spanish (Pozzi-Escot, 1990). Thus, there has been fairly rapid language shift in Peru over the past 65 years. Mufwene (2004: 207) has described language shift among Native Americans in ecological terms, as 'an adaptive response to changing socioeconomic conditions, under which their heritage languages have been undervalued and marginalized'. He argues that it is caused in large part by speakers' recognition of the economic value of the European colonial languages, which has increased as a result of globalization.

This language shift has resulted in the acquisition and use of a contact variety of Spanish, Andean Spanish, which has developed into a stable sociolect in Peru acquired as a first language by monolingual Spanish speakers. The characteristics of Andean Spanish have been amply documented (cf. Pozzi-Escot, 1973; Lozano, 1975; A. Escobar, 1978; Luján, Minaya and Sankoff, 1981; Godenzzi, 1986, 1991; Klee, 1989, 1990, 1996; A. M. Escobar, 1988, 2000; Rivarola, 1990; Caravedo, 1992, 1999; De Granda, 1995; Cerrón-Palomino, 2003, among others) and include a number of features that contrast with the more prestigious variety of Spanish spoken on the Peruvian coast, including object/verb word order, the use of the archmorpheme *lo*, duplication of direct objects, *leísmo*, the use of the present perfect in place of the preterite, evidential use of the past perfect, the double possessive (for example 'su casa de Juan'). Some of the phonological features of this dialect have evolved in a way contrary to the historical development of the Spanish language. Consonants, for example, tend to be retained in syllable-final position, while in coastal Spanish they are weakened or deleted; the lateral palatal /λ/ is largely maintained; and /r/ is frequently assibilated.

Migration from the Andean region to Lima during the twentieth century has followed the pattern observed elsewhere in which inhabitants of rural areas migrate to the city in search of jobs and a better standard of living. In addition, in Peru in the 1980s and early 1990s many *campesinos* sought refuge in Lima from the political violence that raged in many parts of the Andes. As a result of migration, Lima grew from a city of 645,000 inhabitants in 1940 to 6.5 million residents by the early 1990s. Approximately 60 per cent of Lima's population currently comes from other regions of the country, a fact that has brought about major changes in the city during the past three decades.

From a linguistic perspective, migration has increased the rate of language shift to Spanish as it is the principal language in Peru and also because indigenous languages are stigmatized in the capital city. Indeed, these languages are rarely transmitted by Andean migrants to their offspring. For example, Paerregaard (1997:72) found that only 1 per cent of the second generation migrants he studied in Lima spoke Quechua. The effect of the loss of Quechua is the extension of the acquisition and use of the Andean Spanish variety.

Andean groups exhibit distinguishing sociocultural and linguistic characteristics that receive subjective negative evaluation from native inhabitants of Lima, or *limeños*. Specifically, they often speak Quechua or Aymara as a mother tongue and have learned Spanish as a second language, frequently without systematic instruction and often in adulthood. In addition, Andean migrants have a minimal level of schooling, and some have had no formal instruction and arrive in Lima in conditions of extreme poverty. They often have nowhere to live and as a result they 'invade' uninhabited lands on the outskirts of Lima where they construct homes with precarious materials. On the periphery of the city the first spaces of social coexistence arise in neighbourhoods pejoratively called *barriadas*, and euphemistically known as *pueblos jóvenes* or 'human settlements'. In these new spaces conditions for social integration are created through relationships between migrants, both those from the same region and those from different regions, who converge in the capital (Golte and Adams, 1987). The integration of migrants into the greater city begins with the development of informal or provisional unskilled survival occupations from which short-term, fortuitous and unstable relationships with natives of Lima are created. This same process also ensues in the context of migration across national borders in the sense that it often supposes a process of adaptation of individuals who are less advantaged economically and who are marginalized by the receiving society.

Thus as a result of migration, Andean Spanish has come into direct contact with coastal *limeño* Spanish, which is the most prestigious variety in Peru. Migration has created opportunities for face-to-face communicative situations among speakers of different varieties, which can result in the gradual blurring of boundaries between the two dialects or in the creation of new forms. In Peru it has been documented that migration has resulted in the emergence of new patterns manifested in social and economic behaviour (Golte and Adams, 1987), urban life, and diverse cultural expressions (Ramos-García, 1998).[1] It is likely that new linguistic patterns have emerged as well.

Methodology

The purpose of this study is to determine the degree to which contact between Andean and *limeño* Spanish modifies the structure of both varieties of Spanish, and specifically which linguistic aspects are vulnerable to change and which aspects resist change (cf. Klee and Caravedo, 2000). The following social variables of the participants were taken into account:

- Native language (Quechua/ Aymara vs Spanish).
- Family ancestry (Andean vs Non-Andean).

- Generation of migration (generation of Andean migrants: parents/ children).
- Neighbourhood (migrant neighbourhoods vs *limeño* neighbourhoods).
- Level of education (Ø/some primary school/completed primary school/some secondary education/high school diploma/ some higher education).
- Occupation (unemployed vs unskilled/semi-skilled workers).
- Sex.

Neighbourhoods are crucial for a socio-spatial microanalysis of urban change in which speakers are considered to be members of spatially interrelated groups (cf. Labov, 1994, 2001; Milroy, 1980; Milroy and Milroy, 1992; Williams and Kerswill, 1999). Consequently, we have used the migrant/native dichotomy to group the informants according to their membership in Lima's migrant and non-migrant neighbourhoods.

As can be seen, social class is not listed as a factor, not because it is irrelevant, but because in Lima the migrant condition alone appears to be an indicator of lower social status. *Limeños*, on the contrary, are generally situated in higher strata of the social spectrum than migrants. Nevertheless, with regard to *limeños* we have focused on the lower middle class as we hypothesized that the symmetrical communicative relationship between those *limeños* and Andean migrants is likely to favour the transmission of characteristics from one dialect to the other in a double direction (Caravedo, 1996). The relationship between Andean migrants and middle and upper-class *limeños* is, on the contrary, hierarchical and much more complex in a way that makes it unlikely that Andean features can directly transfer to these groups or vice-versa. Additionally, the inclusion of only elementary and intermediate levels of education and of lower occupational categories (unemployed and unskilled or semi-skilled workers) reflects the social characteristics of the targeted groups.

To determine whether Andean Spanish is transmitted to the second generation in Lima both migrants and their adult children were included in the corpus. The inclusion of both generations is crucial to enable an analysis of the transmission of features in *apparent time* (Labov, 1972) and to be able to predict what is happening in *real time*. In the most recent Labovian approaches, the principle of *vernacular reorganization*, the process by which 'the child must learn to talk differently from his mother' (Labov, 2001: 415), which is fundamental to the process of change, functions precisely in the context of contact between different linguistic varieties. It can be defined as the progressive distancing of the new generations from the forms of their parents, if it is a distancing that does not completely abandon its point of departure. We will attempt to ascertain how this principle is manifested in the society under examination. The basic questions posed by this investigation are the following:

1   What is the direction of change: convergence toward the prestigious coastal form or divergence through the creation of a new hybrid form that combines certain traits of one or both native forms?
2   What is the role of social factors in the process of change and in the internal variation of Spanish in the area under study?

To answer these questions a judgment sample of 108 sociolinguistic interviews was conducted.[2] We conducted interviews in several shanty towns inhabited by Andean migrants, interviewing both first-generation migrants as well as adults who had been born in Lima but whose parents had migrated from the Andean region. In addition, we conducted interviews in poor, but 'traditional' (that is, non-migrant) neighbourhoods in

Table 6.1   Characteristics of speakers

Speaker	Generation in Lima	Family background	Neighbourhood	Sex	1st lng	Education	Occupation
3AG	1	Andean	Shantytown	M	Quechua	Some primary	Retired
4GT	1	Andean	Shantytown	M	Quechua	Primary	Retired market vendor
8FT	2	Andean	Shantytown	M	Spanish	Secondary	Military
9FA	1	Andean	Shantytown	F	Quechua	Some primary	Unemployed
10JG	1	Andean	Shantytown	M	Quechua	Some primary	Building caretaker
11BI	1	Andean	Shantytown	F	Quechua	Primary	Unemployed
12BM	1	Andean	Shantytown	M	Quechua	Some primary	Unemployed
13CC	2	Andean	Shantytown	F	Spanish	Some secondary	Unemployed
14EF	2	Andean	Shantytown	M	Spanish	Some secondary	Unemployed
15JF	2	Andean	Shantytown	F	Spanish	Secondary	Unemployed
16LS	2	Andean	Shantytown	F	Spanish	Some college	Factory worker
17MC	Non-migrant	Non-Andean	Established Neighbourhood	F	Spanish	Some college	Nurses' assistant
18JN	Non-migrant	Non-Andean	Established neighbourhood	F	Spanish	Secondary	Unemployed
19JE	Non-migrant	Non-Andean	Established neighbourhood	M	Spanish	Secondary	Unemployed
20JT	Non-migrant	Non-Andean	Established neighbourhood	M	Spanish	Secondary	Security guard

Lima. The individuals in those neighbourhoods and their parents were born in Lima and the consultants had resided there all their lives.

For this study we have analysed a subset of data representing the speech of 15 speakers, including speakers of Andean Spanish as well as native *limeños*. Table 6.1 includes a detailed description of their characteristics.

The analysis centred on phonological and morphological features that are characteristic of the Andean variety of Spanish and represent the most fundamental differences between the Andean and *limeño* dialects. The phonological phenomena include the lateral palatal and assibilated vibrants typical of Andean Spanish and the aspiration and elision of /s/ typical of the coast, as noted below:

(1) Distinction vs non-distinction between palatal lateral /λ/ and non-lateral /y/ [kaλó] [kayó] (*calló – cayó*)
(2) assibilation vs non-assibilation of multiple vibrants [řóxo] [Róxo] (*rojo*); [péřo] [péRo] (*perro*)
(3) elision vs aspiration of sibilants [kántaØ] [kántah] (*cantas*); [káØko] [káhko] (*casco*).

Morphological features include direct and indirect object pronouns, specifically *leísmo*, and the use of archmorpheme *lo*, which have been widely documented in Andean Spanish.

The linguistic variables were quantified and, when appropriate, statistical tests (that is, VARBRUL) were conducted to determine in what linguistic environments features of Andean Spanish are maintained and to identify correlations between linguistic variables and social variables. In subsequent phases we will analyse additional morphosyntactic features (double possessive, order of sentence constituents, verbal system variation) as well as textual organization and pragmatic features.

Results

Palatal lateral

The distinction between /y/ and /λ/, traditionally a prestigious characteristic of peninsular Spanish, is in the process of loss even among younger generations in Castile (Quilis, 1965; Hernández, 1996; Moreno, 1996) who are replacing the lateral palatal with /y/. The same linguistic change is in progress in some South American regions, although the motivation for the change may be different. In Peru, for example, where traditionally this opposition has been maintained in

Table 6.2 The use of the palatal lateral vs the non-palatal lateral by first-generation Andean migrants

Informant	lateral /l/		No lateral /y/	
	N	%	N	%
3AG	53	50	53	50
4GT	6	12	44	88
9FA	0	0	20	100
10JG	0	0	20	100
11BI	6	20	24	80
12BM	28	47	32	53

Andean Spanish from colonial times to the present, it is not positively evaluated, at least not by speakers of the prestigious form in the capital, which is completely *yeísta*.

The negative evaluation of the palatal lateral is apparent in our data from Lima. Only four out of fifteen speakers maintain the lateral palatal form and all those who do maintain it correspond, as expected, to the first generation group of migrants. Furthermore, palatal laterals in this group are not *categorically* used in expected contexts; in addition, they occur with less frequency overall than non-laterals in variable contexts. Thus, it appears that there is a tendency toward *yeísta* production, even among Andeans in Lima. Table 6.2 shows the percentages of production of both phonemes by the six first-generation Andean informants, two of whom (9FA, 10JG) do not use any lateral palatals.

Although it has been asserted that Andean Spanish speakers maintain the distinction between /y/ and /λ/, this aspect of Andean Spanish in Peru has not been studied with exhaustive and systematic methods in representative corpora.[3] For this reason, we are not certain if our first-generation Andean migrants were already experiencing variation in the distinction between the lateral and the non-lateral at the time they moved to the capital. Such uncertainty is justified by previous studies (Caravedo, 1999) in which a loss of palatal laterals was found among Andean speakers who had not moved to Lima. Thus, the presence of variation between palatal lateral and non-laterals in our corpus, even among first-generation Andeans whose mother tongue is Quechua, does not seem surprising. However, the lack of the palatal lateral in the speech of two Andean migrants (9FA and 10 FG) requires explanation. A socio-historical examination of these two individuals, whose results diverge from the rest, assists in the understanding of their language use.

These individuals arrived at the capital during adolescence and are also presently employed in occupations that allow diverse and constant contact with *limeño* speakers, the first as a domestic employee who has lived with a *limeño* family since a young age and the second as a caretaker who works at the most important drama school in Lima.

It is interesting to note that the only speakers who maintain the palatal lateral are first-generation Andeans whose mother tongue is Quechua and who also have very low levels of educational attainment (that is, incomplete primary school). Meanwhile second-generation migrants, who were born in the capital and became socially integrated through their occupations, have completely lost the palatal lateral, adopting the *yeísta* patterns of the capital. Consequently, variability has been converted into categorical invariability at the new site of contact. The migratory period along with the level of social integration, obviously higher among migrant children than their parents, plays a major role in the loss of this distinction.

Assibilation of vibrants

Unlike the loss of laterals, assibilation does not constitute a phonological distinction, but rather solely involves allophonic variation. While in some regions of Mexico (Perissinotto, 1975) and Argentina (Donni de Mirande, 1996), assibilation is not negatively evaluated and has spread to middle-class and formal situations (Rissell, 1989; Matus-Mendoza, 2004; Caravedo, 2001), in Lima this variant is highly stigmatized because it is perceived as characteristic of Andean Spanish.

In the analysis of assibilated vs non-assibilated /r/ we first took into account whether the r appeared in initial position, as in *río*, or in internal position, as in *carro*. As can be seen in Table 6.3, the percentage of assibilation is equivalent in the two linguistic contexts; roughly 30 per cent of the variants are assibilated. However, it is clear that non-assibilated forms occur with greater frequency than the assibilated variant in Lima. These results contrast with those found in Calca, Peru, a town in the Andean region of Peru, roughly 50 kilometers from Cuzco. There /r/ is

Table 6.3 Linguistic factors and /r/ assibilation

Position	Assibilated		Non-assibilated	
Initial	94	30%	217	70%
Internal	67	29%	165	71%

assibilated in initial position 56 per cent of the time and in internal position the assibilated variant was used even more frequently, 69 per cent (Alvord, Klee and Echávez-Solano, 2006). It is clear that there is less frequent use of the assibilated form in Lima than in at least one part of the Peruvian Andes, which is to be expected given the high degree of stigmatization of this variable in Lima.

A multiple regression analysis, VARBRUL, was conducted to determine which social factors correlate with assibilation. Table 6.4 shows the values for each independent variable that was statistically significant. Values higher that 0.500 favour assibilation, while those that are less than 0.500 disfavour it.

The social factors are listed in the order of importance in the statistical analysis. Thus, the factor that contributes most heavily to the use of the assibilated variant is the generation of migration. It is clear that Andean migrants strongly favour the use of assibilated forms, as the VARBRUL weight of 0.744 indicates. However, both the children of migrants and the *limeños* rarely use this variant (3 per cent and 1 per cent, respectively) and the VARBRUL weight indicates that assibilation is strongly disfavoured in these two groups (0.267 and 0.082 respectively). In fact, assibilation is almost absent in the speech of *limeños*. Caravedo (1990) had found that among native *limeños* more assibilation was found among males over 45 years of age than in other *limeño* groups. She attributes the decrease in assibilation in younger generations to their desire to distance themselves from Andean migrants; her results are indirectly confirmed in the present study. Paredes (1992) found that migrants were aware of the stigmatization of the assibilated variant in Lima and had begun to replace that variant with a retroflex /r/ which was more acceptable to *limeños*.

Table 6.4 Social factors and assibilation of /r/

Factor groups	Factors	Occurrence	%	Weight
Generation of migration	Andean migrants	156/ 325	48	**0.744**
	Children of migrants	4/ 128	3	0.267
	limeños	1/ 90	1	0.082
Occupation	Unemployed	160/ 433	36	**0.672**
	Semi-skilled work	1/110	1	0.056
Sex	Male	154/ 344	44	**0.723**
	Female	7/ 199	3	0.160

The next most important social variable is occupation, which is a fundamental factor for social integration. As is apparent in Table 6.4, unemployed individuals who do not have stable communication networks with people from the capital are precisely those who register higher percentages of the assibilated variant (36 per cent) compared to those who are unemployed (1 per cent).

Sex is the final significant social variable. Men register much higher proportions of assibilated forms than women (44 per cent vs 3 per cent). This confirms research in other contexts which has shown that women tend to prefer prestigious varieties and are more innovative (in this case with non-assibilation) (cf. Labov, 2001). Education level was not a significant variable.

Aspiration and elision of /s/

Reduced sibilants have been widely studied in Hispanic contexts, above all in the cities of the Caribbean, the Canaries, Lima, Buenos Aires (Cedergren, 1978; Terrell, 1978a, 1978b; López Morales, 1983; Caravedo, 1983, 1990; Lafford, 1986; Samper, 1990; Alba, 1990; among many more). Aspiration in implosive internal position is widespread in the Spanish-speaking world, while elision, which can occur in word final position and thus affect nominal and verbal morphology, has been concentrated with greatest intensity in the Caribbean and southern Spain. Studies carried out in Lima support the hypothesis that aspiration is the most widespread variant among *limeños* of all social classes and therefore does not receive negative social evaluation, while elision constitutes an incipient process that is confined primarily to the lower social classes in Lima (Caravedo, 1990). In Andean Spanish, the sibilant has tended to be retained, although as far as we know, this has not been verified with an empirical analysis that can be compared with our results.

The results of the VARBRUL analysis of linguistic factors are perfectly consistent with the general tendencies of reduced sibilants and elision in other dialects of Spanish, as can be seen in Table 6.5. In final

Table 6.5 /s/ elision according to position and number of syllables

Int. factors	Occurrences	%	Weight
Final	774/1027	75	**0.601**
Interior	87/208	42	0.116
Monosyllabic	237/394	60	0.255
Polysyllabic	624/840	74	**0.623**

Table 6.6 /s/elision vs /s/ aspiration according to social variables

Factor groups	Factors	Occurrences	%	Weight
Generation of	Andean migrants	283/370	76	0.579
migration	Children of migrants	383/516	74	0.577
	Limeños	195/349	56	0.311
Sex	Male	577/795	73	0.566
	Female	284/440	65	0.382

position /s/ elision is favoured, while aspiration is favoured in internal position. Polysyllabic words favour the appearance of elision with a weighting of 0.623, while in monosyllabic words /s/ tends to be retained.

Table 6.6 summarizes the results of the VARBRUL analysis on the social variables. As in the case of assibilation, generation of migration is the most significant variable. It can be noted that both Andean migrants and their children favour elision to a similar degree with weightings of 0.579 and 0.577 respectively, while native *limeños* disfavour elision (0.311). This result is surprising as it shows that Andean migrants and their adult children use a phonetic variant characteristic of lower-class *limeño* speech to a greater degree than the native *limeños* in this study. Males tend to elide somewhat more than females with weightings of 0.566 and 0.382 respectively, as has been found in studies of /s/ deletion in other areas (Cedergren, 1978; Lafford, 1986; Samper, 1990; and others). Education and occupation were not significant factors and therefore are not included in the table.

It is surprising that Andean migrants exhibit a higher proportion of sibilant elision than the *limeños* in the study, although elision is not characteristic of Andean Spanish. Curiously, Andean speakers are in the most advanced stage of sibilant reduction initiated by *limeños*. Our results indicate that this process is not related to migrant generation, as both the Andean migrants themselves and their adult children exhibit similar proportions of elision.

To explain these results, we begin with the characteristics of the linguistic features we have analysed up to the point. In the case of the laterals and assibilates, migrants are confronted with a stable and categorical *limeño* form; the variants characteristic of Andean Spanish are not used by *limeños* and moreover are stigmatized. In the case of /s/, which is a highly frequent phoneme in discourse, migrants are faced with a complex system of variation, which includes [s], [h] and [Ø]. One of these variants, [Ø], occurs with a higher frequency (55 per cent) than aspiration among the lower middle-class *limeños* in our sample and is the variable chosen with even higher frequency by Andean migrants. This fact lends support to our hypothesis that Andean speakers' most frequent exposure to *limeño* Spanish occurs through symmetrical contact with speakers from the lower middle class rather than through middle or upper middle-class speakers who exhibit elision to a much smaller degree (that is, 5 per cent in Caravedo, 1990: 136). Thus, social integration of Andean migrants in Lima begins in relatively symmetrical relationships rather than in hierarchical relationships and this influences the linguistic variants that they adopt. Clearly, in future studies it will be necessary to explore in more depth the types of social networks and links that occur between migrants and inhabitants of the city. For all three phonological variants Andean migrants and their adult children abandon their native varieties and adopt variants typical of lower middle-class *limeños*.

Given the heightened perception and negative valorization of two of the Andean variants, assibilated /r/ and the lateral palatal, it is not surprising to find that Andean migrants adopt the *limeño* variants within one generation. It is more surprising to discover their high frequency use of elision, as the more common variant in Lima is aspiration, and both aspiration and the sibilant are evaluated as more prestigious than deletion. However, elision is used more frequently by lower-class speakers in Lima with whom the Andean migrants and their children have more contact and their speech likely serves as the primary model of *limeño* Spanish. Although Andean migrants and their children appear to assimilate to *limeño* phonological norms, the question arises as to whether new hybrid forms come into being, as we hypothesized in the introduction. The next two sections, which focus on clitic pronouns, provide some evidence of this.

Leísmo[4]

Leísmo, the use of *le(s)* as an accusative, is widespread in some parts of the Spanish-speaking world, such as in Castile. When its use is restricted to a human male referent, it is officially accepted by the Real Academia de la Lengua Española (Lapesa, 1981: 471–2), although its use with feminine or inanimate referents is considered nonstandard. Conversely, the Spanish of Lima, as is the case with most of continental Spanish America, is governed by the so-called etymological system, which differentiates case, gender, and number. Thus, *leísmo* is not a common variant among *limeños* (DeMello, 2002). However, it is characteristic of Andean Spanish (Caravedo, 1999; Paredes, 1996; Valdez Salas, 2002), along with other clitic phenomena, such as *loísmo* and the use of *lo* as an archmorpheme for the direct object pronouns.

While the overall rate of *leísmo* among the speakers in our study was 15 per cent (that is, 104 tokens of *leísmo* out of a total of 693), individual speakers showed large differences as can be seen in Table 6.7.[5] Speakers 11, 16, 15, 4 and 9 (in that order) used the highest frequency of *leísmo*. In general, first-generation migrants tend to have higher rates of *leísmo*, although many second-generation migrants, such as speakers 15 and 16, but also speakers 13 and 14, have relatively high rates of non-standard usage. In contrast, the native lower middle-class *limeños* rarely use *leísmo*; their rate of usage ranges from 3 to 7 per cent.

Clitic choice for the third person object can be conditioned by features of the object referent (for example information status, definiteness of the NP referent, animacy, specificity of the object referent) and the interaction of pragmatic strategies (cf: García and Otheguy, 1977, 1983; Klein-Andreu, 2000). We will examine these aspects in future analyses; however, for now we focus on the use of *leísmo* with [+human], [+animate, −human], and [−animate] direct objects.

In our corpus, *leísmo* occurs primarily when the direct object is [+human], as can been seen in Table 6.8 and in examples (1)–(3) below.

Migrants

(1) *como es el único mi nietecito que tengo, ya pues,* **le quiero** *bastante.*
     (11BI: 10)

Table 6.7 Leísmo

Migrants			Children of migrants			Limeños		
Speaker	No. cases	%	Speaker	No. cases	%	Speaker	No. case	%
3AG	6/40	15	8FT	0/44	0	17MC	3/78	4
4GT	5/25	20	13CC	9/75	12	18JN	2/72	3
9FA	6/31	19	14EF	5/30	18	19JE	1/15	7
10JG	3/22	14	15JF	16/57	28	20JT	3/71	4
11BI	17/44	39	16LS	24/62	39			
12BM	4/27	15						
Total	41/189	22	Total	54/268	20	Total	9/236	4
	Total for all speakers			104/693	15			

Children of migrants

(2) *a veces cuando hay cumpleaños de cada chica le sa ... le sacan a almorzar.* (16LS:5)

Limeños

(3) *incluso la mujercita también, que se enamoró, también me dijo y, pero no, no más allá que la, le he limitado, ¿no?* (17MC: 6)

As is revealed in Table 6.8, native *limeños* in this sample only used *leísmo* with human direct objects, never with inanimate objects. However, both migrants and their children use *le* on occasion with inanimate direct objects, as in examples (4)–(6).

Migrants

(4) *ella estaba estudiando, estaba estudiando administración, pero, de ahí conoció, ya pues, le dejó el estudio[6] y ahí vino el hijo, ya pues, se quedó en nada.* (11BI: 8)

(5) *Porque nuestra idioma [xxx] allá es pues la madre del idioma. Ah ... claro, posiblemente los de acá en Lima también podemos decir, pero también tiene sus fallos, ¿no? Bah ... no sé cómo le llaman eso ...* (12BM: 13)

Children of migrants

(6) *antes nosotros a veces nos íbamos de paseo a un sitio que le llamábamos la Grama.* (15JF: 5)

The children of migrants use *leísmo* to a lesser degree with inanimate direct objects than the migrants themselves (11 per cent vs 22 per cent

Table 6.8 *Leísmo* and animacy

	Human		Animate		Inanimate		Inanimate	
	M	F	M	F	M	F	w/llamar	Total
Migrants	24/41	8/41	0/41	0/41	3/41	1/41	5/41	9/41
	(59%)	(20%)	(0%)	(0%)	(7%)	(2%)	(12%)	(22%)
Children	41/54	7/54	0/54	0/54	1/54	1/54	4/954(7%)	6/54
of migrants	(76%)	(13%)	(0%)	(0%)	(2%)	(2%)		(11%)
Limeños	7/9	2/9	0/9	0/9	0/9	0/9	0/9(0%)	0/9(0%)
	(78%)	(22%)	(0%)	(0%)	(0%)	(0%)		

respectively). Both groups frequently use *le* with the verb *llamar*, as in examples (4) and (5). The children of migrants in this study maintain *leísmo* at a rate equivalent to their parents (20 per cent vs 22 per cent respectively). They use *leísmo* primarily when referring to male human direct objects at a rate similar to that of *limeños* (76 per cent vs 78 per cent respectively). Unlike *limeños*, they sometimes use *leísmo* with inanimate direct objects, but the rate at which they do so is less than that of the first-generation migrants (11 per cent vs 22 per cent). The *limeños* in the study never used *leísmo* in this context. In addition, the occurrence of *leísmo* among *limeños* is very limited (at 4 per cent of the sample). Unlike some of the phonological variables, such as the lateral palatals and assibilation of vibrants examined above, *leísmo* seems to be one feature of Andean Spanish that is brought to Lima by migrants and is being passed on to their children.

The use of the archmorpheme *lo*

In areas where Andean Spanish is spoken the use of the archmorpheme *lo* in place of the direct object pronouns *la, las* and *los* is frequent. As can be seen in Table 6.9, the migrants tend to use singular *lo* in plural contexts. In addition, they use the pronoun *lo*, and sometimes *los*, for feminine direct-object pronouns the vast majority of the time. The children of migrants also neutralize number and gender distinctions, but do so to a lesser degree than first-generation migrants. In our sample, the rate of neutralization of the plural by children of migrants was 57 per cent compared to 64 per cent by first-generation migrants. This compares to a rate of 22 per cent by *limeños*.

With regard to the neutralization of feminine direct-object pronouns, the migrants' rate is quite high at 76 per cent. They tend to have a partial clitic system (as defined by García and Otheguy, 1983); that is, one that includes case but not gender, as in examples (7) and (8):

(7) […] *no solamente acá en todas partes hay, las malcriadeces de los mucha-chos, **lo pintan la calle, lo ponen la piedra pa' jugar**.*[7] (3AG: 33)

(8) [*hablando de su esposa*] *Sí, claro, que **lo ayudaba** yo todo, porque, desde que se operó de la cadera, cuando se operó de la cadera estaba como dos años en cama, y **yo lo atendía** a su, su gente, de-pués de ahí.* (4GT: 28)

In contrast, the children of migrants have more complex clitic systems, which seem to be a combination of first-generation migrants' partial system and the *limeños'* full system in which there are clear distinctions between case, number and gender. Some speakers, such as 16LS or 8FT,

Table 6.9   Archmorpheme *lo*

Speaker	No. of cases of lo for plural	%	No. of cases of lo(s) for feminine	%
Migrants				
3AG	1/3	33	6/7	86
4GT	2/2	100	5/5	100
9FA	3/6	50	5/5	100
10JG	6/7	86	4/6	67
11BI	5/8	62	5/6	83
12BM	1/2	50	6/12	50
Total	18/28	64	31/41	76
Children of migrants				
8FT	9/17	53	0/3	0
13CC	1/4	25	3/14	21
14EF	3/4	75	2/4	50
15JF	0/0	–	5/24	21
16LS	3/3	100	1/8	12
Total	16/28	57	11/53	21
Limeños				
17MC	2/9	22	0/26	0
18JN	1/3	33	0/8	0
19JE	1/2	50	1/6	17
20JT	0/4	0	0/23	0
Total	4/18	22	1/63	2

have systems that approximate that of *limeños*. It should be noted that both of these speakers have achieved a higher level of educational attainment than the others in their group. The following are examples from speaker 16LS who has the highest incidence of *leísmo* among second-generation speakers:

(9)   *desde acá estoy ya estoy un año y ya* **las veo pues a mis amigas**. (16LS: 8)

(10)   *siempre constantemente* **voy a verlas a mis primas**.[8] (16LS: 14)

Other children of migrants seem to vacillate between the first-generation migrants' partial system and the *limeños'* full clitic system, as in examples (11) and (12) from speaker 13CC below:

(11)   *mi suegro también ... se buscó otra y se fue a vivir con otra. Mi suegra se murió y ahí mismo se casó él con otra. [...] Entonces ya* **la casa lo dejó**.

Entonces, como no estaba tan construida, así era de ... medio construir, entonces lo repartió pa' sus cinco hijos. (13CC: 10)

(12) *mi padrastro dijo que mejor mi mamá se fuera a vivir, esto en Viñedo, por Surco; él* **se la llevó ahí** *... y* **la casa de mi mamá que está en Villa María, la dejó** *...*(13CC: 3)

Whether this hybrid system will be passed on to future generations or whether future generations adopt the system used by *limeños* remains to be seen.

Conclusions

Our results demonstrate that the outcome of dialect contact in Lima is different for the phonological variables examined than for clitics. Andean migrants begin with a variable phonological system, which permits either laterals vs non-laterals and assibilated vs non-assibilated variants as alternative forms. However, migrant children who are purportedly sensitive to *limeño* negative evaluation do not maintain the variable pattern used by their elders. They select only the non-lateral and non-assibilated variants, both of which correspond to the *limeño* patterns.

Something different happens with the elision and aspiration of /s/, because this feature forms part of the system of stable variation present in *limeño* Spanish. In this system, aspiration, especially in pre-consonant position in the middle of the word, has spread to all social classes, while elision, particularly in final position, only occurs in the lower sectors of society. Neither aspiration nor elision have been recognized as characteristic of Andean Spanish. However, the Andean migrants in this study have at least partially learned this variation from communicative relationships with other social sectors, and they adopt it at an even higher rate, even though it is contrary to their original articulatory patterns. Previous studies (Caravedo, 1990) have indicated that the proportion of elision to aspiration is only 25 per cent among upper middle-class speakers, compared to 65 per cent among lower-class *limeños*. Because Andean migrants and their adult children tend to interact more frequently with lower-class *limeños*, it is likely that elision is more salient to them than aspiration and for this reason is the variant that they adopt with highest frequency in their own speech.

The three phonological features analysed share a common characteristic. That is, they entail transformation and change in a single direction: from Andean patterns toward *limeño* patterns, a direction compatible with a tendency towards standardized or prestigious forms in line with the processes of globalization. Andeans tend to abandon the features of their native varieties, even though they maintain strong family ties, and end up acquiring forms that are more commonly used by the *limeños* with whom they have the most frequent contact. Despite this fact, we can, if we so wish, assert that *limeño* Spanish will remain unaltered in the process of social coexistence, but we believe that changes are not likely to occur when features are highly stigmatized. Although the *limeños* who have contact with Andean migrants did not indicate a tendency to adopt any of the features studied that were perceived as typically Andean, it is possible that characteristic Andean variants that are below the level of consciousness may be adopted in more subtle ways.[9] We will explore this hypothesis in future studies that focus on syntax and pragmatics, rather than the phonological level.

Our analysis of the clitic system demonstrated that unlike other phenomena such as lateral palatals or assibilated /r/, *leísmo* appears to be a variable that is not overtly stigmatized, and, as such, is passed on to many second-generation migrants. The native *limeños* in the study do not use *leísmo* to the same degree as migrants and their children. However, the fact that *leísmo* occurs in *limeño* Spanish in some formal styles with certain verbs, such as *considerar, denominar* (frequently combined with impersonal *se*, as in *se le considera, se le denomina*) and *invitar, saludar* (in written pseudo formal styles as in invitations), may contribute to the expansion of Andean *leísmo* among *limeños*, perhaps in certain contexts and with certain types of referents.

With regard to the archmorpheme *lo*, there is maintenance by first-generation migrants who tend to neutralize gender and number differences in the direct-object pronoun. Their clitic system can be defined as a partial system based on case alone, while the *limeños* have a full clitic system, which includes both case and gender. The children of migrants tend to have hybrid clitic systems, which include elements of both. Whether the hybrid system will be transmitted to future generations of migrants remains to be seen; it does not seem likely that this system will be adopted by *limeños*.

The results of this study need to be interpreted with some caution given the small number of speakers and the overlap of some of the variables (for example, first-generation migrants tend to have only primary education). Future studies will incorporate a larger number of speakers in each of these neighbourhoods and will attempt to identify the social networks of each of the speakers to explain the wide variance in the use of these variables.

Without a doubt, the creation of new varieties in Lima will come about as a result of the linguistic system acquired by migrant children as an innovative group. They are confronted with at least two different patterns: that of their parents, which is their native Andean variety, and that of the *limeño* lower classes. This confrontation results in a hybrid form in which only original variants that are not stigmatized and are not susceptible to negative perception are maintained, while stigmatized traits are eliminated. At the same time, features of *limeño* Spanish, such as the elision of /s/ are adopted, although they may not be directly perceived. It is clear, although it will require subsequent investigation with a larger corpus, that the descendants of migrants, who are new and legitimate members of metropolitan Lima, are the true protagonists of change and the creators of a new form of Spanish. Thus, in Lima while the forces of globalization combined with negative attitudes toward indigenous languages are bringing about an end to Quechua within the city, at the same time the contact of Andean and coastal Spanish may result in the creation of a new variety of Spanish – different from the traditional coastal model – by the descendants of Andean migrants.

Notes

1   Gruzinski (1999) has studied *mestizo* features in relation to migration in different societies from a social anthropological perspective.

2   The number of interviews is similar to those used in urban sociolinguistic research in large cities, as noted by Labov (2001: 39), who has utilized a corpus of 81 informants for New York and 118 informants for Philadelphia. The author mentions corpus dimensions in the study of different cities, such as Panama (100), Montreal (120), Paris (109), São Paolo (40), Tokyo (88), and so on.

3   Godenzzi (1991) noted some variation in the use of /ʎ/ vs /y/ among Puneños (inhabitants of the high Ander) with the highest socioeconomic status and among highly educated middle class speakers in the city. The migrants in our study are not from these social strata. He notes that Puneños with little education and who are of middle to low socioeconomic status are not *yeístas*.

4   The sections on *leísmo* and the archmorpheme *lo* are revised versions that appeared originally in Klee and Caravedo (2005).

5   Due to large differences between individual speakers, a Varbrul analysis that included extralinguistic variables could not be conducted.

6   *Le* is a reduplicated direct object pronoun which refers to *el estudio*.

7   *Lo* in this context is a reduplicated direct object pronoun which refers first to *la calle* and then to *la piedra*.

8 This speaker also exhibits one case of fluctuation: LS: ... *las chicas no, no las veo, no las veo a las chicas.* [N: *La señora, la ingeniera?*] LS: *No tampoco no, no no da, no no lo veo.* Additionally, both speakers use direct object doubling.

9 In fact our project includes a perception test that allows us to identify if speakers of different groups are able to perceive the analysed features (Klee and Caravedo, 2000).

7
Spanish as L2 on the Dominican/Haitian Border and Universal Processes of Acquisition*

Luis A. Ortiz López

Introduction

Recently, the Spanish language has come to figure prominently, in the debate over economic globalization (Del Valle and Gabriel-Stheeman, 2004). This has led to a reconceptualization and reevaluation of the traditional symbolic value of Spanish and other languages as an ethno-cultural instrument serving to 'bond' and 'unify' peoples in addition to their linguistic value as means of communication. In today's globalized world, Spanish is a marketable product which generates economic capital. This new economic dimension is becoming increasingly important in contexts where Spanish is in contact with other languages, as, for example, in the USA (Zentella, 2000). This instrumental value of Spanish has contributed to the development of a variety of degrees of bilingualism in different speech communities, not only amongst Spanish speakers, but also amongst other groups, for example, amongst students in universities in the USA and elsewhere in the world. The majority of studies which examine the role of Spanish in a global era have thus far focused on the role of Spanish in contact with English in the USA, although more recently there have been a number of works about the political and commercial pressures brought to bear by external agents on global speakers or 'users' of Spanish (Del Valle and Gabriel Stheeman, 2002, 2004; Del Valle, 2004; Lacorte, forthcoming). The majority of these works either analyse the possible loss of Spanish in Latino communities in the USA on account of historical, political and socioeconomic factors; or examine attitudes towards Spanish not only on the part the English-speaking majority but also by the groups which make up the 'Hispanic community'; or, finally, cast a critical eye over the selection and promotion of given standard varieties to be taught in a particular academic context (Ortiz López and Lacorte, 2005c).

Although the border region between the Dominican Republic and Haiti is at the margins of the global economy, it is not exempt from these sociolinguistic trends. Dominicans, in their invariably coerced encounters with the *other*, have hammered out a variety of types of contact which imply that it is almost always the Haitian who adopts the language and the culture of their host country, for, like all foreigners, they are impelled to do so for their own economic survival. Here Spanish, in its various forms, becomes the instrumental language as can be seen from the extracts below taken from interviews with two Haitians, interviews which reflect what typically occurs in contexts of migration:

I1 *Poque si uno ehtá aquí, obligatolamente hay que sabel el dominicano poque si no cómo tú, cómo tú puedeh buhcal tu comida y si una pelsona te necesita un favol de ti, tú no entiende nada, como quiera obligatolamente hay que hablal.* (H/M/25)
(Because if you're here, you must speak Dominican Spanish because, if not, how are you going to go out and get food and if someone needs you to do them a favour, you don't understand a thing, you just must speak it.)

I2 *Con, cuando una, una persona dominicano quiere comprá yo hablal dominicano con él. Y por eso sabe más. Hablo más oíhte ... Sí. Viene mucha gente que vende aquí y sabe hablá, no sabe hablal bien, pero un chin.* (H/M/19)
(When a Dominican wants to buy something I speak Dominican Spanish with him. And then he finds out more. I speak more, you see, I do. A lot of people come and sell here and can speak Spanish, they can't speak it well, but a bit.)

Linguistic studies of contact between Spanish and other languages in the Americas were relatively rare until the end of the twentieth century. Those works that have appeared have focused mainly on contacts between Spanish and indigenous languages (Zimmermann, 1995; Silva Corvalán, 1995; Klee, 1996; Sánchez, 2003) as well as between Spanish and English, chiefly amongst Hispanics in the United States

(Silva Corvalán, 1994; Torres Caucoullos, 2000), and have neglected other sites of language contact, notably the Caribbean (see also, for example, Díaz *et al.*, 2002). In the Caribbean, a number of ethno-linguistic groups have lived together for extended periods of time and, although there have not been prolonged periods of stable bilingualism, as has been the case in other parts of the Americas, linguistic traces of mutual influence have been left in the languages which have been in contact. In the Caribbean many languages coexist – varieties of Spanish, English and French are spoken many alongside a number of Creole languages which are a product of contact from the sixteenth century onwards between the lexifying languages (Spanish, Portuguese, French, English and Dutch), and African languages spoken by slaves. This multilingualism, as well as the extra-linguistic factors which have contributed to its existence, are the subject of important current research, including that which focuses on the role played by metropolitan languages in the global economy (see Freeland, this volume). The origins and development of the different varieties of creole in contexts such as these, is just one factor which has helped to fuel the debate over the genesis of the varieties of Spanish spoken in the region.[1] Nonetheless, apart from instances of Afro-hispanic linguistic contact in the Caribbean which have been the focus of research since the end of the twentieth century, there has been little research into the significant and growing contact between Hispanic groups and non-Hispanic groups in the region. For example, Haitians are to be found in the south-east of Cuba and along the border between Haiti and Santo Domingo, *cocolos* (English-speaking immigrants) in the Dominican Republic[2] and in Cuba, Dominicans and immigrants from the Lesser Antilles in Puerto Rico (Río Piedras and Santurce). Within this context it is particularly surprising, indeed quite astounding, how little attention has been devoted to ethno-sociolinguistic contact between Haitians and Dominicans on the border dividing Hispaniola into the Dominican Republic and the republic of Haiti. To date, there have been no synchronic studies of the ethno-linguistic situation of this particular speech community, known as *La Raya* and made up of the border provinces of *Pedernales, Independencia, Elías Piña* and *Dajabón* (see Map 7.1 in the Methodology section), and extending to other areas of the country, including the historic Dominican *bateyes* (sugar plantations), inhabited by Haitians and their descendants.

Given the absence of studies in this area, I have chosen to carry out an ethno-linguistic study[3] – from the theoretical perspective of languages in contact (Thomason and Kaufman, 1988; Silva Corvalán, 1994; Lass,

1997; De Graff, 1999, in press; Winford, 2003) – into the speech community which resides along the border between Haiti and the Dominican Republic focusing particularly on the variety of Spanish spoken by Haitians and their descendants in the Dominican Republic. In a previous work on the Spanish spoken as L2 by Haitians, both in the East of Cuba (Ortiz López, 1999a, 1999b, 2001b), and on the border between Haiti and the Dominican Republic (Ortiz López, 2001a, 2004, 2005a), I have carried out a qualitative study of certain aspects of the noun and verb systems of both speech communities.

   On this occasion, I shall carry out a quantitative study of the use of the infinitive (see 1–4 below), from the perspective of languages in contact, paying special attention to the acquisition of L2, in a sample of Haitians and people of Haitian ancestry in the Dominican Republic.

1   *Cómo tú **preguntar** (preguntas) cualquier cosa que tú te venga a la mente.*
    (M19, Haitian, Pedernales)
2   *Aquí no ha vida, no vale uno **bucal** (que busque uno) trabajo.* (M36, Haitian, Pedernales)
3   *Y para (por) un vehículo así, ¿(en) cuánto uno **alquilar**? (lo alquila).* (F 15, Arayana, bilingual, Pedernales)
4   ***Sembrar** (siembro) lah habichuera y trabajo en sembra (de) guineo y café. Y **sube** (subo) aquí cada rato; no **sube** (subo) todo, todo el tiempo.* (M30, Dominican-Haitian, Pedernales)

My principal aim is to study the role of certain linguistic variables including the semantic class of the verb, the presence or absence of subject pronouns, adverbial reference, as well as extra-linguistic factors such as ethnic group, in the use of these elements of the verbal system. In particular, I address the question of why these and other phenomena, such as the invariant third person (see 5–8 below) appear to behave like second language acquisition universals in situations of language contact.

5   *Yo **habla** en dominicano con ella, alguna vez yo **habla** en haitiano. Si lo do muchachi chiquit etai **cría** (se crían) con dominicano no **va hablá** en haitiano.* (M60, Haitian, Pedernales)
6   ***Tiene** (tengo) trentisei año.* (M36, Haitian, Pedernales)
7   *Yo no **sabe** poque se me quemó el nacimiento (el acta de nacimiento). No tengo otro poque ya cuando que yo, ya que yo lo **hace** señorito yo me **coge** pa Santo Domingo con mi esposo y cuando **viene** me jaya mi mamá y mi papá se mueren.* (F55, Haitian, Pedernales)
8   *Yo casi no **come** carne.* (F55, Haitian, Pedernales)

These phenomena have been identified, and reproduced in literary texts, in *bozal*, the Spanish spoken by Africans and their descendants in the Greater Antilles (Lipski, 1999, 2005; Ortiz López, 1998), as well as for speakers of Spanish as a second language (Ortiz López, 1999a, 2001a, 2001b). In this study, I provide data from yet another contact speech community in support of the thesis that speakers pass through a number of stages before they acquire a given target language and that, during these stages, they follow universal processes of language acquisition which override other variables, such as, for example, the linguistic typology of the language in question, the age of speakers when they first come into contact with L2, ethnic group and degree of bilingualism. I also attempt to identify those semantic, syntactic and pragmatic factors which may cause certain linguistic structures – for example, the infinitive, the third person and the gerund – to be utilized universally in the course of second-language acquisition, with particular reference to Spanish as L2. Before going on to discuss the results, I wish to position this study within the field of second-language acquisition.

Theoretical framework

This work situates itself within the study of languages in contact, and in particular the study of the processes of L2 acquisition in contexts where there are differing degrees of bilingualism, specifically on the DH border. Situations of sociolinguistic contact are very favourable to language change, whether through lexical borrowing, linguistic transfer between one system and another or through the generation of linguistic 'innovation' brought about by the proximity of the two systems. This type of linguistic change has been the subject of theoretical investigation into whether it is the result of universal linguistic processes, influence from L1, influence from L2, or some combination of these factors.

Universalist positions are supported by the general trends in linguistic theory over past 50 years (Chomsky, 1986, 1995). The last five decades have been of considerable importance for linguistic theory, as they have ushered in a new paradigm in the ways of conceptualizing and researching language. The (E)xternal approach, based on the theories first of the neo-grammarians, and later of the structuralists, who explained language variation and change from an extra-linguistic perspective, that is by factors external to the language itself, has been superseded by an (I)nternal approach to language. This new model, based on largely on the work of Noam Chomsky, sees languages as an 'element of the mind of the person who knows the language, acquired by the learner, and used by the speaker-hearer' (Chomsky, 1986: 22). This approach sees human language as a part of the innate human capacity to process language which transcends all elements of social context.

Starting from this view of language, one of the main aims of linguistics at the end of the twentieth century and the beginning of the current one has been to create a grammatical model of the linguistic competence or internalized knowledge of the language (L1) held by a speaker/listener, as well as the principles which govern this competence. Chomsky (1986: 3) argues that language and how it is used is dependent on intra-linguistic factors which are part of the human mind and which follow universal processes:

> those aspects of form and meaning that are determined by language faculty, which is understood to be a particular component of the human mind. The nature of this faculty is the subject matter of a general theory of linguistic structure that aims to discover the framework of principles and elements common to attainable human languages; this theory is now often called *universal grammar* (UG).

Within this view of language, UG 'may be regarded as a characterization of genetically-determined language faculty' (1986: 3). Consequently, this theory seeks to establish a model of how grammars are constituted, or, more precisely, of the language universals which make up these grammars which then capture the regularities in these grammars, which reflect our linguistic competence, rather than describing languages or collating superficial details about these languages (Chomsky, 1986, 1995). This approach, which transcends both linguistic and socio-cultural specificities of natural languages, has played an increasingly important role in the study of bilingualism, of second-language acquisition, and of Creole genesis.

Within this theoretical framework, language acquisition involves the setting of binary parameters to conform to those settings that typify the target language (Chomsky, 1986). It is assumed that the universal principles that apply uniformly to all languages are sufficiently restrictive for Primary Linguistic Data (PLD) to be all that is required to set the values of the parameters for a particular language (Chomsky, 1995: 87). In acquisition studies there has been considerable debate over the role of the innate principles of UG on the one hand, and that of external stimulus on the other. In the case of adults learning a second language, the debate revolves around whether they use the Principles and Parameters (P&P) of Universal Grammar (UG) to the same extent as children acquiring their first language (Chomsky, 1986), or, alternatively, whether L1 and L2 learning involves two distinct acquisition processes.

In the case of L2 speakers, a key issue has been to determine which of two basic roles UG plays in the acquisition of functional and formal categories: (1) 'direct access' to UG, that is, the transfer of L1 parameters, including functional categories, which are set into the interlanguage grammar (L2) (Schwartz and Sprouse, 1996; Eubank, 1993/1994; Vainikka and Young-Scholten, 1996), and (2) indirect 'partial access' to UG, where L1 plays an intermediary role in the setting of L2 parameters (Beck, 1998; Hawkins and Chan, 1997). Those who defend the view of direct access to UG argue that speakers of L2 are aware of the abstract properties of language including functional categories and their syntactic results, but are unaware of how these properties are marked morphologically (Gavruseva and Lardiere, 1996). On the other hand, those who defend partial access use *interlanguage* data from adults to show, for example, that the lack of functional and formal features indicate, incomplete access to UG (Beck, 1998) implying that direct access to UG is not available after a critical age (Hawkins and Chan, 1997). In this indirect access model, L2 speakers can use the morphology of the target language with the specifications of their L1. As we can see, both these L2 acquisition hypotheses predict different morphosyntactic and semantic strategies adopted by speakers in the task of L2 learning. Leaving aside disagreements such as these, the debate over similarities and differences in the acquisition of L1 and L2 has had implications for language contact theory in general, regardless of the particular outcome of language contact: *interlanguages* (Selinker, 1972 [1992]), *pidginization, creolization, partial restructuring* (Holm, 1988, 1989, 2004; Sebba, 1997), *bilingualism, multilingualism* and *linguistic variation*.

Some twenty years ago, Bickerton (1984: 173–88) noted that the 'simplicity' of creoles resided in the universal processes of language acquisition inherent in learning a L2, processes which are replicated in *interlanguages, pidgins, creoles* and other L2 contexts as universal acquisition properties. More recently, *creolization* itself has been argued to be an acquisition phenomenon, where the normal mechanisms of language acquisition are reproduced in the processes of pidginization and creolization (DeGraff, 1996, 1999, 2005; Lumsden, 1999). By extension, *pidginization* and *creolization* are increasingly being considered as acquisitional models for other types of language contact located beyond the colonial era context of plantation slavery. Take, for example, the ethnic exchange between immigrants that occurs in classrooms and during the natural process of learning an L2 (Blackshire-Belay, 1990). It appears that there is a close relationship between the natural learning of varieties of L2 and the processes of *pidginization* and *creolization*, for in both processes there is evidence of universal processes such as 'bootstrapping' (Bates and Goodman, 2000).

Levin and Rappaport-Hovay (1995) have pointed to a causal link between certain semantic functions and certain syntactic expressions, which supports the idea that the semantic class of the verb determines the syntactic structure of the utterance. When the morphosyntactic properties of the verb such as TMA inflection are not acquired, then it is the role of the semantic class of the verb to mark those missing or absent syntactic features. If it is true that the acquisition of the grammar of a language, whether it be L1 or L2, depends on the development of the lexicon, then it follows that there are common processes and universal trends in language acquisition that come into play in all situations of language contact.

During the stages of *pidginization* and/or *creolization* involving Ibero-Romance languages and other European language, TMA inflection processes are eroded and even lost, as can be seen in the case of *bozal* (Lipski, 1998, 2005; Ortiz López, 1998, 2005b). These processes are not dissimilar to the strategies employed by adults when acquiring a second language. DeGraff (1999, 2005) notes that inflectional reduction appears even more dramatic in the variants of L2 that develop in situations where language contact is not friendly, that is where it occurs under pressure and allows limited access to the native language. A case in point is the use of the infinitive by informants who have Spanish as L2, specifically the varieties of Spanish used by Haitians and their descendants living on Dominican side of the border between Haiti and the Dominican Republic.

Methodology

Area of the study

The borderland which is the focus of this study lies between two sovereign nations, Haiti and the Dominican Republic. These two nations are divided essentially by language and culture due, in the view of Castor (1987: 15), to historical events which shaped the internal structure of each nation, determining the nature of settlements, development, and the social, economic, cultural and ideological makeup of each. These two nations have been in constant geographic, political, ethnic and linguistic conflict for more than four centuries. They are two nations which have experienced continuous migratory flows. The emigration of

Haitians to the Dominican Republic which originated with the need for Haitian labourers on the sugar plantations, known as *bateyes*, has continued unabated up until the present day with Haitians now working in the construction industry, agriculture and as domestic help. The greatest concentration of Haitians in the DR is in the borderlands, a region otherwise referred to as La Raya. La Raya is home to various emigrant communities including: (1) the *congó*, recently arrived Haitians who do not speak Spanish; (2) the *viejo*, migrants who have lived in the Dominican Republic for a considerable length of time, but who have retained strong links with Haiti and who, consequently, have resisted cultural and linguistic assimilation; (3) the DH, a Dominican of Haitian descent, who was born in the Dominican Republic and who is generally bilingual to a certain extent, and (4) the *rayano* or *arayano*, who is of mixed Haitian and Dominican ancestry, was born in the Dominican Republic and is almost always bilingual. The further away from the border you go, the more hostile and conflictual are the relationships between Haitians and Dominicans. Alongside the strong rejection of Haitians on racial grounds, language proves an additional barrier; with Haitians being compelled to acquire Spanish in a context marked by linguistic stress and pressure. In spite of the fact that on the border these groups live together with a degree of harmony (albeit with inequalities) which involves various degrees of language contact, away from the border there is increasing discrimination and rejection of ethno-linguistic contact. Haitians and Dominicans of Haitian descent are integrated to differing degrees into Dominican society and culture and this has implications relating to language use, language loyalty, linguistic attitudes and beliefs, as well as to the maintenance or loss of the heritage language.

In the border area two languages coexist which are typologically different: on the Eastern side of the border there is Dominican Spanish and on the Western side, Haitian Creole. The area is characterized by socioethnic contact. Language has not been exempt from this cultural encounter, and since the last century there has been talk, but no direct evidence, of the biculturalism and bilingualism of the *arayanos* (border inhabitants). There are many social variables which could be responsible for this cultural and linguistic mix: geographical location, immigration, the population of Haitian origin who reside legally in the Dominican Republic, family ties, commerce, agricultural labour, church attendance, and so on. It was the lack of ethno-sociolinguistic studies of contact in the region which led me to carry out fieldwork in La Raya over the summers of 1998 and 1999.

Sample and methodology

This study forms part of a fieldwork project which I am carrying out in the four provinces along the border between Haiti and the Dominican Republic: *Pedernales, Elías Piña, Independencia* and *Dajabón* (Map 7.1).

In this study, I used both participant observation and recordings of conversational speech from a random selection of informants to examine the linguistic behaviour of the members of the border speech community. The data presented in this work were collected from four groups of informants (Table 7.1), subdivided by ethnicity, whom I recorded during

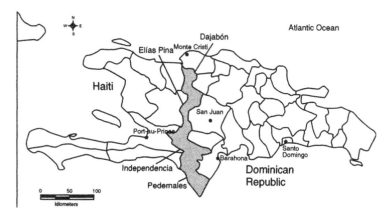

Map 7.1 The border area between the Dominican Republic and Haiti

Table 7.1 Informants, according to social variables

Ethnic group	Gender	Age	Language proficiency
1 Haitians (H)	1 F 5M	(3) 15–25 (3) + 30	Bilingual: Creole L1 *interlanguage* Spanish
4 Dominican- Haitians (DH)	(4) M	(1) –15 (2) 15–25 (1) +30	Bilingual: Creole L1 Spanish L2
2 *Arayanos* (AY)	(2) M	(2) 30–50	Bilingual Creole L1 Spanish L1 or L2
4 Dominicans (D)	(2) F (2) M	(1) 15–25 (3) +30	Monolingual Spanish L1

sessions of spontaneous and semi-spontaneous conversation that lasted between 20 and 40 minutes.

The Hs have lived for between five and thirty years on the border in La Raya and their dominant language is Haitian Creole; they speak Spanish with varying degrees of proficiency, but mainly speak it as an interlanguage. The DHs are Haitians who were born in the Dominican Republic; they are strongly attached to Haitian culture, but have had significant exposure to Dominican culture and are bilingual to varying degrees, although Creole is the language of the home. The AYs are ethnically mixed and have experienced strong contact with both Spanish and Haitian Creole since childhood, through a Dominican father and a Haitian mother. They form the group of most balanced bilinguals in La Raya. In addition to this sample, I included four monolingual Ds who speak a Dominican variety Spanish and who live on the border, as a control group.

Interviews were carried out in a variety of contexts: in homes, on the road, on farmsteads, in grocery stores, and so on. The main topics of conversation revolved around the history of the border and what things are like now, the relationships between Dominicans and Haitians, lifestyles, working practices and how both nations get on with each other. These topics proved extremely interesting and stimulating and the informants took every opportunity to describe and denounce the subhuman conditions that Haitians and their descendants are forced to endure. After transcribing the 16 interviews,[4] I identified the verb forms (both standard and non-standard), codified the data according to the linguistic and extra-linguistic variables selected and ran the findings through an SPSS program to identify correlations between variables.

The verbal system of *creoles*

Haitian Creole (HC) follows the verbal patterns of languages from the West African substrate (not Bantu). For example the TMA system of HC is closer to Fongbe (9–10), a substrate language, than it is to French, the lexifier (Lefebvre, 1998: 111) which follows the morphosyntactic patterns of Romance languages, as in 11 below.

9   Mari kò tùn Jan (Lefebvre 1998: 117) Fongbe
    Mary ANT know Jan.
    (Mary knew John or Mary had known John.)
10 Mì nì ɖù. (Lefebvre 1998: 119) Fongbe
    You (pl) SUB eat.
    (You must eat.)
11 Jean va manger. (Lefebvre 1998: 113) French
    (John will eat (in the near future).)

In HC (12), as in other varieties of Ibero-romance creole, for instance *palenquero* (13–14) and *papiamento* (15), the SV is marked by a preverbal particle + an invariant verb in the infinitive:

12 Dye pou proteje u (Lefebvre 1998: 120) Haitian Creole
   God SUB protect you
13 i *tá kumé* (I am eating) (Dieck 2000: 89) (5) *palenquero*
   bo *tá miná-nda* ele nu?
   (Are (you) not seeing her?)
14 Suto á ten kanatulé (Dieck 2000: 21) *palenquero*
   (We are hungry.)
15 E ta papya (*papiamento*)
   He IMP to speak
   (He speaks.)
   (He is speaking.)

In all these examples, the preverbal particles contain the TMA information.

The system of Haitian Creole (HC)

As Lefebvre (1998: 112) shows, in HC the mark of past time (past or present perfect) is *te*, that of unreality (definite or indefinite future or the subjunctive) is *ap, a-va, pou* (21, 22, 24 and 25 respectively), that of the imperfect or uncompleted action (habitual or imperfective) *ap* (19 and 20):

te marks past time/perfectivity (+punctual/+perfective o aorist/+/− dynamic(16–18):

16 Boukinèt te renmen Bouki (DeGraff, 2005: 8).
   Boukinèt loved (ANT) Bouki.
   (Boukinèt loved Bouki.)
17 Mari te wè volè a   (Lefebvre, 1998: 116).
   Mary ANT catch -sight- of thief DET
   (Mary caught sight of the thief or Mary had caught sight of the thief)
18 Mari te kònnèn Jan. (Lefebvre 1998: 116).
   Mary ANT kònnèn John.
   (Mary knew John or Mary had known John.)

ap marks imperfectivity (+habitual/ +/-simultaneous/+dynamism) (19–22):

19 Mari ap manje krab la (Lefebvre 1998: 120).
   (Mary is eating the crab.)

20 Mari ap joure toutan (Lefebvre 1998: 120).
    Mary IMP swear all-the time.
    (Mary swears all the time.)
21 Jan ap konnen Mari (Lefebvre 1998: 120).
    John IMP know Mary
    (John knows Mary.)
22 Boukinèt ap renmen Bouki (DeGraff, 2005: 8).
    Boukinèt FUT Bouki
    (Boukinèt will love Bouki.)
23 #Jan ap wè vole a. (Lefebvre 1998: 120).
    John IMP catch-sight-of thief DET.
    (Lit.: John is catching sight of the thief.)

pou marks unreality (+neutral/+/−dynamism (23–24), as in the case
of desire, obligation or the *subjunctive*:

24 Mari pou prepare pat (Lefebvre 1998: 118).
    Mari dwe prepare pat la (bilingual Haitian)
    Mary SUB prepare dough.
    (Mary should prepare dough.)
25 Tut sòlda pou vini laplas kunyè a   (Lefebvre 1998: 118).
    All soldier SUB come square now DET.
    (All soldiers must come to the square now.)

These preverbal particles may modify tense or aspect depending on
the verb they accompany. That is, the semantic class of the verb, along
with the preverbal particle (*te/pou/ap*) will determine the TMA of HC.
According to Damoiseau (1988), HC has three types of verb: *dynamic* or
of development, such as *manje* (to eat) and *plante* (to sow); *resultative*, the
outcome of a given process, such as *we* (to catch sight of), *jwenn* (to find)
and *stative*, such as *konnen* (to know), *bezwen* (to need). Thus, the particle *te* + *dynamic* is interpreted as a perfect tense, while *te* + *resultative* is
ambiguous, as it could mark either the preterite or the perfect, depending on context (Lefebvre, 1998: 116). *Ap* + *dynamic* can be interpreted
as + *continuous*/+ *progressive*, as in 19, but *ap* + *resultative* must be interpreted as +*unreality* as in 21–22 and not as +*continuous*/+*progressive* as
in 23. *Ap* can also mean +*habitual*, but it requires the adverb *tutan* (all
the time) as in 20. We can conclude that *ap* marks +*imperfect*, with the
value of +*simultaneous*, that is +*habitual*/+*continuous*, and also+*neutral*/+*unreality*, for example, +*future*/+*conditional*.

In short, HC and Spanish differ in the formal categories they use to
mark TMA: HC uses auxiliary verbs, while Spanish primarily uses

affixation alongside auxiliaries. Nonetheless, both systems employ the properties of tense (± *punctual, simultaneous, succession*), of aspect (± *perfective/aorist, imperfective, neutral* or *unreality*) and mood (± *stative, dynamic, telic, atelic,* etc.).

Analysis

In situations of language contact, it is the verbal system which experiences the greatest amount of change throughout the process of acquisition of a contact language. There is evidence for this in the different stages of acquisition. According to Thomason and Kaufman (1988: 157), a process of language accommodation appears to take place in learners who attempt to learn the dominant language by 'accommodating' the L2 to their own language. Various factors come into play in this accommodation process, including access both to L1 and to L2, the typological distance between L1 and L2, the motivation to learn the language and the natural tendency towards unmarked universal forms, especially where differences between the two languages most pronounced.

As we shall see, the Spanish verbal system of speakers dwelling on the border displays different degrees of L2 acquisition. In principle, there are differences between the two groups of speakers who are most distant from each other: Hs vs DHs, AYs and Ds. The first group of Hs have learnt a variety of Spanish which has been affected by many of the processes we mentioned previously. There is, on the one hand, the use of an *interlanguage* among recent arrivals and among those who, despite having lived in the Dominican Republic for a considerable period of time, have remained on the margins of the dominant culture for a variety of reasons including the ethnic discrimination they have been subjected to, the age they were when they emigrated (the 'critical period' according to Krashen, 1973–74), isolation in rural areas which frequently have been abandoned by the Dominicans themselves, linguistic loyalty towards HC as the mother tongue, etc. And there also is the learning of Spanish as L2, basically amongst those who have overcome barriers of this nature and created a space for themselves amongst the Dominican community. Conversely, amongst Dominicans of Haitian descent there is evidence of the acquisition of the grammar of Dominican Spanish with few traces of creole; although we do find some informants who, having remained, along with other older members of their family, isolated in marginal, rural, agricultural communities, acquire, along with creole, an *interlanguage* or *approximate system* of Spanish. Many of these inhabitants display a range of mastery of the verbal system going from the extended use of infinitives and progressives to the generalization of the third-person singular as an unmarked form and the use of the local variety of Dominican Spanish. The 16 interviews provided a corpus of 2,310 verb forms, of which 1,906 corresponded to the group of Haitians and their descendants (Table 7.2). Of these, 1,648 (86%) were grammatical and 258 (14%) non-standard. These data place the informants on the continuum of acquisition of the Spanish verbal paradigm, where Hs, as was expected, make up the group which is farthest from the Dominican Spanish system with 17 per cent of non-standard forms, followed by the DHs with 12 per cent and the AYs with 11 per cent. These figures are significantly different from those for the sample of Dominicans with Spanish as L1, who account for barely 3 per cent of non-standard forms.

For the purposes of this study, I will focus on the non-standard forms of the verb. Of these, 217 (84%) relate to three specific phenomena: non-standard use of the infinitive, the third person of the verb and the gerund (Table 7.3). The patterns of use of these three features enabled me to investigate the processes of language acquisition, specifically in relation to the verbal system, within the La Raya speech community.

Infinitives

As can be seen in Table 7.3, it is the Hs who use these forms with greatest frequency (49%). Furthermore, this group shows a particularly frequent use of the infinitive (84%), as shown below in examples 26–29.[6]

26 *Ese muchacho yo llevai (llevar a) Haití.* (H, M36, Pedernales)
27 *Casi siempre yo llevarlo para allá porque yo, ese es un pobrecito.* (H, M36, Pedernales)

Table 7.2 Corpus of verbs, according to ethnicity

Ethnic group	Verbs		
	standard (%)	non-standard (%)	Total (%)
Haitians	651 (83%)	130 (17%)	781 (100%)
%	36%	50%	41%
Dominican-Haitians	312 (88%)	43 (12%)	355 (100%)
%	19%	17%	19%
Arayanos	685 (89%)	85 (11%)	770 (100%)
%	42%	33%	40%
Total	1648 (86%)	258 (14%)	1906 (100%)
Dominicans	392 (97%)	12 (3%)	404 (100%)

Table 7.3 Use of the infinitive, the third person of the verb and the gerund, according to ethnic group

Ethnic group	Infinitive %	3rd person of the verb %	Gerund %	Total %
Haitians	21 (20%)	59 (55%)	27 (25%)	107 (100%)
%	84%	36%	71%	49%
Dominican-Haitians	3 (7%)	31 (76%)	6 (15%)	40 100%
%	12%	19%	16%	18%
Arayanos	1 (.01%)	67 (95%)	2 (.02%)	70 (100%)
%	4%	41%	5%	32%
Total	25 (12%)	157 (72%)	35 (17%)	217
%	100%	100%	100%	100%
Dominicans	–	7	3	10
%		4%	8%	4%

28 *Yo vivir para (en) la Frontera. El no vivir más lejos.* (H, F39, Pedernales)
29 *Si tú mandarla (mandas) a buscar un chin de agua, él no va a saber. Si tú mandarla buscar la comida, él no va a saber.* (H, F, 39 Pedernales)

The infinitive, in most Romance languages, has over time extended its verbal functions and has become the canonical form of the verb. For example, in Spanish, utterances such as those in 30–32, albeit common in the Caribbean, can also be found in the Canaries, and in Andalusian, Galician and other varieties of Spanish (Lipski, 1994):

30 *Para nosotros **llegar** a la fiesta, necesitamos suficiente tiempo.* (PR, L1)
31 Antes de ustedes viajar, tenemos que despedirnos. (PR, L1)
32 *Recibían muchos juguetes en Navidad para los nenes **divertirse**.* (PR, L1)

These infinitival structures which depart from standard Spanish, in addition to being of particular interest to those who study the Spanish of the Caribbean (Navarro Tomás, 1948; Henríquez Ureña, 1982 [1940]), have also been the subject of debate amongst generativists (Suñer, 1986; Morales, 1986; Pérez Leroux, 1999).

Nonetheless, the use of the infinitive by Hs is much more extreme than the use of infinitival structures with an overt subject in L1 we mentioned before; in the former a full verb is replaced by an infinitive principally in main clauses, while in the case of speakers of Spanish as L1, the infinitive replaces the subjunctive. As we can see in Table 7.4, the verbs which appear in the infinitive are mainly verbs of activity (88%) and all are atelic, verbs of development or less punctual action.[7] Here we can see that both the infinitive (88% of occurrences) and the gerund (90% of occurrences) co-occur with dynamic verbs or verbs of activity,

Table 7.4   Non-standard uses, according to verb type

Verb class	Infinitive	−Person*	Gerund	−TMA**	Other	Total
Stative	3 (3%)	77	4 (4%)	15	4 (4%)	103
1158	12%	(75%)	10%	(15%)	50%	100%
50.1%		49%		45%		40%
Dynamic	22 (14%)	79	34 (22%)	18	3 (2%)	155
1152	88%	(51%)	(90%)	(12%)	50%	100%
49.9%		51%		55%		60%

* Principally use of the 3rd person; ** Problems with tense, mood or aspect.

and that the use of the third person represents the greatest number of occurrences (77%).

In many cases, these structures characterize a preliminary stage in language acquisition where speakers display a marked reduction in the use of inflection; in others, they reflect forms which have become fossilized as a result of incomplete acquisition of Spanish as L2. The infinitive becomes the verbal marker which, while lacking *tense, mood, aspect, person* and *number*, retains enough meaning to enable communication to take place. Compared with the complex verbal morphology that typifies Spanish, Haitian Creole [8] uses a very different system of auxiliaries (*te, ap* and *pou*) instead of affixes to indicate TMA. Many of our informants used uninflected verbal forms which are largely sufficient for communication during the initial stages of acquisition, although some of these may fossilize and become part of a non-standard L2 grammatical system.

What is more, Haitian Creole has the syntactic structure *preposition + pronoun + infinitive*, as in 33, which is similar to utterance 30 for L1 speakers:

33   *Pou non rive nan fèt la nou bezwen you bon tan.*
    Para nosotros llegar a la fiesta, necesitamos suficiente tiempo.
    (In order to get to the party, we need sufficient time.)

Influence from the verbal system of Haitian Creole, which lacks inflections, morphemes (Lefebvre, 1998; DeGraff, 2005) (see examples 16–22) may be contributing to the fossilization of the acquisition of the infinitive in place of an inflected verb. Nonetheless, for some informants, (for example the DHs and the AYs, who have greater contact with the target language through a bilingual context within which they acquire both languages, although almost always with a degree of imbalance) the verb gradually incorporates the inflections of the language which is being acquired, albeit with traces of the L1 system, as is the case with the non-standard use of third person, which is the least marked form of the Spanish verbal paradigm (Table 7.3).

In the acquisition of both L1 and L2, there is a clear natural tendency to adopt universal, unmarked forms. In such instances the non-standard use of the infinitive reflects a universal of language acquisition in the speech of those who are learning Spanish principally, although not exclusively, as a second language. Furthermore, there is evidence in favour of a greater frequency of the infinitive (77%) over the subjunctive (7%) in subordinate clauses which allow either the infinitive or the subjunctive (23a and 23b), amongst L2 speakers of Caribbean Spanish (Morales, 1986; Rivera Alamo, 1989):

34a *Tenían toda clase de juegos para* **los muchachos divertirse.** (PR, Rivera Alamo 1989)
34b *Tenían toda clase de juegos para que* **se divirtieran** *los muchachos.*
35a *Lo hizo sin* **yo saberlo.** (PR, Rivera Alamo 1989)
35b *Lo hizo sin que yo lo* **supiera.**

The question which now arises is whether and how our informants compensate for the morphosyntactic information which has been 'lost' when they fail to use standard Spanish verbal morphology. With verbs of activity, non-standard infinitival forms are used 88 per cent of the time and with verbs of development such as *sembrar, comprar, llevar, vivir, mandar a buscar*, etc. they are used 100 per cent of the time. This indicates that in many cases time reference is not completely lost, as the semantic element of these verbs contains – movement/+ progress in a given direction. The preference for the infinitive, and later for the invariant third person form of the verb (5–8), as can be seen in the data (Table 7.3), responds to a natural tendency on the part of speakers to use the least marked forms, where semantic elements are retained in the meaning of the verb. In line with the work of Levin and Rappaport (1995), we contend that in our data the semantic class of the verb often determines much of the syntactic structure of the utterance so that when certain features of the verb are not marked morphosyntactically, such as TMA inflection, then it is the semantic class of the verb which determines these features. It is dynamic verbs and verbs of activity with the features [−movement, +development] which appear to supply the information lost with the verbal affixes. These data appear to support the argument that during the acquisition of the grammar of a language, whether L1 or L2, lexical and semantic proficiency precede syntactic proficiency.

The TMA interpretation of verbs of activity is frequently supported by other discursive resources such as the presence of adverbials (for example

Table 7.5 Class of verb, according to presence/absence of pronouns or subject NPs in Haitians, Dominican-Haitians, Arayanos and Dominicans

Class of verb	Pronoun present	Pronoun absent	NP present or referential	Total
Stative	502 (44%)	356 (31%)	284 (25%)	1142 (100%)
	55%	36%	57%	49.7%
Activity	411 (36%)	544 (47%)	199 (17%)	1154 (100%)
	45%	60%	41%	50.3%
Total	913	900	483	2296/2310
	100%	100%	100%	

ahora, después, en la mañana), in the same clause or in the speech act. These adverbial references syntactically help to retrieve TMA information lost morphologically, although retained to a certain extent by verbal semantics.[9] Also, most non-standard instances of the infinitive (50%) occur in environments where an inflected verb would be in the present tense. Non-standard infinitives also replace verbs which would otherwise be in the subjunctive, which situates itself midway between the atemporality of the infinitive and the temporal precision of the indicative. Indeed, the use of subjunctive is in gradual decline even by L1 speakers, as shown in 34–35 above. Furthermore, the data show a fairly high rate of occurrence of subject pronouns or explicit subject noun phrases with 69 per cent of the stative verbs and with 53 per cent of the verbs of activity (see Table 7.5); the figures for the infinitive are similar. These markers, either accompanying the verb or occurring earlier in the speech event, help to furnish information about person and number which is lost with the morphology, and appears to serve a pragmatic function.

Invariant third person[10]

The extension of the third-person singular to other verbal contexts which demand a verb marked for person and number, in standard varieties (see 5–8 above), appears to be a fairly generalized phenomenon in the processes of second-language learning (Table 7.3), to the extent that it has been considered a language universal which characterizes speakers of L1 as well as speakers of vestigial varieties and of *pidgins* and *creoles*. In the process of learning L2, this feature represents an advance on the use of the infinitive and the gerund, for here we have a full verb which is marked for TMA and which amply meets the semantic demands of the utterance. This is a frequent phenomenon amongst Hs and for many of these speakers it has become fossilized as the sole verbal marker. For the DHs and the AYs, although invariant third-person forms are used, there is some evidence of acquisition of verbal forms with +person and +number as marking required by standard varieties of Spanish. The generalization of the third-person singular is one of the strategies adopted by speakers who are immersed in the process of contact while they are learning a second language. This strategy, in turn, corresponds to a particular stage of L2 acquisition, which appears to be superseded in contexts which are favourable to learning. In these speakers, this generalization may be supported by an absence of marking of verbal forms by morphemes and by the widespread presence of an unmorphologically-marked infinitive, supported by preverbal particles and subject pronouns, all characteristics of HC. Consequently, a language universal supported in turn by a characteristic feature of L1, here HC, tends to promote the generalization of the third person. An even more striking example of the use of the third person can be seen in the invariant copula *son* in structures 37–38:

37   *Ete son familia mía.* (M60, H, Pedernales)
38   *La libra son a die peso.* (M45, H, Pedernales)

These structures are similar to those of Haitianized Spanish in Cuba (39–40):

39   *Sí (el creol) son la lengua de nusutro.* (Ortiz López 2001b: 181)
40   *El valón son teniente (en) La Habana.* (Ortiz López 2001b: 182)

They also coincide with the forms recorded for Afro-Antillean *bozal* Spanish in the nineteenth century, and which, according to Lipski (1996, 2005), originated in the variant *sã/são* which emerged from of contact between Africans and the Portuguese. In the case of the Hs, as much in Cuba as on the border between the Dominican Republic and Haiti, rather than a vestige of an Afro-Portuguese *pidgin* or *creole*, it is a widespread generalization of the third person which, in many cases, has become grammaticalized amongst those Hs who have only learnt an *interlanguage*.

The generalization of the third-person singular to other verbal contexts is different, in our view, from the phonological reduction of /s/ and /n/ which produces the simplification of the verbal forms corresponding to the second and third person in non-standard Dominican Spanish and Caribbean Spanish in general. Such reduction is also found in Haitianized Spanish in both Cuba and La Raya and border Spanish (41–45):

41   *A vece no **echa** uno (nos echan a uno) y no jaya ni la comía poque a vece viene lo dueño no que mañana te pago, que pasa'o, y así se va (el tiempo).* (M36, H, Pedernales)

42   *En Haití hay las habicheras **ehtá** barata.* (M30, DH, Pedernales)
43   *Lo único que **tiene** ello que son medio baratero.* (M36, H, Pedernales)
44   *No por mucho trabajo no porque tú **sabe** to lo parto **tiene** la brujería.* (F45, H, Pedernales)
45   *Después **llega** cuarto y se lo paga.* (F45, H, Pedernales)

This simplification is a result of the process of phonetic erosion which occurs in many varieties of Spanish from Spain, the Americas and the Caribbean (López Morales, 1992) and which appears to become accentuated in speakers of *interlanguages*, mainly those whose mother tongues do not have verbal inflection as is the case with many creoles, including Haitian Creole. This feature has been associated with the descendants of speakers of slave languages who acquired Spanish imperfectly, and who through their learning of the language transferred structures from African languages to Afro-Hispanic Caribbean varieties and/or of a hypothetical Pan-Caribbean *pidgin* or *creole* (Granda, 1976; Megenney, 1985; Perl, 1985; Green, 1997). I contend that this is a natural process of phonetic erosion which frequently takes place in L2 acquisition, which is supported by the fact that consonant elision and lack of verbal inflection typify Haitianized Spanish in general.

Conclusion

To conclude, the use of the infinitive and invariant third person among people of Haitian descent in La Raya, can be considered to be due to the operation of universals of language acquisition for speakers of Spanish as L2. The infinitive is starting to gain ground as a variant for the subjunctive in subordinate clauses, principally in contexts where alternation between the infinitive and the subjunctive is possible for speakers of Spanish as L1. In this regard, there is a need for variationist studies to be carried out to determine the extent to which the infinitive is used in subjunctive contexts and of the linguistic and extra-linguistic variables which determine its use. The data in the present study support the argument that, during the acquisition of L2, the reduction of the verbal inflectional paradigm is even greater than is the case for L1 speakers; this is true for the use of both the *infinitive*, as well as of the *invariant third person of the verb*. As we have tried to demonstrate in this study, these processes of *inflectional reduction* are influenced and/or compensated for as much by linguistic variables as by extra-linguistic factors. These linguistic variables include: (1) the semantics of the verb; (2) the use of adverbial phrases; (3) the use of pronouns in subject position; (4) the lack of verbal inflection in L1 (HC); (5) fixed SVO word order in L1 (HC); and (6) the existence of similar constructions in L1 (HC). Among the extra-linguistic factors we find firstly, the degree of contact with Spanish which ranges from the *congó* or *viejo* Haitian on one side of the continuum, who has little access to the L2 or target language, and on the opposite end the *arayano* who is always bilingual to some extent and, secondly, the ethno-linguistic attitudes which arise from this contact which is always stressful and almost never amicable due to the rejection on ethnic, cultural and linguistic grounds to which Haitians and their descendants are invariably subjected. In La Raya, any variety of Spanish (even the Haitianized variety discussed in this chapter) provides an entry into the global marketplace which paradoxically promises a better chance of economic survival in a context of extreme poverty and great human injustice. It is by using these varieties of Spanish that Haitians and their descendants manage to negotiate, albeit not on equal terms, with *forces of domination*, in a way which mirrors the experience of the indigenous peoples in Latin America, and Latinos in the USA. The stressful context of language contact found in La Raya gives rise to conflicts of ethno-linguistic identity in which the Spanish language becomes the discourse of progress or indeed the 'rhetoric of progress' (Del Valle and Gabriel-Stheeman 2004), relegating to the margins any sentimental values attached to HC.

Notes

* An early version of this chapter was presented at the Second UK Symposium of Hispanic Linguistics held at the University of Southampton, 15–17 April 2004. I am grateful to Miranda Stewart and Nicholas Faraclas (University of Puerto Rico) for the translation.

1 See Ortiz López (1998) for a summary of positions on this issue.
2 For an historical account of the different groups of immigrants in the Dominican Republic, see Inoa (1999).
3 For an overview of the project, see research proposal (manuscript available for those interested).
4 I am grateful for the support during this stage of the research of graduate students Melvyn González and Rose Vázquez from the Linguistics Programme and from the Dean's Office for Graduate Studies and Research of the University of Puerto Rico.
5 In *palenquero* two functions have been identified for *tá*: one which is closer to that found in other creoles *I tá kumé* (I am eating) and another similar to Spanish: *bo tá miná-nda ele nu?* ((you) are not seeing her), which, according to Dieck (2000: 9), on account of its form, distribution and function, appears to be a loan from the Spanish gerund. The semantic information contained in *-ndo* is the same as that of *tá* (continuous or progressive): there appears to be no difference of meaning between *bo tá miná-ndo ele nu?* and *bo tá miná-lo nu?*

6 For the purposes of this analysis, I shall mainly focus on the infinitive.

7 These findings are in line with those of a study of a Chinese speaker with Spanish as her L2 (Clements, 2003).

8 In recent decades Haitian creole has been the subject of much research and debate. For a diachronic and synchronic account of Haitian creole, see Lefebvre (1998) and DeGraff (1999, 2001, 2005).

9 I shall return to the issue of adverbial reference in future work, given that I currently possess only qualitative data.

10 In work in progress, we carried out a detailed analysis both of the use of the invariant third person as of the gerund in the sample of speakers from the border between Haiti and the Dominican Republic.

8
Whose Story Is It Anyway? Representing Oral Testimony in a Multilingual 'Contact Zone'*

Jane Freeland

Introduction

One discipline area which has arguably always been 'globalized' is anthropology, in particular its ethnographic methodology. Until relatively recently, 'the historic mission of ethnology [was] to find the universals of human language and human culture' (Foley, 2002: 470). Its unexamined assumption was that the generalizations (Western) anthropologists drew from their ethnographies would be universal. In the 1970s, in the context of decolonization and postcolonial criticism, anthropology entered a state of crisis, acknowledging that it rested on 'liberal, humanist doctrines of ameliorism, orientalism, colonialism, and racism' (*ibid.*).

Since then, reflection upon and deconstruction of the interaction between ethnographic field researchers and 'their subjects' (both the noun and the possessive are revealing) have become an increasingly overt part of ethnographic research, and of other social sciences which use similar methods. They have also stimulated experiments in the writing of

* This chapter and the articles it comments on (Freeland, 2003, 2005) arise from work with my students on the *Licenciatura* (BA) in Intercultural-Bilingual Education at the University of the Autonomous Regions of the Caribbean Coast of Nicaragua (URACCAN) in 2000 and 2001. I am deeply indebted to them for their insights into the communicative practices of the Coast and for permission to cite their 'linguistic autobiographies'. I thank the Sahwang Project for financing that teaching as part of its development of the Licenciatura, and the URACCAN's Institute for the Promotion and Investigation of Languages and Cultures (IPILC), especially its director, Guillermo McLean Herrera, for constant moral, intellectual and logistical support.

ethnography, to expose these relationships in ways the conventional academic genre can not (see for example Clifford and Marcus, 1986; Rosaldo, 1989; Hall, 1997; Chopra, 2001; Foley, 2002). This chapter explores such issues as they affect an article I first published in English (Freeland, 2003) and then translated into Spanish (Freeland, 2005).

The original article concerned the problems of realizing linguistic human rights (LHR) in intercultural, plurilingual regions like Nicaragua's Caribbean Coast. It discussed how the LHR discourse itself can paradoxically impede the realization of its own aspirations, to the extent that it is embedded in the linguistic ideology of European nation-building, whose construction of language and identity may obscure important aspects of indigenous/ethnic intercultural practices, from which there is much to learn. Its argument rested on evidence from a series of 'linguistic autobiographies', narrated by members of several indigenous and ethnic groups of the Coast, during sessions of a course I was teaching there on the Sociolinguistics of Multilingual Societies in 2000 and 2001.

The article first appeared in a special number on indigenous education of the British journal *Comparative Education*, whose guest editors were concerned to represent 'authentic' indigenous voices, alongside work by indigenous and non-indigenous scholars, including a 'linguistic autobiography'. The Spanish translation was for a Nicaraguan journal whose aim is to make academic research on the Coast accessible to Coast people (Costeños) themselves (Freeland, 2005). I had several reasons to welcome the chance to publish the paper in Spanish. It would enable me to discuss it with the narrators themselves, in the developing tradition of 'critical ethnography' (Foley, *ibid.*). Moreover, since the autobiographies had been narrated in Spanish, the language of the classroom and the *lingua franca* of the Coast, I imagined that I would be able to restore the authenticity of the narrators' own voices, which became lost in the English version. So I undertook to translate the paper myself.

I had reflected elsewhere (Freeland, 2001) on the relationship between my researcher self and the Coast people (Costeños) I had consulted, and imagined that reflexivity had become built into my research. In writing the English article, I had been aware of the many borders the autobiographies had crossed in their passage from classroom discussion in Nicaragua towards becoming 'my data' in an academic article in English, but had found no way to deal with the issue within the confines of that paper.[1] Translating it into Spanish made me more acutely aware of those crossings, not only as they affected my paper and its conclusions, but as they might appear to the autobiographers themselves. Moreover, it brought me up against one key aspect of the relationship between researcher and researched, which writing in English had completely obscured: my innocent assumptions about Spanish as the Coast's *lingua franca*. This aspect, as I shall show, adds a new dimension to the discussion of language rights on the Coast, and has a general significance in relation to this book.

In fact, the notion of 'border crossings' oversimplifies the complexity of what happened to these narratives; it implies something too orderly, well signposted and too unidirectional. More appropriate is Pratt's notion of 'contact zones' (1992) which incorporates notions of exchange and interaction. Pratt uses it to refer to 'the space of colonial encounters ... in which peoples geographically and historically separated come into contact with each other and establish ongoing relations, usually involving conditions of coercion, radical inequality, and intractable conflict' (Pratt, 1992: 6). She applies it particularly to the way such encounters become re-presented in colonial and postcolonial texts, particularly of travel and 'discovery'. Taking a 'contact perspective' reveals 'relations among colonizers and colonized, or travelers and "travelees" [or here, researchers and researched] not in terms of separateness or apartheid, but in terms of ... interaction, interlocking understandings and practices' (Pratt, 1992: 6–7).

Contact zones, one might say, are zones where 'invisible cultures' (Garcez, 1998) come into invisible but powerful interactions. I would suggest that the meetings between indigenous and non-indigenous people discussed by Hamel (this volume) are another such contact zone, and that both chapters are attempts to make that interaction more visible. This seems particularly necessary in the globalized world of today, where we can make too facile assumptions about our intercultural knowhow, *and its exchange through apparently neutral 'world languages'*.

I shall first describe the several linguistic and social 'contact zones' through which the Costeño linguistic autobiographies negotiated their passage, starting with their originating context, the Caribbean Coast region of Nicaragua, a contact zone shaped by globalizing processes that began in the Spanish and British colonial enterprises, and continued through the nation-building and neocolonialism of the modern and postmodern worlds.

I shall then discuss some ways in which the linguistic autobiographies were shaped by the encounter between the 'invisible cultures' of narrators and audience at the time of their narration, and subsequently by their treatment as academic 'data'. Finally, I shall draw out some implications *of these encounters* both for doing linguistic ethnography in such complex circumstances, and for globalized communication in general.

'Contact zones' between oral testimony and 'data'

Figure 8.1 shows the 'contact zones' through which these autobiographies passed in their transformation from oral narrative to written 'data'. Firstly, they originated in the multiethnic, intercultural and twice-colonized region of Nicaragua's Caribbean Coast, almost an archetypal 'contact zone'. Secondly, the events, which transpired in the narrators' various languages, were recounted in a 'contact language': Spanish used as the region's *lingua franca*, the second or third language of most tellers and listeners, myself included. This, I shall show, proved to be perhaps the most treacherous and least visible of all the contact zones. Just how treacherous only became clear when the narrators' speaking voices were transcribed into fixed, examinable writing, and dragged into a contact zone bristling with conflicting assumptions

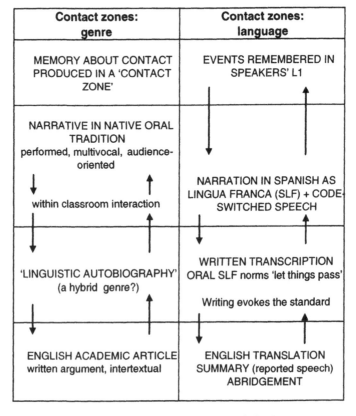

Figure 8.1 Contact zones between oral testimony and 'data'

about speech and writing, local norms and 'standards'. Finally, they became 'my data', quoted or summarized as reported speech in an academic article. The narratives also negotiated several zones of contact between genres, as conversational story-telling became classroom discourse, was re-presented as 'linguistic autobiography' (a sociolinguistic genre), and finally became 'data' in the genre 'academic article'.

I shall attend particularly to four of these 'contact zones', but treat only two in full detail. After describing the Caribbean Coast region itself and the classroom where the autobiographies were narrated, I shall home in on the zone of contact where genres meet, and its implications for the narratives' truth value as 'data'. Finally, I shall explore the linguistic contact zone between speech and writing that must be negotiated when oral testimony is transcribed. Reflection on this revealed an aspect of the Coast's linguistic inequalities that the English article had erased: the conflict between the function of Spanish as the *lingua franca* of the Coast and as the mythified national language of Nicaragua and Nicaraguan-ness. This last is the aspect of the chapter with most significance for this book. However, I would argue that its full complexities emerge most clearly when it is seen in the context of the others.

The Caribbean Coast as 'contact zone'

The most obvious 'contact zone' in the odyssey of these linguistic autobiographies is their originating context: Nicaragua's multiethnic, plurilingual Caribbean Coast region, a region shaped by interethnic contacts since well before the irruption of Europeans into Central America (Offen, 1999; González Pérez, 1997; Romero Vargas, 1995), and subsequently by its subsequent double colonization by Hispanic and Anglo powers and their postcolonial economic and political successors.

This region once formed part of the so-called Mosquito Coast, which extended northwards through present-day Honduras to Belize and southwards through Costa Rica towards Panama. From the seventeenth century its strategic position in the Caribbean Basin, its potential as the site for a transoceanic canal, and its rich natural resources, made it the arena of competition first between the Spanish and British Empires, and after Nicaraguan independence (1838) between Hispanic and Anglo America. Within the changing forcefield of this superpower competition, the Coast's peoples have historically constructed and reconstructed their identities, in relation both to each other and to the process of Nicaraguan nation-building. The cooption into the US-backed counter-revolutionary war of indigenous and ethnic conflict with the Sandinista revolution in the early 1980s was but the latest episode in this history.

Today, four indigenous minorities, two Afro-Caribbean minorities, and the Mestizos (of mixed Indian and Spanish descent), who constitute the dominant group in the Nicaraguan state, now inhabit overlapping or closely contiguous territories, interacting through four languages, of unequal power and range (see Table 8.1).

At the same time, Costeños (even some Spanish-speaking Mestizos) acquire dynamic bi-, tri- and even quadrilingual repertoires, which can include Sumu-Mayangna, Miskitu, various forms of Creole English, and Spanish, and code switching is frequent in identity negotiation (Freeland, 2003).

The sessions in which the autobiographies were originally narrated, during my teaching of a unit on the Sociolinguistics of Multilingual Societies, were a virtual microcosm of this larger contact zone. They brought together students from different indigenous and ethnic groups – Sumu-Mayangna, Miskitu, Creole and Mestizo in one grouping, Ulwa, Rama, Creole and Mestizo in another. Most of them were teachers or *técnicos* in the Coast's Intercultural-Bilingual Education Programme (PEIB). They were taught in Spanish as the putative *lingua franca* among

Table 8.1 Demography of Nicaragua's Caribbean Coast Region

Ethnic group	Population	% CC total%	nat. total	Language	Orgin
Mestizo	117,143	46.11	95.6	Spanish	Country's inland
Miskitu	70,122	27.5	1.7	Miskitu	Indigenous mixed Amerindian/African/ European
Creole	50,000	19.6	1.3	Mosquito Coast Creole	Afro-Caribbean
Sumu/ Mayangna	13,204	5.19	0.8	Sumu	Indigenous Amerindian
Ulwa (Sumu sub-group)	600	1.0	>0.5	Miskitu	Indigenous Amerindian
Garifuna	3,068	1.2	0.07	English Creole	Amerindian/ Afro-Caribbean (St Vincent)
Rama	1,023	0.4	0.02	Rama Coast Creole	Amerindian, possibly from South America
Total	254,560	100	100	(3.89% non-Mestizo)	

Source: Adapted from Holm (1978) and González Pérez (1997: 32–41).

us all and the students' language of secondary and higher education. Interactions, especially between the students themselves but also between some students and myself, were characterized by code-switching – a point to which I shall return later.

At a less obvious level, the classes brought into contact a student body and a teacher perceived as an 'expert' on Coast sociolinguistics, imported from England, a former colonial metropolis for the Coast. Over time, Costeño memories of the colonial relationship with England have become positively idealized (see for example Freeland, 1995), which did not make for egalitarian relationships. Moreover, as many of the narratives make plain, students' educational experience had taught them to expect student-teacher interactions embodying profound inequalities of power, especially symbolic power.

I strove to balance these inequalities as much as possible. I conceived and presented the course as a collaborative enterprise: the students' multilingual practices were to be our primary material, whilst I offered a set of tools with which we could jointly examine them. My interest in learning from the students must have been clear as I took notes and made recordings with their permission. I also continually drew attention to the fact that I, too, was not a native speaker of Spanish: I consulted the native-speakers among them about Spanish terms, and pointed out minor errors in my materials. Whilst these efforts were helpful, it will become clear from my analysis that they created only approximations to equality.

Linguistic contact zones

Much could be made of the translation issues raised by several of the linguistic contact zones negotiated by these autobiographies: between the first languages of their narrators and the *lingua franca* Spanish in which they were told; between this Spanish and the English of the first article; and between that version and its Spanish translation, not to mention issues associated with code-switching. However, that would require another, and very different article. I shall deal with code-switching, but as an aspect of genre rather than as a translation problem. Similarly, I shall address the unequal power of Spanish and the narrators' first languages as it emerges in the contact zone between speech and writing.

Genre as contact zone

I place genre first because I believe, with Bakhtin (1986), that it shapes most of our language learning and language choice. This may be the most complex 'contact zone' of all. As Tonkin (1998: 2) suggests, it constitutes an almost imperceptible 'horizon of expectation', determining the 'different conventions of discourse through which speakers tell history and listeners understand them'.[2] It is therefore fundamental to any interpretation of the narratives as research 'data' or as discourse for analysis. During the narration of these autobiographies, I shall argue, several different 'horizons of expectation' must have been operating. Did they produce misinterpretations and misrecognitions of what was happening? And how does this possibility affect the standing of the narratives as 'data'?

The autobiographies were elicited during a course session on multilingual repertoires and multilingual competences, which I consider important for curriculum design and classroom practice in intercultural bilingual education programmes for this region. I wanted to ground our exploration of these phenomena in the students' own experience of Coast multilingual practices, and decided to tap into the Costeño tradition of treating moral, philosophical and other abstractions through story. The way I framed the request for narratives implicitly encouraged students to place them within this tradition, to treat their own experience as *ejemplos* (exemplary narratives). I then asked them to recount how, when, and for what purposes they had acquired the languages they now spoke or had spoken in the past, confident that this would yield an interesting range of multilingual profiles to explore.

There was no prior discussion of what was meant by 'speaking language X'; this was to come later through our discussion of the profiles. The narratives suggest that students took it for granted that certain competences might be quite limited, acquired for highly specific purposes. The most striking example of this occurs in Perla's account of her acquisition, as a novice primary school teacher, of a quasi-fictitious, 'defensive' Creole, and in the corroborative chorusing by her listeners of the appropriate range of Creole expressions. (See Appendix for transcription conventions.)

(1)   yo tenía que trabajar en una escuela primaria donde la mayoría era niños criollos - entonces yo tenía que aprender - por lo menos **good marnin** - **how aar yu** - [*at this point several listeners join in chorus*] **gudbai** - **yu wan waata? yu wan milk? yu uokie?**[3] porque tenía que trabajar con niños pequeños – entonces dominamos algunas palabras para trabajar con niños de habla inglés --
[**intervention in Miskitu** *by a woman listener*]
no tía nooo – yo por ejemplo le digo a mi [??] usted no va a hablar detrás de mi porque yo entiendo todo ...

(I had to work in a primary school with a majority of Creole children – so I had to learn – at least **good marnin - how aar yu** - [at this point several listeners join in chorus] **gudbai - yu wan waata? yu wan milk? yu uokie?**[3] Because I had to work with small children – so we learn a few words to work with English-speaking children **[intervention in Miskitu** by a woman listener] no girl, nooo – for example I say to my [pupils?] you're not going to talk behind my back because I understand everything ...)

No doubt my framing of the narrative task influenced the way speakers recalled and recounted their linguistic experience. As Tonkin points out (1998: 39), we understand our experience differently over time, influenced by memory, conversations, and the ideological climate. So narratives, especially autobiographical ones, will alter according to the particular intersection of time, place, and audience where they are told.[4] Throughout the course, I had encouraged a positive, socio-historically based evaluation of the Coast's multilingual, interethnic communicative practices, to set against the 'received wisdom' of idealized, monolingual native-speaker norms and 'one-nation/ethnicity-one-language' assumptions. In such a context, narrators might well have revalued their own multilingualism.

The students responded readily to my proposal – indeed, narration quickly took over the class.[5] However, a number of different generic 'horizons of expectation' appear to have interacted, in both the telling and the hearing. For instance, examples (1) above and (2), from Perla's narrative, both show that the students were engaged in a genre we might call 'conversational story telling', in which joint performance and development of the narrative, also a characteristic of the oral traditions of both Miskitu and Creoles, are evident. In both these examples audience participation involves a switch into Miskitu. In (1), although Perla switches back into Spanish, she continues to interact with the intervention, using the colloquial expression and intonation 'no tía nooo'.

JF's (my) contributions, are of a different order. They slide between three stances: that of teacher, framing or encouraging activities, or making teaching points from the narratives; that of researcher, checking and clarifying 'information'; and that of something like participant audience, but differentiated from it by its relation to the other two, and perhaps by its enthusiasm, compared to the rather teasing nature of other audience contributions. These shifts produce a hybrid interactive genre related to the way I had set up the course – between seminar discussion and fieldwork interview.

This is where the first zone of genre contact emerges. JF responds to these narratives as if they were *already* 'linguistic autobiographies', a genre familiar to her but probably not to the narrators, and so from a different 'horizon of expectation' from theirs. How far this second genre is constructed jointly with the narrators or is the product of JF's individual interpretation is not easily judged. Much depends on the place occupied (or not) by this kind of 'exemplary' first person narrative within the oral traditions of these Miskitu and Creole students, and on how it might be interpreted. All this needs further research, whose findings may well colour any interpretation of these narratives as 'data' on language use or language attitudes; the narrative moment and the audience expectations that a genre sets up both constitute aspects of the truth value of the events recounted (Tonkin, 1998: 11). Take example (2):

(2) **Perla:** Bueno - mi lengua materna es miskita {JF: mm} y - yo aprendí -- en una escuela -- de monjas --
    JF: {mhm} ¿monolingüe? ¿de español?
    P: No
    Marcos: [*P's husband*] sí – monolingüe
    JF: de español
    P: sí monolingüe de español y me costó mucho porque en mi casa *toditos -- de habla miskita* y -- para enfrentarme -- con la gente tenía mucho temor mucho miedo -- em -- cuando yo comencé a trabajar -- no tuve tantos miedos para dar clase -- porque me encontraba - *todo mi comunidad* -- era de de de mi etnia -- de habla miskita -- entonces -- en la escuela - no - no tuve tanto temor --- pero -- cuando yo comencé a estudiar en las universidades - en la universidad -- entonces tuve mucho temor porque cuan - el grupo [¿con el que?] estoy estudiando su lengua materna es - es - el español -- entonces *ciertos momentos hasta para lectura* yo tenía miedo -- en la exposiciones – me acuerdo en una exposición que yo hice por no pronunciar bien una palabra - *entonces profesor me dijo* – - siéntese porque una universitaria no tiene que pronunciar así -- entonces yo me senté ya reflexioné y le dije -- gracias le digo yo domino dos o tal vez tres lenguas {{y usted}} {{JF: muy bien}} -- y usTED sólo {{domina UNA --- }} {{JF: muy bien dicho, sí sí}} español -- mas sin embargo yo estoy entre ustedes - estudiando y eso me alegra y usted a ese nivel usted sí nunca va llegar
    JF: Pero hay muy poca persona que tiene el empuje que tiene usted para atreverse a decir eso ¿verdad? {{P: así me dijo}} -- un profesor - un profesor - de -- historiografía --- entonces — pero - yo - yo sentí que mis compañeros no me apoyaron ....[6]

(**Perla:** Well - my mother tongue is Miskitu {JF: mm}I - I learned - in a - a convent school --
JF: {mhm} monoligual? in Spanish?
P: No
Marcos: [P's husband] yes - monolingual
JF: in Spanish
P: yes monolingual in Spanish and I struggled a lot because in my home **everyone** - **Miskitu speaking** and -- to stand up to -- I was very afraid of people very frightened -- em -- when I began work -- I wasn't so afraid of teaching -- because I was - **all my community**[7] -- were from my etnia -- Miskitu speakers -- so -- in school – I wasn't – so afraid -- but - when I began university studies – then I was very frightened because whe - the group [with which?] I'm studying their mother tongue is - is - Spanish -- so **certain moments even for reading** I was afraid -- in presentations – I remember in one presentation I made for not pronouncing a word properly – **then teacher said** -- sit down because a student shouldn't pronounce like that -- so I sat down and after thinking a bit I said -- thank you I said I command two or even three languages {{and you}} {{JF: very good}} -- and **YOU** have only {{ONE -- }} {{JF: very well said, yes, yes}} Spanish -- but even so I am among you – studying and that makes me glad and you'll **NEVER** reach that level
JF: but not many people have your guts to dare to say that, do they? {{P: that's what he said}} -- a teacher - a teacher - of historiography --- so -- but I – I felt that my fellow students didn't support me.).

How should we assess whether at the time of the event Perla voiced her reaction to her teacher's cruel put-down quite so boldly? This is not to suggest that her narrative is 'untrue', but to ask two kinds of question: whether in *this* narrative, and in the context created by our positive discourse on multilingualism, she felt able to express anger that she originally had to suffer silently. This question relates to the next: whether the narrative genre itself induced some kind of tailoring to her audience. The answers here will affect any assessment of Costeño discourse on multilingualism and whether it has changed over time.

Another aspect of the performance element, evident in even the most restrained and laconic of these narratives, is their multivocality (in Bakhtin's terms). They resound with the voices of parents, grandparents, sisters, teachers, which give them both emotional vitality and temporal depth. Usually, this multivocality appears within the Spanish *lingua franca* (SLF), the different voices sometimes marked in advance, sometimes only after they enter. Of many examples, the most striking is Rachel's narrative (3), where voices also enter as code-switches, which would carry for the audience more complex significance than for JF:

(3) **JF:** ... tú sabes por qué será que - que te has puesto del lado miskito que no del otro? {**Rachel:** pues} ¿cuál fue la atracción?[8]
R: la atracción fue lo siguiente por mi abuela {mm} (...) y también -- una muchacha que vivía con nosotros de - de mi edad y era miskita ella {mm} (..) - y ella me enseñaba todo - todititITo - todo lo que ella sabía cuento yo sé cuentos en miskito como sesenta cuentos - a entonces (...) - o sea que me ponía bastante con ella - todos los trabajos que a mí me daban **OK yu go an do dis go an cliin di gaaden go an do dis go an wash – go** [??] ella me ayudaba (...) - y yo le daba comida a ella por cambio de mi trabajo porque a ella le gustaba comer bastante - y yo no - yo hasta esta altura yo casi no como - poquito {*JF laughs at the tone*} – carne no me gusta – entonces toda la carne {la pasabas a ella} sí – pescado [??] **winka abris yahkja abris** todo se le amontonaba **fruut you doon iit yes sir!**..
{JF: ... do you know – what made you – take your Miskitu side and not the other? {**Rachel:** well} what was the attraction?
R: the attraction was the following for my grandmother {mm} and also -- a girl who lived with us my - my age and she was Miskitu {mhm} (...) and she taught me everything - *EVERything – all she knew stories I know stories in Miskitu like sixty stories – so then (...) I went a lot with her – all the jobs they gave me* **OK yu go an do dis an cliin di gaaden go an do dis go an wash – go** [??] she helped me (...) – and I gave her food in exchange because she liked eating quite a lot - and I didn't - even now I hardly eat anything - little (...) I don't like meat – so all the meat {you passed it to her} yes - fish [??] **winka abris yahkja abris** all piled on her **fruut you doon iit yes sir!**..}

Yet by the time they appear as 'my data' the narratives are stripped of all these generic characteristics, unquestioningly (re)presented as 'linguistic autobiographies' and re-contextualized within a third genre: the 'academic article in English'. As example (4) shows, this third genre imposes its own multivocality, that of intertextuality (Fairclough 1992).

(4) Both Amelia's and Rachel's homes spoke their father's Creole rather than their mother's Miskitu. Rachel's father also taught her to read Standard English. Spanish was the third-acquired language of both, Miskitu their second. Amelia acquired hers 'with my neighbours in

the *barrio* [district /S] here (...) and with Miskitu children at school'. Rachel acquired hers from her mother and grandmother, against her father's will: 'I always got stick from my Dad because I'd do all my activities round the house in Miskitu (...) My Granny – on my mother's side – used to visit and (...) she'd take me off to [the River Coco] for the holidays (...) and every time (...) he'd grumble "when my daughter comes back she can't speak proper English any more".' Now Rachel's preferred language is Miskitu. (Freeland 2003: 245)[9]

Re-contextualized, these narrators' voices are also re-presented. Often they are summarized, since speech is redundant, whilst journal word limits impose terseness. As reported speech, though, they are invisibly mediated. Direct quotations are selected, often from different parts of the narrative sequence, abridged and dropped into the text, sometimes in bunches. In this way, they come to resemble other academic textual references, all selected *post hoc* from the totality of the narratives to legitimate an argument about 'mother tongues' in multilingual regions. Their performance elements are all erased, even from consideration of the truth value of the stories.[10]

Transcribed speech as 'contact zone'

This final contact zone proved to be the most complex of all, because it's the least visible. Yet arguably it frames all the others. It might seem that being able to quote from the original recordings in the Spanish version of my paper would release the 'authentic voices' of the narrators, which in the English version could be approximated only through translation style. However, as the quotations above already suggest, quoting in Spanish in fact raised thorny problems of representation: when speech takes an unorthodox form, as theirs did, what constitutes 'authenticity' in its transcription?

As several writers have pointed out, transcriptions reflect not only a transcriber's theoretical stance towards the speech transcribed (Ochs, 1979), but also their ideological position (Preston, 1982, 1985). Jaffe (2000), introducing her *Journal of Sociolinguistics* special number on non-standard orthography and non-standard speech, highlights how writing recalls the standard and so draws attention to any deviation from it. In the same issue, Jaffe and Walton (2000) demonstrate this empirically, showing how readers of transcribed non-standard speech generally stigmatize it (see also Miethaner, 2000).

The 'deviations' here are in the students' Spanish. I said earlier that our classroom interaction took place in Spanish, the *lingua franca* of the Coast. Its Spanish transcription, however, revealed aspects of this statement which writing in English had masked. In particular it threw into stark relief how different was my experience of Spanish as a *lingua franca* from that of my students, and it alerted me to social and power differences between the functions of Spanish as a *lingua franca* (SLF) and Spanish as the dominant national language. These have implications for the topic of this book which go beyond the context of the Coast. At the heart of this difference is their relation to 'native-speaker' norms, and their role in nationalism.

House (2003) has usefully collated recent research into a description of '*lingua franca* talk' which is relevant here, though her focus is on English. In (E)LF talk, she says, 'participants appear to adopt a principle of "let it pass", an interpretive procedure which makes the interactional style both "robust" and explicitly consensual' (House, 2003: 559). Consequently, LF speaker competence 'is not measurable by native speaker competence', but rather by a notion of 'multi-competence', 'a distinctive state of mind' deriving from 'the possession of ... more than one set of linguistic and socio-cultural knowledge' (House, 2003: 557–8, referring to Cook, 1993). A LF may be elaborated *ad hoc* among strangers, or it may become a distinct variety, as indeed is happening with 'World Englishes'. The students in my classes, indeed most Costeños, have precisely this kind of multi-competence; it was, indeed, what we had set out to explore through their autobiographies. Through my very different trajectory, so did I, but as we shall see, it did not match theirs.

As the highlighted sections (in bold italics) in the cited extracts illustrate, the Spanish the students spoke was clearly SLF according to House's definition. Indeed, my emphasis on the fact that many of us were not Spanish native-speakers positively sanctioned this, and explicitly related it to our exploration of Costeño multi-competence Yet, judged by monolingual standard norms it is 'full of errors'.

It is clear from their narratives that the students' previous experience of Spanish in the classroom had been governed by those norms. Examples (2) above, and (5) and (6) below are just three of many accounts of stressful, even traumatic experiences of monolingual, Spanish-medium education and of the deep linguistic insecurities they induced (bilingual education on the Coast dates only from 1985; these students are the successes of the old system).[11]

(5) **Carlos:** ... francamente - me costó - o sea - porque la misma profesora - en esos tiempos era - creo que se llamaba Alicia - - me regañaba - o sea - - me - en cuanto hacía a hablar – no me salía bien y siempre hablaba mal español - - pero en el examen *salía buenas notas* - ya escrito

JF: escrito?

C: sí - sí salía buena nota pero - al expresar - - comía muchas preposiciones [??] entonces los maestros - vos te hablás mal el español - pero cuando tenía escrito algunas cosas que me enseñaron en la lectura y en el examen *si eso los ponía porque a esa lectura tiene* y entonces *yo los ponía algunas* de memoria *me los había memorizado* entonces no fallaba en el examen – entonces como usted escribe bien me dice la profesora pero no puede hablar bien - entonces así llamaba mi mama mi papa les decía su hijo el examen de escritura dice sale bien pero la verdad - o entonces ustedes procuren para que - dicen sí procuro pero - así le pasa dicen pero tal vez más adelante dicen ...

(**Carlos:** ... frankly – it cost me – that is – because the teacher herself (...) - - would tell me off – that is - - she – as soon as I started to speak – it didn't come out right and I always spoke bad Spanish - - but in the exam **I came out good marks** – written

JF: written?

C: yes – yes I got good marks but – speaking - - I swallowed a lot of prepositions [??] then the teachers – you speak Spanish so badly – but when I wrote down a few things they taught me in reading and in the exam **if I put those I got from reading** and then **I'd put some of those** from memory (...) then I didn't fail the exam – then how well you write the teacher says to me but you can't talk properly – then she'd call my Mum my Dad she'd tell them your son in the written exam she says does well but really – or so you try to – they say yes I try but – that's what he's like they say but maybe later on they say ...).

(6) **Rachel:** ... pero cuando yo voy a la Morava tercer grado ya niña grande yo no puedo hablar ni entiendo el español {mhm} - - ya – pero nada NADA {mm} - - nada – ni artículo ni preposición ni nada ni na DA yo SÉ en español - entonces mi papa explica que mi hija sólo inglés sabe - - entonces me baja a segundo grado - - - ya – y segundo grado pero también mi padre saca un **ticha** para que me enseñe – español [??] - - pero yo no podía me era imposible y más de una vez cuando yo estoy leyendo - cancañando [*makes gagging noises*] me - se - c - e - los compañeros se rieron de mí – por eso hasta esta altura - yo para levantar a este examen en español yo tengo que

pensarlo dos tres veces porque me queDÉ con ESO psicológica-
mente *me quedé dañado* porque - lo - si me levanto se van a reírse
de mí si me levanto voy a hacer un error ... [12]
(**Rachel:** ... but when I go to the Moravian School third grade
already a big girl I can't speak nor understand Spanish {mhm} - -
but nothing NOTHING - - nothing – not article nor preposition nor
nothing noTHING (...) so my Dad explains that my daughter only
speaks English - - so they put me down to second grade - - - and
second grade but my Dad gets a **ticha** to teach me – er – Spanish
[??] – – but I couldn't it was impossible and more than once when
I'm reading – gagging [makes gagging noises] I – it – c – e – my fellow students laughed at me – so even now – to do this exam in
Spanish I have to think about it two or three times because this
LEFT me psychologically **I was damaged** because – if I get up
they're going to laugh at me if I get up and make a mistake ...).

In these students' learning experience, the classroom language was never
SLF, freely available to all, but Spanish, as defined by *monolingual* Mestizo
teachers (as they mostly were then), for whom multilingualism was a
problem and whose authority lay in being native-speakers. They applied
idealized native-speaker norms, ostensibly to overcome the students'
multilingualism and help them become 'proper members' of the Spanish-
speaking community. In fact, the narratives suggest, these norms operated
as shibboleths, masking racist attitudes that made the entry bar to that
community impossibly high.[13] A notable effect of this educational experience is the narrators' tendency to feel more confident in writing, which
can be revised and corrected to get good grades (see examples (5) and (6)
above), and to discuss competence in terms of grammatical elements.
This, of course, affects their approach to their pupils' Spanish.[14]

In example (2) above, Perla clearly distinguishes the two situations:
with other Miskitu speakers she feels less fear; with Spanish native
speakers she is nervous even of reading aloud. Indeed, it was Perla's
warning at the start of the course, that students might feel too inhibited
to participate in Spanish, which prompted me to emphasize our shared
multilingualism. Later (7 below), referring to another instance of her
nervousness about speaking Spanish to monolingual native-speakers,
Perla confirms that we had created in our seminars a community of
practice where 'multi-competence' was acknowledged and Spanish
could be used as a *lingua franca*.[15] The extract comes at the end of her
narrative, shortly after quotation (1) above. Even so, she still diagnoses
our multilingualism as a shared *problem*.

(8) **Perla:** ... ante la gente trilingüe bilingüe eso es una experiencia que uno vive - y hasta - *hasta momento* - - yo tengo miedo para participar - pero con este grupo que son lingüistas no me da miedo
JF: {{pues me alegro}}
P: {{porque ya sabemos}} ya manejamos – ya manejamos que todos tenemos ese problema.

(P: ... with trilingual bilingual people that is an experience one shares – and – up to – up to now - - I am afraid to participate – but with this group who are linguists I have no fear
JF: {{well I'm glad}}
P: {{because we know}} we're aware – we're aware that we all have this problem).

We had, in fact, begun to create what Kramsch (1993: 205) terms a 'sphere of intercultural activity' (quoted in Roberts *et al.*, (2001: 30–1), freely appropriating Spanish as its *lingua franca*, as part of the multilingual repertoires and competences we were discussing. Indeed, SLF enabled us to contrast these competences with the idealized monolingual 'native speaker' norms that had caused the students such troubles, and to set them aside. Once speech passed into closely examinable writing, however, this was no longer possible. If I chose to transcribe the narrators' speech 'authentically', I would merely highlight its differences from those norms, inviting a stigmatized reading and betraying all the principles upon which the classes were conducted. I would thus undermine the speakers' public authority both as educated teachers and as informants.

Paradoxically, by transcribing the stories in Standard Nicaraguan Spanish I could respect these principles. After all, the issue was not the narrators' Spanish, but how their stories illustrated Costeño multilingual practices, their implications for the Bilingual Intercultural Education Programmes and for minority language rights in general. All these issues had come through untroubled in the English version of the paper. However, in doing so, I was also conniving in a manipulation of the differences between SLF and native norms which has serious implications for those very language rights.[16]

The expression 'language/linguistic rights' focuses attention on a hierarchical relationship between a dominant *language* and 'other' subordinated or minority *languages*. As in Nicaragua, it often leads to the creation of unidirectional programmes to help speakers of subordinated languages to integrate into the national culture, hopefully without losing their original languages. The PEIB, in addition, seeks to develop 'interculturality'. In the articles we are discussing here (Freeland, 2003, 2005) I suggest, that this notion, as constructed by the PEIB, takes no account of long-standing intercultural practices on the Coast. It now appears that 'interculturality' should also shape its approach to Spanish.

Instead of 'linguistic rights', Kubchandani (1994) proposes 'communication rights' as a framework for education in multilingual societies. This concept encompasses the whole linguistic repertoire of speakers as it functions in their context (see also Stroud and Heugh, 2004, on 'linguistic citizenship'). Such a framework for the Coast would recognize explicitly that SLF and national standard Spanish have different functions, and make it less easy to manipulate slippage between them. Then intercultural-bi-/multilingual teacher training would alert teachers not only to the linguistic but also the social power differences between SLF and Standard Spanish, and require them to make, and to teach, appropriate use of each. Otherwise, they can only perpetuate the norms they have internalized and their own linguistic insecurity, and unwittingly close the gates of linguistic equality that the PEIB is supposed to open.

Conclusion

In the introduction to his edited volume on *Representation in Ethnography*, Van Maanen (1995: 17–18) suggests that reflexivity may be useful 'to refute the truth claims of others, but [not] to make new truths ... [T]he results of this work do not provide a better way to do ethnography'. I would argue that, in this chapter, reflexivity emerges not just as a demolition tool, but as a probe towards further truths.

I have shown that the interpretation of oral testimony as academic 'data' is always a hybrid process involving subliminal interactions between researcher and researched, making knowledge together in 'contact zones' complexly grounded in their different social histories. Sometimes these zones are fairly obvious: it would be foolish to ignore the colonial history of Nicaragua's Caribbean Coast and the potential effects of a researcher's place within it, or language differences and their power implications. Here, the borders between zones are relatively well-marked. Our assumptions about genre are less obvious, more taken for granted, and this is especially so when we seem to be speaking a *lingua franca*. Yet on reflection, this may be the most conflict-laden of all the zones. As we saw, Spanish as the putative *lingua franca* of Nicaragua's Caribbean Coast region does not bridge differences for minority speakers.

According to House (2003), successful 'lingua franca talk' is consensual, communication-oriented and tolerant of imperfection. Could it be that this is possible only when the lingua franca is a *foreign* language, but not when it is the language that gives passage to full participation in a national culture? As a foreign speaker of Spanish, I innocently generalized this tolerance and consensuality, unaware that it was denied to my students.

This is a situation unlikely to be confined to the Coast; it is certainly observable in other parts of Latin America. It has, I think, serious implications for our assumptions about 'world languages' as bridges in our globalizing times. Other chapters in this book (notably Hamel's examination of differing indigenous and Mestizo norms of what constitutes 'a meeting', and Mar Molinero's discussion of the nationalistic possessiveness of Spanish, manifest by the Instituto Cervantes) also suggest that we may use the term *lingua franca* with too much facility, unaware that, like any other contact zone, it conceals as Pratt (1992: 6) shows: 'conditions of coercion, radical inequality and intractable conflict'.

Appendix

Narrators

Despite the protestations of some, all names are anonymized. Pseudonyms reflect the linguistic tendency of the original names. The three narratives were selected as particularly clear illustrations of the issues under discussion, from a total of 18. The full range of 18 autobiographies included one *mestizo* narrative, one Sumu-Mayangna, and one Ulwa. Ethnicities are self-ascribed; ages where not known are surmized from internal evidence; L1 to L^n ascriptions are the students' own.

Perla – 50+, *Miskita*, L1 Miskitu (monolingual home); L2 Spanish (monolingual schooling); L3 Creole English (acquired as an adult for (elementary) communication with primary school pupils).

Carlos – 30s, *Miskitu*. L1 Miskitu (both parents Miskitu, father (local pastor) also spoke Spanish and Creole English, mother spoke Spanish); L2 Spanish (acquired with parents' friends, learned at monolingual school); L3 Creole English (acquired with neighbourhood friends).

Rachel – early 30s, *Miskita*. L1 bilingual: Creole + Miskitu (Creole father, Miskitu mother); L2 Standard Caribbean English (early schooling with private teacher and reading with father); L3 Spanish (Spanish-medium schooling from 3rd grade + English taught as a subject)

Transcription conventions

For the purposes of this chapter, a broad transcription is used. For instance, overlaps and 'interruptions' are recorded with enough precision for the discussion of genre, but not for a detailed study of turn-taking, which the chapter does not treat.

- - -   pause: relative length conveyed impressionistically by number of dashes

[*some chit-chat*]   explanatory comments or summaries of omitted sequences

{mhm}   backchannelling, brief interjections

me queDÉ con Eso   heightened pitch/ increased stress

{{como le decía}}
{{sí pues}}   overlaps / interruptions
[??] [¿mis hermanos?]   inaudible sections, likely approximations
(...)   section of text omitted
gud maarnin   code-switched text (emphasis in bold)
entonces profesor me dijo   non-standard forms in Spanish as *lingua franca*
                              (SLF) (emphasis in bold italics)

Notes

1   Between writing and translating Freeland (2003), I attended a meeting of the Linguistic Ethnography Special Interest Group of the British Association for Applied Linguistics, where Rosaleen Howard and Lindsey Crickmay discussed an Andean Quechua autobiographical narrative within Pratt's 'contact perspective'. This chapter owes much to that (Howard, 2005).

2   See also Hanks (1987): 670–1: 'genres can be defined as the historically specific conventions and ideals according to which authors compose discourse and audiences receive it. In this view, genres consist of orienting frameworks, interpretive procedures, and sets of expectations that are not part of discourse structure, but of the way actors relate to and use language ... genres are an integral part of linguistic habitus'.

3   To transcribe Perla's Creole phonology here I have adopted the Nicaraguan Kriol orthography now being developed on the Coast (Woods, 2003).

4   See also Pavlenko and Blackledge's (2003: 19) account of identities as 'social, discursive and narrative options offered by a particular society in a specific-time and place to which individuals and groups appeal in an attempt to self-name, to self-characterize, and to claim social spaces and social prerogatives'.

5   When after about four contributions I moved to draw out their pedagogical implications, students who had not yet contributed protested vehemently. Although giving them more space upset the teaching schedule, I was happy as a researcher to gather more 'data'. Some students opted to write narratives for a folder of work to be presented (see Freeland, 2003, for details).

6   Extract (2) precedes extract (1) in Perla's narrative sequence, with only a few phrases of intervening speech.

7   Translating these quotations back into English takes them again into the linguistic contact zone. In the translations I have continued to highlight non-standard (Spanish) sections in bold italics, to enable readers to match them to the Spanish originals.

8   The V form of address is conventional in classroom discourse. JF's switch to the T form follows a passage of a rather personal nature, here omitted, and may express the sense of increased intimacy it induced. JF realizes the T form of address as *tú*, whereas Nicaraguan Spanish uses *vos*.

9   The transcript of this part of Rachel's narrative reads: 'pero mi mami es – este miskita – de - - - de de de – de una comunidad que se llama X {mhm} – entonces mi abuelita de parte de mi madre ella nos visitaba ... entre los nietos parece que le cayó bien más a mi persona - y ella me llevaba a Waspam - pero para las vacaciones y mi padre me regañaba mucho - y me pegaba mucho él tenía serios problemas con la suegra porque cada vez que ella quería sacarme el permiso dice no dice porque cuando mi hija viene de esa comunidad ella no puede ni hablar inglés decía ...'

10 This argument, moreover, draws on the temporal depth given by the multi-vocality of the stories to legitimate my contention that Costeño intercul-tural-multilingual practices are not a new phenomenon. Paradoxically, in this chapter the narratives pass through another cycle of the kind I have just described. Given its argument, it should feature a larger sample of narratives, quotations should not be cited out of their original narrative sequence, nor abbreviated. Yet the genre 'academic chapter' dictates otherwise.

11 Indeed, there appears to be a higher concentration of these 'errors' at points where the narrative treats these experiences.

12 This section precedes the citation at (4). The intervening narrative concerns Rachel's self-identification as a Miskitu, which prompts JF's first question in extract (4). 'La Morava' refers to the fee-paying Moravian College, held to be one of the best on the Coast, especially for English. Rachel had transferred there from a small, English-medium school – hence her lack of Spanish.

13 See Rampton (1995: 340) on the potency and influence of the folk concept of the 'native speaker'.

14 PEIB evaluations frequently criticize indigenous teachers for their unwilling-ness to depart from teaching texts, especially in Spanish, and to focus on the written language (see Freeland, 2003).

15 The relative frequency of code-switching may be a further indication that SLF norms were in operation here.

16 Hence the decision recorded in note 9. In contrast, for this discussion of relations between SLF and 'native' Spanish, differences between them must be highlighted. I have indicated here only the most striking syntactical errors (lexical errors do not occur), anything else would need linguistic and ideo-logical justification. It should be clear from the whole argument that it would be virtually impossible to publish this paper in Spanish translation; it would need to be completely rewritten.

9
Spanish-Speaking Latin Americans in Catalonia: Reflexivity and Knowledgeability in Constructions of Catalan

Steve Marshall

Introduction

During the past twenty years, there has been remarkable change in the sociolinguistic make-up of Catalonia, and of Barcelona in particular, where many allochthonous 'new migrants' (Turell, 2001a) have settled. Spanish-speaking Latin Americans are of particular interest: allochthonous new migrants who speak marked varieties of the majority language of the Spanish state, settling in Catalonia, during a key stage in the normalization of the Catalan language. Their presence in large numbers not only represents a new and interesting twist in the age-old conflict between Catalan and Castilian, it also threatens to contribute to the rolling back of the progress that the Catalan language has made in recent years through policies of linguistic normalization.

Many sociolinguistic studies have analysed issues related to bilingualism and codeswitching in Catalonia, focusing mainly on interactions between speakers of Castilian and Catalan.[1] Woolard (1989) described the prevalent 'accommodation norm': Catalan speakers switching to Castilian in interactions with Castilian speakers. Woolard also described a 'bilingual norm' – described as 'passive bilingualism' in Pujolar (2001) – to describe a form of 'reciprocal bilingualism' in which no switch is made: each interlocutor continues in their own language. Pujolar (2001: 211) cites several studies which found that little 'passive bilingualism' was being practised (Tusón, 1990; Bastardas, 1985, 1986; Erill *et al.*, 1992; Boix, 1989; Pujolar, 1993). Pujolar (2001) follows a discourse analysis approach (Fairclough, 1989, 1992) in a study of young people in Barcelona. He focuses on gender as the key aspect of social identity in the peer-group context, highlighting ethnicity and class as important in understanding young people's cultural practices, especially in their management of heteroglossia, 'the socially stratified diversity of speech forms' (Pujolar, 2001). A more structural-descriptive approach can be found in Turell (2001b), where the focus is on the language use of established and new linguistic minorities in Spain, including chapters focusing on Catalonia.

One key group on which little literature has focused yet is Spanish-speaking Latin Americans. This may be because their mass migration into Catalonia is relatively recent. Moreover, as allochthonous Spanish-speakers arriving in Catalonia during the linguistic normalization of the Catalan language, they do not fit tidily into many of the existing paradigms of sociolinguistic analysis, nor into the ideological frameworks of many writers on linguistic minorities and Catalonia.

The two key analytic concepts that I focus on in this chapter are 'knowledgeability' and 'reflexivity' (Giddens, 1984) in Spanish-speaking Latin Americans' constructions of Catalan. The data that I present is part of a wider study carried out between 2000 and 2004 (Marshall, 2005), in which I analysed the sociolinguistic agencies of Spanish-speaking Latin Americans in Catalonia from an analytic perspective of 'language as recursive social practice'. As part of the approach, I frame my analysis around 'structure' and 'agency' (Giddens, 1984). In terms of 'structure', my focus is on the representation of Catalan in present-day language policies, as well as the 'structures' of new migrants' Latin American countries of origin. In terms of 'agency', I focus on two key areas of the sociolinguistic agencies of Spanish-speaking Latin Americans: (1) *how* individuals build Catalan into their lives through incorporation into repertoire in-group and inter-group, and (2) *how* and *why* individuals form conflicting constructions of being addressed in Catalan.[2]

I argue that individuals' constructions of Catalan are in many cases transitional, taking place within the new structures of Catalonia, yet still influenced by the old structures of Latin American countries of origin; and encountered via interactions with Catalan speakers, who in turn are making linguistic choices as expressions of their own 'agency within structure'. Whilst both groups' respective 'agencies within structure' may converge in a synchronic sense at the level of social and linguistic interaction in daily life-paths, they are often based upon distinct diachronic perspectives and epistemological grounding. Many Spanish-speaking Latin Americans may be basing their agency upon sociolinguistic histories, or structures, grounded in Latin American countries where the sense of Spanish monolingualism and nationhood are closely linked, and where 'other' minority languages, in particular the indigenous minority languages of the Americas are socially excluded. In contrast, the agency of many Catalan speakers may be based upon very distinct diachronic perspectives and epistemologies: those of a linguistic minority group that has undergone centuries of oppression and exclusion within the Spanish state. Thus, constructions and misconstructions of *the code of the other* may take place from both sides, often in interactions involving codeswitching.

In this chapter, my specific focus is on *how* and *why* individuals form conflicting constructions of being addressed in Catalan, and on individuals' 'knowledgeability' and 'reflexivity' (Giddens, 1984). Giddens (1984) emphasizes the key role of the knowledgeability and reflexivity of human agents in the recursive ordering of social practice. In a similar vein, Bourdieu (1984) argues that knowledgeable, reflexive agents assess market conditions in anticipation of responses, as part of the process of engaging with market forces. Central to Giddens' theory of 'structuration' is the view that all agents are knowledgeable (Giddens, 1984), in that they know a vast amount about what a system is, and about its normative procedures. In order to 'bring off' an interaction, participants are seen to make use of their knowledge of the institutional order in which they are involved, in order to make their interchange meaningful (Giddens, 1984: 330–1). 'Reflexivity' is defined by Giddens (1984: 3) as both 'self-consciousness', and the monitored character of the ongoing flow of social life, grounded in the continuous monitoring of action which human beings display and expect others to display. Giddens argues that actors continuously monitor the flow of their activities and that they expect others to do the same for their own activities. The key issue in this case is individuals' applications of sociolinguistic knowledge (knowledge of norms of sociolinguistic practice): how interlocutors' knowledgeability affects the reflexive linguistic choices that they make when selecting/switching codes, and specifically here, when Spanish-speaking Latin Americans interpret being addressed in Catalan.

Globalization: *'ensaladilla rusa en el barrio chino'*[3] (Russian salad in Chinatown)

The manifestations of new multiculturalism are everywhere to be seen in Barcelona, particularly in *Ciutat Vella* (the Old Town) and its neighbourhoods, such as the so-called *barrio chino* ('Chinatown': an unfortunate term based on a misguided concept of vice rather than any historic presence of East Asian culture and cuisine). Pakistani shopkeepers speak Urdu, and switch between English, Spanish and Catalan as I buy my bread and decide between the somosas and *ensaladilla rusa* (Russian salad, of the Spanish variety). Traditionally in Barcelona, buying 'Russian salad' in 'Chinatown' never involved any Russians or Chinese. Today, however, it is sold by Pakistanis, and there *are* Russians and Chinese, as well as many other much larger new migrant groups. In fact, the rate of immigration over the last two decades has been unprecedented, as the following statistics illustrate. Whilst in 1996 foreigners made up 1.9 per cent of the population of Barcelona, by 2005 the figure rose to 14.6 per cent (*Departament d'Estadística*, Ajuntament de Barcelona, 2005). Between 1996 and 2005, the number of Ecuadoreans, for example, officially registered as living in Barcelona rose from 202 to 31,828. Similar growth patterns have taken place for many other non-EU groups: Moroccans (1996 – 3,196; 2005 – 14,508); Pakistanis (1996 – 614; 2005 – 11,997); Colombians (1996 – 703; 2005 – 13,935) (*Departament d'Estadística*, Ajuntament de Barcelona, 2005). Added to 'official' Town Hall figures, which are based on local lists of residents, are an unknown number of *'sin papeles'* (immigrants without legal 'papers'). An article in the Colombian national newspaper *El Tiempo* (30 December, 2004) cited figures from the Spanish *Instituto Nacional de Estadística* suggesting that there were more than one million 'illegal' foreigners in Spain in 2003; the same article stated that 300,000 (70%) of Colombians living in Spain are *sin papeles*, or non-regularized with residence applications in process (Vargas, 2004); whilst the largest concentration of Colombians is in Madrid, many also live in Catalonia.

Policy-makers are attempting to address the challenges of globalization by performing a difficult political juggling act: politically and economically pushing Catalonia forward in the global arena; culturally and linguistically striving for greater recognition of the Catalan language in the expanding multilingual, multicultural European Union; and paradoxically, socially, culturally and linguistically pulling individual agents away from the 'multi', and towards the 'uni', in which the Catalan language is legislated as *the* defining feature of Catalanness, and in which its use in many institutional settings enjoys preferential status over that of Castilian. For example, the 1998 Llei de Política Lingüística (Language Policy Law) accords both Catalan and Castilian co-official status, yet the Catalan language is also accorded the additional status of defining the Catalan people: 'Catalan is Catalonia's own language and distinguishes it as a people' (Preliminary Chapter: Article 2.1). Moreover, Catalan is given preferential status in key areas: 'The language preferentially used by the State Administration in Catalonia ...' (Preliminary Chapter: Article 2.2b; Llei de Política Lingüística, 1998).

Tied to the programme of linguistic normalization have been a series of campaigns promoting the social use of Catalan. In 2003, the Generalitat (the Catalan government) launched a TV and press campaign, *Tu ets mestre* (You're the teacher). The campaign aimed to increase the social use of Catalan by encouraging Catalan speakers to address visible minorities in Catalan, rather than Castilian, '*la qual pot provocar que els immigrants que aprenen el català trobin poc útil el seu esforç o se sentin exclosos o discriminats*' (which can make immigrants who learn Catalan feel that their efforts to have been of little use, or feel excluded and discriminated against) (novessSL, 2003). The campaign raises interesting questions about new migrants' constructions of Catalan. How will 'visible-minority' new migrants interpret being addressed in Catalan by strangers? Are there really immigrants who feel excluded and discriminated against because Catalan speakers address them in Castilian rather than Catalan? And can Catalan speakers rise to the challenge of taking on the role of agents for sociolinguistic change by changing their own practice, in particular the 'accommodation norm' as described above?

Conflicting constructions of being addressed in Catalan[4]

In interviews, I asked informants to describe how they use Catalan in their daily lives, and then how they interpreted being addressed in Catalan: the focus was on in-group and inter-group interactions, with known and unknown interlocutors. In terms of incorporation of Catalan into daily repertoire (not presented in this chapter), informants described a very wide range of functional and rhetorical practices, ranging from those who neither understood nor used any Catalan in their daily lives to those who used Catalan regularly, in-group and inter-group, and for a variety of purposes. Most informants' descriptions were somewhere in between these two opposite ends of the spectrum.

Informants also described very conflicting constructions of being addressed in Catalan by Catalan speakers, in a general sense, and also in the specific terms of mid-interaction switches to from Castilian to Catalan. A distinction needs to be made here between being addressed by *known* and *unknown* interlocutors. With known interlocutors, an interpersonal norm will often have been established, guiding the linguistic choices made in interactions. In contrast, interactions with unknown interlocutors are first-time interactions with no interpersonal norm. In these cases, interlocutors' linguistic choices will be guided by a range of other factors: for example, interlocutors' sociolinguistic knowledge, domain, appearance or sound of voice of other interlocutor, and previous experience in similar interactions, to name but a few. Several informants interpreted being addressed in Catalan as normal, natural, unconscious, or as the result of confusion. Paulo is Ecuadorian from the Pacific coast and has been in Barcelona for a year:[5]

> Paulo: *verdaderamente estamos en Cataluña y es el dialecto de ellos, el idioma de ellos, y ya no se lo puede cambiar ¿eh?*
> (Paulo: we're actually in Catalonia and it's their dialect, their language, and it can't be changed, right?)

Paulo understands little, and speaks no Catalan. Of additional interest, is Paulo's reference to Catalan first as a dialect and second as a language. The roots of such usage could be traced to the nationalist monolingual discourses of his Latin American country of origin. Yet later, he also uses the same two terms to describe his own variety of Ecuadorian Spanish:

> Paulo: *yo soy ecuatoriano y yo hablo mi lengua mi dialecto y ya ya está*
> (Paulo: I'm Ecuadorian and I speak my language my dialect and that's it)

This would suggest that Paulo's usage of the term *dialecto*, then *idioma/lengua*, can also be seen as a linguistic manifestation of his changing sociolinguistic knowledge; in this instance, a 're-construction' of his existing variety of Latin American Spanish. Paulo, like most other informants, regularly self-corrected in interviews when unsure of what term to use with me: switches from **Girona** to *Gerona*, from *español* to *castellano* (often *espa ... castellano*), for example, in the same sentence.

In a response echoed by several other informants, Hilda and Emi (Colombian teenagers), with their Colombian friend, Diana, describe being addressed in Catalan as normal, in this case, mid-utterance switches to Catalan:

> Diana: *yo pienso que no es por por nada malo ni por discriminación sino o no sé*
> Emi: *que se confunden*
> Hilda: *normal*
> [...]
> Diana: *a mí me pasa, en esa tienda que voy, y pido algo y digo '¿cuánto es?' y me dan el precio en catalán, con números catalanes [...] yo pienso que es porque la señora, a lo mejor está atendiendo a otra persona en catalán, y empieza a hablar conmigo y se le olvida y automáticamente me dice el*

precio o lo que me va a decir me lo dice en catalán, pero no por nada especial,
yo pienso que es que es inconscientemente que lo hacen
(Diana: I don't think it's for for any bad reason or because of discrimination, but that they..
Emi: they get confused
[...]
Diana: it happens to me, in that shop I go to, I ask for something and say 'how much is it?' and they give me the price in Catalan, with numbers in Catalan [...] I think it's because the lady, maybe she's looking after another person in Catalan, and she starts talking to me and she forgets and automatically gives me the price or what she's got to say to me in Catalan, but not for any special reason, I think they do it unconsciously.)

Hilda, Emi and Diana have all taken Catalan classes, and feel that being addressed in Catalan is normal and/or unconscious. Several informants who have never studied Catalan offered similar interpretations.

In contrast, a minority of informants reported negative constructions of being addressed in Catalan, linking it to discrimination and to a sense that Catalan speakers were using Catalan so that they would not be able to understand. One such informant was José Luis, from the Atlantic coast in Colombia. José Luis had been in Barcelona for three years at the time of interview and was working in a hardware store. He spoke no Catalan and only understood a little. José Luis would be normally recognised as Latin American: he speaks a very marked variety of Colombian *costeño* Spanish, and he is of African appearance.[6]

In an interview, José Luis described mid-utterance switches to Castilian at work:

José Luis: *están hablándome y me hablan en castellano, o sea, español normal,[7] y de pronto, hmm, se pasan al catalán*
[...]
José Luis: *me manejan así de esa broma ... me confunden, o sea, tratan de confundirme, eso sí sí*
SM: *¿y por qué crees que hacen eso?*
José Luis: *por discriminación*
[...]
José Luis: *claro, cuando les he molestado entonces se cambian*
SM: *¿sí?*
José Luis: *para que uno no les entienda*
SM: *y ¿qué haces tú?*

José Luis: *digo frases que se usan allá que ellos no las conocen aquí*
SM: *sí, ¿por ejemplo?*
José Luis: *por ejemplo, 'no joda'*
[...]
José Luis: *si vienen acompañados se hablan en catalán entre.., que me parece molesto también*
SM: *¿sí?*
José Luis: *en catalán en catalán, empiezan a hablarlo en catalán entonces no entiendo y es tan fácil hablarlo, en español, para que entendamos los tres*
(José Luis: they're talking to me, and they talk to me in Castilian, or um, normal Spanish, and suddenly, mm, they switch to Catalan
[...]
José Luis: they manipulate me like that with that kinda wind-up, they confuse me, I mean, they try to confuse me, that's for sure, for sure
SM: and why do you think they do that?
José Luis: because of discrimination
[...]
José Luis: of course, when I've annoyed them then they change
SM: yeah?
José Luis: so that you can't understand them
SM: what do you do?
José Luis: I use expressions that are used over there that they don't know here
SM: yeah, for example?
José Luis: for example, 'stop fucking about'
[...]
José Luis: if they come together they speak Catalan among.., which seems annoying to me as well
SM: yeah?
José Luis: in Catalan in Catalan, they start saying it in Catalan then I can't understand and it's so easy to say it, in Spanish, so that the three of us can understand)

In contrast, Claudia is Dominican, married to a Catalan, has a Catalan-speaking daughter, and has been in Catalonia for over 20 years. In two interviews, Claudia described in detail her mixed African and European origins, which included Catalan ancestors. She also equated the historical suffering of the peoples of Hispaniola under Castilianization with that of the Catalans. When I asked her opinion of negative perceptions such as those of José Luis, her construction of such switches to

Catalan was the opposite:

> SM: *¿pensarías que* [to switch to Catalan] *tiene otro significado?*
> *Claudia: no, no suelo ser negativa en ese sentido, no yo no, no, porque es su idioma y lo veo lo más, lo más normal que lo hagan*
> [...]
> Claudia: *yo tengo 19 años aquí en Cataluña, y jamás un catalán-catalán, o sea decir, nunca jamás te hace sentir lo que, por lo menos, me han hecho sentir a mí, lo que me han hecho sentir unos de otra parte de España*
> (SM: do you think it [to switch to Catalan] has any other meaning?
> *Claudia:* no, I'm not usually negative in that sense, no not me, no, because it's their language and I see it as, as completely normal for them to do it
> [...]
> Claudia: I've been here for 19 years in Catalonia, and a Catalan-Catalan has never, or um, they never ever make you feel what, at least, I've been made to feel, how people from other parts of Spain have made me feel)

I was to find similarly conflicting constructions of being addressed in Catalan when I asked informants their views on the *Tu ets mestre* campaign.

Tu ets mestre: Catalan speakers maintaining Catalan with unknown immigrants

When I first heard about the *Tu ets mestre* campaign, its stated aims seemed to contradict my ongoing findings from informants: no new migrant informant had expressed feeling excluded or discriminated against on the grounds that a Catalan speaker has spoken Castilian to them. However, this was only my assumption, my pre-construction of informants' possible responses – I had not actually asked any informants about the campaign. When I did, I was to find that the aims of the campaign would ring true to a certain extent among some Latin Americans, but not all.

Pati, a Colombian domestic worker, brought up the TV campaign *Tu ets mestre* on our way to do a recording of her interactions. She described a phone call to the house where she works, during which the Catalan-speaking interlocutor continued in clear Catalan, while she continued in her marked variety of Colombian Costeño Spanish. She said that this was the first time she could remember this happening in 12 years in Catalonia:

> Pati: *yo me sentí, con mi hermana quizá no* [puts on high exaggerated voice] *'estos catalanes, no sé qué, son muy mal educados', mi hermana, sabes, te has dado cuenta que mi hermana es un poco así, protestor,* [high exaggerated voice] *'que son unos mal educados y que' pero yo me sentí bien, como, integrada*
> SM: *entonces ¿que te hablara en catalán así te gustó?*
> Pati: *sí, yo me sentí muy integrada, en ningún momento me sentí mal*
> (Pati: I felt, my sister probably wouldn't, [puts on a high exaggerated voice] 'those Catalans, you know, they're really rude', you know my sister, you must have realised that she's a bit like that, always protesting, [high exaggerated voice] 'they're so rude, and you know', but I felt good, like, integrated
> SM: so you liked [him] speaking to you like that in Catalan?
> Pati: yeah, I felt really integrated, I didn't feel bad for a moment)

Pati's unelicited response fascinated me, as it forced me to consider my role as a researcher and the pre-constructions (mentioned above) that I had formed around informants' possible constructions. Somewhat unexpectedly for me, Pati's response matched exactly the aims of the *Tu ets mestre* campaign – clearly she had been feeling excluded as Catalan speakers did not allow her to exploit her 'cultural capital': the large passive knowledge of Catalan that she had acquired and which would allow her to feel included by maintaining reciprocal bilingual interactions with no switches either side. Yet her interpretation was the complete opposite of her sister, Iliana, who offered mainly negative constructions of being addressed in Catalan.

I asked Andreína, a Venezuelan student, what she felt about the campaign, referring to the case of Pati:

> Andreína: *una persona que quiere quedarse a vivir en en Cataluña, que quiere interaccionar en la lengua, el que usa el catalán con ella significa que la inserten, que la tomen en cuenta, mientras para otras personas podría ser una manera de de complicarle la vida [...] yo creo que que que van a haber reacciones negativas y positivas, y creo que van a ser más negativas que positivas*
> (Andreína: a person who wants to stay and live in Catalonia, who wants to interact in the language, if someone uses Catalan with her it means that they're including her, they're acknowledging her, whilst for other people it could be a way of making their lives difficult [...]

I think there are going to be negative and positive reactions, and I think they're going to be more negative than positive)

Andreína's view that the campaign did have some worth, but that it would cause more problems than it solves, was one echoed by the majority of other informants. However, I gained an additional perspective while I was recording lunch one day at Claudia's (Dominican-Catalan) house (with her husband, Miquel, and her daughter, Fernanda) The topic of addressing immigrants in Catalan was brought up by Claudia; all present were in favour of the campaign:

Claudia. *hi ha un anunci de la tele que surt un noi que és marroquí, un negre i un altre de, ¿de qué país? que le dicen 'hola Hassan, hola bon dia, parla'm el català, que jo vull aprendre el català'*
[...]
SM: *¿y qué opinan de eso que hay que dirigirse al inmigrante en catalán en vez de en castellano?*
Fernanda: me parece bien
[...]
Miquel: *per ajudar-li a que es trobi millor, perquè és veritat que un immigrant, encara que sigui immigrant, si parla en català, puja la seva ..., no sé*
Fernanda: *qualitat de vida*
Miquel: *qualitat de vida [...] i a la feina si saps parlar català, malgrat que siguis estranger, i sobretot si ets negre, africà, que es vegi, que la gent es dongui compte que sí està parlant català, uf! puja punts, un montón, un montón*
[...]

SM: *pero esa clase de campaña, también, si todos los catalanoparlantes se pusieran así, a hablar catalán con los extranjeros, puede causar problemas también, ¿no?*
Miquel: *no, ¿por qué? [...] no, canvies d'idioma i parles en castellà o en qualsevol idioma, si veus que ell respon bé, pues segueixes parlant en català; si veus que ell et respon en castellà, doncs canvies*
(Claudia: **there's an advert on TV, a guy who's Moroccan, a black guy and another from, what country is it? and they say to him 'hi Hassan, hi, good morning, let's speak Catalan, cos I want to learn Catalan'**

[...]

SM: and what do you think of the idea that you should speak to immigrants in Catalan instead of Castilian?

Fernanda: I think it's good

[...]

Miquel: **to help them to improve their situation, because it's true that immigrants, even though they're immigrants, if they speak Catalan it raises their ... I don't know**

Fernanda: **quality of life**

Miquel: **quality of life** [...] **and at work if you know how to speak Catalan, despite being a foreigner, and especially if you're black, African, you can see, people realise if you're speaking Catalan, uf! you gain points,** loads, loads

[...]

SM: but that type of campaign, also, if all Catalan speakers did that, speaking Catalan with foreigners, it can cause problems too, right?

Miquel: no, why? [...] **no, you change language and speak Castilian or any language, if you see that he responds well, then you carry on in Catalan, if you see that he responds in Castilian, then you change**)

Informants' responses to questions about the *Tu ets mestre* campaign presented me with more conflicting constructions of being addressed/addressing in Catalan. What I found particularly challenging was that the responses of these informants seemed to be valid in terms of distinct sociolinguistic positions that were grounding their constructions.

Reasons for conflicting constructions: knowledgeability and reflexivity

In an attempt to throw some light on the reasons behind such conflicting constructions, I focused my analysis on José Luis's and Claudia's responses above, and considered the conflicting epistemologies that were grounding their constructions. The first thing that came to mind was that José Luis is single, male, newly-arrived, a monolingual speaker of very marked Colombian Spanish, and in a precarious situation as an immigrant. In contrast, Claudia is female, and very settled, married to a Catalan, bilingual, with a bilingual daughter, and living in Catalonia for over a decade. However, I found that other informants who had similar characteristics did not necessarily form associated positive or negative constructions. Equally, both José Luis and Claudia expressed very strong senses of increasing Latino identity, which meant that I could not point to any simple correlation with identity formation.

In order to gain further insight, I began to ask informants why they felt that other Latin Americans were forming such conflicting constructions of being addressed in Catalan. Several informants mentioned linguistic competence, and changes with time:

Andreína (Venezuelan):
SM: *y y ¿cómo te sientes, así, cuando cambian así?*
Andreína: *pues yo,* [laughs] *yo no me siento ni bien ni mal porque como yo entiendo la lengua*
(SM: and, and how do you feel, like, when they change like that?
Andreína: well I, [laughs] I don't feel good or bad as I understand the language)

Emi, Hilda, Diana (Colombians):
Hilda: *antes cuando no entendía me daba rabia porque no lo entendía, pero ahora que lo entiendo me gusta que me hablen en catalán*
Diana: *pero yo pienso que es porque no lo entiendes*
Emi: *porque no lo entienden no se comunican* [...]
Hilda: *para mí se me fue la rabia, para mí el proceso fue así*
(Hilda: before when I couldn't understand it it really annoyed me because I couldn't understand it, but now that I understand it I like them to speak to me in Catalan
Diana: but I think it's because you don't understand
Emi: because they don't understand they can't communicate [...]
Hilda: for me I stopped getting angry, that was how the process was for me)

Tania (Venezuelan):
Tania: *yo a veces me he sentido incómoda, porque sí me ha pasado que en plena conversación cambian al catalán, sobre todo porque no lo manejo del todo bien y la gente que hace el cambio sabe que no lo manejo del todo bien [...] no entendía de pronto lo que querían decir con eso, no lo sabía interpretar [...] después voy entendiendo que es un cambio natural, en la medida de que son bilingües pues es absolutamente normal*
(Tania: sometimes I've felt uncomfortable, because it has happened that right in the middle of a conversation they change to Catalan, especially as I don't speak it very well and the people who make the change know that I don't speak it very well [...] I didn't understand what it might be that they meant by that, I didn't know how to

interpret it [...] afterwards I started to understand that it's a natural change, in keeping with their being bilingual it's absolutely normal)

Iliana (Colombian) mentioned age and location:

> Iliana: *si tú vas a una lencería, por ejemplo, te digo por mi casa, la gente mayor, en español entras hablando español, ellos te siguen hablando catalán, y por aquí la gente te sigue hablando en catalán*
> (Iliana: if you go to a fabric shop, for example, I mean the ones near my house, the old people, you enter speaking Spanish, they carry on speaking to you in Catalan, and round here people keep talking to you in Catalan)

Education, culture, and lack of progress were mentioned by Josep (Catalan) and his Peruvian wife, Karina:

> Karina: *yo creo que es por educación*
> Josep: *es educación, de la cultura*
> Karina: *sí*
> Josep: *la cultura propia que está propia de su país, que es si viene de allí educados de una manera*
> (Karina: I think it's to do with education
> Josep: it's education, the culture
> Karina: yeah
> Josep: the actual culture of their country, it's if they come from there educated in a particular way)

I found informants' perspectives interesting as, viewed together, they brought up issues that related to two wider factors that I felt were underpinning informants' construction processes: changing perceptions along paths of migration and paths of identity; and changing sociolinguistic knowledge, in a new complex, heteroglossic sociolinguistic environment. For example, Karina and Josep mentioned the structures/ culture of the home country which continue to frame the agencies of some individuals after migration; and several informants mentioned how perceptions change with increased competence in Catalan, which can be linked to the changing sociolinguistic knowledge that comes with increased competence.

I found, however, that these perspectives of my informants could not be applied consistently to others' constructions of being addressed in Catalan. For each case where one factor could be linked to another informant, another factor could not. I consequently tried to link the explanations above to wider conceptual factors that could be applied more generally to informants with both positive and negative constructions of being addressed in Catalan.

Two concepts which I believe can account for conflicting constructions of being addressed in Catalan, as presented by José Luis and Claudia above, are their knowledgeability and reflexivity (Giddens, 1984) as social agents. In such terms, a common view of individuals such as José Luis would be as follows: a newly-arrived migrant lacking sociolinguistic knowledge (of the complex sociolinguistic dynamic between Spanish/Castilian and Catalan speakers), whose reflexive monitoring and expectations lead to unsuccessful interactions with Catalan speakers, and to negative, oppositional interpretations (misconstructions even) of social meanings of interactions involving Catalan.

In contrast, a common view of Claudia would be the following: someone who has become more knowledgeable of the sociolinguistic situation in Catalonia over the years due to her high degree of socialization in the Catalan–Castilian dynamic in Catalonia, whose reflexive language use leads to more successful interactions and to positive interpretations of being addressed in Catalan.

My view of José Luis and Claudia, however, is that they are both knowledgeable social agents, albeit at opposite ends of a spectrum of sociolinguistic knowledge, and with distinct epistemological groundings. Whilst José Luis may be less sociolinguistically knowledgeable in terms of certain wider social realities, this does not mean that he is not knowledgeable about the specific interactional strategies that he employs, and about his aims therein in reproducing or challenging the social realities that *he* perceives. Claudia clearly has a higher degree of sociolinguistic knowledge of the Catalan–Castilian dynamic, and she too is knowledgeable of the interactional strategies that she employs. In Claudia's case, however, this does not lead to her challenging what she perceives as social realities.

José Luis and Claudia are also reflexive social agents. They both show the key characteristics of reflexive social practice, as defined by Giddens (1984): (1) they are clearly aware of how they use socially-situated language; (2) their responses would suggest that they monitor their own language use and have clear expectations about the language use of others; and (3) they are able to use language to succeed in interactional aims. In terms of reflexivity, José Luis' reflexive monitoring of interactional situations and his language use would commonly be viewed as unsuccessful and negative. However, my view is that José Luis describes an interaction in which he does reflexively monitor situations and adapts strategies, succeeding in his own interactional aims; these aims appear to have more to do with putting up barriers and maintaining boundaries in order to emphasize non-membership of the other interlocutors' group, even though these aims may have been the opposite at the outset of an interaction. Claudia also monitors situations and adapts strategies, although in her case, success in her interactional aims can be judged in terms of successful inter-group communication, and a sympathetic and mutually-inclusive interpretation of being addressed in Catalan.

A 'new-Catalan' perspective of constructing Catalan

As very able Catalan speakers, who are often visible minorities, 'new-Catalans' constructions of Catalan can be subtle and interesting. One informant, Yanet, would meet the common defining features of a 'new-Catalan'. She is a university student, born and educated in Barcelona, who describes her nationality as Catalan. Yanet's parents are Colombian and she is of mixed African and European appearance. During the interview, Yanet explained that she normally speaks Catalan with her school and university friends, but Castilian/Spanish at home. I referred to negative constructions such as those of José Luis, assuming that, as an able Catalan speaker, Yanet would contradict any negative perception. I was basing this pre-construction on the responses of several informants (as described above) who had explained to me that, as their knowledge of Catalan increases, negative perceptions decrease. However, in asking the question, I had unwittingly struck a rather raw nerve:

Yanet: *a veces sí que notas cierta agresividad como en la manera de diri-girte hacia ti en el idioma como diciendo 'a ver, a ver si hablas catalán'*
[...]
Yanet: *están haciendo una entrevista también de trabajo en castellano, y la persona en un momento dado, cambiar de lengua ¿no? y hablar el catalán peor que yo,* [laughing] *que también te hace gracia una persona de aquí que hablaba el catalán bastante peor que yo*
[...]
SM: *y ¿cuál es la reacción cuando tu catalán es mejor que el catalán de ellos?*
Yanet: *sorpresa, siempre, 'ah ostras, hablas catalán, ah, pues pensaba que no ¿no? y a mí lo, el dolerme el decir pues 'si pensabas que no ¿por qué te diriges a mí en catalán de esta manera' ¿sabes?*
[...]
Yanet: *pero es algo que puede doler, aparte, yo lo digo porque lo he vivido también*
[...]

Yanet: *y he trabajado de camarera ¿no? y pues esto lo vives, y que te hablen en, que tú te diriges a ellos en, en castellano porque no los has oído hablar tampoco, y que te hablan en catalán muy cerrado y mirándote incluso mal, ¿no? entonces allí yo creo que empieza a rozar la discriminación, un poco*
[...]
Yanet: *hay muchos extranjeros y muchos inmigrantes que le cogen manía a la lengua, al catalán, mi tía por ejemplo no habla catalán y lleva 20 años aquí, no lo habla*
(Yanet: sometimes you notice a certain aggression like in the way of being spoken to in the language as if they're saying 'let's see, let's see if you speak Catalan'
[...]
Yanet: they're speaking in Castilian in a job interview, and the person at a given moment, changes language, yeah? and speaks Catalan worse than me [laughing] and it's also amusing someone from here who speaks Catalan quite a lot worse than me
[...]
SM: and what's the reaction when your Catalan is better than theirs?
Yanet: surprise, always, 'wow, you speak Catalan, ah, well, I didn't think you could', you know what I mean? and the thing that, that hurts me, to say like 'if you didn't think I could, why do you address me in Catalan in that way?' you know?
[...]
Yanet: but it's something that can hurt, and also, I'm saying it because I've also been through it
[...]
Yanet: and I've worked as a waitress, right? and well you live through that, that they speak to you in, that you speak to them in, in Castilian as you haven't heard them speak, and they speak to you in a really closed Catalan and even give you dirty looks, you know? then that's when I think it borders on racism, a bit
[...]
Yanet: there are lots of foreigners and lots of immigrants who develop a dislike of the language, of Catalan, my aunt for example doesn't speak Catalan and she's been here for 20 years, she doesn't speak it)

The example of Yanet clearly shows that linguistic competence alone is not the sole determining factor in informants forming positive constructions of being addressed in Catalan – what you look like can be as important as what you sound like. In the example of the service encounter she describes, she addresses unknown informants in Castilian as a normal practice, and gets a response in Catalan, which she constructs negatively. In a separate interview, Yanet's friend, Sara, a white, 20-year-old Catalan-speaking student from a small Catalan-speaking village in the Pyrenees, describes an interesting mirror-image of being a waitress in Barcelona:

Sara: *era camarera de discoteca [...] yo de normal me dirigía en español, en castellano, porque la mayoría de clientes eran castellanos, y lo que me hacía mucha gracia [...] venían catalanes, y los catalanes siempre siempre siempre siempre me pedían lo que querían en español, pero yo me daba cuenta que eran catalanes porque oía, o porque les oía hablar en catalán o por el acento o por lo que fuese, entonces yo les respondía en catalán porque sabía que para ellos les era más cómodo ¿no?, como un poco por educación, y ellos seguían hablando conmigo en castellano, porque una camarera siempre es* [laughing] *un tipo de mujer que.* [...] *les contesto en, pero no es, no les sale, no preguntes por qué* [laughs]
(Sara: I was a waitress in a disco [...] I normally spoke to people in Spanish, in Castilian, because most of the customers were Castilian, and the thing that really made me laugh was [...] Catalans would come, and the Catalans always always always always ordered what they wanted in Spanish, but I realised they were Catalans because I could hear, or because I would hear them speaking in Catalan or by their accent or whatever, so I replied in Catalan because I knew it was more comfortable for them, yeah? kind of to be courteous, and they would carry on talking to me in Castilian, because a waitress is always [laughing] a type of woman that. [...] I answer them in, but no, they can't do it, don't ask me why [laughs])

The two cases above present an interesting 'heteroglossic paradox' that links code selection, place and appearance. The reasons why customers do not speak Catalan back to Sara or Castilian back to Yanet are very complex. However, I would speculate that much of it can be attributed to ascription of ethnolinguistic identity according to physical appearance, setting, and the perceived associated social positions: key factors in the heteroglossic construction processes of Catalan speakers, Spanish-speaking Latin Americans, and 'new Catalans'.

Conclusion

Through the interview data analysed in this chapter, I have illustrated a range of conflicting constructions of being addressed in Catalan, and have presented a number of reasons why informants felt that conflicting processes may be taking place. I have added my view that all individuals should be considered as valid, knowledgeable, and reflexive social agents irrespective of whether they form positive or negative constructions at this level. What is normal for one may not be for another, yet it is still valid.

The arrival of hundreds of thousands of allochthonous Spanish-speaking new migrants in the territory of the autochthonous Catalan-speaking linguistic minority of the Spanish state has fundamentally challenged what is 'normal' in normalization. In the highly sensitized, heteroglossic sociolinguistic setting that is Catalonia, the linguistic choices that Spanish-speaking Latin Americans and Catalan-speakers reflexively make in their interactions in shared spaces are highly complex, linked to wider issues of national identity and social/linguistic/minority rights. Both sides would appear in many instances to be applying their sociolinguistic knowledge at the synchronic level of interaction from different diachronic perspectives. And these applications of sociolinguistic knowledge can be determined by conflicting epistemologies that evolve and change along individuals' paths of migration and identity formation, most notably when the applications of knowledge take on the form of interactional strategies, in particular code selection and codeswitching.

In conclusion, I highlighted earlier the key role of knowledgeability and reflexivity in recursive social practice. If we are to accept, as I do, Giddens' view that the relation between structure and agency is essentially a recursive one, then at some stage, not only language policies, but also the historical imaginings of the contested Catalan nation at a structural level, will have to respond in a recursive manner, reflecting new sociolinguistic practices. At present, 'structure', in the form of the language policies of linguistic normalization, in particular the positioning of the Catalan language as preferential and as *the* key marker of being Catalan, is responding to new agency 'non-recursively'. In this sense, policy-makers are holding out against external new agencies, attempting to mould them into a linguistic normalization model based on a local autochthonous Castilian–Catalan model, rather than a global–local, allochthonous–autochthonous view of 'normal' practices in a rapidly changing sociolinguistic environment.

Notes

1   I use 'Catalan/Catalan speaker' to refer to individuals whose main language is Catalan; 'Castilian/Castilian speaker' for speakers whose main language is an Iberian variety of Spanish; and 'Latin American Spanish/Spanish speaker' for

speakers whose main language is a variety of Latin American Spanish. This is to distinguish between the three codes and does not take into account the many complexities involved in naming these codes.

2 In Marshall (2005), I also highlight the following: (1) a clear link between the diachronic and the synchronic; and (2) parallel paths of migration and of identity-formation, along which epistemologies evolve and change, playing an important role in determining how individuals apply their sociolinguistic knowledge in interactions.

3 In the main text, Spanish will be presented in italics and Catalan in bold and italics.

4 I interviewed 44 informants, and recorded the interactions (in-group and inter-group) of 11 informants. I have limited the selection of data samples presented here to individuals' self-reporting in interviews of how they interpret being addressed in Catalan. A discussion of the complex issues related to informants' self-report data *vis-à-vis* their recorded interactions can be found in Marshall (2005).

5 Pseudonyms are used throughout, and details changed to anonymize informants. In transcribed text, Spanish/Castilian is presented in italics and Catalan in bold and italics. The English translation employs bold for Catalan. As I am not focusing on intonation, pitch, pausing and so on, I use the following simple transcription conventions in data samples:

[...]   shows that I have edited out sections of text
...   shows that a speaker has stopped abruptly in the middle or at the end of a word
...   and shows a pause of between two and five seconds
[comment/description of setting or manner]
        my comments about the language, the situation, or the manner of speech are presented in brackets.

Commas have two functions: to indicate pauses of less than two seconds, and indicate breaks between chunks of language (as would full stops and commas in written text when there is no notable pause).

6 A number of informants mentioned their physical appearance as being related to their interpretations of being addressed in Catalan, in particular their expectations about which code they should be addressed in. In such cases, I describe the informant's physical appearance, using the term 'Latin American' for those who would readily be identified as Latin American by their appearance, and 'African' for informants of African/African-Caribbean ancestry.

7 Parallels can be drawn between José Luis' use of '*me hablan en castellano, o sea, español normal*' and the two possible interpretations of Paulo's use of the term 'dialect' to refer to Catalan.

10

Language Contact between Galician and Spanish: Conflict or Harmony? Young People's Linguistic Attitudes in Contemporary Galicia

Bernadette O'Rourke

Introduction

Much of Spain's history has been characterized by policies of political centralization and linguistic uniformity which date from the initial consolidation of political unity by the Catholic Kings, Isabel and Ferdinand in the second half of the fifteenth century to the strongly centralist dictatorship of the Franco regime in the twentieth century. Although as Martin (2002: 18) points out, no official linguistic laws were passed during Isabel and Ferdinand's reign, it nonetheless marks the emergence of an implicit link between the Castilian language and a move towards political and administrative power. More explicit references to linguistic uniformity in Spain were to appear during the Bourbon Dynasty in the eighteenth century where the use of languages other than Castilian was prohibited in domains of culture and education (Martin, 2002: 21). In the early years of the Franco dictatorship (1939–75), the use of languages other than Castilian Spanish was prohibited from all areas of public life and penalties were imposed on anyone who disobeyed.

However, policies of linguistic uniformity in the Spanish context, which were closely linked to political centralization failed in that linguistic diversity continued to exist and languages such as Catalan, Basque, Galician and Valencian continued to be spoken. For the communities in which they were spoken, these languages came to be symbolic of the ongoing historic tensions between a Castilian-speaking centre of political and economic power and the socio-economically and politically dominated linguistic communities of the peripheries.

Language survival and decline in the Galician context

The Galician-speaking population in the extreme north-western corner of the Iberian Peninsula would seem to have been most successful in resisting linguistic shift to Castilian. The strong survival of the Galician language can at least in part be explained by Galicia's geographical isolation from the rest of Spain. Galicia borders Portugal to the south, has two long coastlines to the north and west and mountains along the border with other parts of Spain to the east. The geographic isolation of Galicia, which is also linked to its history of poor economic development, did not attract the waves of Spanish-speaking migrants from other parts of Spain which was taking place in Catalonia and the Basque Country (Mar-Molinero, 1997). However, while Galicians were not affected by in-migration, they frequently found the need to migrate to other parts of Spain in search of work or to emigrate to Europe or Latin America.

As well as their peripheral location with respect to the rest of Spain, Galician speakers have tended to be widely dispersed within Galicia itself. An almost entirely agricultural region, at the turn of the twentieth century, over 90 per cent of Galicians continued to live in rural areas with the remaining less than 10 per cent concentrated in Galicia's urban centres (Fernández Rodríguez, 1993: 28), a divide which can be taken to correspond roughly to the linguistic divide between Galician-speaking rural areas and Galicia's predominantly Spanish-speaking cities. The very isolated nature of the Galician-speaking rural population is reflected in the fact that in 1877, over 88 per cent of Galicians continued to be monolingual Galician speakers (Fernández Rodríguez and Rodríguez Neira, 1994: 52-3). Compared to other parts of Spain, the modernization of Galician society occurred at a much later stage and even by the end of the twentieth century, according to Monteagudo and Santamarina (1993: 123), 'the substitution of a precapitalist economy based on agriculture for an economy founded on industry was still far from complete in Galicia'.

The strongly Castilianizing potential of formal functional domains such as education and the written media seemed to have had little direct impact on the linguistic practices of the Galician population, the majority of whom were not exposed to formal education and as a result possessed low levels of literacy (Bouzada, 2003: 326). Therefore, geographic, socio-economic and cultural isolation of Galician speakers to a large extent explain an unusually long period of linguistic sheltering from Spanish. However, as the society began to modernize during the twentieth century, Galician speakers became less isolated and began to come into more direct contact with areas in which Spanish was used. The impact of urbanization and industrialization on geographically isolated language communities, such as the Galician case, is well-documented in the literature on language maintenance and shift (for example Gal, 1979; Dorian, 1981). While Galician and other minority language cases provide support for the thesis that because of the effects of modernization and globalization, our societies are becoming linguistically homogenous, this perspective on language maintenance and shift tends to naturalize the decline of some languages and the rise of others. As Tovey and Share (2003: 333) suggest, the relationship between the majority and a minority language is not one of modernity versus backwardness but one of power.

Therefore, it has not been the modernization or globalization process *per se* that has led to the shift towards Spanish in more recent years, but rather the implicit understanding amongst Galician speakers that Spanish is the language of power and social mobility. The very factors (ignorance, poverty and rurality) which had allowed Galician to survive centuries of linguistic dominance as a subordinate of Spanish, were to provide the rationalization for many Galician migrants to abandon their language as they moved from the countryside to Galicia's cities in search of work during the second half of the twentieth century. Socio-structural changes in Galicia, coupled with the coercive linguistic policies of the Franco regime (1939–75), therefore, seemed to be working simultaneously against the language in the second half of the twentieth century.

However, decentralization policies in Spain since the 1980s, in line with changes in political ideologies which support difference and pluralism as opposed to unity and monoculturalism, have helped create a new environment for Galician along with the other languages of Spain including Catalan, Basque and Valencian (see, Casesnoves, Sankoff and Turell, this volume). The Galician language now enjoys constitutional protection under Article 3 of the 1978 Spanish Constitution and holds co-official status with Spanish within the Autonomous Community of Galicia. Article five of the Galician Autonomous Statutes, approved in 1981, confirms the status of the language as Galicia's 'own language' (*lingua propia*) and guarantees its 'normal' and official use along with Spanish in all domains of public and cultural life.

Measures to increase the 'normal' use of Galician have taken the form of what can be referred to as *normalization planning* (Mar-Molinero,

2000: 80). The concept of *normalization*, which is very specific to the Spanish context, was first coined by Catalan sociolinguists, Aracil, Ninyoles and Vallverdú and was subsequently used as a model for language planners within Catalonia itself as well as in Galicia and the Basque Country (see, Hamel, this volume). Although the concept is widely used in the Spanish context by academics, policy makers and even amongst the general public, the way in which the term is interpreted across and amongst these different groups is not always the same. This had led to the somewhat confusing array of both technical and common sense meanings which have come to be associated with the term.

In Spanish linguistic terminology normalization (*normalización*) and normativization (*normativización*) often appear in discussions of *normalization planning*. On the one hand, normalization tends to refer to the extension of a standardized language to all areas of public life, corresponding to the concept of 'status planning' commonly used in English language terminology (Kloss, 1969; Cooper, 1989). On the other hand, normativization involves the selection and codification of a standard language and corresponds more specifically to the concept of 'corpus planning' in the terminology used in English.

According to Cobarrubias (1987: 60 cited in Mar-Molinero, 2000: 80), normalization consists of three specific tasks. The first of these involves empowering minority languages so as to allow them to satisfy the communicative needs of a modern society. In the Galician context, such empowerment is being facilitated through the inclusion of the language in the education system, the media and administration, domains of public life in Galicia which were previously dominated by Spanish. These measures can be understood in the context of the normalization or status planning aspect described above. Some of the most significant provisions in the process of linguistic normalization in Galicia have been in the education system (Portas, 1997: 186). With the drawing up of the 1983 Linguistic Normalization Act (*Lei de Normalizión Lingüística*), the Galician autonomous government (*Xunta de Galicia*), issued a decree making Galician a compulsory subject along with Spanish, at all levels of education up to but not including university. The extension of the Galician language to a key area of public life such as the school, has the potential of raising the status of the language and instilling more positive attitudes towards it, especially amongst the younger generation. The increased presence of the language in the media further extends the presence of Galician to a domain which was previously dominated entirely by Spanish. The Galician language channel (*Televisión Galega*, TVG) broadcasts entirely in the Galician language and provides an important public space in which the local language can now be heard.

The second task in normalization according to Cobarrubias is to increase the number of speakers of a language and to raise the communicative competence of its current users. Although the majority (68 per cent) of Galicians continue to be active users of the language (Fernández Rodríguez and Rodríguez Neira, 1994), the number of younger speakers has declined dramatically over the past fifty years and less than half of those in the 16–25 age category report regular use of the language. There has also been a notable decline in the intergenerational transmission of the language of parents to children within the home, a trend which is especially acute amongst those living in urban areas. Therefore, particularly in these urban areas, the school can be seen to play a critical role in the production of new speakers of the language. For existing Galician speakers, especially amongst the younger generation, formal education in the language also has the potential to increase their communicative competence in other formal domains such as science and technology. This of course also has a status planning function whereby the social domains of use are extended in line with the 'normal' functioning of a modern society.

The third task of normalization according to Cobarrubias involves expanding the geographic scope of the language within a given area. The predominantly rural nature of Galicia's population is being gradually eroded by increased migration to Galicia's cities, traditional Spanish-speaking strongholds. As already highlighted, the inclusion of Galician in the education system since the 1980s is seen to have an important role in the spread of Galician amongst the younger generation within predominantly Spanish-speaking urban environments (Bouzada *et al.*, 2002). The Galicianization of institutions and the training of public administrative employees and officials who form part of the Galician autonomous structure also has the potential to increase the presence of the language across a broader geographical area. Similarly, the inclusion of the language in the mass media increases its presence in Spanish-speaking homes in urban areas. Moreover, because of modern technology, the transmission of television and radio programmes through internet and satellite can potentially extend the presence of the language beyond the Galician borders.

The effects of linguistic policy in Galicia

The initial effects of language policies in Galicia are well-documented in the findings of the Sociolinguistic Atlas of Galicia (*Mapa Sociolingüístico de Galicia*, MSG), an extensive sociolinguistic study of the Galician population (Fernández Rodríguez and Rodríguez Neira, 1994, 1995, 1996). The first volume of the report points to high levels of proficiency in the Galician language across all sectors of the Galician population. Over 97 per cent understand the language and as many as 86 per cent report an ability to speak it. Comparatively, however, more formal skills such as reading and writing are much lower with only 45 per cent of the population report an ability to read Galician and as few as 27 per cent report written competence in the language. Low literacy levels in Galician can of course be explained by the historical absence of the language from formal education and as a written medium prior to the 1980s. The positive reinstatement of Galician in the area of education since then does seem to have brought about a considerable increase in literacy levels in the language amongst the younger generation. Almost three-quarters of those in the 16–25 age group report being able to read Galician well or quite well and a majority (64 per cent) report high levels of written competence in the language.

Despite generally high levels of oral language proficiency amongst the entire Galician population, not all Galicians put their skills into actual language use. Active use of the language is highest amongst the oldest age category, with 85 per cent reporting 'habitual' use of the language. The lowest levels of reported use are to be found amongst the 16–25 age group, less than half of whom use the language habitually. Galician speakers continue to be concentrated in lower socio-economic groups, amongst those with low levels of education and living in most rural areas. Spanish speakers, on the other hand, tend to be predominantly within the upper middle class sectors of Galician society, possess high levels of education and reside in more urban settings.

Perhaps more telling of the relative success of recent linguistic policies in Galicia are the findings on changes in attitudes towards the language within the population. The third volume of the MSG report is dedicated to the findings of attitudinal research which was used to measure Galicians' attitudes towards and perceptions of the language, its speakers and its presence within Galician society. On a five-point scale where one represents most negative and five most positive attitudes, Galicians score a 3.6 average (MSG, 1996: 80) in their ratings of the Galician language. Although positive attitudes are to be found across all sectors of Galician society, the younger generation (those between 16 and 25 years old) score highest on the attitudinal scale (3.75 on the five-point scale). Those with high levels of education and from middle-class backgrounds also show more consolidated support for the language, especially in attitudes towards the transmission of Galician to the next generation

(MSG, 1996: 559) and towards Galician as a symbol of identity. Nevertheless, as the MSG (1994) report on language behaviour clearly shows, positive attitudes are not being matched by increased language use amongst these sectors of the population. However, given the mediating import of symbolic values, it can be hypothesized that the more positive attitudes expressed by the younger generation of Galicians as well as middle-class educated sectors of Galician society provide an indicator of future linguistic change amongst these groups. Linguistic attitudes tend to be more usefully interpreted as pre-behavioural changes which may not have as yet become apparent through actual language use (Baker, 1992: 16; Woolard and Gahng, 1990: 312). The fact that Galician is most highly supported by younger age groups, on whom the future of the language depends, provides an indication of the direction that changes for the language are likely to take.

It is also significant that middle-class sectors of Galician society are attaching a high symbolic value to the language and are supportive of the need to transmit the language to the next generation, given that such groups were in the past least supportive of the language in these areas. Language maintenance and shift theorists (Boyd, 1985; Crystal, 1999) highlight the importance of engaging support from higher social classes in society in the process of language recovery as these groups are often instrumental in providing the necessary leadership that can bring about mobilization for language change to occur. Moreover, changes in attitudes and behaviour tend to filter down through the social hierarchy, with those at the upper end of the social scale providing role models for the rest of society. The ideas about what constitute prestige and status symbols tend to be developed amongst upwardly mobile or dominant groups. The attitudes towards and perceptions of the Galician language amongst these groups, therefore, can be extremely powerful in defining the terms on which other members of society evaluate their situations and the meanings which come to be attached to cultural symbols such as language.

The MSG report clearly indicates that the new socio-political context in which Galicia has autonomous status within Spain and the co-official status which the language now enjoys is being internalized by key social groups within Galician society. Most consolidated support is to be found amongst the younger generation, amongst sectors of the population with highest levels of education and the middle classes. Paradoxically, these are the very groups which show lowest levels of language use. The remainder of this chapter, therefore, looks within these three social groups and explores in some more depth, the possible reasons why language support is highest amongst these sectors of Galician society. In analyzing these sub-groups in isolation, further insights are gained into the factors which are determining language attitudes amongst young, middle class, educated sectors of the Galician population. Such an analysis also seeks to understand the paradoxical mismatch between language attitudes and language use which seems to be most pronounced within these social groups.

The sociolinguistic study and methodology employed

The following sections report on the findings of a piece of sociolinguistic research carried out at the University of Vigo, situated close to the southern coastal city of Vigo, Galicia's largest and most industrial centre. In linguistic terms it is also one of the most Castilianized areas of Galicia with two-thirds of the Vigo population reporting exclusive or predominant use of Castilian (Vaamonde *et al.*, 2003).

Quantitative data were collected from a representative sample of undergraduate students attending this institution during the academic year 2002–03. The sample was stratified according to the four main academic disciplines offered at the university which included students pursuing degrees in the areas of humanities, technology, business and science. A total of 725 respondents completed a self-administered sociolingusitic questionnaire within which were included a range of attitudinal statements and questions on different aspects relating to the Galician language, its speakers and its use. A series of in-depth interviews with a further 12 students constituted the qualitative phase of the research.

Choice of respondents

There were several reasons for choosing to carry out the research in a university context and amongst university students. A major one was ease of access to the university by acquaintances who worked in the institution. Additionally, undergraduate university populations are pre-selected for age and a large number of respondents could be tested at the same time. Moreover, the completion of a questionnaire is an activity which is already considered socially appropriate and meaningful in classroom situations. Students were therefore more likely to be able to make sense of the survey as an event and respond with less difficulty than might occur in other settings (Woolard, 1989: 102).

However, as well as the practicalities associated with researching student populations, there are also a number of theoretical considerations which made the choice of this group meaningful as well as expedient for the objectives of this research. The age, social class and educational level of university groups mirror quite closely the three social categories identified in the MSG as having most consolidated positive attitudes towards the Galician language. Firstly, the age range of the student group corresponds to the 16–25 age category in the MSG, that is, the younger generation of Galicians. Secondly, as university students, this group possesses high levels of what Bourdieu (1991) refers to as 'cultural capital' in the form of educational qualifications. Such qualifications can in turn be converted to 'economic capital' through which social mobility can be achieved, gaining these students access to middle-class occupational sectors of the labour market. Amongst these university students are likely to be for example engineers, lawyers, teachers, civil servants and so on of the future.

Linguistic attitudes amongst Vigo students

The statistical technique of factor analysis[1] confirmed two dimensions of meaning underlying the response patterns of Galician informants to attitudinal statements and questions contained within the sociolinguistic questionnaire. The first attitudinal dimension identified in the study combined items related to the transmission of the minority language to the next generation with more general issues such as the level of passive support for the language within the Galician society as well as direct questioning of respondents' perceptions about the future of the Galician language. As an attitudinal dimension it thus represents a broad range of components, incorporating a number of sub-themes which it was hypothesized, could be considered important determinants for the survival of the Galician language (perceived utility, suitability for the modern world, desired future of the language, societal support for the language and the inclusion of the language in education).

The second attitudinal dimension which emerged from a factor analysis of attitudinal items, measured the role of Galician as a symbol of group or ethnic identity. The 'integrative' or 'solidarity' dimension of language attitudes which is being measured in this dimension, stems from the idea that language binds, or integrates people into a community of shared understandings and hence identity. The language and identity perspective as an attitudinal dimension is based on the well-established premise that language can play a key role in defining or symbolizing a sense of 'ethnic' or group identity, thus making it a valuable resource to be protected. Anderson (1991: 133), for example, suggests that language constitutes an important symbol of identity because of its capacity for generating imagined communities and building on solidarities particular to a group. Castells (1997: 52) also highlights the symbolic importance of language in the context of globalization suggesting that

> in a world submitted to cultural homogenisation by the ideology of modernization and the power of global media, language, as a direct expression of culture, becomes the trench of cultural resistance, the last bastion of self-control, the refuge of identifiable meaning.

It was thus hypothesized that insights into the vitality of Galician could be gained by analyzing the degree to which respondents valued the language as a symbol of group or ethnic identity.

Support for the societal presence of the Galician language

The responses given by Vigo students to the range of the attitudinal statements contained within the first attitudinal dimension highlight generally strong support for the Galician language. Of the different options provided, 61 per cent of respondents would like to see a bilingual Galicia in which Galician would be the main language. The number of students who wish to see Galician discarded or forgotten was negligible (less than 1 per cent) as was the number who opted for complete mono-lingualism in Galician (5 per cent). The second most popular option was bilingualism with Spanish as the main language but this constituted a minority of students (19 per cent).

A number of items within this attitudinal dimension point to the positive effect that the process of linguistic normalization seems to be having on the younger generation of Galicians. It is for example significant that 86 per cent of students queried disagree with the statement that 'Galician is not suitable for business, science and technology'[2] given that up until a few decades ago these were domains from which Galician was excluded. While it is unlikely from a linguistic point of view that languages are more or less equipped to fulfil different societal functions, such value judgements are frequently made (Edwards, 1994). The status planning element of linguistic policy which has led to the more explicit presence of the Galician language in public spaces such as the school, the media and administration seems to have put in place new social conventions influencing perceptions about the relative prestige of the language.

The relative success that the process of linguistic normalization seems to be having is also clear from the fact that 81 per cent disagree that 'The extension of Galician in all areas of public life is impossible' and that the language should be included in areas where it has not yet become normalized with 60 per cent agreeing that 'Shop signs should be in Galician'. The perceived relevance and importance of Galician in contemporary Galician society is also highlighted in the overwhelming disagreement with statements suggesting that the maintenance of the language is a waste of time (93 per cent) or that there should be cuts in financial support for efforts to maintain the language (84 per cent).

Another key finding in this study is the explicitly expressed desire amongst respondents to transmit the Galician language to the next generation. While few opt for a monolingual upbringing in either Galician or Spanish, there does seem to be strong support for some form of bilingualism. The preferred option is one in which both languages are equally present – 69 per cent in the case of the language that should be transmitted in the home and 77 per cent in the case of formal schooling. The fact that the majority of students surveyed were between the ages of 18 and 24, and thus in the transitional stage between adolescence and adulthood, provides insights into possible behavioural patterns of Galicia's parents of the future. It is worth noting that 51 per cent of the students queried at the University of Vigo were brought up in Spanish-speaking homes. Thus, the positive dispositions held by this group of students may very well be indicative of behavioural change and increased use of Galician in the future.

Language as a symbol of ethnic identity

Responses to items contained within the second attitudinal dimension point to strong support for Galician as a symbol of a Galician identity. As many as 87 per cent agreed that 'Without Galician, Galicia would lose its identity as a separate culture', and 79 per cent of students were of the opinion that Galicia would not really be Galicia without a Galician-speaking population. Even more significant is that for the majority (70 per cent) of Vigo students, language constitutes the most important element in the construction of a Galician identity, thus acting as what Smolicz (1995) refers to as a 'core value' in demarcating a sense of Galicianness.

Factors influencing language attitudes
amongst Vigo students

Although students at the University of Vigo are generally supportive of the measures to ensure the presence of Galician within Galician society and value the language as a symbol of identity, closer analysis identified certain sub-groups within the student population as having more consolidated positive attitudes than others.[3] The three variables on which attitudes towards Galician were found to be most clearly distinguishable were, firstly, the way in which students defined themselves as part of a collective ethnic group; secondly, their political ideology; and finally, the degree to which Galician formed part of students habitual linguistic practices.[4] Most positive attitudes were to be found amongst those who define their sense of collective identity in terms of a Galician as opposed to a Spanish collective identity. This strong sense of 'Galicianness' was also closely related to support for the Galician Nationalist Party (*Bloque Nacionalista Galego*, BNG) as opposed to support for Galician branches of the two main political parties, the centre-right Popular Party (*Partido Popular*, PP) and the centre-left Socialist Party (*Partido Socialista Obrero Español*, PSOE) or amongst those students who did not support any particular political ideology. Finally, a strong identification with a Galician national collective was also related to higher levels of use of Galician, with those who defined themselves in terms of a Galician ethnic identity generally reporting Galician as their habitual language.

The role of nationalist movements and the conscious organization of language loyalty resulting from such movements have been credited with upgrading the value of minority languages in many parts of the world (for example Roberts and Williams, 1980, for Wales; Woolard, 1989, and Paulston, 1994, for Catalonia). Strong identification with and recognition of a Galician ethnic or national identity amongst Vigo students would seem to have increased significantly the value these students attach to the language compared with those who define their sense of collective identity, partially or fully in the context of the Spanish State. Moreover, more favourable attitudes towards the language as a result of a strongly held nationalist ideology also take on what Smolicz and Secombe (1988) refer to as a *personal positive evaluation* whereby language commitment (as expressed by a favourable disposition towards language) is put into practice.

The fact that identity is more strongly related to the 'habitual' language of the speaker as opposed to the first language in which these Galician students learned to speak in the home is also significant and would seem to indicate that language loyalty is not necessarily strongest amongst young Galicians whose mother tongue is Galician.[5] Instead, what seems be more important is the degree to which the language forms part of their 'habitual' linguistic repertoire with those reporting predominant or exclusive use of Galician showing most favourable attitudes. This finding points to a possible trend in language shift amongst those brought up speaking Spanish, a trend which is possibly being influenced by the conscious organization of language loyalty through an ideological orientation towards Galician nationalism. The findings of the current study also revealed that attitudes are strongly influenced by students' political orientation, with supporters of the politics of the Galician Nationalist Party (*Bloque Nacionalista Galego*, BNG) displaying most favourable attitudes towards the language.

In explaining the relationship found in this study between ethnicity, habitual language, political ideology and language attitudes, Paulston's (1994) conceptual model for the prediction of maintenance or loss of a minority language provides a particularly useful framework. This framework has previously been used by Del Valle (2000) as a means of understanding the trend towards the substitution of Spanish for Galician in contemporary Galician society as a whole. The model characterizes different types of social mobilization adopted by minority groups on a four-point continuum ranging from *ethnicity* to *geographic nationalism*. Paulston (1994) uses the concept of social mobilization to describe firstly, the level of recognition amongst members of a minority group of certain cultural features (including language) particular to the group, and, secondly, the perception that the minority group has of its relation with some dominant 'other'. In the Galician context, that dominant 'other' is the Spanish State of which Galicia, as one of Spain's Autonomous Communities, forms a part. Over one-third of the students queried in this study defined themselves as Galician compared to the remaining two-thirds who defined their identity partially or exclusively in the context of the Spanish State. The type of social mobilization which characterizes the latter group can be defined as *ethnicity* which, within Paulston's (1994: 30–1) framework, is a form of mobilization based on learned behaviour associated with a common past and common cultural values and beliefs but in which there is no perceived power struggle with another ethnic group. Rather than seeing their relationship with the Spanish State as a point of tension, this group of students sees themselves as forming part of that political entity. Paulston (1994) predicts that the closer a minority group's social mobilization comes to *ethnicity* the more likely they are to lose the minority language and to assimilate to the dominant group. This trend amongst the majority of these Vigo students reflects what Del Valle (2000: 117) sees as also being the predominant type of social mobilization at work in Galicia and which explains the ongoing shift in the direction of Spanish.

However, language use as an aspect of identity increases for minority groups where *ethnicity* turns 'militant' (Paulston 1994: 32), and where the form of social mobilization adopted resembles that of *ethnic movement*, the second point on Paulston's continuum. In addition to identifying with common cultural values such as a specific language, the members of minority groups who fall into the *ethnic movement* category see themselves competing with another ethnic majority for scarce goods and resources. As a result, language becomes symbolic of the power struggle between the minority and the dominant group. According to Del Valle (2000: 117), a small though significant percentage of the Galician population participates in this type of social mobilization and might even be described as moving towards Paulstons's (1994) third point on the social mobilization continuum, namely *ethnic nationalism*. The latter type of social mobilization incorporates the demand for territorial access on the part of the minority group and a possible move towards independence. In this group Del Valle (2000: 117) includes Galician nationalists, a group which he sees as being well-articulated around a political coalition of parties which include the Galician Nationalist Party (*Bloque Nacionalista Galego*, BNG).

Vigo students who define themselves as Galician and who are also supportive of the BNG would seem to recognize more explicitly their participation in a power struggle with another ethnic group. This sub-group of the student population appears to move beyond the more passive position of *ethnicity* and towards a more militant stance, whereby ideological support for the language is converted to language use. In effect therefore, this sub-group expresses a *personal positive evaluation* (Smolicz and Secombe, 1988) of the minority language whereby language commitment is put into practice. This interpretation is also supported by the comments made by students such as Alexandra from the city of Vigo who was brought up speaking Spanish but who like an increasing number of young urban Galicians, made a conscious decision to switch to Galician. Alexandra's desire to use Galician may be interpreted as a way of constructing a specifically Galician identity, not only in opposition to the Spanish nation-state, but also as a strategy which allows her to maintain her sense of identity and to challenge the threat of homogenization in the context of an increasingly globalized world:

> when you begin to become aware of where you live, of the problems that they suffered historically, you realise what the situation is that it is not normal ... that it is not logical to lose our language, our culture ... you see that everywhere we are being bombarded with

things from outside Galicia ... then you say, well perhaps things will have to change in some way then if you see that your language in being lost what do you to prevent this ... well use it! (My translation)[6]

Manuel Castells (1997: 66) characterizes the emergence of challenges from below as evidence of the increasing influence of 'identities of resistance', arguing that they are defensive reactions to modernization and globalization. He suggests that

When the world becomes too large to be controlled, social actors aim at shrinking it back to their size and reach. When networks dissolve time and space, people anchor themselves in places and recall their historic memory.

Although ethnicity, political ideology and habitual language constitute the three factors which best explain attitudinal variation amongst students at the University of Vigo, a number of other factors were also found to affect attitudes towards Galician, albeit in a more minor way. There were, for instance, differences between students on the basis of the degree course being pursued, with those in the humanities reporting more positive attitudes than, for example, technology students. At this early stage in their career paths, differences in attitudes towards Galician across Vigo students according to their academic field of study seem to be emerging. When asked about the perceived utility of Galician in their job prospects, 63 per cent of students taking humanities-type courses were returned as saying that the language was very or fairly important. This figure compares with 17 per cent in the case of technology students, 29 per cent for those in science and 33 per cent of business students. Thus, for students of humanities, amongst whom we are likely to find the potential teaching and cultural professionals of the future, Galician would seem to be recognized as a valued commodity. Linguistic policies appear to be having some success in changing the 'rules' of the social mobility process (Ó Riagáin, 1997) in certain sectors of the Galician labour market. However, as yet these policies do not appear to be broad enough to affect sectors outside of those most closely connected to the administrative structures of the Galician Autonomous Community. Therefore, according to Bouzada (2003: 332) the identification of upward social mobility with Spanish continues to be dominant and that

the sensibilities of the business world, in general removed from the expressive caprices of the cultural world are routinely well-ensconced within a favourable instrumental concept of Spanish.

The continued link between upward social mobility and Spanish can also perhaps be used to explain some of the underlying stigmas which continue to be at least implicitly associated with the Galician language (González *et al.*, 2003; Bouzada *et al.*, 2002; Iglesias, 2002). Although explicit prejudices against the language were not detected amongst Vigo students, certain discourses point to the continued presence of some of the former stigmas associated with knowing and speaking Galician. It would seem from the findings of this study that the full dissolution of deep-rooted prejudices against the language has not yet been fully achieved given that a very sizeable minority of Vigo students (41 per cent) agree that 'Most people see things associated with Galician as old-fashioned'. Even more pertinent were comments made during in-depth discussions with students on these issues which further highlighted some of the stigmas which continue to be associated with Galician and Galician speakers. Adjectives such as 'ugly', 'inferior', 'uncultured', 'stupid' were among those which appeared in the discourses produced by students. Eliminating these more deep-rooted stigmas would seem to be the greatest challenge facing language planners in their efforts to curb the ongoing trend of language shift to Spanish.

Nevertheless, although these tensions continue to exist in the Galician-Spanish language contact situation, from the data analysed in this research there are also signs that speaking Galician has become more acceptable and students at the University of Vigo report tolerance towards speakers of both languages in conversational interaction. The reported behaviour amongst this particular group of students was that one's habitual language was maintained and that young Galician speakers, especially, no longer felt obliged to switch to Spanish in interpersonal interaction. May (2001: 14) points out that long-term success of minority language policies rests on gaining a sufficient degree of support from majority language speakers or what Grin (2003), terms increased levels of 'tolerability' to facilitate the use of the language amongst the minoritized group. Bilingual conversations are of course facilitated in the Galician-Spanish language contact situation by the closeness in linguistic terms between the two languages in contact. Almost all (99 per cent) of students at the University of Vigo reported being able to understand Galician very or fairly well. Therefore, when the majority (93 per cent) of students said 'I prefer to speak Castilian with people who do not understand Galician', students probably had non-Galicians rather than Galicians in mind, in which they included people from other parts of Spain and outside of Spain. With non-Galicians, linguistic accommodation through the use of Spanish was the reported linguistic norm amongst Vigo students and continued use of Galician in such contexts was seen as largely radical and unwanted behaviour. It is also significant that more than half of the students disagree that 'People from outside Galicia who come to live here should learn Galician'. The students interviewed during the study appeared to take pride in their 'open' attitude to the use of Spanish with those who were unwilling or unable to speak in Galician and regarded this 'linguistic openness' as a marker of Galician 'humility' and 'friendliness'. These latter characteristics were seen as key elements in the construction of a specifically Galician identity. Respondents made frequent reference to the Catalan context and Catalans' unwillingness (as perceived by students) to use Spanish with non-Catalans was strongly condemned (for some comparisons, see, Casesnoves, Sankoff and Turell, this volume).

However, while a switch to Spanish with outsiders is considered 'polite' behaviour, Bourdieu (1977: 662) points out that politeness in itself is not a neutral act but instead 'contains a politics, a practical immediate recognition of social classifications and hierarchies'. In the Galician context, these hierarchies can be understood at three different but interrelated levels. Firstly, at a political level, despite recent decentralization policies in Spain which have given Galicia along with the other Spanish regions a form of self-government, political power ultimately lies with the Spanish State. Secondly, despite increased political autonomy, in economic terms, Galicia continues to be strongly dependent on central Spain. Thirdly, the legal status of the Galician language is lower than that awarded to Spanish. Although Article 3 of the 1978 Spanish Constitution grants Galician co-official status with Spanish this status is only within the territorial confines of the Galician Autonomous Community. In the context of the Spanish State and Galicia's position as part of that state, Spanish is the only official language. Galician remains but a constitutional right, not an obligation and is restricted to Galicia itself. Thus, it is perhaps the case that these considerations are at least implicitly impinging on linguistic accommodation to Spanish speakers on the part of these Vigo students.

Conclusion

The MSG clearly indicates that the new socio-political context in which Galicia has autonomous status within Spain and the co-official status which the language now enjoys is being internalized by key social groups within Galician society. Most consolidated support for the language is to be found amongst the younger generation, sectors of the population with highest levels of education and certain sectors of

Galicia's middle class. These are, paradoxically, the very groups which show the lowest levels of language use. The present study sought to explore in some depth the attitudinal patterns of these social groups through an analysis of university students within one of Galicia's largest cities. The findings of this piece of research seem to largely confirm those of the MSG (1996) report, pointing to generally strong levels of support for the language amongst young, educated sectors of Galician society who are likely to become the future middle classes in Galicia. The majority of students queried in the study were found to be strongly supportive of measures to increase the presence of the language within Galician society and attach a high value to the language as a symbol of ethnic identity. The evidently high level of support amongst the middle class sectors of the future in Galicia is instrumental in providing the necessary leadership that can bring about mobilization for language change to occur. Their positive attitudes can be extremely powerful in defining the terms on which other members of society evaluate their situations and the meanings which come to be attached to cultural symbols such language.

Most consolidated support for the language within the Vigo student population was found amongst those who expressed a strong allegiance to a specifically Galician ethnic identity and support for the political ideologies of the Galician nationalist party. Given the increased support for nationalist ideologies amongst emerging middle class sectors of Galician society we might predict the emergence of a new dominant political class in Galicia and a movement away from the more conservative and more centralist ideologies of the Popular Party which has dominated the political arena in Galicia for the past two decades. Indeed, their recent loss of power to the newly elected Socialist Party and Galician Nationist Party coalition in the Galician Autonomous 2005 elections is perhaps indicative of this new current.

While the study clearly highlights grassroots desire to maintain the local language, it also highlighted the underlying tensions caused by the global pull of a world language such as Spanish. Despite explicitly favourable attitudes towards Galician amongst these Vigo students, perceptions about the language as a status symbol tend to be more ambiguous. Although Vigo students do not explicitly voice prejudice against the language, certain negative social meanings formerly associated with speaking Galician continue to be at least implicitly recognized. Although linguistic policy seems to have to some degree altered the rules of social mobility within Galician society, students who seem to be most affected by these changes are amongst those pursuing degrees in the humanities, a group which is likely to constitute Galicia's future cultural professionals. For students entering the world of business and technology, however, such policies have less effect as the instrumental value of (global) Spanish clearly continues to be strongly recognized.

Notes

1 The basic aim of factor analysis is to examine whether, on the basis of people's answers to questions, a smaller number of more general factors or dimensions that underlie answers to individual questions can be identified (De Vaus, 1991: 257).

2 In the questionnaire, this and other statements and questions are in Galician (see O'Rourke, 2005).

3 The effect of different distinguishing background variables such as place of origin, ethnicity, linguistic practices and so on student attitudes was determined using techniques of analysis of variance (ANOVA). This procedure compared the mean scores of sub-groups in a sample in order to determine whether they differ significantly from each other.

4 A three-way ANOVA found all three variables to have statistically significant ($p < .001$) effects on attitudes towards Galician. These three background variables together account for forty per cent of the total variance in attitudinal responses amongst these students.

5 The study by Iglesias' and Áevcwez (1998) of linguistic attitudes and behaviour amongst older school pupils in Vigo also found attitudinal variation to depend on ethnicity and habitual language.

6 The original quote in Galician can be found in O'Rourke (2005).

11
Linguistic Shift and Community Language: The Effect of Demographic Factors in the Valencian Region, Balearic Islands and Catalonia

Raquel Casesnoves Ferrer, David Sankoff and M. Teresa Turell

Introduction

The language normalization programmes adopted by several Autonomous Communities of Spain between 1982 and 1986 involve efforts to restore the status and vitality of Basque, Catalan and Galician as historic languages of these communities, which had been undermined over the 40 years of Francoist dictatorship (see, Hamel; O'Rourke, this volume). As Map 11.1 illustrates, Catalan is the historic and official language of Catalonia, the Valencian Region and the Balearic Islands; Basque is the historic and official language of the Basque Country and Navarra; and Galician is the historic and official language of Galicia (see, Hamel; O'Rourke, this volume). There are other traditional languages in Spain, such as Asturian, Aranese and Aragonese, which do not (yet) have status as official languages, as well as many other languages of thriving speech communities both longstanding (for example Portuguese, Berber, Caló) and of recent immigrant origin (such as Arabic, English, Serbian), but Basque, Catalan and Galician are the only three to benefit from recognition as official languages of Spain and concerted normalization programmes fostered by their community governments (Mar-Molinero, 2000; Siguan, 1992; Turell, 2001).

Many factors may contribute to advancing or reversing the process of linguistic shift in a community: language education, government

Map 11.1 Autonomous communities with historic and official languages

practices, incentives and regulations, measures to assimilate immigrants, the relative prestige of the competing languages. In Spain, any evaluation of the efforts made since the late 1970s to halt or reverse the imposition of Spanish is complicated by factors that vary enormously from community to community. These include:

- At a purely linguistic level, the fact that Basque does not bear any relationship with Spanish, while Catalan, Galician and Spanish share common sources within the Romance family.
- The Valencian Region has a more ambiguous economic, social and political relationship with Spanish centralism than is the case between Catalonia and Madrid where there is historical rivalry.
- Galicia is losing population to external migration and hosts hardly any immigration. This is completely different from the situation in the Valencian Region and Catalonia, which in recent years have seen huge waves of immigration, mostly from North Africa, Eastern Europe and South America (see Marshall, this volume), and also from the migration affecting the Balearic Islands, which in certain areas are effectively colonized by European holiday-makers and tourists.

In this chapter we present a comparative study of the changes that have taken place between 1991 and 2001 in the competences of understanding, speaking, reading and writing in Catalan, drawing from the 1991 and 2001 census data collected in the communities where Catalan is the official language: Catalonia, the Valencian Region and the Balearic Islands. We compare overall distributions by gender, age, birthplace and county and document changes in the four linguistic skills as a function of these demographic factors. In a country which has invested heavily in promoting the status of minority languages in the face of the dominance of the global language, Spanish, it is interesting to observe to what extent the language planning legislation of the last twenty years has succeeded in achieving parity between the majority and the minority languages.

This analysis is part of an on-going overall demolinguistic project on all the Autonomous Communities in Spain that have a historic and official language other than Spanish. Our goal is to characterize and evaluate in an objective and precise way the evolution of language planning by comparing data from successive censuses; here we present the results derived from this comparison.[1]

Historical and political background

The process of linguistic shift from the historic languages to Spanish did not, of course, begin with the Franco period. In the sixteenth century, for example, by virtue of the status associated with the Spanish monarchy, and the prestige and power of its speakers, including local officials of the Church and the Inquisition, the use of Spanish began to make inroads into the aristocracy and clergy, particularly in the city of Valencia (Ninyoles, 1972, 1995). By the second half of the nineteenth century, the use of Spanish had extended throughout the new dominant class, the landed oligarchy and the petite bourgeoisie. A contemporaneous process operated to some extent in the Balearic Islands as well, but not in Catalonia, as we shall discuss below.

Among the factors favouring linguistic transfer during the intervening centuries were prohibitions against using Catalan in official and formal domains. Catalan was the target of repression throughout the eighteenth century in all domains of public life (Ferrer i Gironés, 1985). With the unification of Spain, and the abolition of the laws and institutions of self-government in the Catalan-speaking territories, Spanish became the sole official language, as in all regions of the Spanish state, at the expense not only of Catalan, but also Galician and Basque. In education, for example, the Spanish monarchy ordered the use of Spanish exclusively in primary education, and the establishment of a Spanish-only university in Cervera to supplant all existing Catalan universities and to have a publishing monopoly on educational materials (Marcet i Salom, 1987).

This repression continued unabated throughout the nineteenth century; in 1857 the *Real Academia Española* (Spanish Royal Academy) became the sole authority on matters of language taught in public schools, in 1867 the Office of the Censor was prohibited to authorize any work written only in the 'provincial dialects of Spain' as they were referred to at that time, and in 1870, inscriptions in Catalan were no longer permitted in the civil registry.

Predictably, the imposition of these measures by the Spanish state met resistance, especially in Catalonia. The period starting in 1833 is considered the Catalan 'Renaissance', when various cultural and ideological movements promoted the revival of the literary use of Catalan, in the first instance, and then the institutionalization of an autonomous cultural policy restoring the public and official use of the language (Argenter, 2002). The industrial and economic strength of Catalonia and the divergence of its interests from those of the Spanish state were such that, especially after 1898 when Spanish hegemony was weakening, the emergence of a middle-class Catalan nationalism became very evident. This extended to political action, especially in the urban areas, and provided ideological support which was particularly intense from 1906–23 for the project of restoring, modernizing and codifying the Catalan language.

In Valencia, however, the Renaissance did not make much headway among the Spanish-speaking bourgeoisie and the landed oligarchy (except to some extent in the city of Valencia itself). This historical difference between the two territories is fundamental to understanding the current differences in the linguistic demography between the Autonomous Communities of Valencia and Catalonia that we present here.

It must be stressed, however, that despite differences in the processes of language shift between Catalonia, Valencia and the Balearic Islands, in all these Catalan-speaking territories the populace maintained the cultural continuity of the Catalan language (Pradilla, 2004). Despite all the prohibitions against Catalan accumulated since the eighteenth century pertaining to official and public domains, and despite the increasing tendency of the Valencian elite and sectors of the Balearic upper class to speak Spanish, this had relatively little impact on the daily life of the citizens in general and the majority remained monolingual in Catalan until the first half of the twenty century.

It was against this background that in the mid-twentieth century the substitution of Catalan by Spanish became a coercive, all-encompassing process under the Franco regime, in Catalonia as well as the other communities. It was then that Catalan monolingualism began to disappear.

The linguistic objectives of Franco's (1937) promulgation:

Spain is organized through the imposition of a totalitarian concept, by means of national institutions which ensure its totality, its unity and its continuity. The character of each area will be respected, but without prejudice to national unity, which must be absolute, with only one language, Castilian, and only one identity, Spanish (Francisco Franco, 1939, cited in Cucó 1989)

were achieved through various means over the next forty years:

- Mandatory schooling exclusively in Spanish, starting in the 1960s, effectively ensured that the younger generations who spoke Catalan would be illiterate in the language, although they would all have basic competence in Spanish.
- An increase in the influence of the media (especially television), government activities and advertising, all in Spanish, so that for the first time, the Spanish language became an inescapable presence in the daily life of the citizenry.
- A high rate of immigration into the three communities from the less-developed Spanish-speaking regions of Spain as a consequence of urbanization, industrialization and, especially in the Balearics, the development of tourism, which doubled their population. As there was no incentive for Spanish speakers to integrate linguistically in the coercive political climate of the time, a new working class emerged with no knowledge of Catalan. Bilingualism became a one-way process (a similar phenomenon exists in Galicia and the Basque-speaking areas) – all Catalan speakers are bilingual, while a majority of Spanish speakers are monolingual.

Despite these commonalities, two processes have been prevalent in Valencia and to some extent in the Balearics that are not operative in Catalonia. One is the complete interruption of intergenerational transmission of Catalan in the major cities such as Palma, Alicante and Valencia, a process that has not been reversed to this day and may even be intensifying (Querol, 1990). The second is a feeling of linguistic inferiority experienced by many Catalan speakers, Spanish being associated with economic progress, education and urban sophistication. Feelings such as these lead to a reluctance to use Catalan in public and sometimes to its abandonment in the quest for social mobility (Aracil, 1982; Ninyoles, 1971). By contrast, in Catalonia, the system of linguistic values functions differently. While Spanish is still important for daily life in public, it is also associated with elements of the working class, principally immigrants, while Catalan is the language of both the working and middle classes and socially mobile groups, and thus has undeniable prestige value.

After the death of Franco in 1975, official recognition of the historic languages in their territories enabled the development of linguistic normalization programmes. These programmes were largely inspired in all three communities by longstanding popular movements, many of which emerged during the 1960s and spread rapidly in the late 1970s. Indeed, all the six Autonomous Communities with official historic languages adopted normalization legislation between 1982 and 1986, thus constituting, for observers of language planning, a veritable 'natural laboratory' where, within a single state, six independent experiments are being conducted at the same historical moment and for similar reasons, all with the goal of reversing, or at least slowing down, the tendency towards Spanish monolingualism. These programmes differ, of course, even among the Catalan-speaking communities, because of their different histories and current status of Catalan, as we have described above, and because they were all initiated by different regional authorities.

Demographic and political changes during the 1990s

The demographic, social and political changes taking place during the 1990s have had major effects on the use of the historic languages of Spain. The most important demographic change that Spanish society has faced over the last years, in common with the majority of areas observed in other chapters of this volume and the strongest sign of the impact of globalization, is the flux of immigrants from abroad. From a situation where emigration abroad predominated during the 1960s and 1970s, Spain has become primarily a receiving country for immigration.

This change accelerated dramatically from 1997 as is shown in Figure 11.1. However, it is important to note here that the data derive from official sources (*Instituto Nacional de Estadística*: Statistics on Residence Changes Online) where only registered arrivals during the past year are counted and where illegal migrants are not considered, so that the true number of immigrants could be as high as double this figure.

There are, however, other official information sources[2] on foreign migration that can be very useful in assessing its significance and magnitude, especially in the Balearic Islands where the annual flow of foreigners has not increased as spectacularly as it has in the other two

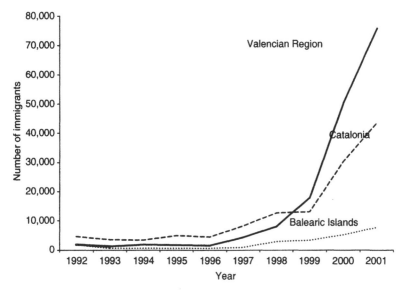

Figure 11.1 Evolution of foreign migration during the 1990s

Catalan-speaking communities. These sources are the Register of Foreigners (*Registro de Extranjeros*), the Municipal Census (*Padrón Municipal de Habitantes*) and the Population Census (*Censo de Población*). The Register of Foreigners is restricted to data on the population holding a residence permit, that is, foreigners whose status is legal. The Municipal Census, on the other hand, is an administrative register updated annually, and is compulsory for all residents of Spain, whether Spanish or foreign, and whether or not they hold a residence permit.[3] Finally, the Population Census, updated like the Municipal Census every ten years, includes records on all people living in Spain, and contains more sociological information. Thus, within the limits inherent in official sources, Figure 11.2 shows the evolution, from 1996 to 2003, of the flow of foreign population by continent of origin registered in the three communities under consideration and its percentage of the overall foreign immigration in each of these communities.

In 1996 migrants from the EU amounted to 70 per cent of the foreign population of the Valencian Region and the Balearic Islands, and in 2003 they still appeared to constitute the biggest group but had begun to show a clear downward trend. The increase in Latin American migrants and Africans, particularly from the Maghreb, breaks with the stereotyped tradition of predominantly European retirees, attracted by

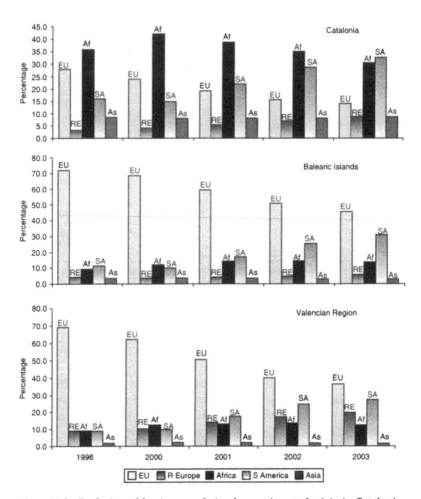

Figure 11.2 Evolution of foreign population by continent of origin in Catalonia, the Valencian Region and the Balearic Islands (1996–2003)[4]

the seaside and the mild Spanish climate. The composition of foreign immigration in Catalonia is quite different and has changed considerably during this period (see Marshall, this volume). Europeans are no longer the most numerous group, giving way to Africans who, in turn, have been overtaken by the Latin Americans. The proportion of Asian migrants, more significant in Catalonia than in the other two communities, has remained stable.

These relative changes do not involve a decrease in the absolute number of any of these immigrant groups. In fact, the proportion of foreign residents in the overall population in each community has been increasing continuously in line with global trends: in 1996 it involved 1.6, 2.2 and 4.2 per cent of the population in Catalonia, the Valencian Region and the Balearic Islands respectively, and 8.1, 9.3 and 13.4 per cent in 2003. Only the Canary Islands and the two Autonomous Communities of Madrid and Murcia have comparable proportions of foreign residents (INE, 2004).

Other changes, namely decrease in birthrate and increase of life expectancy, are not new but have been consolidated during this period. It is only in the twenty-first century that the birthrate has begun to increase slightly, but significantly, owing to a disproportionately large number of births to foreign women. This suggests then that the future of Catalan will very much depend on the linguistic integration of new immigrants.

In terms of the political context of each community, while Catalonia has been governed by a nationalist party since 1977, this is not the case in either the Valencian Region, where a centralist, pro-Spanish political party has been in power since 1995; or in the Balearic Islands, governed since 1983 also by this party with the exception of the period from 1999 to 2003. Accordingly, the linguistic policy implemented in each of these three Catalan-speaking communities differs. This ties in with our description of Catalan as being more prestigious, more socially wide-spread and enjoying more institutional support in Catalonia than in the other two Catalan-speaking communities.

Changing abilities in Catalan

Linguistic censuses provide exhaustive information on the demo-graphic, economic and social characteristics of the population and allow systematic correlations between them and the linguistic variables surveyed in the census. Moreover, to the extent that similar protocols are followed from one census to the next, we can observe not only the relationship between the variables, but also how language competence and use evolves over time.

The first general official data on Catalan competence in Catalonia, the Valencian Region and the Balearic Islands (Reixach, 1990) are from 1986. The linguistic questions are standardized in the three territories and specified for the four abilities of linguistic competence (understanding, speaking, reading and writing), the only difference being the name of the language.[5] The questions refer solely to competence in Catalan rather than to use, and do not differentiate between different degrees of competence. Respondents were asked to select only one of the following answers:

1 Does not understand Catalan
2 Understands Catalan, but does not speak it
3 Understands and reads Catalan, but does not speak it
4 Can speak Catalan
5 Can speak and read Catalan
6 Can speak, read and write Catalan

The classification made in view of these questions is as follows:

Does not understand Catalan (1)
Understands Catalan (2+3+4+5+6)
Can speak Catalan (4+5+6)
Can read Catalan (3+5+6)
Can write Catalan (6)

In the bilingual regions the census questionnaires are bilingual. The main way of administering the written questionnaire is by door-to-door delivery and collection by the same official, with provision made for assistance in completing the form for persons requiring it. Telephone and internet services are also available. Although there may be certain regional differences in administration and certainly some changes from one census to the next, there is as yet no published information on these inconsistencies that we could factor into the interpretation of our results in the ensuing sections.[6]

According to the results of the 2001 Census,[7] illustrated in Figure 11.3, the majority of the population understands Catalan (94.5%, 86.7% and 87.6% in Catalonia, the Valencian Region and the Balearic Islands, respectively). The differences between these three communities are found in the other linguistic abilities: 75 per cent of the population in Catalonia speak and read in Catalan and only half of the people write it, while in the Balearic Islands all these values decrease by 15 per cent and in the Valencian Region, by 25 per cent.

Figure 11.4 shows the change in knowledge of Catalan between 1991 and 2001. In all three Catalan-speaking communities it is the reading-writing ability that increases the most, demonstrating the effect of the teaching and learning of Catalan and in Catalan. The ability to speak Catalan increases six points in Catalonia but it decreases two points in

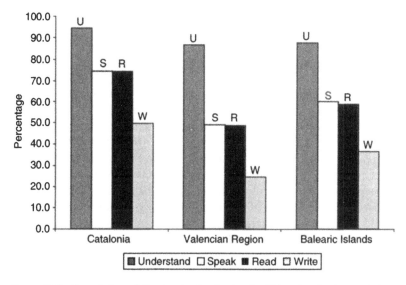

Figure 11.3 Knowledge of Catalan in Catalonia, the Valencian Region and the Balearic Islands

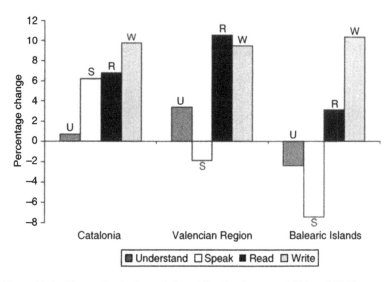

Figure 11.4 Change in the knowledge of Catalan between 1991 and 2001

the Valencian Region and seven points in the Balearic Islands, where the ability to understand Catalan also declines.

Changing abilities in Catalan according to age

Turning to changes in the ability to speak and understand Catalan according to age group, as illustrated in Figure 11.5, it can be seen that understanding is increasing in all age groups in Catalonia and, in particular, the Valencian Region, whereas in the Balearic Islands it is decreasing slightly in general except in the case of children between the ages of 6 and 14. The ability to speak Catalan is evolving positively and in a generalized way in Catalonia, in particular in the age cohort between 20 and 54 years of age. In the other two communities, however, while young people between the ages of 10 and 24 are increasing their knowledge of Catalan, particularly in the Valencian Region, adults over 30 in the latter community and over 40 in the Balearic Islands, are actually displaying a decrease in knowledge.

We will refrain from commenting on the first age group, children between 2 and 4 years of age, because of possible methodological differences between the 1991 and 2001 census. In any case, for this age group,

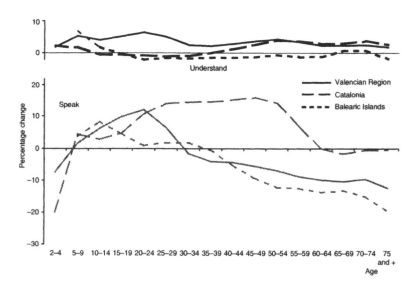

Figure 11.5   Changes in the abilities to understand and speak Catalan according to age

it is more likely that it is parents' projections which are reflected in the responses than children's current competences.

In the Valencian Region, the ability to read and write (Figure 11.6) increases in the 15 to 34 age group. In Catalonia and the Balearic Islands the ability to write Catalan is also increasing, particularly in the 20 to 39 age group. The greatest improvement in reading can be observed in the Catalan 40 to 54 age group, while little change is observed in the Balearic Islands. Thus, among young poeple the ability to write Catalan has improved the most, while among the adults, particularly in Catalonia and the Balearic Islands, it is reading ability that has increased.

To sum up, then, understanding has only improved slightly or remained relatively stable in all age groups. This is due largely to the fact that almost the whole of the population in these communities is able to understand Catalan and so is approaching an upper limit. The key role of education in the processes of linguistic revitalization is here shown by the spectacular increase in reading and writing abilities, particularly among young people in the Valencian Region. This latter effect, which is also observed in the ability to speak Catalan among Valencian youth, seems to disappear in adulthood, in contrast to what is happening in Catalonia but similar to the case for the Balearic Islands.

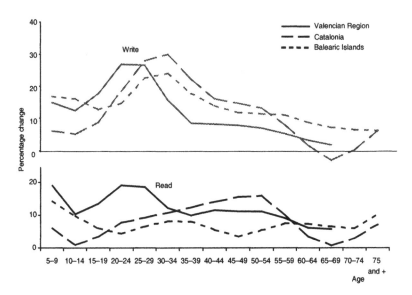

Figure 11.6 Changes in the abilities to read and write Catalan according to age

Changing abilities in Catalan according to gender and age

Gender does not have a significant effect on the degree of linguistic competence, although it is the case both in 1991 and 2001 that women claim a somewhat lower degree of competence in Catalan than men in the three Catalan-speaking communities. This does not mean, however, that women's competence is increasing at a slower rate; on the contrary, as well as showing the change between the two censuses in the abilities to understand and speak, Figure 11.7 illustrates the differences between men and women by age. Where the plotted percentages are positive, women are overtaking men; where they are negative, men are improving more than women.

Women aged 20 to 49 have increased their understanding of Catalan more than men in the three communities, although the differences are not substantial. There are, however, dramatic differences between men and women related to the ability to speak Catalan; in Catalonia women between 30 and 44 are overtaking men of the same age; in the Balearic Islands and the Valencian Region this positive pattern is extended to the age groups of 20-year-olds and 15-year-olds, respectively.

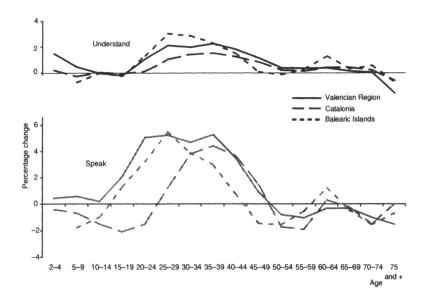

Figure 11.7 Gender differences in changing abilities to understand and speak Catalan

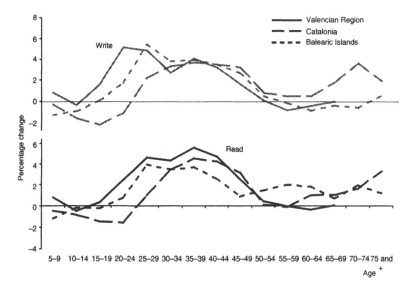

Figure 11.8 Gender differences in changing abilities to read and write Catalan

Figure 11.8 contrasts men's and women's changing abilities to read and write Catalan. Once again, women have acquired more linguistic knowledge than men over the 10 years, in particular those women whose schooling was in Catalan.

To sum up, post-school-age working women are increasing their competence in Catalan more than men, particularly in relation to their abilities to speak, read and write Catalan. If this tendency continues, women will soon be more competent than men in these areas.

Changing abilities in Catalan according to birthplace

One of the variables that, together with age, greatly affects a speaker's degree of competence in Catalan is birthplace, as can be observed in Figure 11.9, which illustrates the results of the 2001 census. For all birthplaces, the degree of competence in Catalan is always higher among the population living in Catalonia than in the Balearic Islands and the Valencian Region. In all three communities, the highest levels are attained by the indigenous population, followed by those from other Catalan-speaking communities, those from the rest of Spain, and finally those from abroad. Moreover, for each birthplace, the competence values are always higher in Catalonia, followed by the Balearic Islands,

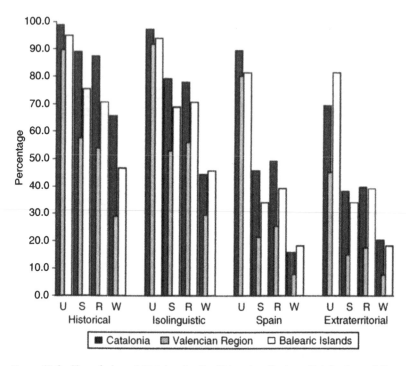

Figure 11.9 Knowledge of Catalan in the Valencian Region, Catalonia and the Balearic Islands, according to birthplace

while the Valencian Region consistently shows the lowest competence levels. It is of interest that in 1991 foreign-born people living in any of these Catalan-speaking communities had a higher degree of knowledge of Catalan (except for the ability to understand) than the population born in the rest of Spain; 10 years later this pattern has been reversed.

In the three Catalan-speaking communities, foreign-born competence in Catalan has decreased (Figure 11.10) especially the ability to understand (by 25% in the Balearic Islands and by almost 10% in Catalonia and the Valencian Region). The ability to speak Catalan has also decreased: by around 30 per cent in the Balearic Islands and 10 per cent in the Valencian Region. However, for those people born in non-Catalan-speaking areas of Spain competence has increased (except in Catalonia with respect to the ability to understand). On the other hand, it is worth mentioning that the decrease in the ability to speak Catalan in the Valencian Region and the Balearic Islands is not only due to the effects of migration, since the indigenous population is also losing some

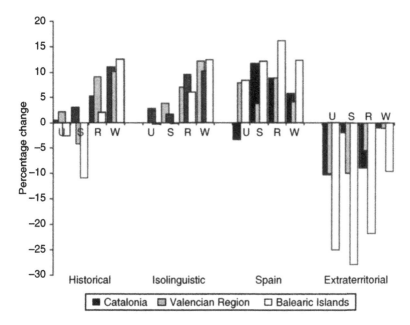

Figure 11.10 Change in the knowledge of Catalan in the Valencian Region, Catalonia and the Balearic Islands, according to birthplace

competence (4% and 10% respectively). Furthermore, in general, it is the abilities to read and write Catalan that are evolving more positively.

The foreign-born competence level in Catalan has been affected by the new wave of immigration; the negative evolution of linguistic competence in Catalan is related to the sudden and accelerated changes in the migration pattern into the three communities in recent years (see, Marshall, this volume).

Changing abilities in Catalan by county

We next turn to the evolution of linguistic competence in Catalan in the different counties of the Valencian Region (34, out of which 11 belong to the historically Spanish-speaking area), Catalonia (41) and the Balearic Islands (Minorca, Eivissa-Formentera and Majorca, where the capital, Palma, also known as Ciutat de Mallorca, has been distinguished from rest). Place of residence within the autonomous community has a significant effect on degree of competence in Catalan, especially in the Valencian Region where two linguistic areas co-exist, a historically Catalan-speaking area and a Spanish-speaking one. We will focus our analysis on data related to oral ability, both active and passive, since it is these that underwent the most significant change during the 1990s.

Figure 11.11 shows the general ability to understand and speak in Catalan, where counties and/or islands are ordered from left to right to indicate more or fewer Catalan-speaking people in 1991 (continuous line), while the dashed lines represent the results from the 2001 census.

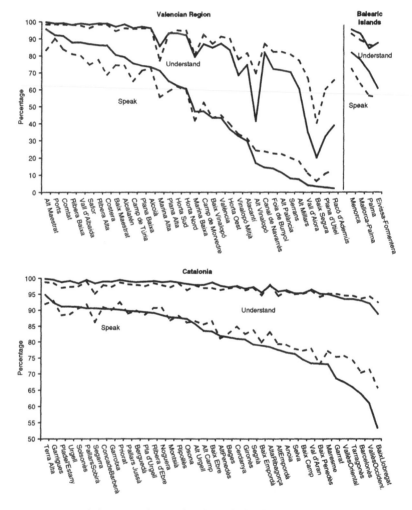

Figure 11.11   Ability to understand and speak Catalan according to counties in the Valencian Region, Catalonia and the Balearic Islands

In Catalonia and the Balearic Islands the ability to understand changes little throughout the territory, whereas in the Valencian Region, the counties with fewer Catalan speakers in 1991 have increased their ability to understand Catalan by more than 10 per cent. The same tendency can be observed in both Catalonia and the Valencian Region with respect to speaking competence in the historic language, which has increased more in the counties with fewer Catalan speakers in 1991. Strikingly, some of the counties that have increased their linguistic abilities in Catalan have welcomed a large number of foreign migrants; on the other hand, the decrease in oral competence, especially in the Valencian Region, is not observed in the counties with fewer foreign people. In the Balearic Islands, however, oral competence has declined independently of the island of residence although to different degrees: by 15 points in Majorca and its capital Palma, 10 points in Minorca and 6 points in Eivissa-Formentera.

It is also worth mentioning that the competence level in Catalan varies widely in the Valencian Region where the differences by county are substantially higher than in Catalonia and the Balearic Islands (here, the lowest value is usually greater than 50%).

In order to establish more precisely the effect of migration on the changing abilities to speak Catalan we illustrate in Figure 11.12 the variation observed between the two censuses according to birthplace.

There is a remarkable difference between Catalonia, on the one hand, and the Valencian Region and the Balearic Islands, on the other: In the Valencian Region and the Balearic Islands the decline in the ability to speak affects the Catalan-speaking region, not only among the foreign-born but also among the indigenous people, although to a different degree; in Catalonia, however, in spite of the fact that the foreign population has also lost a degree of competence, no change is observed in the ability to speak Catalan by the indigenous population. On the other hand, a pattern observed in the three communities affects people born in the Spanish-speaking areas of Spain: their competence to speak Catalan has improved.

It has sometimes been assumed that rates of loss of competence will be highest in those areas with a high level of immigration. Indeed, in Catalonia the decrease in the ability to speak is mainly due to recent immigration. In the Valencian Region and the Balearic Islands, however, it is not clear that the new wave of migration is the main cause for this decrease, basically because some locally born people have also been losing this competence.

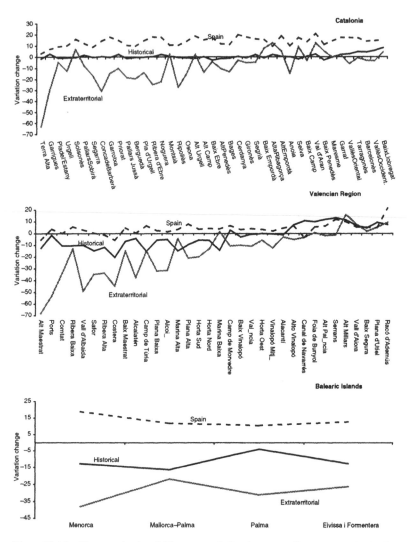

Figure 11.12   Changes in the ability to speak Catalan according to counties in the Valencian Region, Catalonia and the Balearic Islands and birthplace

As a general comment it could be added that these results seem to indicate that there is a trend towards de-regionalization in Catalonia and the Valencian Region, since it is in the most Catalan-speaking counties where the loss of competence is greatest and in the least Catalan-speaking where there is an actual increase of competence. In the Balearic Islands, however, the decrease in oral competence can be observed as a general trend in all the islands.

Discussion and conclusions

Throughout this chapter we have highlighted the similarities and differences in the evolution of Catalan competence in three Catalan-speaking communities engaged in a process of linguistic revitalization and sharing similar demographic patterns. The most significant are:

- The population in Catalonia is the most linguistically competent in Catalan followed by the Balearic Islands and lastly the Valencian Region which enjoys the lowest competence levels in all linguistic abilities.
- The ability to speak Catalan is decreasing in the Valencian population over the age of 30, and also in the Balearic population of 40 and more years of age, while in Catalonia it is increasing for all age groups.
- The pattern observed for the ability to read and write in Catalan appears to show the significance of schooling, particularly in the Valencian Region.
- The role of women in linguistic revitalization contexts is key, owing to the spectacularly higher degree of acquisition among post-school-age women, in contrast to men, a pattern that has been confirmed in the Basque Country as we have documented elsewhere (Casesnoves Ferrer, 2005).
- Another common pattern, although not as spectacular, is the change in the ability to speak Catalan in the regions that 10 years ago included a higher proportion of Catalan speakers: both in Catalonia and the Valencian Region the degree of competence has not improved the way it has in those with a smaller proportion of Catalan speakers.
- The most remarkable difference between the three territories under analysis pertains to variation according to birthplace. Although it is true in all three communities that foreign-born competence levels in Catalan have decreased, why is this also true for the indigenous population in the Valencian Region and the Balearic Islands?

One plausible explanation seems to be located in the differing linguistic policies implemented by the governments in the three communities. In the Valencian Region the most effective language planning measures are confined to the compulsory teaching of Catalan in schools and the development of non-compulsory and little utilized educational programmes entirely in Catalan. This explanation is not enough, however, since the adult population of Valencia and the Balearic Islands appears to be losing Catalan. In Catalonia, however, the positive evolution of the competence level in all age groups may indicate that compulsory education in Catalan constitutes a guarantee for language maintenance. The degree of institutional support that Catalan enjoys differs considerably among the three communities. While in the Valencian Region the governments of the last few years have actively obstructed the diffusion of Catalan (for example, cutting down on financial support for the written media and for cultural initiatives), in Catalonia the aim of the new Linguistic Policy Law passed in 1998 aims at extending the use of Catalan in all domains. While politicians from Catalonia struggle for Catalan to be recognized by the European Union, in the Valencian Region politicians do not even speak Catalan in their own Parliament. In the Balearic Islands, even when the political party in power was centralist and pro-Spanish, the diffusion of Catalan was never interrupted and the obstruction to its normalization was not as strong as in the Valencian Region. Between 1999 and 2003 with a social democratic party in power some steps forward were made. This trend seems to be continuing at present since the Balearic government in power, once again centralist and pro-Spanish, has endorsed, with some hesitation, the creation of and participation in the Ramōn Llull Institute (2003).[8] However, in the case of the Balearic Islands, and as has been mentioned above, the apparent decrease in competence level in Catalan of the indigenous population may be due to methodological issues regarding data collection and the availability of census data.

Be that as it may, the trend we have sketched towards a degree of de-regionalization in all areas where traditionally Catalan was strongest, and despite strenuous efforts, particularly in the case of Catalonia, to revitalize the language, could be seen as evidence of the globalizing power of Spanish, and this within its traditional homeland.

Notes

1   A second approach not considered in this article is a demolinguistic projection protocol, which can predict how the linguistic situation will evolve if current values of demographic factors and acquisitional rates remain constant in the future. For these purposes we have developed demographic projection soft-ware called DMLX (Casesnoves and Sankoff, 2004; Casesnoves, Turell and Sankoff, 2004).

2 Official sources do not encompass all illegal foreigners, a rather large group. Estimates on their number have been calculated by non-governmental organizations (NGOs) and trade unions that work directly with them.

3 It is important to mention that, given the fact that this census reflects the number of residents at a particular moment (1 January every year), it can fall short due to elements of the foreign population who do not register, and/or overcount, since it includes registered foreign migrants who migrate to other countries and never cancel their registration.

4 In the data from Catalonia, the official statistics on Central Americans are conflated with those on North Americans, so we have not been able to include them in a category of Latin Americans. In the Valencian Region and the Balearic Islands migrants from Central America are counted separately and we have included them with the South Americans. Asia and Oceania are grouped together in all three communities.

5 In the Valencian Region the official and most popular name used is 'Valencian' (*'valencià'*). In the Balearic Islands, the official name is 'Catalan' (*'català'*), but people use the terms 'Majorcan' (*'mallorquí'*), 'Minorcan' (*'menorquí'*), 'Ibizan' (*'eivissenc'*). In fact, the 1991 Census results are skewed, as the director of the Balearic Institute of Statistics explained (personal communication), because instead of asking about knowledge of the 'language of the islands', as in 1986, respondents were questioned about knowledge of the 'Catalan language', something that could have influenced the answers given by the respondents, depending on educational level. To compound the problem of interpreting the data, in the 2001 Census the name was changed again to the 'Catalan language (the Balearic variety or other varieties)'.

6 According to several sociolinguists, a problem with the 2001 Census, affecting all three territories to some extent, is the lack of reliability of the linguistic data. In the Balearic Islands 23 per cent of the questionnaires which had been distributed were never collected (*Diari de Balears*, 18 June 2004). In Catalonia, for the 0–4 age group, the method of calculating competence percentages seems to have changed from 1991 to 2001.

7 The age range included varies from community to community: in Catalonia, 2 or more years of age; in the Valencian Region, 3 or more years of age, and in the Balearic Islands, 6 or more years of age. The sources for the Census data are Institut d'Estadística de Catalunya (Idescat, on-line) for Catalonia, Institut Valencià d'Estadística (IVE, 1996 and IVE, on-line) for the Valencian Region, and Govern de les Illes Balears (1993) and Institut Balear d'Estadística (IBAE, on-line) for the Balearic Islands.

8 The Ramōn Llull Institute (IRL) is a consortium created by the governments of Catalonia and of the Balearic Islands, with the collaboration of the Ministry of Foreign Affairs of the Spanish Government. Its aim, as established in its statutes, is 'the external promotion of Catalan and the culture expressed therein, especially literature, in all its forms, subjects and means of expression and its learning outside the linguistic area, respecting the contributions of all the lands which share it' (http://www.llull.com).

References

Alba, O. (1996) *Variación fonética y diversidad social en el español dominicano de Santiago* (Santiago de los Caballeros: Pontificia Universidad Católica 'Madre y Maestra').

Alvar, M. (1986) *Hombre, etnia, estado: actitudes lingüísticas en Hispanoamérica* (Madrid: Gredos).

Alvar, M. (ed.) (1996) *Manual de Dialectología Hispánica. El español de América* (Barcelona: Ariel).

Álvarez, C. (1991) 'Code-switching in narrative performance: Social, structural, and pragmatic function in the Puerto Rican speech community of East Harlem', in Klee, C.A. and Ramos-García, L.A. (eds), *Sociolinguistics of the Spanish-speaking World: Iberia, Latin America, United States* (Tempe, AZ: Bilingual Press/Editorial Bilingüe): 271–98.

Alvord, S., Klee, C.A. and Echávez-Solano, N. (2006) 'La (r) asibilada en el español andino: un estudio sociolingüístico', *Lexis*, XXIX (1): 27–45.

Anderson, B. (1982) *Imagined Communities: Reflections on the Origin and Spread of Nationalism* (London: Verso).

Anderson, B. (1991) *Imagined Communities*, 2nd edn (London and New York: Verso).

Anzaldúa, G. (1999) *Borderlands/La Frontera*, 2nd edn (San Francisco: Aunt Lute Books).

Aracil, L.V. (1982) *Papers de sociolingüística* (Barcelona: La Magrana).

Argenter, J. (2002) 'Le processus de standardisation et de modernisation du catalan', *Terminogramme*, 103–4: 11–22.

Auer, P. (ed.) (1998) *Code-Switching in Conversation: Language, Interaction and Identity* (London: Routledge).

Baker, C. (1992) *Attitudes and Language* (Clevedon and Philadelphia: Multilingual Matters).

Bakhtin, M.M. (1981) *The Dialogic Imagination: Four Essays by M.M. Bakhtin* (Austin: University of Texas Press).

Bakhtin, M.M. (1986 [1952–3]) 'The problem of speech genres', in Emerson and Holquist (1986): 60–102.

Bakhtin, M.M. (1986) *Speech Genres and Other Late Essays* (Austin: University of Texas Press).

Barbour, S. and Carmichael, C. (eds) (2000) *Language and Nationalism in Europe* (Oxford: Oxford University Press).

Baron, D. (1991) *The English-Only Question: An Official Language for Americans?* (New Haven: Yale University Press).

Barth, F. (ed.) (1969) *Ethnic Groups and Boundaries: The Social Organisation of Cultural Difference* (Oslo: Universiteforlaget).

Bastardas, A. (1985) *La bilingüització de la segona generació immigrant: realitat i factors a Vilafranca de Penedès* (Barcelona: La Magrana).

Bastardas, A. (1986) *Llengua i immigració: la segona generació immigrant a la Catalunya no-metropolitana* (Barcelona: La Magrana).

Bates, E. and Goodman, J.C. (1990) 'On the emergence of grammar from the lexicon', in MacWhinney, B. (ed.), *The Emergence of Language* (Mahwah, NJ: Lawrence Erlbaum Associates): 29–79.

Beck, M.L. (1998) 'L2 acquisition and obligatory head movement: English-speaking learners of German and the local impairment hypothesis', *Studies in Second Language Acquisition*, 20: 311–48.

Berdugo, Ó. (2001) 'El español como recurso económico: anatomía de un nuevo sector' http://cvc.cervantes.es/obref/congresos/valladolid/ponencias/activo_del_espanol/1_la_industria_del_espanol/berdugo_o.htm.

Bereiter, C. and Scardamalia, M. (1987) *The Psychology of Written Composition* (Hillsdale, NJ: Erlbaum).

Bernal-Enríquez, Y. and Hernández-Chávez, E. (2003) 'La enseñanza del español en Nuevo México, ¿Revitalización o erradicación de la variedad chicana?' in Roca, A. and Colombi, C. (eds), *Mi Lengua: Spanish as a Heritage Language in the United States, Research and Practice* (Georgetown University Press): 96–119.

Bickerton, D. (1984) 'The language bioprogram hypothesis', *The Behavioral and Brain Sciences*, 7: 173–221.

Bierbach, C. (1989) 'La lengua ¿compañera del imperialismo? – Nebrija (1492) au service de la politique linguistique du Franquismo', in Py, B. and Jeanneret, R. (eds), *Minorisation linguistique et interaction. Actes du Symposium organisé par AILA et CISLA* (Genève: Droz): 217–32.

Bills, G.D., Hernández-Chávez, E., and Hudson, A. (1995). 'The geography of language shift: distance from the Mexican border and Spanish language claiming in the U.S.' *International Journal of the Sociology of Language*, 114, 9–27.

Blackshire-Belay, C. (1990) *Language Contact: Verb Morphology in German of Foreign Workers* (Tübingen: Gunter Narr Verlag).

Bley-Vroman, R. (1990) 'The logical problem of foreign language learning', *Linguistic Analysis*, 20: 3–49.

Blommaert, J. (2003) 'Commentary: A Sociolinguistics of Globalization', *Journal of Sociolinguistics*, 7(4): 607–24.

Boix, E. (1989) *Tria i alternança de llengües entre joves de Barcelona: normes d'ús i actituds* (PhD Thesis: Universitat de Barcelona).

Bonfil Batalla, G. (1990) *México profundo* (Mexico: Grijalbo-CNCA).

Bourdieu, P. (1977) 'The Economics of Linguistic Exchanges', *Social Science Information*, 16: 645–68.

Bourdieu, P. (1979) *La distinction. Critique sociale du jugement* (Paris : Éditions de Minuit).

Bourdieu, P. (1980) *Le sens pratique* (Paris: Éditions de Minuit).

Bourdieu, P. (1991) *Language and Symbolic Power* (Cambridge, Mass.: Harvard University Press).

Bourdieu, P. (2001) *A contre-feu 2* (Paris : Liber-Raison d'agir).

Bouzada, X.M., Fernández Paz, A. and Lorenzo Suárez, A. (2002) *O Proceso de Normalización do Idioma Galego 1980–2000. Volume II. Educación* (Santiago de Compostela: Concello da Cultura Galega).

Bouzada Fernández, X.B. (2003) 'Change of values and the future of the Galician language', *Estudios de Sociolingüística*, 4(1): 321–4.

Boyd, S. (1985) *Language Survival: A Study of Language Contact, Language Shift and Language Choice in Sweden* (Göteborg: University of Göteborg).

Boyer, H. (1991) *Langues en conflit. Études sociolinguistiques* (Paris: L'Harmattan).

Boyer, H. and Lagarde, C. (eds) (2002) *L'Espagne et ses langues* (Paris: L'Harmattan).

Brecht, R.D. and Ingold, C.W. (1998) 'Tapping a national resource: Heritage languages in the United States' http://www.cal.org/resources/digest/brecht01.html (accessed July 5, 2004).

Brutt-Griffler, J. (2002) *World English: A Study of its Development* (Clevedon: Multilingual Matters).

Bybee, J.L., Perkins, R. and Pagliuca, W. (1994) *The Evolution of Grammar, Tense, Aspect, and Modality in the Languages of the World* (Chicago: University of Chicago Press).

Callahan, L. (2001) Spanish/English Codeswitching in Fiction: A Grammatical and Discourse Function Analisis (Doctoral Thesis, Berkeley, University of California).

Calvet, L-J. (1999) *Pour une écologie des langues du monde* (Paris: Plon).

Calvet, L-J. (2002) *Le marché aux langues. Essai de politique linguistique sur la mondialisation* (Paris: Plon).

Camagarajah, A.S. (ed.) (2005) *Rethinking the local in Language Policy and Practice* (New Jersey/London: Lawrence Erlbaum).

Cameron, D. (1995) *Verbal Hygiene* (London: Routledge).

Cameron, D. (2000) *Good to Talk: Living and Working in a Communication Culture* (London: Sage).

Caravedo, R. (1983) *Estudios sobre el español de Lima. I Variación contextual de la sibilante* (Lima: Pontificia Universidad Católica del Perú).

Caravedo, R. (1990) *Sociolingüística de la ciudad de Lima* (Lima: Pontificia Universidad Católica del Perú).

Caravedo, R. (1992) 'Espacio geográfico y modalidades lingüísticas en el español del Perú', in Hernández, C. (ed.), *Historia y presente del Español de América* (Valladolid: Junta de Castilla y León): 719–41.

Caravedo, R. (1996) 'Variedades en contacto: propuestas para una investigación del español del Perú', *Signo y Seña*, 6: 493–511.

Caravedo, R. (1999) *Lingüística del corpus: cuestiones teórico-metodológicas aplicadas al español* (Salamanca: Ediciones Universidad de Salamanca).

Caravedo, R. (2001) 'Norma y variación fonética del español de América'. II Congreso Internacional de la Lengua Española. Valladolid: Real Academia de la Lengua Española, Instituto Cervantes (www.cervantes.es).

Carreira, M. (2002) 'The media, marketing and critical mass: Portents of linguistic maintenance', *Southwest Journal of Linguistics*, 21 (2): 37–54.

Casesnoves Ferrer, R. (2005) 'La competencia lingüística de las mujeres durante los procesos de revitalización', in M. Lusia Carrió (ed.), *Perspectivas interdiciplinarias de la Lingüística Aplicada*, Proceedings of the XXII Congreso Internacional de la Asociación Española de Lingüística Aplicada, Universitat Politècnica de València: pp. 191–202.

Casesnoves Ferrer, R. and Sankoff, D. (2004) 'Transmission, Education and Integration in Projections of Language Shift in Valencia', *Language Policy* 3: 107–31.

Casesnoves Ferrer, R., Turell, M.T. and Sankoff, D. (2004) 'La base démolinguistique pour évaluer l'aménagement linguistique dans un contexte bilingue' Paper presented at the LINGUAPAX conference on *Linguistic diversity, sustainability and peace* (Barcelona: Fòrum de les Cultures, May 2004) Online http://www.linguapax.org/congres04/pdf/3_turell.pdf.

Casilda Béjar, R. (2001) 'Una década de inversiones españolas en América Latina (1990–2000) El idioma como ventaja competitiva' http://cvc.cervantes. es/obref/congresos/valladolid/ponencias/activo_del_espanol/1_la_industria_de l_espanol/casilda_r.htm.

Castells, M. (1997) *The Power of Identity* (Oxford: Blackwell).

Castor, S. (1987) *Migración y relaciones internacionales (el caso haitiano-dominicano)* (Editorial Universitaria UASD: Santo Domingo).

Cedergren, H. (1978) 'En torno a la variación de la s final de sílaba en Panamá: análisis cuantitativo', in López Morales, H (ed.), *Corrientes actuales en la dialectología del Caribe hispánico: actas de un simposio* (Hato Rey, Puerto Rico: Editorial Universitaria, Universidad de Puerto Rico): 35–50.

Cerrón-Palomino, R. (1993) 'El Inca Garcilaso o la lealtad idiomática', *Políticas del lenguaje en América Latina. Iztapalapa* 29: 75–108.

Cerrón-Palomino, R. (2003) *Castellano andino: aspectos sociolingüísticos, pedagógicos y gramaticales* (Lima: Pontificia Universidad Católica del Perú).

Chomsky, N. (1986) *Knowledge of Language* (New York: Praeger).

Chomsky, N. (1995) *The Minimalist Program* (Cambridge, Mass.: MIT Press).

Chomsky, N. (2003) *Hegemony or survival. America's quest for global dominance* (New York: Metropolitan Books, Henry Holt and Co).

Chopra, P. (2001) 'Betrayal and solidarity in ethnography on literacy: revisiting research homework in a north Indian village', *Street* (2001): 78–91.

Cifuentes, B. (1998) *Letras sobre voces. Multilingüismo a través de la historia* (México, D. F.: CIESAS-INI).

Cifuentes, B. and Pellicer, D. (1989) 'Ideology, politics and national language: a study in the creation of a national language in 19th century Mexico', *Sociolinguistics*, 18: 7–17.

Cifuentes, B. and Rosmeso, M.C. (1993) 'Oficialidad y planificación del español: dos aspectos de la política del lenguaje en México durante el siglo XIX', *Políticas del lenguaje en América Latina. Iztapalapa*, 29: 135–46.

Clements, C. (2003) 'The tense-aspect system in pidgins and naturalistically learned L2', *SSLA*: 245–83.

Clifford, J. and Marcus, G. (eds) (1986) *Writing Culture: The Poetics and Politics of Ethnography* (Berkeley: University of California Press).

Clyne, M. (ed.) (1988) *Australia, Meeting Place of Languages* (Canberra: Australian National University).

Clyne, M. (ed.) (1992) *Pluricentric languages* (Berlin, New York: de Gruyter).

Cobarrubias, J. (1987) 'Models of language planning for minority languages', *Bulletin of the CAAL, 9*: 47–70.

Cooper, R. (1989) *Language Planning and Social Change* (Cambridge: Cambridge University Press).

Coupland, N. (2003) 'Introduction: Sociolinguistics and Globalization' *Journal of Sociolinguistics*, 7(4): 465–73.

Crystal, D. (1997) *English as a Global Language* (Cambridge: Cambridge University Press).

Crystal, D. (1999) 'Millennium of briefing: the death of language', *Prospect* 46. http://www.prospect-magazine.co.uk.

Crystal, D. (2000) *Language Death* (Cambridge: Cambridge University Press).

Crystal, D. (2003) *English as a Global Language*, 2nd edn (Cambridge: Cambridge University Press).

Cucó, A. (1989) *País i Estat: la qüestió valenciana* (Valencia: 3 i 4).

D'Andrade, R. and Strauss, C. (eds) (1992) *Human motives and cultural models* (Cambridge: Cambridge University Press).

Damoiseau, R. (1988) 'Éléments pour une classification des verbaux en créole haïtien', *Études créoles*, 11: 41–64.

De Genova, N. and Ramos-Zayas, A.Y. (2003) *Latino Crossings: Mexicans, Puerto Ricans, and the Politics of Race and Citizenship* (London: Routledge).

De Granda, G. (1995) 'El influjo de las lenguas indoamericanas sobre el español. Un modelo interpretativo sociolingüístico de variantes areales de contacto lingüístico', *Revista Andina*, 25: 173–98.

De la Peña, G. (1995) 'La ciudadanía étnica y la reconstrucción de los indios en el México contemporáneo', *Revista Internacional de Filosofía Política*, 6: 116–40.

De la Peña, G. (1999) 'Territorio y ciudadanía étnica en la Nación Globalizada', *Desacatos*, 1: 13–27.

De Oliver, M. (2004) 'Marketing Latinos as development policy: San Antonio and the reproduction of underprivilege' *Latino Studies*, 2(3): 385–422.

De Swaan, A. (2001) *Words of the World: The Global Language System* (Cambridge: Cambridge University Press).

De Swaan, A. (1993) 'The emergent world language system: An introduction', *International Political Science Review*, 14 (3): 219–26.

DeGraff, M. (1996) 'UG and acquisition in pidginization and creolization', in Epstein et al., *Second Language Acquisition: Theoretical and Experimental Issues in Contemporary Research, Behavioral and Brain Sciences*, 19: 724.

DeGraff, M. (1999) 'Creolization, language change, and language acquisition: A prolegomenon', in DeGraff, M. (ed.), *Language Creation and Language Change. Creolization, Diachrony, and Development* (Cambridge: The MIT Press): 1–46.

DeGraff, M. (2005) 'Morphology and word order in creolization and beyond', in Clinque, G. and Kayne, R. (eds), *The Handbook of Comparative Syntax* (Oxford: Oxford University Press).

Del Valle, J. (1999) 'Monoglossic policies for a heteroglossic culture: misinterpreted multilingualism in Modern Galicia', *Language and Communication*, 20 (1): 105–32.

Del Valle, J. (2004) 'El español como recurso económico: ¿para quién?', paper delivered at the Second Hispanic Linguistics, Southampton, UK, 14–16 April.

Del Valle, J. (2005) 'La lengua, patria común: política lingüística, política exterior y el post-nacionalismo hispánico', in Wright and Ricketts (eds) (2005): 391–416.

Del Valle, J. and Gabriel-Stheeman, L. (eds) (2004a) *La batalla del idioma: la intelectualidad hispánica ante la lengua*. (Frankfurt and Madrid: Vervuert/ Iberoamericana).

Del Valle, J. and Gabriel-Stheeman, L. (2002b) ' "Codo con codo". Hispanic community and the language spectacle' in del Valle, J. and Gabriel-Stheeman, L. (eds) (2002a): 195–216.

Del Valle, J. and Gabriel-Stheeman, L. (eds) (2004) *La batalla del idioma. La intelectualidad hispánica ante la lengua* (Frankfurt, Madrid: Vervuert).

DeMello, G. (2002) 'Leísmo in contemporary Spanish American educated speech', *Linguistics*, 40: 261–83.

Departament d'Estadística, Ajuntament de Barcelona, (2005) http://www.bcn.es/estadistica/catala/dades/inf/est/pobest/pobest05/pobest05.pdf, (accessed 07/05/05).

Díaz, N. (2002) 'La diáspora haitiana: desde la periferia hacia la periferia. Contacto en "Hispaniola" ', in Díaz, N., Ludwig, R. and Pfänder, S. (eds): 279–326 (Frankfurt am Main/Madrid: Vervuert/Iberoamericana).

Díaz, N., Ludwig, R. and Pfänder, S. (eds) (2002) *La Romania americana. Procesos lingüísticos en situaciones de contacto* (Frankfurt am Main/Madrid: Vervuert/Iberoamericana).

Díaz-Polanco (2000) 'El conflicto cultural en el umbral del tercer milenio', *Memoria*, 131: 34–42.

Dieck, M. (2000) 'La Negación en el Palenquero. Análisis Sincrónico, Estudio Comparativo y Consecuencias Teóricas' (Frankfurt am Main/Madrid: Vervuert/Iberoamericana).

Donni de Mirande, N. (1996) 'Argentina-Uruguay', in Alvar M. (ed.) (1996): 209–21.

Dorian, N.C. (1981) *Language Death: The Life Cycle of a Scottish Gaelic Dialect* (Philadelphia: University of Pennsylvania Press).

Edwards, J. (1994) *Multilingualism* (London and New York: Routledge).

Emerson, C. and Holquist, M. (eds) (1986) *M.M. Bakhtin, Speech Genres and Other Late Essays* (Austin, Texas: University of Texas Press).

Epstein, S., Flynn, S. and Matohardjone, G. (1996) 'Second Language Acquisition. Theoretical and Experimental Issues in Contemporary Research' *Behavioral and Brain Sciences*, 19: 677–758.

Erill i Pinyot, G., Farràs i Farràs, J., and Marcos i Moral, F. (1992) *Ús del català entre els joves a Sabadell* (Barcelona: Departament de Cultura, Generalitat de Catalunya).

Escobar, A. (1978) *Variaciones sociolingüísticas del castellano en el Perú* (Lima: Instituto de Estudios Peruanos).

Escobar, A.M. (1988) *Hacia una tipología del bilingüismo en el Perú.* (Lima: Instituto de Estudios Peruanos).

Escobar, A.M. (2000) *Contacto social y lingüístico: el español en contacto con el quechua en el Perú* (Lima : Pontificia Universidad Católica del Perú).

Eubank, L. (1993/94) 'On the transfer of parametric values in L2 development', *Language Acquisition*, 3: 183–208.

Fairclough, N. (1989) *Language and Power* (London: Longman).

Fairclough, N. (1992) *Discourse and Social Change* (Cambridge: Polity Press).

Fairclough, N. (2000) *Language and Power*, 2nd edn (Edinburgh: Pearson Education / Longman).

Fairclough, M. (2001), 'Expresiones de modalidad en una situación de contacto'. '*Deber (de)* vs. *Tener que* en el español hablado en Houston', *Southwest Journal of Linguistics*, 19 (2): 19–30.

Fairclough, M. (2003) 'El (denominado) *Spanglish* en Estados Unidos: polémicas y realidades', *Revista Internacional Lingüística Iberoamericana*, 2: 185–204.

Fasold, R.W. (1984) *Sociolinguistics of Society* (Oxford: Oxford University Press).

Ferguson, C.A. (1959) 'Diglossia', *Word*, 15: 325–40.

Fernández Rodríguez, M.A. (1993) 'La lengua materna en los espacios urbanos gallegos', *Plurilinguismes: Sociolinguistique Galicienne*, 6: 27–53.

Fernández Rodríguez, M.A. and Rodríguez Neira, M. (1994) *Lingua inicial e competencia lingüística en Galicia* (Real Academia Galega: Vigo).

Fernández Rodríguez, M.A. and Rodríguez Neira, M. (1995) *Usos lingüísticos en Galicia* (Real Academia Galega: Vigo).

Fernández Rodríguez, M.A. and Rodríguez Neira, M. (1996) *Actitudes lingüísticas en Galicia* (Real Academia Galega: Vigo).

Ferrer i Gironés, F. (1985) *La persecució política de la llengua catalana* (Barcelona: Edicions 62).

Fisher, S. (2000) 'O fim do português', *Veja*, 05.04. 2000, São Paulo.

Fishman, J.A. (1964) 'Language maintenance and language shift as fields of inquiry', *Linguistics*, 9: 32–70.

Fishman, J.A. (1967): 'Bilingualism with and without Diglossia; Diglossia with and without bilingualism', *Journal of Social Issues*, 23, (2): 29–38.

Fishman, J.A. (1980): 'Bilingualism and Biculturalism as Individual and Societal Phenomena', *Journal of Multilingual and Multicultural Development*, 1: 3–15.

Fishman, J.A. (1991) *Reversing language shift* (Clevedon: Multilingual Matters).

Fishman, J.A. (ed.) (2001) *Can threatened languages be saved?* (Clevedon, Philadelphia: Multilingual Matters).

Foley, D.E. (2002) 'Critical ethnography: the reflexive turn', *Qualitative Studies in Education*, 15(5): 469–90.

Francis, N. and Hamel, R.E. (1992) 'La redacción en dos lenguas: escritura y narrativa en tres escuelas bilingües del Valle del Mezquital', *Revista Latinoamericana de Estudios Educativos*, 22 (4): 11–35.

Franco, F. (1939) *Palabras del Caudillo* (Barcelona: Ediciones Fe).

Freeland, J. (1995) ' "Why go to school to learn Miskitu?": changing constructs of bilingualism, education and literacy among the Miskitu of Nicaragua's Atlantic Coast', *International Journal of Educational Development*, 15(3): 214–32.

Freeland, J. (2003) 'Intercultural-bilingual education for an interethnic-plurilingual society? The case of Nicaragua's Caribbean Coast', Special Number 27: *Indigenous Education: New possibilities, ongoing constraints, Comparative Education*, 9(2): 239–60.

Freeland, J. (2005) 'La educación intercultural-bilingüe y su relación con las prácticas interétnicas y plurilingües de la Costa Caribe nicaragüense', *Wani*, 37: 25–44.

Gal, S. (1979) *Language Shift. Social Determinants of Linguistic Change in Bilingual Austria* (New York: Academic Press).

Gal, S. and Woolard, K. (eds) (2001) *Languages and Publics: The Making of Authority* (Manchester: St. Jerome).

Garcez, P.M. (1998) 'Invisible culture and cultural variation in language use: Why language educators should care', *Linguagem and Ensino*, 1(1): 133–86.

García Canclini, N. (1999) *La globalización imaginada* (Buenos Aires, Barcelona, México: Paidós).

García Canclini, N. (2004) *Diferentes, desiguales y desconectados: Mapas de la interculturalidad* (Barcelona: Gedisa).

García Canclini, N. (ed.) (2002) *Iberoamérica 2002. Diagnóstico y propuestas para el desarrollo cultural* (México, Madrid: OEA – Santillana).

García Delgado, J.L. (2001) 'El activo del español: presentación' http://cvc.cervantes.es/obref/congresos/valladolid/ponencias/activo_del_espanol/1_1 a_industria_del_espanol/garcia_j.htm.

García, E. and Otheguy, R. (1977) 'Dialect variation in leísmo: a semantic approach', in Fasold, R.W. and Shuy, R.W. (eds), *Studies on Language Variation* (Washington, D.C.: Georgetown University Press): 65–87.

García, E. and Otheguy, R. (1983) 'Being polite in Ecuador: Strategy reversal under language contact', *Lingua*, 61: 103–32.

Gardt, A. and Hüppauf, B. (eds) (2004) *Globalization and the Future of German* (Berlin/New York: Mouton de Gruyter).

Gardy, P. and Lafont, R. (1981) 'La diglossie comme conflit; l'exemple occitan', *Bilinguisme et diglossie. Langages*, 61: 75–92.

Gavruseva, E. and Lardiere, D. (1996) 'The emergence of extended phrase structure in child L2 acquisition' in Stringfellow, A., Cahana-Amitay, A., Hughes, D.E. and Zukowski, A. (eds), *BUCLD 20 Proceedings*: 223–36.

Generalitat Valenciana (ed) (1990) *Miscel•lània 89* (Valencia: Generalitat Valenciana).

Giddens, A. (1991) *Modernity and Self-Identity: Self and society in the Late Modern Age* (Cambridge: Polity Press).

Giddens, A. (1984) *The Constitution of Society: Outline of the Theory of Structuration* (Cambridge: Polity Press).

Giddens, A. (1990) *The Consequences of Modernity* (Cambridge: Polity Press).

Giles, H., Robinson, W. and Smith, P. (eds) (1980) *Language: Social Pscyhological Perspectives* (Oxford: Pergamon: Oxford).

Givón, T. (1975) 'Serial verbs and syntactic change: Niger-Congo', in Li, C. N. (ed.), *Word order and word order change* (Austin: University of Texas Press): 47–112.

Glaser, B.G. and Strauss, A.L. (1967) *The Discovery of Grounded Theory. Strategies for Qualitative Research* (London: Weidenfeld & Nicolson).

Godenzzi, J.C. (1986) 'Pronombres de objeto directo e indirecto del castellano en Puno', *Lexis* X: 197–202.

Godenzzi, J.C. (1991) 'Variantes sociolectales de español en el espacio andino de Puno, Peru', in Klee, C.A. and Ramos-García, L.A. (eds), *Sociolinguistics of the Spanish-speaking World: Iberia, Latin America, the United States* (Tempe, AZ: Bilingual Press): 182–206.

Goffman, E. (1974) *Frame analysis. An essay on the categorization of experience* (New York: Harper and Row).

Golte, J. and Adams, N. (1987) *Los caballos de Troya de los invasores: estrategias campesinas en la conquista de la Gran Lima* (Lima, Perú: Instituto de Estudios Peruanos).

Gómez Dacal, G. (2001) 'La población hispana de Estados Unidos' in Instituto Cervantes (2001) *Anuario 2001*, Centro Virtual Cervantes.

González, M. *et al.* (2003) *O galego segundo a mocadide* (A Coruña: Real Academia Galega).

González, N. (2001) *I Am My Language: Discourses of Women and Children in the Borderlands* (Tucson: University of Arizona Press).

González Echevarría, R. (1997) 'Kay Possa? Is 'Spanglish' a language?', *The New York Times* (28 March 1997).

González Pérez, M. (1997) *Gobiernos Pluriétnicos: La constitución de regiones autónomas en Nicaragua* (Mexico/Managua:URACCAN/Plaza y Valdes SA).

Graddol, D. (1997) *The Future of English* (London: British Council).

Granda, G. de (1976) 'Algunos rasgos morfosintácticos de posible origen criollo en el habla de áreas hispanoamericanas de población negra', *Anuario de Letras*, 14: 5–22.

Green, K. (1997) *Non-standard Dominican Spanish: evidence of partial restructuring* (Ann Arbor: University Microfilm International).

Grin, F. (2003) *Language Policy Evaluation and the European Charter for Regional or Minority Languages* (New York: Palgrave Macmillan).

Grosjean, F. (1997) 'Processing mixed language: Issues, findings, and models', in de Groot, A.M.B. and Kroll, J.F. (eds), *Tutorials in Bilingualism: Psycholinguistic Perspectives* (Mahwah, New Jersey: Erlbaum): 225–54.

Gruzinski, S. (1999) *El pensamiento mestizo* (Barcelona: Paidós).

Gumperz, J.J. (1982) *Discourse strategies* (Cambridge: Cambridge University Press).

Gumperz, J. and Wilson, R. (1977) 'Convergence and Creollization', in D. Hymes (ed.), *Pidginization and Creolization of Languages* (Cambridge: Cambridge University Press): 151–67.

Gumperz, J.J. (1982) *Discourse Strategies* (Cambridge: Cambridge University Press).

Gutiérrez, M. (1994) *Ser y estar en el habla de Michoacán, México* (México: UNAM).

Gutiérrez, M.J. (1994) 'Simplification, Transfer, and Convergence in Chicano Spanish', *The Bilingual Review/La Revista Bilingüe*, XIX (2): 111–21.

Gutiérrez, M.J. (1996) 'Tendencias y alternancias en la expresión de condicionalidad en el español hablado en Houston', *Hispania*, 79 (3): 568–77.

Gutiérrez, M.J. (1997) 'Discurso irreal de pasado en el español de Houston: la disputa continua', *Bulletin of Hispanic Studies*, LXXIV (3): 257–69.

Gutiérrez, M.J. (2001) '*Estar* Innovador en el Continuo Generacional Bilingüe de Houston' in *Proceedings of the VII Simposio Internacional de Comunicación Social* Santiago de Cuba: 210–13.

Hakuta, K. and D'Andrea, Daniel (1992) 'Some properties of bilingual maintenance and loss in Mexican background high-school students', *Applied Linguistics*, 13 (1): 72–99.

Hall, S. (1997) 'The work of representation', in Hall, S. (ed.) (1997) *Representation: Cultural Representation and Signifying Practices* (London: Sage/Milton Keynes: Open University): 13–74.

Hamel, R.E. (1982) 'Constitución y análisis de la interacción verbal', *Estudios de Lingüística Aplicada*, 2: 31–80.

Hamel, R.E. (1988a) *Sprachenkonflikt und Sprachverdrängung. Die zweisprachige Kommunikationspraxis der Otomi-Indianer in Mexico* (Berne, Frankfurt, Paris, New York: Verlag Peter Lang).

Hamel, R.E. (1988b) 'Las determinantes sociolingüísticas de la educación indígena bilingüe', *Signos*: 319–76.

Hamel, R.E. (1993) 'Políticas y planificación del lenguaje: una introducción', *Políticas del lenguaje en América Latina. Iztapalapa*, 29: 5–39.

Hamel, R.E. (1994) 'Linguistic rights for Amerindian peoples in Latin America', in Skutnabb-Kangas, T. and Phillipson, R. (eds) (1994) *Linguistic Human Rights: Overcoming Linguistic Discrimination* (Berlin: Mouton de Gruyter): 289–05.

Hamel, R.E. (1996) 'The inroads of literacy in the Hñähñú communities of Central Mexico', *International Journal of the Sociology of Language*, 119: 13–41.

Hamel, R.E. (1997) 'Language conflict and language shift: a sociolinguistic framework for linguistic human rights', *International Journal of the Sociology of Language*, 127: 107–34.

Hamel, R.E. (2000) 'Políticas del lenguaje y estrategias culturales en la educación indígena', IEEPO (ed.) (2000) *Inclusión y diversidad. Discusiones recientes sobre la educación indígena en México* (Oaxaca: Colección Voces del Fondo): 130–67.

Hamel, R.E. (2001) 'Políticas del lenguaje y educación indígena en México. Orientaciones culturales y estrategias pedagógicas en una época de globalización', in Bein, R. and Born, J. (eds) (2001) *Políticas lingüísticas – norma e identidad* (Buenos Aires: UBA): 143–70.

Hamel, R.E. (2003a) 'Regional blocs as a barrier against English hegemony? The language policy of Mercosur in South America', in Maurais, J. and Morris, M.A. (eds) (2003) *Languages in a globalising world* (Cambridge: Cambridge University Press): 111–42.

Hamel, R.E. (2003b) *The Development of Language Empires* (Universidad Autónoma Metropolitana, México, D.F.) (unpublished working paper).

Hamel, R.E. (in press) 'The development of language empires' in Ammon, U., Mattheier, K. Nelde, P. and P. Trudgill (eds), *Sociolinguistics. An International Handbook of the Science of Language and Society*, 2nd edn, Vol. 3 (Berlin, New York: de Gruyter).

Hamel, R.E. and Muñoz Cruz, H. (1982) 'Conflit de diglossie et conscience linguistique dans des communautés indiennes bilingues au Mexique', in Dittmar, N. and Schlieben-Lange, B. (eds). *Die Soziolinguistik in den romanis-chsprachigen Ländern – La sociolinguistique dans les pays de langue romane* (Tübingen: Narr): 249–70.

Hamel, R.E. and Muñoz Cruz, H. (1988) 'Desplazamiento y resistencia de la lengua otomí: el conflicto lingüístico en las prácticas discursivas y en la reflexividad', in Hamel, R.E., Lastra de Suárez, Y. and Muñoz Cruz, H. (eds), *Sociolingüística latinoamericana* (México: UNAM): 101–46.

Hamel, R.E. and Sierra, M.T. (1983) 'Diglosia y conflicto intercultural', *Boletín de Antropología Mexicana*, 8: 89–110.

Hanks, W. (1987) 'Discourse genres in a theory of practice', *American Ethnologist*, 14(4): 668–92.

Hart, S. and Rowe, W. (eds) (2005) Studies in Latin American Literature and Culture in Honour of James Higgins, *Bulletin of Hispanic Studies*, Special Issue.

Haugen, E. (1972) *The Ecology of Language* (Stanford: Stanford University Press).

Hawkins, R. and Chan, C. (1997) 'The partial availability of Universal Grammar in second language acquisition: the "failed functional features hypothesis" ', *Second Language Research*, 13 (3): 187–226.

Heath, S.B. (1972) *Telling tongues. Language policy in Mexico: from colony to nation* (New York: Teacher's College Press).

Heine, B. (1993) *Auxiliaries: Cognitive forces and grammaticalization* (Oxford: Oxford UP).

Heller, M. (1994) *Crosswords: Language, Education and Ethnicity in French Ontario* (Berlin, New York: Mouton de Gruyter).

Heller, M. (1999) 'Alternative ideologies of la francophonie', *Journal of Sociolinguistics* 3 (3): 336–59.

Heller, M. (1999) *Linguistic Minorities and Modernity: A Sociolinguistic Ethnography* (London: Longman).

Heller, M. (2003) 'Globalization, the new economy, and the commodification of language and identity', *Journal of Sociolinguistics*, 7(4): 473–93.

Henríquez Ureña, P. (1940 [1982]) *El español en Santo Domingo* (Santo Domingo: Editorial Taller).

Hernández, C. (1996) 'Castilla La Vieja', in Alvar, M. (ed.) (1996): 197–212.

Hernández-Chávez, E. (1993) 'Native language loss and its implications for revitalization of Spanish in Chicano communities', in Merino, B.J., Trueba, H.T.

and Samaniego, F.A. (eds), *Language and Culture in Learning: Teaching Spanish to Native Speakers of Spanish* (London: The Falmer Press): 45–57.

Hill, J.H. and Hill, K.C. (1986): *Speaking Mexicano. Dynamics of a syncretic language in Central Mexico* (Tucson: The University of Arizona Press).

Himmelmann, N.P. (2004) 'Lexicalization and grammaticization: opposite or orthogonal?', in Wiemer, B., Bisang, W. and Himmelmann N. (eds), *What makes grammaticalization – a look from its components and its fringes* (Berlin: Mouton de Gruyter): 21–42.

Hispanic Market Weekly (August 7, 2000) 'American as apple flan', *The HMW Research Page* www.awool.com/hmw/rp080700.pdf (November 18, 2004).

Holland, D. and Quinn, N. (eds) (1987) *Cultural models in language and thought* (Cambridge: Cambridge University Press).

Holm, J. (1978) *The Creole English of Nicaragua's Miskito Coast* (London: University College, unpublished PhD dissertation).

Holm, J. (1988/89) *Pidgins and Creoles* (Vols 1–2) (Cambridge: Cambridge University Press).

Holm, J. (2004) *Languages in Contact. The Partial Restructuring of Vernaculars* (Cambridge: Cambridge University Press).

Hopper, P. (1991) 'On some principles of grammaticalization', in Traugott, E. Closs and Heine, B. (eds), *Approaches to Grammaticalization*, 2 vols. (Amsterdam/Philadelphia: Benjamins): 17–35.

Hopper, P. and Traugott, E. (1993) *Grammaticalization* (Cambridge: Cambridge UP).

Hornberger, N.H. (ed.) (1997) *Indigenous literacies in the Americas: Language planning from the bottom up* (Berlin, New York: Mouton de Gruyter).

House, J. (2003) 'English as a lingua franca: A threat to multilingualism?', *Journal of Sociolinguistics* 7(4): 556–78.

Howard, R. (2005) 'Translating hybridity: a case from Southern Peru', *Bulletin of Hispanic Studies*, Special Issue: 159–72.

Hudson, A., Hernández Chávez, E. and Bills, G.D. (1995) 'The many faces of language maintenance: Spanish language claiming in five Southwestern states', in Silva-Corvalán, C. (ed.) (1995) *Spanish in four continents: Studies in language contact and bilingualism* (Washington, DC: Georgetown University Press, 1995): 165–83.

Hudson, A., Hernández-Chávez, E. and Bills, G. (1995) 'The many faces of language maintenance: Spanish language claiming in five Southwestern states', in Silva-Corvalán, C. (ed.), *Spanish in four continents* (Washington DC: Georgetown UP): 165–83.

Huntington, S.P. (1996) *The clash of civilizations and the remaking of world order* (New York: Simon and Schuster).

Huntington, S.P. (2004) *Who are we? The challenges to America's national identity* (New York: Simon and Schuster).

Huppauf, B. (2004) 'Globalization: Threats and opportunities', in Gardt and Hüppauf, 2004: 3–25.

Iglesias, E.V. (2001) 'El potencial económico del español' http://cvc.cervantes.es/obref/congresos/valladolid/ponencias/activo_del_espanol/1_la_industria_del_espanol/iglesias_e.htm.

Iglesias Álvarez, A. (1998) *Actitudes lingüística dos emigrantes do rural no medio urbano* (Unpublished MA thesis. Universidade de Santiago de Compostela).

Iglesias Álvarez, A. (2002) *Falar galego "no veo por qué." Aproximación cualitativa á situación sociolingüística de Galica* (Vigo: Xerais).

Inoa, O. (1999) *Azúcar, árabes, cocolos y haitianos* (Santo Domingo: Editorial COLE y FLACSO).

Institut Balear d'Estadística (1993) *Cens de Població 1991. VII. Tales sobre el coneixement de la llengua de la CAIB* (Palma de Mallorca: Governs de les Illes Balears).

Institut Balear d'Estadística (2005) http://www.caib.es/ibae/demo/catala/index.htm.

Institut d'Estadística de Catalunya (2005) http://www.idescat.es.

Institut Valencià d'Estadística (1996) *Info Censos de Població, Habitatges, Edificis i Locals de la Comunitat Valenciana 1990–91* (Valencia: Institut Valencià d'Estadística).

Institut Valencià d'Estadística Online (2005) http://ive.infocentre.gva.es.

Instituto Cervantes (2000) *El español en el mundo; Anuario 2000* Centro Virtual Cervantes http://cvc.cervantes.es/obref/anuario/.

Instituto Nacional de Estadística (2004) *Los extranjeros residentes en España. 1998–2002* http://www.ine.es/prodyser/pubweb/ext_espa/ext_espa.htm.

Irvine, J.T. and Gal, S. (2000) 'Language ideology and linguistic differentiation', in Kroskrity, P.V. (ed.) (2000): 35–83.

Jaffe, A. and Walton, S. (2000) 'The voices people read: Orthography and the representation of non-standard speech', *Journal of Sociolinguistics*, 4(4): 561–87.

Jaffe, A. (2000) 'Introduction: Non-standard orthography and non-standard Speech', *Journal of Sociolingustics*, 4(4): 497–513.

Joseph, J.E. and Taylor T.J. (eds) (1990) *Ideologies of Language* (London: Routledge).

Journal of Sociolinguistics (November 2003) Themed issue: *Sociolinguistics and Globalization*, 7, (4).

Kachru, B.B. (1986) *The alchemy of English: The spread, functions and models of non-native Englishes* (Oxford: Pergamon Press).

Kachru, B.B. and Nelson, C.L. (1996) 'World Englishes', in McKay, S.L. and Hornberger, N.H. (eds) (1996) *Sociolinguistics and language teaching* (Cambridge: Cambridge University Press): 71–102.

Klee, C.A. (1989) 'The acquisition of clitic pronouns in the Spanish interlanguage of Quechua speakers: A contrastive case study', *Hispania*, 72: 402–08.

Klee, C.A. (1990) 'Spanish-Quechua language contact: The clitic pronoun system in Andean Spanish', *Word*, 41: 35–46.

Klee, C.A. (1996) 'The Spanish of the Peruvian Andes: The influence of Quechua on Spanish language structure', in Jensen, J.B. and Roca, A. (eds), *Spanish in contact: Studies in bilingualism* (Somerville, MA: Cascadilla Press): 73–91.

Klee, C.A. and Caravedo, R. (2000) *Language Change as a result of Andean Migration to Lima Peru* Unpublished manuscript.

Klee, C.A. and Caravedo, R. (2005) 'Contact-Induced Language Change in Lima-Peru: The case of Clitic Pronouns', in Eddington, D. (ed.), *Selected Proceedings of the 7th Hispanic Linguistics Symposium* (Somerville, ME: Cascadilla Press): 12–21.

Klein-Andreu, F. (2000) *Variación actual y evolución histórica: los clíticos le/s, la/s, lo/s* (Munich: LINCOM EUROPA).

Kloss, H. (1969) 'Research possibilities in group bilingualism: a report', *Quebec: International Center for Research on Bilingualism*.

Kramsch, C. (1993) *Context and Culture in Language Teaching* (Oxford: Oxford University Press).

Krashen, S. (1973–1974) 'Lateralization, language learning, and the critical period: Some new evidence', *Language Learning*, 22: 3–74.

Kroskrity, P.V. (2000) 'Regimenting Languages: Language Ideological Perspectives', in Kroskrity (ed.) (2000) *Regimes of language: ideologies, polities, and identities* (Santa Fe, New Mexico: School of American Research Press): 1–34.

Kubchandani, L.M. (1994) ' "Minority" cultures and their communication rights', in Skutnabb-Kangas, and Philipson (eds) (1994): 317–34.

Kulick, D. (1992) *Language shift and cultural reproduction* (Cambridge: Cambridge University Press).

Labov, W. (1972) *Sociolinguistic Patterns* (Philadelphia: University of Pennsylvania Press).

Labov, W. (1994) *Principles of Linguistic Change: Internal Factors* (Oxford: Blackwell).

Labov, W. (2001) *Principles of Linguistic Change: Social Factors* (Oxford: Blackwell).

Lacorte, M. (in press) 'Política y lenguaje en el español de Estados Unidos: ¿Globalidad o falta de realidad?', in Teborg, R. and García Landa, L. (eds), *Los retos de la política del lenguaje en el siglo XXI* (México, DF: Universidad Nacional Autónoma de México).

Lafford, B. (1986) 'Valor diagnóstico-social del uso de ciertas variantes de /s/ en el español de Cartagena, Colombia', in Núñez Cedeño, R. et al. (eds), *Estudios sobre la fonología del español del Caribe* (Caracas: La Casa de Bello): 53–74.

Lang, M. (1980) 'Sprachenpolitik. Einige Bemerkungen zur mühsamen und doch notwendigen Kooperation von Sehern und Bastlern', *Osnabrücker Beiträge zur Sprachtheorie*, 14: 75–9.

Lapesa, R. (1981) *Historia de la lengua española* (Madrid: Gredos).

Lass, R. (1997) *Historical Linguistics and Change* (New York: Cambridge University Press).

Le Page, R. and Tabouret-Keller, A. (1985) *Acts of identity: Creole-based approaches to language and ethnicity* (Cambridge: Cambridge University Press).

Leáñez Astimuño, C. (2002) '¿Competir con el inglés o emigrar a él?', *Argos*, 36: 127–44.

Lefebvre, C. (1998) *Creole Genesis and the Acquisition of Grammar: The Case of Haitian Creole* (Cambridge: Cambridge University Press).

Lehmann, C. (1982) *Thoughts on Grammaticalization. A Programmatic Sketch*. Vol 1, akup 48, (Universität zu Köln [2nd edn 1995, Munich: Lincom]).

Lehmann, C. (1989) 'Grammatikalisierung und Lexikalisierung', *ZPSK*, 42: 11–19.

Levin, B. and Rappaport-Hovay, M. (1995) *Unaccusativity* (Boston, MA: MIT Press).

Lippi-Green, R. (1997) *English with an Accent: Language, Ideology and Discrimination in the United States* (London/New York: Routledge).

Lipski, J. (1982) 'Spanish-English language switching in speech and literature: Theories and models', *The Bilingual Review*, 3: 191–12.

Lipski, J. (1993) 'Creoloid phenomena in the Spanish of transitional bilinguals', in Roca, A. and Lipski, J. (eds), *Spanish in the United States: Linguistic contact and diversity* (Berlin: Mouton de Gruyter): 155–82.

Lipski, J. (1994) *Latin American Spanish* (London and New York: Longman).

Lipski, J. (1996) 'Génesis y evolución de la cópula en los criollos afro-ibéricos', paper delivered at the Seminario Internacional "Palenque, Cartagena y Afro-Caribe: conexiones históricas y lingüísticas", Cartagena de Indias, (6 August, 1996.)

Lipski, J. (1998) 'Perspectivas sobre el español bozal', in Perl, M. and Schwegler, A. (eds) *América Negra: Panorámica Actual de los Estudios Lingüísticos sobre*

Variedades Hispanas, Portuguesas y Criollas (Frankfurt am Main/Madrid: Vervuert/Iberoamericana).

Lipski, J. (1999) 'El sufijo –ico y las palabras agüé/awe y aguora/ahuora: rutas de evolución y entorno dialectológico', in Ortiz López (ed.), *El Caribe Hispánico: Perspectivas Lingüísticas Actuales* (Frankfurt am Main/Madrid: Vervuert/Iberoamericana): 17–42.

Lipski, J. (2005) 'A History of Afro-Hispanic Language: Five Centuries and Five Continents' (Cambridge: Cambridge University Press).

Lipski, J. (2002) 'Génesis y evolución de la cópula en los criollos afro-ibéricos', in Moñino, Y. and Schwegler, A. (eds), *Palenque, Cartagena y Afro-Caribe: historia y lengua*: 65–101 (Tübingen: Niemeyer).

Llei de Política Lingüística (1998) http://cultural.gencat.es//llengcat/legis/act1.html (English version), (accessed 26/04/03).

Lodares, J.R. (2001) *Gente de Cervantes: la historia humana del idioma español* (Madrid: Taurus).

López García, A. (1985) *El rumor de los desarraigados* (Barcelona: Anagrama).

López Morales, H. (1992) *El español del Caribe* (Madrid. Editorial MAPFRE).

López Morales, H. (1983) *La estratificación social del español de San Juan de Puerto Rico* (México: Universidad Nacional Autónoma de México).

López, L.E. and Jung, I. (eds) (1998) *Sobre las huellas de la voz* (Madrid: Morata).

Lozano, A.G. (1975) 'Syntactic borrowing in Spanish from Quechua: The noun phrase', in Avalos de Matos, R. and Ravines, R. (eds), *Lingüística e indigenismo moderno de América. Actas y memorias del XXXIX congreso internacional de americanistas* (Lima, Perú: Instituto de Estudios Peruanos): 297–305.

Luján M., Minaya, L. and Sankoff, D. (1984) 'Implicational universals as predictors of word order acquisition stages in the speech of Quechua/Spanish bilingual children', *Language*, 60: 343–71.

Lumsden, J.S. (1999) 'Language Acquisition and creolization', in DeGraff (ed.), (1999): 129–57.

Marcet i Salom, P. (1987) *Història de la llengua catalana* (Barcelona: Teide).

Mar-Molinero, C. (1997) *The Spanish-Speaking World: A Practical Introduction to Sociolinguistic Issues* (London and New York: Routledge).

Mar-Molinero, C. (2000) *The politics of language in the Spanish-speaking world: from colonization to globalization* (London, New York: Routledge).

Mar-Molinero, C. (2004) 'Spanish as a world language: Language and identity in a global era', *Spanish in Context*, 1 (1): 3–20.

Mar-Molinero, C. (2006) 'The European Linguistic Legacy in a Global Era: Linguistic Imperialism, Spanish and the Instituto Cervantes', in Mar-Molinero, C. and Stevenson, P. (eds) (2005) *Language Ideologies, Policies and Practices: Language and the future of Europe*, (Basingstoke/New York: Palgrave Macmillan): 76–91.

Marshall, S. (2005) *Spanish-speaking Latin Americans in Catalonia: constructions of Catalan* (PhD thesis, Institute of Education, University of London).

Martin, F. (2002) 'Patrimoine et plurilingue et faiblesse de l'État: l'émergence des nationalismes autour de la question linguistique', in Boyer and Lagarde (eds) (2002): 17–40.

Maschler, Y. (1998) 'On the transition from code-switching to a mixed code', in Auer, P. (ed.), *Code-switching in conversation: Language, interaction and identity* (London: Routledge): 125–49.

Mather, P.-A. (2000) *Crosslinguistic Influence in Second Language Acquisition and in Creole Genesis*, Ph.D Dissertation, University of Pittsburg.

Matus-Mendoza, M. (2004) 'Assibilation of /-r/ and Migration among Mexicans', *Language Variation and Change*, 16: 17–30.

Maurais, J. and Morris, M.A. (eds) (2003) *Languages in a Globalising World* (Cambridge: Cambridge University Press).

May, S. (2001) *Language and Minority Rights: Ethnicity, Nationalism and the Politics of Languages* (Essex and New York: Longman).

McClure, E. (1981) 'Formal and functional aspects of the codeswitched discourse of bilingual children', in Durán, R. (ed.), *Latino language and communicative behavior* (Norwood, NJ: Ablex): 69–92.

Meeuwis, M. and Blommaert, J. (1998) 'A monolectal view of code-switching: Layered code-switching among Zairians in Belgium', in Auer, P. (ed.), *Codeswitching in conversation: Language, interaction and identity* (London: Routledge): 76–100.

Megenney, W. (1985) 'La influencia criollo-portuguesa en el español caribeño' *Anuario de Lingüística Hispánica* (Valladolid), 1: 157–80.

Miethaner, U. (2000) 'Orthographic transcriptions of non-standard varieties: The case of Earlier African-American English', *Journal of Sociolinguistics*, 4(4): 534–60.

Milroy, J. (2001) 'Language ideologies and the consequences of standardization' *Journal of Sociolinguistics*, 5 (4): 530–55.

Milroy, J. and Milroy, L. (1999) *Authority in Language: Investigating Standard English* 3rd ed. (London: Routledge).

Milroy, L. (1980) *Language and social networks* (London, Blackwell).

Milroy, L. and Milroy, J. (1992) 'Social networks and social class: toward an integrated sociolinguistic model', *Language in Society*, 21: 1–26.

Monteagudo, H. and Santamarina, A. (1993) 'Galician and Castilian in contact: historical, social and linguistic aspects', in Posner and Green (eds) (1993): 117–73.

Montes Alcalá, C. (2001) 'Written codeswitching: Powerful bilingual images', in Jacobson, R. (ed.), *Codeswitching Worldwide II* (Berlin: Mouton de Gruyter): 193–22.

Montes-Alcalá, C. (2000) *Two languages, one pen: Socio-pragmatic functions in written Spanish-English code switching* (Doctoral Thesis, Santa Barbara: University of California).

Morales, A. (1986) *Gramáticas en contacto: Análisis sintácticos sobre el español de Puerto Rico* (Madrid: Editorial Playor).

Morales, A. (1996) 'El español de Puerto Rico: aspectos sintácticos', *Boletín de la Academia Puertorriqueña de la Lengua Española*. Segunda Epoca.

Morales. E. (2002) *Living in Spanglish: The Search for Latino Identity in America* (New York: St. Martin's Press).

Morales-Gónzalez, D. and Torres, C. (eds) (1992) *Educational Policy and Social Change: Experience from Latin America* (Westport/London: Praeger).

Moreno, F. (1996) 'Castilla La Nueva', in Alvar, M. (ed.) (1996): 213–32.

Mufwene, S.S. (2004) 'Language birth and death', *Annual Review of Anthropology*, 33: 201–22.

Muñoz Cruz, H. (1987) 'Testimonios metalingüísticos de un conflicto intercultural: ¿Reivindicación o sólo representación de la cultura otomí?', in Muñoz Cruz, H. (ed.) (1987) *Funciones sociales y conciencia del lenguaje. Estudios sociolingüísticos en México* (Xalapa: Universidad Veracruzana): 87–118.

Muysken, P. (2000) *Bilingual speech: A typology of code-mixing* (Cambridge: Cambridge UP).

Navarro Tomás, T. (1948) *El Español de Puerto Rico* (Río Piedras: Editorial de la Universidad de Puerto Rico).

Ninyoles, R.L. (1969) *Conflicte lingüística valencià* (València: Tres i Quatre).

Ninyoles, R.L. (1971) *Idioma i prejudici* (Palma: Moll).

Ninyoles, R.L. (1972) *Idioma y poder social* (Madrid: Tecnos).

Ninyoles, R.L. (1995) *Conflicte lingüístic valencià* (València: Tres i Quatre).

Noves, S.L. (2003) La Generalitat emprèn una campanya per facilitar la integració lingüística de les persones immigrades (*Noticies*) http://cultural.gencat.net/llengcat/noves/noticies/campanya.htm (accessed 21/03/03).

ó Riagáin, P. (1997) *Language Policy and Social Reproduction in Ireland 1893–1993* (Oxford: Clarendon Press).

O'Rourke, B. (2005) *Attitudes towards Minority Languages: An Investigation of Young People's Attitudes towards Irish and Galician* (Unpublished PhD thesis) (Dublin: Dublin City University).

Ocampo, F. (1990) 'El subjuntivo en tres generaciones de hablantes bilingües', in Bergen, J. (ed.), *Spanish in the United States: Sociolinguistic Issues* (Washington, DC: Georgetown University Press): 39–48.

Ochs , E. and Schieffelin, B. (eds) (1979) *Developmental Pragmatics* (New York: Academic Press).

Ochs, E. (1979) 'Transcription as theory', in Ochs and Schieffelin (eds) (1979): 43–72.

Oesch Serra, C. (1998) 'Discourse connectives in bilingual conversation: The case of an emerging Italian-French mixed code', in Auer, P. (ed.), *Code-switching in conversation: Language, interaction and identity* (London: Routledge): 101–24.

Oesterreicher, W. (2002) 'El español, lengua pluricéntrica: perspectivas y límites de una autoafirmación lingüística nacional en Hispanoamérica. El caso mexicano' *Lexis*, 26 (2): 275–04.

Ortiz López, L.A. (1998) *Huellas Etno-sociolingüísticas Bozales y Afrocubanas* (Frankfurt am Main/Madrid: Editorial Vervuert/Iberoamericana).

Ortiz López, L.A. (ed.) (1999a) *El Caribe Hispánico: Perspectivas Lingüísticas Actuales. Homenaje a Manuel Alvarez Nazario* (Frankfurt am Main/Madrid: Editorial Vervuert/Iberoamericana).

Ortiz López, L.A. (1999b) 'La variante hispánica haitianizada en Cuba: otro rostro del contacto lingüístico en el Caribe', in Morales, A., Cardona, J., Forastieri, E. and López Morales, H., (eds), *Estudios de Lingüística Hispánica. Homenaje a María Vaquero* (Editorial Universidad de Puerto Rico): 428–56.

Ortiz López, L.A. (1999c) 'El español haitiano en Cuba y su relación con el habla bozal', in Zimmermann (ed.), *Lenguas Criollas de Base Lexical Española y Portuguesa* (Frankfurt am Main/Madrid: Vervuert/Iberoamericana): 145–76.

Ortiz López, L.A. (2001a) 'Contacto lingüístico en la frontera dominico-haitiana: hallazgos preliminares de un proyecto en marcha' *Anuario 1* (Centro de Altos Estudios Humanísticos y del Idioma Español, República Dominicana): 327–56.

Ortiz López, L.A. (2001b) 'El sistema verbal del español haitiano en Cuba: implicaciones para las lenguas en contacto en el Caribe', *Southwest Journal of Linguistics*, 20 (2): 175–192.

Ortiz López, L.A. (15–17 October 2004) ' "No llevando nada, deja todo allá": usos del gerundio en la frontera Domínico-haitiana', paper delivered at the The Eighth Hispanic Linguistics Symposium Together With the Seventh

Conference on the Acquisition of Spanish and Portuguese as First and Second Languages, University of Minnesota.

Ortiz López, L.A. (24–26 March 2005a) 'Huellas del habla bozal en el español de la frontera domínico-haitiana: ¿contacto de lenguas y/o universales lingüísticos de adquisición?', paper delivered at the colloquium *El habla bozal: Spanish in contact with African languages*, at the XX Spanish in the U.S./Spanish in Contact with Other Languages Conference, University of Illinois, Chicago.

Ortiz López, L.A. (24–26 March 2005b) 'La negación en la frontera domínico-haitiana: variantes y usos (socio)lingüísticos', paper delivered at the XX Spanish in the U.S./Spanish in Contact with Other Languages Conference, University of Illinois, Chicago.

Ortiz López, L.A. and Lacorte, M. (eds) (2005) *Contactos y contextos lingüísticos: el español en los Estados Unidos y en contacto con otras lenguas* (Frankfurt am Main/Madrid: Vervuert/Iberoamericana).

Otheguy, R. (1993) 'A reconsideration of the notion of loan translation in the analysis of U.S. Spanish', in Roca, A. and Lipski, J. (eds), *Spanish in the United States. Linguistic contact and diversity* (Berlín: Mouton de Gruyter): 21–45.

Otheguy, R. (2001) 'Simplificación y adaptación en el español de Nueva York', Ponencia – II Congreso Internacional de la lengua española – Valladolid. http://cvc.cervantes.es/obref/congresos/valladolid/ponencias/unidad_diversidad_del_espanol (accessed August 4, 2003).

Otheguy, R., García, O. and Fernández, M. (1989) 'Transferring, switching, and modelling in West New York Spanish: An intergenerational study', in Wherritt, I. and García, O. (eds), *US Spanish: The language of Latinos. International Journal of the Sociology of Language*, n°. 79: 41–52.

Paerregaard, K. (1997) *Linking separate worlds: urban migrants and rural lives in Peru* (New York: Berg Publishing Ltd.).

Paredes, L. (1992) 'Assibilation of /r/ in the Andino-Spanish Variety in Lima'. Presented at the Second Annual Conference on Spanish in Contact with Other Languages, University of Minnesota, October 1992.

Paredes, L. (1996) The Spanish continuum in Peruvian bilingual speakers: A study of verbal clitics (Quechua) (Los Angeles, CA: University of Southern California dissertation).

Paulston, C.B. (1994) *Linguistic Minorities in Multilingual Settings: Implications for Language Policies* (Amsterdam and Philadelphia: John Benjamins).

Pavlenko, A. and Blackledge, A. (eds) (2004) *Negotiation of Identities in Multilingual Contexts* (Clevedon, Avon: Multilingual Matters).

Pennycook, A. (1998) *English and the Discourses of Colonialism* (London/New York: Routledge).

Pérez Leroux, A.T. (1999) 'Innovación sintáctica en el español del Caribe y los principios de la gramática universal', in Ortiz López (ed.) (1999a): 99–118.

Perissinotto, G. (1975) *Fonología del español hablado en la Ciudad de México: ensayo de un método sociolingüístico* (México: El Colegio de México).

Perl, M. (1985) 'El fenómeno de descriollización del "habla bozal" y el lenguaje coloquial de la variante cubana del español', *Anuario de Lingüística Hispánica* (Valladolid) 1: 191–201.

Pfaff, C. (1982) 'Constraints on language mixing: Intrasentential code-switching and borrowing in Spanish/English', in Amastae, J. and Elías-Olivares, L. (eds),

Spanish in the United States: Sociolinguistic aspects (New York: Cambridge University Press): 264–97.

Philips, S.U. (1998) 'Language ideologies in institutions of power: a commentary', in Schieffelin, Woolard, and Kroskrity (eds) (1998): 211–25.

Phillipson, R. (1992) *Linguistic Imperialism* (Oxford: Oxford University Press).

Phillipson, R. (2003) *English-Only Europe: Challenging Language Policies* (London/New York: Routledge).

Pike, F. (1971) *Hispanismo, 1898–1936* (Notre Dame: University of Notre Dame Press).

Poplack, S. (1982) ' "Sometimes I'll start a sentence in Spanish y termino en español": toward a typology of code-switching', in Amastae, J. and Elías-Olivares, L. (eds), *Spanish in the United States: Sociolinguistic aspects* (New York: Cambridge University Press): 230–63.

Poplack, S. and Meechan, M. (1998) 'How languages fit together in code-mixing', *International Journal of Bilingualism*, 2 (2): 127–38.

Poplack, S. and Tagliamonte, S. (1999) 'The grammaticization of *going to* in (African American) English', *Language Variation and Change* ,11(3): 315–42.

Portas, M. (1997) *Língua e sociedade na Galiza* (A Coruña: Bahía).

Posner, R. and Green, J.N. (eds) (1993)*Trends in Romance Linguistics and Philology. Volume 5: Bilingualism and Linguistic Contact in Romance* (Berlin and New York: Mouton de Gruyter).

Pozzi-Escot, I. (1973) *Apuntes sobre el castellano de Ayacucho. Documento de Trabajo No. 21* (Lima: Centro de Investigación de Lingüística Aplicada, Universidad Nacional Mayor de San Marcos).

Pozzi-Escot, I. (1990) 'Reflexiones sobre el castellano como segunda lengua en el Perú', in Ballón Aguirre, E. and Cerrón-Palomino, E. (eds), *Diglosia linguo-literaria y educación en el Perú*, (Lima: Multiservicios Editoriales): 51–72.

Pradilla, M.A. (2004) 'La llengua catalana: un miratge de normalitat', in Pradilla, M.A. (coord) (2004) *Calidoscopi lingüístic* (Barcelona: Octaedro-EUB): 53–110.

Pratt, M.L. (1987) 'Linguistic Utopias' in Fabb, N., Attridge, D. Durant, A. and McCabe, C. (eds) (1987) *The Linguistics of Writing: Arguments between Language and Literature* (Manchester: Manchester University Press): 48–66.

Pratt, M.L. (1992) *Imperial Eyes. Travel Writing and Transculturation* (London/ New York: Routledge).

Pratt, M.L. (2005) 'Why the Virgin of Zapopan went to Los Angeles: Reflections on Mobility and Globality' in Andermann, J. and Rowe, W. (eds) (2005) *Images of Power: Iconography, culture and the State in Latin America* (New York/Oxford: Berghahm): 271–91.

Preston, D.R. (1982) ' "Ritin' fowklower daun rong": Folklorists' failures in phonology', *Journal of American Folklore* 95(377): 330–39.

Preston, D.R. (1985) 'The Li'l Abner Syndrome', *American Speech*, 60 (4): 328–36.

Pujolar, J. (1993) 'L'estudi de les normes d'ús des de l'Analisi Crítica del Discurs', *Treballs de Sociolingüística Catalana* (11), (València: Editorial Tres i Quatre): 61–78.

Pujolar, J. (2001) *Gender, Heteroglossia and Power: a sociolinguistic study of youth culture* (Berlin: Mouton de Gruyter).

Querol, E. (1990) 'El procés de substitució lingüística: la comarca dels Ports com a exemple' in Generalitat Valenciana (ed.): 85–196.

Quilis, A. (1965) 'Description phonétique du parler madrilène actuel', *Phonetica* 12: 19–24.

Ramos-García, L.A. (1998) 'El teatro callejero peruano: proceso de cholificación', *Gestos*, 25: 105–16.

Rampton, B. (1995) *Crossing: Language and Ethnicity among Adolescents* (London/New York: Longman).

Rampton, B. (1999): 'Language crossing and the redefinition of reality', in Auer, P. (ed.), *Code-switching in conversation: Language, interaction and identity* (London: Routledge): 290–320.

Reixach, M. (1990) *Difusió social del coneixement de la llengua catalana. Anàlisi de les dades lingüístiques del padró d'habitants de 1986 de Catalunya, Illes Balears i País Valencià* (Barcelona: Generalitat de Catalunya).

Ricento, T. (ed) (2000) *Ideology, Politics and Language Policies* (Amsterdam/Philadelphia: John Benjamins).

Rissell, D. (1989) 'Sex, Attitudes, and the Assibilation of /r/ among Young People in San Luis Potosí, Mexico', *Language Variation and Change*, 1: 269–83.

Rivarola, J.L. (1990) *La formación lingüística de Hispanoamérica* (Lima: Pontificia Universidad Católica del Perú).

Rivera Alamo, R. (1989) 'Interferencia lingüística: Algunas de sus manifestaciones en el sistema verbal del español en Puerto Rico', *Asomante*, XXXVII: 163–70.

Roberts, C. and Williams, G. (1980) 'Attitudes and ideological bases of support for Welsh as a minority language', in Giles, H., Robinson, W. and Smith, P. (eds) (1980): 227–32.

Roberts, C., Byram, M., Barro, A., Jordan, S., and Street, B. (2001) *Language Learners as Ethnographers* (Clevedon, Buffalo, Toronto, Sidney: Multilingual Matters).

Robinson, L. (1998, May 11) 'Hispanics don't exist', *U.S. News* http://www.usnews.com/usnews/issue/archive/980511/19980511003893_brief.php (accessed July 5, 2004).

Romero Vargas, G. (1995) *Las sociedades del Atlántico de Nicaragua en los siglos XVII y XVIII* (Managua: Fondo de Promoción Cultural, BANIC).

Rosaldo, R. (1980) *Culture and Truth: The remaking of social analysis* (Boston: Beacon Press).

Rosaldo, R. (1994) 'Ciudadanía cultural en San José, California', in García Canclini, N. et al. (eds) (1994) *De lo local a lo global. Perspectivas desde la antropología* (México: UAM): 67–88.

Salvador, G. (1987) *Lengua española y lengua de España* (Barcelona: Ariel).

Salvador, G. (1992) *Política lingüística y sentido común* (Madrid: Istmo).

Samper, J.A. (1990) *Estudio sociolingüístico del español de Las Palmas de Gran Canaria* (Las Palmas: La Caja de Canaria).

Sánchez, A. and Dueñas, M. (2002) 'Language Planning in the Spanish-Speaking World', *Current Issues in Language Planning*, 3 (3): 280–305.

Sánchez, L. (2003) *Quechua-Spanish Bilingualism. Interference and convergence in functional categories* (Amsterdam/Philadelphia: John Benjamins).

Sankoff, G. (2002) 'Linguistic outcomes of language contact', in Chambers, J.K., Trudgill, P. and Schilling-Estes, N. (eds), *The handbook of language variation and change* (Oxford: Blackwell): 638–68.

Schieffelin, B.B., Woolard, K. and Kroskrity P.V. (eds) (1998) *Language ideologies: practice and theory* (Oxford: Oxford University Press).

Schiffman, H.F. (1996) *Linguistic culture and language policy* (London: Routledge).

Schwartz, B. and Sprouse, R. (1996) 'L2 cognitive states and the full transfer/full access model', *Second Language Research*, 12: 40–72.

Scott, J. (2002) 'In simple pronouns, clues to shifting Latino identity', *The New York Times*, December 5, 2002, B1.

Sebba, M. (1997) *Contact Languages: Pidgins and Creoles* (New York: St Martin's Press).

Selinker, L. (1972) 'Interlanguage', *IRAL*, 10: 209–31.

Selinker, L. (1992) *Rediscovering Interlanguage* (New York: Longman).

Sierra, M.T. (1990) 'Lenguaje, prácticas jurídicas y derecho consuetudinario indígena', in Rodolfo Stavenhagen and Diego Iturralde (eds), *Entre la ley y la costumbre. El derecho consuetudinario indígena en América Latina.* (México: Instituto Indigenista Interamericano – Instituto Interamericano de Derechos Humanos): 231–58.

Sierra, M.T. (1992) *Discurso, cultura y poder. El ejercicio de la autoridad en los pueblos hñähñús del Valle del Mezquital* (México-Pachuca: CIESAS-Gobierno del Estado de Hidalgo).

Sierra, M.T. (1995) 'Indian rights and customary law in Mexico: A study of the Nahuas in the Sierra de Puebla', *Law and Society Review*, 29 (2): 227–54.

Siguan, M. (1992) *España plurilingüe* (Barcelona: Ariel).

SIL, Summer Instiute of Linguists (2005) *Ethnologue*, 5th edn. www.ethnologue.com.

Silva-Corvalán, C. (1986) 'Bilingualism and Language Change: The Extension of *Estar* in Los Angeles Spanish', *Language*, 62: 587–608.

Silva Corvalán, C. (1994) *Language contact and change. Spanish in Los Angeles* (Oxford: Clarendon Press).

Silva Corvalán, C. (ed.) (1995) *Spanish in the four continents. Studies in language contact and bilingualism* (Washington: Georgetown University Press).

Silva Corvalán, C. (2001) *Sociolingüística y pragmática del español* (Washington: Georgetown University Press).

Silverstein, M. (1992) 'The uses and utility of ideology: A commentary', in Schieffelin, B., Woolard, K.A. and Kroskrity, P.V. (eds) (1998) *Language Ideologies. Theory and Practice* (Oxford: Oxford University Press): 123–45.

Skutnabb-Kangas, T. and Philipson, R. (eds) (1994) *Linguistic Human Rights: Overcoming Linguistic Discrimination* (Berlin/New York: Mouton de Gruyter).

Smolicz, J. (1995) 'Australia's language policies and minority rights', in Skutnabb-Kangas and Phillipson (eds) (1994): 235–52.

Smolicz, J.J. and Secombe, M. (1988) 'Community languages, core values and cultural maintenance: the Australian experience with special reference to Greek, Latvian and Polish groups', in Clyne (ed.) (1988): 11–38.

Spolsky, B. (2004) *Language Policy* (Cambridge: Cambridge University Press).

Stavans, I. (2003) *Spanglish: The Making of a New American Language* (New York: HarperCollins).

Stroud, C. (2004) 'Rinkeby Swedish and semilingualism in language ideological debates: a Bourdieuean perspective', *Journal of Sociolinguistics*, 8 (2): 196–214.

Stroud, C. and Hengh, K. (2004) 'Linguistic human rights and linguistic citizenship', in D. Patrick and J. Freeland (eds), *Language Rights & Language Survival: a Sociolinguistic Exploration* (Manchester: St Jerome): 191–219.

Suárez, D. (2002) 'The paradox of linguistic hegemony and the maintenance of Spanish as a heritage language in the United States', *Journal of Multilingual and Multicultural Development*, 23 (6): 512–31.

Suñer, M. (1986) 'Lexical subject of infinitives in Caribbean Spanish', in Jaegglie, O. and Silva Corvalán, C. (eds), *Studies in Romance Linguistics* (Dordrecht: Foris): 189–203.

240   *References*

Tamarón, Marqués de (ed.) (1995) *El peso de la lengua española en el mundo* (Valladolid: INCIPE).

Terrell, T. (1978 b) 'La aspiración y la elisión de /s/ en el español porteño', *Anuario de Letras*, 16: 41–66.

Terrell, T. (1978a) 'Constraints on the aspiration and deletion of final /s/ in Cuban and Puerto Rican Spanish', *The Bilingual Review*, 4: 35–51.

Therrien, M. and Ramírez, R. (2000) *The Hispanic Population in the United States: March 2000* Current Population Reports 520–35, US Census Bureau, Washington D.C.

Thomason, S. and Kaufman, T. (1988) *Language Contact, Creolization, and Genetic Linguistics* (Berkeley: University of California Press).

Tonkin, E. (1992) *Narrating our Pasts: The social construction of oral history* (Cambridge: Cambridge University Press).

Torres, L. (1997) *Puerto Rican discourse: A sociolinguistic study of a New York suburb* (Mahwah, NJ.: Erlbaum).

Torres Cacoullos, R. (1999) *Grammaticization, synchronic variation, and language contact: A study of Spanish progressive –ndo constructions* (Unpublished doctoral dissertation, Albuquerque: University of New Mexico).

Torres Cacoullos, R. (2000) *Grammaticization, synchronic variation, and language contact. A study of Spanish progressive –ndo constructions* (Amsterdam/ Philadelphia: John Benjamins Publishing Company).

Torres Cacoullos, R. (2001) 'From lexical to grammatical to social meaning', *Language in Society*, 30 (3): 443–78.

Tovey, H. and Share, P. (2003) *A Sociology of Ireland* (2nd edition) (Dublin: Gill and Macmillan).

Tsitsipis, L.D. (2004) 'A sociolinguistic application of Bakhtin's authoritative and internally persuasive discourse', *Journal of Sociolinguistics*, 8 (4): 569–94.

Turell, M.T. (2001a) 'Spain's Multilingual Make-up: Beyond, Within and Across Babel', in Turell (ed.) (2001b): 1–57.

Turell, M.T. (ed.) (2001b) *Multilingualism in Spain: Sociolinguistic and Psycholinguistic Aspects of Linguistic Minority Groups* (Clevedon: Multilingual Matters).

Tusón, A. (1990) 'Catalan-Spanish code-switching in interpersonal communications', *Papers for the Workshop on Impact and consequences: broader considerations* (Brussels: European Science Foundation, Network on Code-switching and Language Contact): 167–87.

U.S. Census Bureau (2001) *United States Census 2000: Population tables and reports.* http://www.census.gov/main/www/cen2000.html (accessed May 29, 2001).

Urciuoli, B. (1996) *Exposing Prejudice: Puerto Rican Experiences of Language, Race, and Class* (Boulder: Westview Press).

Vaamonde et al. (eds) (2003) *Estudio Sociolingüístico sobre o uso da lingua galega no Concello de Vigo 2002* (Vigo: Universidade de Vigo).

Vainnika, A. and Young-Scholten, M. (1996) 'Gradual Development of L2 phrase structure', *Second Language Research* 12: 7–39.

Valdés, G. (2000) 'Introduction', in AATSP: Professional development series, Volume 1, *Spanish for native speakers* (Forth Worth, TX: Harcourt College Publishers): 1–20.

Valdés-Fallis, G. (1976) 'Social interaction and code-switching patterns: A case study of Spanish/English alternation', in Keller, G. et al. (eds) *Bilingualism in the bicentennial and beyond* (New York: The Bilingual Press): 53–85.

Valdez Salas, M.L. (2002) *Clitics in the speech of monolingual Andean Spanish speakers* (Pittsburgh, PA: University of Pittsburgh dissertation).

Vallverdú, F. (1973) *El fet lingüistic com a fet social* (Barcelona: Edicions 62).

Vallverdú, F. (1980) *Aproximació crítica a la sociolingüística catalana* (Barcelona: Edicions 62).

Van Maanen, J. (1995) 'An end to innocence: The ethnography of ethnography, in, Van Maanen, J. (ed.) (1995) *Representation in Ethnography* (London: Sage): 1–35.

Vargas, V.M. (2004) 'Miles de colombianos podrán legalizar su situación en España', *El Tiempo*, (December 30th, 2004).

Veltman, C. (1983) *Language shift in the United States* (Berlin, New York: Mouton de Gruyter).

Veltman, C. (1990) 'The status of the Spanish language in the United States at the beginning of the 21st century', *International Migration Review* 24: 124–48.

Veltman, C. (2000) 'The American linguistic mosaic: Understanding language shift in the United States', in McKay, S.L. and Wong, S-L. C. (eds) *New Immigrants in the United States* (Cambridge, UK: Cambridge University Press): 58–93.

Villa, D. (2000) 'Languages have Armies and Economies too: the Presence of US Spanish in the Spanish-speaking World', *Southwest Journal of Linguistics*, 19: 144–54.

Villa, D. (2001) 'A millenial reflection sobre la nueva reconquista', *Southwest Journal of Linguistics* 20 (1): 1–13.

Wallerstein, I. (1983) *Historical Capitalism* (London: Verso).

Weinreich, U. (1953) *Languages in Contact* (The Hague: Mouton).

Williams, A. and Kerswill, P. (1999) 'Dialect levelling: continuity vs. change in Milton Keynes, Reading and Hull', in Foulkes, P. and Docherty, G.J. (eds), *Urban Voices* (London: Arnold): 141–62.

Williams, G. (1992) *Sociolinguistics. A sociological critique* (London, New York: Routledge).

Winford, D. (2003) *An Introduction to Contact Linguistics* (Oxford, England: Blackwell Publishing).

Woods, S. (2003) *YOU can read and write Kriol* (Bluefields, Nicaragua: FOREIBCA-IPILC/URACCAN).

Woolard, K. (1989) *Double Talk. Bilingualism and the Politics of Ethnicity in Catalonia.* (Stanford: Stanford University Press).

Woolard, K. (1998) 'Introduction: Language ideology as a Field of Inquiry', in Schieffelin, B. Woolard, K. and Kroskrity, P. (eds) (1998) *Language Ideologies: Practice and Theory* (New York/Oxford: Oxford University Press): 3–51.

Woolard, K. (2005) 'Language and identity choice in Catalonia: the interplay of ideologies of linguistic authenticity and anonymity' Paper given at the *International Colloquium on Regulations on Societal Multilingualism in Linguistic Policies*, Ibero-Amerikanisches Institut P.K., Berlin.

Woolard, K. and Gahng, T.J. (1990) 'Changing language policies and attitudes in autonomous Catalonia', *Language in Society*, 19: 311–30.

Woolard, K. and Schieffelin, B (1994) 'Language Ideology' *Annual Review of Anthropology*, 25: 55–82.

Wright, R. and Ricketts, P. (eds) (2005) *Studies on Ibero-Romance Linguistics Dedicated to Ralph Penny* (Newark: Juan de la Cuesta).

Wright, S. (2004) *Language Policy and Language Planning* (Basingstoke/New York: Palgrave Macmillan).

Zentella, A.C. (1990) 'Lexical leveling in four New York City Spanish dialects: Linguistic and social factors', *Hispania,* 73 (4): 1094–105.

Zentella, A.C. (1997) *Growing up bilingual: Puerto Rican children in New York* (Malden, MA: Blackwell).

Zentella, A. (2000) 'Puerto Ricans in the US: Confronting the linguistic repercussions of colonialism', in McKay, S. and Wong, S. (eds), *New immigrants in the United States: Readings for second language acquisition* (Cambridge: Cambridge University Press): 137–64.

Zimmermann, K. (ed.) (1995) *Lenguas en contacto en Hispanoamérica* (Frankfurt am Main/Madrid: Editorial Vervuert/Iberoamericana).

Name Index

Alvar, M. 16
álvarez, C. 82
Alvord, S. 102
Anderson, B. 186
'imagined' community 15, 30
Anzaldúa, G. 36, 44
Aracil, L.V. 181
Auer, P. 78, 79
Aznar, J.M. 34, 35, 42

Bakhtin, M.M. 143, 147
Balestra, A. 93n
Barbour, S. 26(n2)
Barro, A. 238
Barth, F. 50
Bates, E. 121
Berdugo, Ó 35, 42
Bereiter, C. 83–4
Bickerton, D. 120
Bills, G.D. 71
Blackledge, A. 156(n4)
Blommaert, J. 9, 11, 12
Bonfil Batalla, G. 58
Bourdieu, P. 30, 44, 160, 221
   cultural capital 186
   habitus concept 56
   'polite' behaviour 194
Bouzada, X.M. 192
Boyer, H. 54
Brutt-Griffler, J. 8, 12–13, 19
Bybee, J.L., et al. (1994) 79, 222
   Pagliuca, W. 222
   Perkins, R. 222
Byram, M. 238

Calvet, L.-J. 74(n2)
Camagarajah, A.S. 3, 6
Cameron, D. 10, 43
Caravedo, R. x, 4–5, 16, 21, 95, 96,
   97, 100–3, 105, 110, 112(n4),
   113(n9), 222
Carmichael, C. 26(n2)
Carreira, M. 24

Carreter, F.L. 38–9
Casesnoves Ferrer, R. x, 7, 180, 194,
   217, 218(n1)
Castells, M. 187
Castor, S. 121
Cerrón-Palomino, R. 73, 95
Chomsky, N. 74(n4), 118–20
Chopra, P. 138
Cifuentes, B. 47, 73
Clements, C. 136(n7)
Clifford, J. 138
Cobarrubias, J. 181–2
Concha, V.G. de la 31, 37
Cortés, M.A. 33–4
Coupland, N. 22
Crickmay, L. 156(n1)
Crystal, D. 8, 45(n1)
Cucó, A. 201

D'Andrea, D. 228
Damoiseau, R. 126
Dartmouth College 38
de Granda, G. 95
de Swaan, A. 48
DeGraff, M. 121, 136(n8)
del Valle, J. x, 2, 3–4, 13, 19, 24–5,
   26(n5–6), 27, 31–2, 46(n4–5),
   47, 73, 190–1, 224
Díaz, N., et al. (2002) 116, 225
   Ludwig, R. 225
   Pfänder, S. 225
Dieck, M. 135(n5)
Dueñas, M. 9, 26(n3, n10), 27

Echávez-Solano, N. 102
Escobar, A. 95
Escobar, A.M. 95

Fairclough, M. x–xi, 4, 24, 93(n2)
Fairclough, N. 77, 148
Faraclas, N. 135n
Fasold, R.W. 54
Fernández, M. 236

243

Fishman, J.A. 51, 54, 74(n6–7), 226
Foley, D.E. 138
Franco, F. 201, 202
Freeland, J. xi, 6, 15, 21–2,
    116, 137n, 138–51, 153,
    156(n1, n5, n7–8),
    157(n10, 12, 14)
classroom discussion/interaction
    138, 140f, 141, 145, 150,
    156(n5)
'not a native speaker of Spanish'
    143, 155
'three stances' 145

Gabriel-Stheeman, L. 26(n5),
    47, 73
Gal, S. 1–2, 4, 31, 42, 54, 68,
    74(n8), 180
García, E. 106, 108
García, O. 236
García Canclini, N. 50
Gardt, A. 8
Gardy, P. 75(n18)
Garrido, A. 38
Giddens, A. 18, 28, 172, 176
'knowledgeability' and 'reflexivity'
    160, 172
structuration 160
Givón, T. 79
Glaser, B.G. 75(n9)
Godenzzi, J.C. 95, 112(n3)
Goffman, E., frame analysis 56
González, M. 135(n4)
González Echevarría, R. 40–1
González Pérez, M. 142n
Goodman, J.C. 121
Graddol, D. 8
Grin, F.
'tolerability' 193
Gruzinski, S. 112(n1)
Gumperz, J.J. 49

Hakuta, K., et al. (1992) 52, 228
    D'Andrea, D. 228
Hall, S. 138
Hamel, R.E. xi, 4, 9, 13–14, 16, 21,
    23, 49, 52, 54, 55, 73, 74(n3),
    75(n11, n16), 139, 155, 181,
    197, 228–9

Hanks, W. 156(n2)
Haugen, E. 45(n3)
Heath, S.B. 73
Heine, B. 79
Heller, M. 10, 28, 74(n8)
Hernández-Chávez, E. 71, 81
Herrera, G.M. 137n
Heugh, K. 154
Hickey, L. xiii
Hill, J.H. 58, 64
Hill, K.C. 58, 64
Himmelmann, N.P. 79
'Hispanic nation' 47
Holm, J. 120, 142n
Hornberger, N.H. 73
House, J. 150, 154
Hudson, A. 71
Huntington, S.P. 36, 37, 48,
    49, 71
Hüppauf, B. 8, 18

Iglesias, E.V. 35
Iglesias Álvarez, A. 196(n5)
Irvine, J.T. 42

Jaffe, A. 149
Jordan, S. 238
Juaristi, J. 33–4
Jung, I. 73

Kachru, B.B. 48
Kaufman, T. 127
Kelly-Holmes, H. ii, ix
Kerswill, P. 97
Klee, C.A. xi, 4–5, 16, 21, 95, 96,
    102, 112(n4), 113(n9), 231
Klein-Andreu, F. 106
Kramsch, C.
'sphere of intercultural activity'
    153
Krashen, S. 127
Kroskrity, P.V. 29
Kubchandani, L.M.
'communication rights' 154
Kulick, D. 54, 68

Labov, W. 97, 103, 112(n2)
Lafont, R. 75(n18)
Lake, J. ix

Leáñez Astimuño, C.   47
Lefebvre, C.   125, 136(n8)
Lehmann, C.   79
Levin, B.   121, 131
Lippi-Green, R.   20
Lipski, J.   77, 133, **232–3**
'transitional bilinguals' (Lipski)   77
Lodares, J.R.   2, 26(n5), 45
López, L.E.   73
López García, Á.   2, 42, 46(n4)
López Morales, H.   37–8, 134
Lozano, A.G.   95
Ludwig, R.   225
Luján, M.   95

Mar-Molinero, C.   xii,   2, 3, 9, 19, 25,
   26(n2, n4–5, n9), 27–30, 31, 47,
   71, 75(n20), 93n, 155, 179,
   180–1, 197
Mar-Molinero, V.   ix
Marcus, G.   138
Marshall, S. (SM) xii,   6, 13, 159,
   164–70, 173–4, 176, 176(n1),
   177(n2, n4–6), 198, 204, 213
Martin, F.   178
Maschler, Y.   77, 78, 80
Maurais, J.   8, 10
May, S.   26(n2),   193
Meechan, M.   80
Miethaner, U.   149
Milroy, J.   43, 44, 97
Milroy, L.   43, 52, 97
Minaya, L.   95
Monteagudo, H.   179
Montes-Alcalá, C.   82, 93(n1)
Morris, M.A.   8, 10
Mufwene, S.S.   94
Muysken, P.   80–1

Nebrija, A. de   47
Nelson, C.L.   48
Nelson, D.J.   44
Ninyoles, R.L.   181

O'Rourke, B. xii,   7, 21,
   196(n2, n6),   197
Oesch Serra, C.   78
Ortiz López, L.A. xii,   5, 50, 117, 118,
   133, 134, 135(n1), **235–6**

Otheguy, R.   81n,   82, 93(n2),
   106, 108
Otheguy, R., *et al.* (1989)   81n,
   82, 236
Fernández, M.   236
García, O.   236

Paerregaard, K.   95
Paglivca, W.   222
Paredes, L.   102
Pastor, B.   38
Patrick, D.   xi
Paulston, C.B.   189, 190–1
Pavlenko, A.   156(n4)
Pennycook, A.   8
Perkins, R.   222
Pfaff, C.   77, 82
Pfänder, S.   225
Philips, S.U.   46(n5)
Phillipson, R.   8, 12
Poplack, S.   80, 82
Poplack and Meechan's typology
   (bilingual discourse,   1998) 80
Pozzi-Escot, I.   95
Pratt, M.L.   5–6, 11, 13–14, 23, 155,
   156(n1)
'contact zones'   139
Pujolar, J.
   discourse analysis   158
   'passive bilingualism'   158

Ramírez, R.   26(n11)
Rampton, B.   157(n13)
Rappaport-Hovay, M.   121, 131
Ricento, T.   8
Rivarola, J.L.   95
Roberts, C.   189
Roberts, C., *et al.* (2001)   153, 238
   Barro, A.   238
   Byram, M.   238
   Jordan, S.   238
   Street, B.   238
Ros Romero, M.C.   47, 73
Rosaldo, R.   138

Salvador, G.   2, 40
Sánchez, A.   9, 26(n3, n10),   27
Sankoff, D. xii-xiii,   7, 95, 180, 194,
   218(n1)

Santamarina, A.   179
Scardamalia, M.   83–4
Schieffelin, B.   9, 25–6(n1)
Schiffman, H.F.   45(n5)
Sebba, M.   120
Secombe, M.
  personal positive evaluation   **189, 191**
Selinker, L.   120
Share, P.   180
Sierra, M.T.   75(n14)
Siguan, M.   26(n5),   197
Silva-Corvalán, C.   75(n20), 80,
  81n, 82, 92, 93(n2)
  'bilingual continuum'   77
Silverstein, M.   75(n18)
Smith, A. xii
Smolicz, J.J.   188
  personal positive evaluation   **189, 191**
Spolsky, B.   12
Stavans, I.   44
Stevenson, P. ii, xii
Stewart, M. xiii,   93n,   135n
Strauss, A.L.   75(n9)
Street, B.   238
Stroud, C.   46(n6),   154

Tamarón, Marqués de   9
Therrien, M.   26(n11)

Tonkin, E.   144, 145, 146
Torres, L.   82
Torres Cacoullos, R.   93n
Tovey, H.   180
Turell, M.T. xiii,   7, 180, 194, 197,
  218(n1)
  'structural-descriptive
  approach'   159

Vallverdú, F.   51, 54, 181
Van Maanen, J.   154
Vázquez, R.   135(n4)
Veltman, C.   71
Villa, D,   28, 44

Wallerstein, I.   48
Walton, S.   149
Weinreich, U.
  'language contact'   51
Williams, A.   97
Williams, G.   74(n6),   189
Woolard, K.A.   1–2, 4, 9, 25–6(n1),
  31, 75(n18), 189, **241**
  'accommodation norm'   158
  'bilingual norm'   158
Wright, S. ii, ix,   8, 11, 26(n2)

Zentella, A.C.   81

Subject Index

ABC 33, 34
abridgement 140f, 149
acceptance 31, **45(n3)**
'accommodation norm' (Woolard) 158, 162
action structure 55, 61–2, 65, 66f, 67, 75(n15)
administration 15, 181
  Catalonia 161
  local 55, 58
  public 9, 187
  regional 58
adults/adulthood 155, 209, 218
  second-language acquisition 119–20
adverbs/adverbial phrases 126, 131–2, 134, 136(n9)
adversative connectives 78
advertising 10, 23, 24, 38–9, 168, 201
affixation/affixes 127, 130
  verbal 131
Africa 204f
African languages 78, 116, 134
African Spanish 118
Africans 133, 168, 169, 173, 203, 204
Afro-Caribbean people (Nicaragua) 142, 142t
Afro-Hispanic Caribbean varieties 134
age 33, 102, 118, 120, 123t, 127, 155, 171, 182–6, 188, 217, 218, 219(n6)
  changing abilities in Catalan 199, **208–11**
agency 12, 14, 159–60
'agency within structure' 159
agents 13, 160
  globalization 8, 23
  language spread 1
  sociolinguistic change 162
agriculture 122, 179
allophonic variation 101

ameliorism 137
Americas 27, 116, 134, 159
  'discovery' 74(n1)
Amerindians 142t
analysis of variance (ANOVA) 196(n3)
Andalusian Spanish 129
Andean Spanish 4–5, 99
Andean Spanish and the Spanish of Lima: linguistic variation and change in a contact situation **94–113**
  archmorpheme *lo* 108–10, 111, 112(n4), 113(n8)
  aspiration and elision of /s/ 103–5
  assibilation of vibrants 101–3
  characteristics of speakers 98t
  children of migrants 107–8
  conclusions 110–12
  extralinguistic variables 112(n5)
  lateral palatal 99–101, 112(n3)
  leísmo 105–8, 112(n4–6)
  migrants 106, 107
  perception test 113(n9)
  social variables 96–7, 98
Andes (Peru) 4
anglicisms 18, 43
animacy 107t
anonymity (ideology) **2**, 6
anthropology 49–50, 58
  'globalized' discipline 137
Anuarios 9
Arabic language 197
Aragonese language 197
Aranese language 197
arayano (mixed Haitian-Dominican ancestry) 5
Arayanos (AY) 117, 122, 123t, 124, 127–30, 132t, 132, 133, 135
archmorpheme *lo* 95, 99, 106, **108–10**, 111, 112(n4), 113(n8)
Argentina 76, 84, 87, 87t, 101
Argentinean Spanish 16

Argentineans 16
aristocracy 199
articles (grammatical) 83
Asia/Asians 204f, 204, 219(n4)
Asociación para el Progreso del Español como Recurso Económico 35
aspiration 99, **103–5**, 110
assibilation 95, 99, 108, 110, 111
  multiple regression analysis 102, 102t
  vibrants **101–3**
assimilation 49, 71, 73, 190
  resisted 122
Association of Academies of Spanish Language 31, 37–8
Association for Development of Spanish as Economic Asset 35
Asturian language 197
Aula Virtual de Español (AVE) 21
authenticity **2**, 4, 138, 149, 153
autobiography
  Andean Quechua 156(n1)
  linguistic 138–44, 146, 148, 150, 155, 157(n11)
auxiliary verbs 126–7
'awareness', linguistic 28
Aymara language 96
Aztec Empire 26(n7), 75(n10)

Balearic Islands 7
  foreign population (1996–2003) 204f, 205
  linguistic shift and community language (effect of demographic factors) **197–219**
Barcelona x, xiii, 158, 163, 164, 173, 175
  foreign population (1996–2005) 161
barriadas 96
barrio (district) 149
Basque Country x, 49, 74(n5), 179, 181, 197, 198(map), 201, 217
Basque language 178, 180, 197, 198, 199
Bates, E. 121
bateyes (sugar plantations) 116, 122
Belize 141
Bernal-Enríquez, Y. 81

bilingual continuum (Silva-Corvalán) 77
bilingual discourse
  Poplack and Meechan's typology (1998) 80
'bilingual norm' (Woolard) 158
bilingualism xiii, 6, 45, 53, 72, 114, 116–19, **120**, 123t, 124, 130, 135, 142, 153–5, 169, 171, 188, 193, 206
  additive 49, 74(n3)
  Catalan 201
  dangers 40
  Galicia 187
  reciprocal 158
birthplace
  changing abilities in Catalan 199, **211–13**, 215, 217
'bleaching' (Givón) 79
  'ideologies affect language change' 9
Bloque Nacionalista Galego (BNG), 189, 190, 191, 195
Bolivia 73
'boot-strapping' (Bates and Goodman) 121
border crossings (notion) 139
Borderlands/La Frontera (Anzaldúa) 36–7
borders/boundaries
  cultural **48–51**
  linguistic 68–9, 74(n5)
  national 74(n5)
  role 5
bozal 118, 121, 133
Brazil xi, 30, 74(n5)
British Association for Applied Linguistics: Linguistic Ethnography Special Interest Group 156(n1)
British Empire 141
Broadway Toyota Fabor/Pleaze 38–9
business meetings 61

cacique 55
Calca (Peru) 101
call centre, 'virtual' 10
Callahan, L. 82

Caló language 197
calques
  bound collocations, idioms,
    proverbs 81f
  conceptual/cultural 81f
  lexico-syntactic 81f
  multiple-word 81, 81f, 84, 85f, **86**,
    89t, 89, 91, 92, 93(n2)
  single-word 84, 85f, **86**, 89t,
    89–92, 93(n5)
campesinos/peasants 58, **59–64**,
  65, 95
Canada xii, 49
Canary Islands 103, 129, 205
Caribbean Basin 103, 116, 141
Caribbean English 155
Caribbean Spanish 129, 131,
  133, 134
case and gender 111
  and number 105, 108–9
  'identities of resistance' 192
Castilian language (Spanish) 19, 20,
  161, 162, 164, 166, 168, 169,
  172–6, 178–9, 193, 201
  age-old conflict with Catalan 158
  definition 176(n1)
  Galicia 179
  'national language' 15, 26(n5)
  standard 36–7
Castilian-speaker 176(n1)
Castilianization 185
Castile 99, 105
Catalan language x, xiii, 1–2, **6–7**,
  51, 178, 180
  age-old conflict with Castilian 158
  census (1986), 219(n5)
  comparative study of
    understanding, speaking,
    reading, and writing **197–219**
  'defining feature of Catalanness'
    161, 176
  definition 176(n1)
  foreign-born competence
    212–13, 215
  future 'depends on linguistic
    integration of immigrants' 205
  intergenerational transmission 201
  normalization 158, 159, 161–2, 176
  prohibited 199, 200, 201

reflexivity and knowledgeability in
  constructions of **158–77**
social use 162
varieties 219(n5)
Catalan-speakers 160
  definition 176(n1)
  maintaining Catalan with unknown
    immigrants **166–9**
Catalan-speaking 176
Catalan-speaking regions
  demographic and political changes
    (1990s) 202–5, 219(n2–4)
Catalans 49
  'Castilian oppression' 51
Catalonia 6–7, 74(n5), 179, 181,
  189, 194
  foreign immigration 204
  industrial and economic
    strength 200
  foreign population (1996–2003)
    204f, 204–5
  linguistic shift and community
    language (effect of demographic
    factors) **197–219**
  sociolinguistic make-up 158
  Latin American immigrants 6
  socio-linguistic situation 6
  Spanish-speaking Latin Americans
    xii, **158–77**
Censo de Población 203
censuses
  Catalan-speaking regions (1991,
    2001) 7, 198–9, 203, 206,
    208–11, 214, 219(n3, n5–6)
  methodological differences 208,
    219(n5–6)
  Mexico (1990) 75(n10)
  Peru (1940-) 94
  US (1990, 2000) 76
Central America 87
  'double colonization' 139, 140, 141
  see also Latin America
Central Americans 219(n4)
  'central imperial states' 74(n4)
centralization, political 178
Cervera 199
children 102, 102t, 104t, 104–12,
  149, 208, 209
  first-language acquisition 119–20

Ciutat de Mallorca (Palma)   201, 213, 214f, 215, 216f
civil registry
  prohibition of inscriptions in Catalan (1870–)   200
clash of civilizations (Huntington)   49
clergy   199
clitic systems   105, 106, 108–11
Coastal Spanish (Peru)   5
cocolos (English-speaking immigrants)   116
code of the other   **160**
code-mixing   4
  Muysken's typology   80–1
code-selection   175, 176
code-switching (CS)   56, 67, 69, 76–86, 88–92, 142, 143, 148, 156, 157(n15), 158, 162, 176
  borrowings   81, 81f, 92
  calques   81, 81f
  calques: multiple-word   81, 81f, 84, 85f, **86**, 89t, 89, 91, 92, 93(n2)
  calques: single-word   84, 85f, **86**, 89t, 89–92, 93(n5)
  functional   79
  intersentential   81f
  intrasentential   81f
  model   81f
  multiple-word   81, 81f, 84, 85f, **86**, 89t, 89
  single-word loans   84, 85f, **86**, 89t, 89, 90
  single-word switches   84, 85f, **86**, 89t, 89
  single-word transfers   81, 81f
  socio-pragmatic functions   82
  terminology   81
  transfer of meaning   81f
Colombia xii,   73, 76, 87, 87t, 164
Colombian *costeño* Spanish   164, 166, 169
Colombians   161, 164, 166, 170, 171, 173
  teenagers   163
colonial encounters   5–6, 139
colonial era   21, 74(n1), 100, 120, 154
colonial texts   139
colonialism   31, 137, 139, 143

colonization   15, 16, 27
  Spanish   75(n10)
commodification (Coupland)   **10**, **18**
commodification of language   42, 45, 46(n6)
communication rights (Kubchandani)   154
communicative practices, interethnic   145
communicative repertoire   **53–5**, 75(n10–11)
communicative schemas   55
communicative systems (Spanish)   73
community language
  linguistic shift and   **197–219**
Comparative Education (journal)   138
competence
  bilingual   24, 82
  communicative   182
  grammatical   152
  intellectual   39
  linguistic   29, 43, 44, 89, 119, 170, 171, 174, 205
  multilingual   144, 153
  native-speaker   150
  oral language (Galician)   183
  written language (Galician)   183
  see also linguistic competence
Complutense University of Madrid   38
compression of time and space (Coupland)   **10**, **18**
comunidad hispanohablante 30
Conference of Linguistic Association of Southwest (Puebla, 2001)   44
conflict   5–6
  cultural   48
congó (new-arrival immigrants, DR)   5, 122, 135
Congreso Internacional de la Lengua Española,   19, 22
conjunctions   83
consonants   95
  elision   134
constitutions   16
constructing Catalan
  'new-Catalan' perspective   **173–5**
contact
  ethno-linguistic   116, 122
  socioethnic   122

contact language 127
'contact zone' (Pratt)
oral testimony **137–57**
contact zones (multilingual): oral
testimony 5–6, **137–57**
abridgement 149
Caribbean Coast as 'contact zone'
141–3
'contact zones' between oral
testimony and 'data' 140–1
further research required 146
genre as contact zone 143–9,
156–7(n2–10)
intermediation by researcher 148–9
linguistic contact zones 143–54,
156–7(n2–16)
transcribed speech as 'contact zone'
149–54, 157(n11–16)
transcription conventions 155–6
control
political and linguistic **13**
conversation analysis 55
conversational story-telling 145
cooperatives 55
settlement of damages
(language-shift case study)
59–64, 75(n13)
copula, invariant 133
corpus linguistics x
corpus planning 181
correctness ideology 22
Costa Rica 87t, 141
Costeños (people of Caribbean Coast,
Nicaragua) 138, 139, 142, 143,
144, 147, 150
intercultural-multilingual practices
157(n10)
multilingual practices 153
council of elderly (Hñähñú) 65
'four key processes' 10, 17–18
Creole English language 142, 155
Creole expressions 144
Creole genesis 119
Creole languages 116, 123t, **132**,
135(n5), 142t, 148
Ibero-romance 125
Pan-Caribbean 134
traces 127
verbal system **124–5**

Creoles 120, 142, 142t, 145, 146
Creolization **120**, **121**
'critical ethnography' 138
'critical period' (Krashen) 127
Cuba 87t, 116, 117, 133
Cuban-Americans 82
cultural brokers 61, 63, 64,
65, 67
cultural capital (Bourdieu)
167, 186
cultural models 53, **68–72**,
75(n17–20)
shift (case-study) **64–8**,
75(n14–16)
cultural models (shift) **64–8**,
75(n14–6)
action structure 65, 66f, 67,
75(n15)
sequential structure 65, 66f,
75(n15)
verbal interaction 66f
cultural models and procedures
(CM), 56–7f, 58, 63, 64, 66f,
67, 69–73
Hispanic community (USA) **71–2**
Hñähñú 56
cultural policy (autonomous) 200
cultural resistance 54, 187
culture 5, 12, 16, 35, 84, 121, 137,
178, 180, 188
Catalan 219(n8)
dominant 24, 127
Dominican 124
East Asian 160
fragmentation 49
Galician 191–2
global 23
Haitian 124
home country 171
indigenous 64
international language 31
'invisible' 139
Latino 23
linguistic 46(n5)
mainstream 58
Mexican 72
national 58, 153, 155
oral, vernacular 55
Cuzco (Peru) 101

Dajabón (province)   116, 123,
    123(map)
damages
    language-shift (case study)   **59–64**,
        75(n13)
data   177(n4), 193, 218
    'contact zones' with oral testimony
        140–1
    Freeland   138, 139, **140–1**,   144,
        146, 148, 154, 156(n5)
    oral   82
    qualitative   136(n9)
    quantitative   185
data limitations   92, 136(n9),
    219(n2–6)
    typology of languages   74(n2)
de-regionalization   7, 216, 218
Decá (village)   65
decentralization (post-Franco)
    180, 194
    'rhetoric of progress'   135
demography   7, 28, 32, 41, 42, 48,
    76, 92, 142t
    linguistic shift and community
        language   **197–219**
demolinguistics xiii,   199, 218(n1)
desemanticization (Heine/Lehmann)
    79
determinism   75(n12)
diachronic perspectives   159, 160,
    176, 177(n2)
dialects   68, 85, 96, 103, 110, 163,
    177(n7)
    limeño 99
    phonological features   95
diglossia   51, 54, 68, 75(n18)
direct object doubling   113(n8)
discourse analysis xiii,   52, 70,
    75(n19), 158
    interactional   72
    language shift   **61–4**,   75(n13)
    micro–macro research
        (integrated)   72
    multi-layer   53, 54, 55, **61–4**,
        75(n13)
    shift in cultural models   **67–8**,
        75(n15–16)
discourse and language structure
    68–72,   75(n17–20)

discourse strategies   56
discourse structures (DS)   53, 56f, 56,
    58, 63–7, 69–73, 156(n2)
    Hispanic community (USA)   **71–2**
discourse-pragmatic functions   92
discovery   139
discrimination   162, 165, 166
    perceived   164
disembedding (Coupland)   10, **18–19**
dispute settlement   64
DMLX software   218(n1)
domain analysis   55
domestic help/workers   122, 166
dominance/domination   10, 12, 14,
    21, 64
    cultural   19
Dominican Catalans   168
Dominican Republic (DR)   5,
    123(map)
    Spanish as L2: universal processes of
        acquisition xii,   **114–36**
Dominican Spanish language   122,
    124, 127, 128, 133
Dominicans (D)   5, 115, 116, 123t,
    124, 127, 132t
    in Barcelona   165
Dominicans of Haitian descent (DH)
    117, 122, 123t, 127–30, 132t, 132,
    134, 135
double possessive   99
Dravidian languages   78
Dutch language   116

Ecuador   87t
Ecuadorean Spanish   163
Ecuadoreans   16, 161, 163
education   112, 155, 171, 178–86,
    188, 201, 209
    bilingual   33, 55, 58, 72, 73, 150
    language medium   186
    monolingual, Spanish-medium
        150
    multilingual societies   154
education system   9, 16, 21, 25,
    181, 182
educational level   96, 194, 219(n5)
educational attainment   97, 98t, 101,
    103, 104, 109t, 109, 112(n3), 186
educationalists   19

efficiency 69
EFL/ELT industry 20
Eivissa-Formentera 213, 214f,
    215, 216f
ejido 59
El País 27, 31, 32–4, 37–40, 44–5
El Salvador 87t
El Tiempo (Colombia) 161
electronic communication 11, 18, 82
    'informal written context' 79
electoral procedures 55
Elías Piña (province) 116, 123,
    123(map)
elision 99, 103–5, 110
elites 11, 15, 16, 19, 21, 23, 24–5,
    29, 200
    'agents of linguistic imperialism' 14
emigration 7, 127, 179, 202
emolinguistic ideology (López García)
    42, 45, 46(n4)
empiricism
    language conflict 51
    language shift 71, 75(n12)
    micro-macro link 52
    pluriculturalism and additive
        bilingualism 49, 74(n3)
    sibilants 103
    stigmatization of non-standard
        speech 149
empowerment
    minority languages 181
encounters
    'invisible cultures' (narrators and
        audience) 139
English language 6, 8, 13, 18, 24, 25,
    26(n4), 36, 38, 40, 44, 45, 45(n2),
    71, 142t, 144–5, 149–53, 156(n7),
    157(n12), 160, 177(n5), 181, 197
    economic and military weight 48
    'hyper-central' language (de Swaan)
        74(n2)
    sole hyper-language 47–8
    standard 37, 148
English-speaking world 10, 48
enrichment orientation 72, 74(n3)
epistemology 159, 160, 169, 172,
    176, 177(n2)
Equatorial Guinea 26(n4)
erasure (semiotic process) 42, 43

español como lengua extranjera
    (ELE) 15
    creating a global language 19–22,
        26(n10)
ethnic fundamentalism 49
ethnic groups/minorities 16, 27, 32,
    118, 190
ethnic loyalty 69
ethnic movement 191
ethnic origins 26(n4)
ethnicism 32
ethnicity 5, 123, 128t, 129t, 158,
    190–1, 192, 196(n5)
    Latino 23
    self-ascribed 155
ethnography 52, 54, 56, 72, 137, 154
    limits of traditional analysis 55
    linguistic 139
ethnolinguistic attitudes 5, 135
ethnolinguistic groups 4, 48, 49,
    57, 116
Ethnologue (Summer Institute of
    Linguists) 26(n4)
ethnology 137
etymology 105
Europe 34, 59, 179
European Union 161, 203,
    204f, 218
Europeans 141, 173, 203–4
experience 145, 153, 157(n11), 163
    educational 152
    historical and biographical 58, 63, 70
    social 64
extra-linguistic perspective 118
EZLN 73, 75(n17)

factor analysis (statistical technique)
    186, 196(n1)
'Fairclough (2001)' 8, 11
family ancestry 96, 98t
film 18, 21
flow ('concept') 14
focused grammar 42
Fongbe (substrate language) 124
forces of domination 135
foreign policy (Spain)
    language policy 34–5
fossilization (use of infinitive)
    130, 132

fractal recursivity (semiotic process) **42**
fragmentation (cultural)   68, 70, 72
frame analysis (Goffman)   56
Franco régime (1939–75)   178, 180, 197, 199, 200–1
Francophones (Canada)   49
francophonie 45
'French-speaking world'   10
French language   78, 116, 124
'super-central' language (de Swaan) 74(n2)
future temporal reference   79

Galicia   7, 197, 198(map), 201
    autonomous status   184
    effects of linguistic policy **182–5**
    external migration   198
    language contact between Galician and Spanish   **178–96**
    language survival and decline **179–82**
    language as symbol of ethnic identity   **188**, 189
    sociolinguistic study (methodology employed)   **185–7**, 196(n1)
Galicia: Autonomous Community x, 180, 190, 192, 194
    elections (2005) 195
Galician Autonomous Statutes (1981) 180
Galician language xii,   7, 21, 197, 198, 199
    active use   183
    constitutional protection (1978–)   180
    contact with Spanish (young people's linguistic attitudes) **178–96**
    geographic scope   182
    inter-generational transmission 182, 183–4, 186, 188
    number of speakers   182
    status under Spanish Constitution (1978) 194
    'strong support' (Vigo students) 187

symbol of ethnic identity 186–7, 195
    utility   186, 187–8
Galician Spanish   129
Galicianness   189
Garifuna (ethnic group)   142t
gender   29, 158
    changing abilities in Catalan 199, **210–11**
gender and number   111
Generalitat   162
generations   29
    future   110, 111
    migrants (to Lima)   97, 98t, 100, 101, 102, 102t, 104t, 104, 106, 106t, 108–11
    new   76
    younger   99, 102, 201
genre as contact zone **143–9**, 156–7(n2–10)
    performance element   147, 149
geography   18, 122, 139, 179, 180
gerund   79, 118, 128–30, 132, 135(n5), 136(n10)
global language, the   *see* English language
global languages/international languages   1, 6, 27, 42, 47, 50
    creation   **19–22**,   26(n10)
    definition   45(n1)
    standardized   29
global Spanish/international Spanish xii,   2, 3, 7, 10, 19–22, 27, 195–6, 199, 218
    conflict-imperialist framework   4
    micro perspective   4
globalization   1, 3, 27, 46(n4), 47, 50, 94, 95, 111, 112, 114, 139, 155, 180, 187, 191, 192, 202
    from below (US Latinos) **22–5**, 26(n11)
    features **19**
    linguistic   24, 48
    literature   11
    metropolitan discourse (preferred metaphor)   13–14
    top-down versus bottom-up   17

globalization in Spanish-speaking
world: linguistic imperialism or
grassroots adaptation **8–26**
contact, shift, competition 14–17,
26(n3–8)
contemporary spread of Spanish
17–19, 26(n9)
creating a global language: role of
Instituto Cervantes 19–22,
26(n10)
globalization from below: US
Latinos 22–5, 26(n11)
language ideology and globalization
9–14, 25–6(n1–2)
glocalization 52
grammar 119, 127, 131
interlanguage 120
non-standard 130
Spanish 77
standard 41
grammatical functions 91
grammatical items 83
grammatic(al)ization 4, 78–80, 86, 92
definition 79
grassroots adaptation: forces of
globalization in Spanish-speaking
world **8–26**
Greater Antilles 118
Grosjean, F. 82
Grounded Theory (Glaser and Strauss,
1967) 75(n9)
Guatemala 87, 87t
Guatemalans 16
discourse versus linguistic
structure 56

habitus (Bourdieu) 56, 69, 156(n2)
Haiti
Spanish as L2: universal processes of
acquisition xii, **114–36**
Haitian Creole (HC) 122, 124, 130,
133–5
diachronic and synchronic account
136(n8)
system **125–7**
verbal system **124–5**
Haitianized Spanish xii, 133, 135
in Cuba 133
typical features 134

Haitians (Hs) 5, 115, 117, 121–4,
127–9, 132t, 132–5
hegemonic constellation (Gramscian
sense) 63
hegemony 12, 14, 20, 43
heritage languages 76, 77, 84, 90,
94, 122
hesitation phenomena 63
heteroglossia **44**, 159, 171, 176
heteroglossic paradox 175
hierarchy 194
high modernity 28
US Latinos, la *hispanofonía* and
language ideologies **27–46**
Hispanic world 48, 71, 73
pluricentric language area, 50
'vigour' **32–4**
Hispanics 49, **71–2**, 115–16
educated 41
largest minority (USA) 76
Hispanidad 15, 47
Hispaniola 116, 165
Hispanism 21
hispanismo 30, 42
Hispanoamérica 30
hispanofonía
language ideologies of high
modernity **27–46**
historic memory 192
historiography 146, 147
history 14–15, 16, 29, 51, 58, 114,
121, 135(n2), 139, 156(n2), 165,
176, 178–9
ethnology 137
ideological 30
linguistic shift (Catalan-speaking
regions) **199–202**
social 154
sociolinguistic 159
Hñähñú language 67
Hñähñú (Otomi) people 4, 53, 54,
59, 62, 63, 65, 69
communicative universe 70
culture 75(n16)
definitions 75(n10)
homogeneity 18, 19, 48
homogenization 187, 191
worldwide economic and
political 49

Honduras   84, 87, 87t, 141
'horizon of expectation'   144, 145, 146
host countries/society   17, 23
Howard, R.   156(n1)
Hoy 37
human agents   160
hybridity   18, 19, 22, 41, 58, 98, 105, 110, 154

'Ibizan' language   219(n5)
iconization (semiotic process)   **42**
'identities of resistance' (Castells)   192
identity   21, 36, 44, 138, 141, 171
   collective   189
   cultural   35
   ethnic   50, 186–7, **188**, 189, 195
   ethnolinguistic   175
   ethnolinguistic conflict   135
   Galician   184, 186–7, 191, 194
   Hispanic   73
   hybrid   45
   immigrants   17
   Latino (in Barcelona)   170
   Latino (in USA)   37, 43–4
   linguistic   15
   national   16, 19, 20, 22, 25, 28, 30, 36, 71, 72, 176, 201
   social   158
   supranational   20
identity-formation   176, 177(n2)
identity-markers   23
ideological climate   145
ideology   2, 6, 12, 20, 43, 51, 73, 74(n3), 121, 157(n16), 159, 200
   diglossic   75(n18)
   linguistic   45, 138
   macro   50
   modernization   187
   nation, empire, Spanish language   47, 74(n1)
   nation-building   138
   nationalist   189, 195
   political   180, 189, 190, 192
   scientific   26(n2)
   support for Galician language   191
'imagined' community (Anderson)   15, 31, 187

immigrants   36, 40, 45, 71–2, 76, 120, 168–9, 173, 197–8, 202, 203f
   American (in Israel)   78
   Dominican Republic   135(n2)
   illegal   24
   Mexican (in USA)   23, 36
   sin papeles   161
   Spanish-speaking Latin American (in Catalonia)   6
immigration   16–17, 26(n8), 122, 201, 213, 215
imperialism   19
   Aztec and Inca   26(n7)
   linguistic   3, 12, 14, 15, 17, 21, 74(n1)
   post-modern   14
   see also 'linguistic imperialism: forces of globalization'
imposition   10
impoverishment (language and thought)   39
Inca (author)   135(n2)
Inca Empire   26(n7)
independence   21, 30, 191
   'decolonization'   137
   post-colonial era   14, 31, 139
Independencia (province)   116, 123, 123(map)
indigenous languages   5, 15, 21, 49, 64, 69, 112, 115
   abandoned   58
indigenous people/s   53, 74(n3), 75(n10), 135, 142
   'authentic' voices   138, 149, 153
   meetings with non-indigenous people   139
   mixed Amerindian/African/European   142t
individuals
   conflicting constructions of being addressed in Catalan   159, 160, **162–6**, 175–6, 177(n4–7)
   reasons for conflicting constructions (knowledgeability and reflexivity)   **169–73**
inequality   139, 155
   linguistic   141, 142, 143
   power   143

infinitives   117, 118, 125, **128–32,** 134, 136(n6–9), 133
   replaces subjunctive   129, 131, 132, 134
inflection   130–1
   verbal   134
inflectional reduction   121, **134**
informants
   random selection   123
   social variables   123t
   see also Freeland; Marshall
institutions
   educational   28
   Galicianization   182
   linguistic power   43
   Spanish   33
   US   28
Instituto Cervantes (1991–)   2, 3, 9, 17, 18, 31, 33–5, 155
   creating a global language   **19–22,** 26(n9–10)
   New York branch   38
Instituto Nacional de Estadística (Spain)   161, 202
instrumental language   115
integration
   immigrants and host society   17
   social   96, 101
   supra-national   48
intentionality   14
interaction
   in-group, inter-group   162, 177(n4)
   reciprocal bilingual   167
   synchronic level   176
interactional strategies   172
Interamerican Development Bank   35
intercultural-bilingual education xi, 137n
intercultural-Bilingual Education Programme (PEIB)   142, 153–4, 157(n14)
interdependence (Coupland)   **10,** **17–18**
intergenerational transmission   72
   Andean Spanish   97
   Catalan   201
   Galician   182, 183–4, 186, 188
   Quechua language (Peru)   95
   Spanish language (USA)   24, 76–7

interlanguage/s (Selinker)   **120,** 123t, **127,** 133, 134
interlocutors
   known versus unknown   **162**
   sociolinguistic knowledge   162–3
International Association for Study of Spanish in Society (SiS) xii, xiii
International Conference on Spanish Language (Valladolid, 2001)   34–5, 37
intertextuality   148

Journal of Sociolinguistics   8, 149

Kannada (Dravidian language)   78
Kikongo language   78
knowledge   3
   linguistic and socio-cultural   150
   sociolinguistic   160, 163, 171, 172, 176
knowledge-telling (Bereiter and Scardamalia)   **84**
knowledge-transformation (Bereiter and Scardamalia)   **84**
knowledgeability   159, 160, 176
   reasons for conflicting constructions   **169–73**
Kupwar (India)   78

L2   *see* second language
La Raya (speech community)   116, 122, 124, 128, 134, 135
labelling   30, 68
labour market   186, 192
landed oligarchy (Spain)   199, 200
language/s
   abstract properties   120
   colonial   95
   'core value' (Galicianness)   188
   correct usage   39
   de Swaan's typology   74(n2)
   dominant   2, 6, 7, 24, 51, 58, 67, 70, 73, 127, 150, **153,** 190–1
   dominated   51
   endangered   8–9
   foreign   22
   global total   94
   'habitual'   189–90, 192, 193, 196(n5)

language/s – *continued*
  hegemonic versus subordinate
    (social relationship) 68–9,
    75(n17–18)
  immigrant 36
  imperialist 15
  Indian 64
  'loyal companion of empire'
    (Nebrija) 47, 74(n1)
  majority 193
  minority 70
  national 58
  new, independent 80
  public 2
  standardized 181
  subordinate 73
  symbol of ethnic identity (Galicia)
    188, 189
  views (modern and
    high-modern) 27
  written 157(n14)
  see also indigenous languages
language academies 25
language accommodation/linguistic
    accommodation 127,
    193, 194
language acquisition 117–18, 128,
    148, 218(n1)
language alternation 77–8
language attitudes/linguistic attitudes
    146, 185
  analysis of variance (ANOVA)
    196(n3–4)
  factors influencing 188–94,
    196(n3–6)
language censuses/linguistic censuses
    26(n4), 205
language change/linguistic change
    x, 13, 14, 53, 99, 118
language choice 143
  functions and effects 55
language as commodity 29
language competition 9, 10, 14–17,
    21, 26(n3–8)
language conflict 6, 48–51,
    121, 155
  framed by Catalan sociolinguists
    (1970s) 51
  Mexican context 52–3,
    74–5(n8–9)

modalities 55
processes (levels of cognitive and
    discourse organization)
    55, 56f
Spanish versus Hñähñú 54, 57f
language contact x–xii, 1, 6, 7, 9,
    10, 14–17, 21, 26(n3–8), 68,
    69, 77, 80, 116–18, 120, 122,
    127, 135
  Andean Spanish and the Spanish of
    Lima 94–113
  French and Italian 78
  Spanish and English (USA)
    4, 36, 71–2, 114–15,
    115–16
  Spanish and indigenous
    languages 115
  Spanish and Quechua xi
  structuralist view 51
  Weinreich's (socio)linguistic
    metonymy 51
language contact between Galician
    and Spanish 178–96
  analysis of variance (ANOVA)
    196(n3–4)
  choice of respondents 185–6
  effects of linguistic policy in Galicia
    182–5
  factors influencing language
    attitudes amongst Vigo students
    188–94, 196(n3–6)
  language survival and decline
    (Galician context) 179–82
  language as symbol of ethnic
    identity 188
  linguistic attitudes amongst
    Vigo students 186–7,
    196(n1)
  support for societal presence of
    Galician language 187–8,
    196(n2)
language distribution 63–4
  post-diglossic 67
language dynamics 51
language education 197
language faculty
  genetically determined 119
Language and Globalization
  series ii, ix
language hierarchy 12, 143

language ideology x, 3, **9–14**, 25–6(n1–2), 31, 35
  convergence 28
  definitions 9
  local, national, global **27–9**, 45(n1–2)
  modernist 29
  Spanglish **41–5**, 46(n4–6)
language loss 52, 57, 76, 114, 209
language loyalty 122, 127, 189–90
language maintenance 51–4, 68, 180, 184, 218
language mavens 38
language minoritization 63, 68
  'not planned consciously' 70
language mixing 4, 43
language planners 181
language planning xiii, 9, 22, 45(n3), 202, 217
  legislation 199
language policing 43
language policy x, 3, 48, 50, 52, 68, 70, 176, 192, 195
  basis (micro-level findings) **72–4**
  foreign policy (Spain) **34–5**
language policy (LP) agents 21, 27
language proficiency 77, 91–2, 93, 123t, 124
language promotion 27
language purity 18–19
  'self-appointed guardians' 19
'language as recursive social practice' (Marshall) 159, 176
language resistance 54, 64
language revitalization 51
language shift 4, 7, 10, **14–17**, 26(n3–8), 51, 72, 180, 184, 190, 193, 200
  in actu and *in situ* 71
  indigenous language to Spanish 95
  macro societal factors 68, **70–2**, 75(n20)
  mechanisms 68, **69–70**, 75(n19)
  Mexican context **52–3**, 74–5(n8–9)
  modalities 53, **55–68**, 75(n12–16)
  processes (levels of cognitive and discourse organization) 55, 56f
  Quechua to Spanish 94
  see also linguistic shift

language shift: settlement of damages in cooperative (case study) **59–64**, 75(n13)
  action structure 61–2
  language distribution 63–4
  sequential structure 61
  social relations 62–3
  traces of language shift in process 63–4
language spread 9, 10, 12–13, 14, 20, 26(n3–4)
  agents 19
  Spanish (in globalized world) **17–19**, 26(n9)
language standardization 20
language structure 53
language subsystems 80
language switching 55
language universals 137
language use 184, 185, 195, 205
language variation/linguistic variation x, xii, xiii, **120**
  extra-linguistic perspective 118
lateral palatal /λ/ 95, **99–101**, 104, 105, 108, 111, 112(n3)
laterals versus non-laterals 110
Latin America/Iberoamérica 21, 30, 31, 34, 49, 74(n3), 135, 155, 179
  countries of origin 163
  independence and nation-forming 15–16
  language policy 72–3
  see also South America
Latin American Spanish x
  definition 176–7(n1)
Latin American Spanish-speaker 176–7(n1)
Latin Americans 166, 204
  migration to Catalan-speaking regions (Spain) 203
Latinoamérica 30
Latinos 114–15, 135
  origins 41
Lehmann, C. 79
leísmo 99, **105–8**, 109, 111, 112(n4–6)
  use of *le(s)* as accusative 105
leisure organizations
  'agents of linguistic imperialism' 14

lengua propia/own language (Woolard) 2, 6
Lesser Antilles 116
lexicalization 4, 78–80, 86, 92
    congruent 81
    definition 79
lifting out (Giddens) 18
Lima xi, 4–5
Lima Spanish (language) **94–113**
    'most prestigious variety' (Peru) 96
limeños (native inhabitants of Lima) 5, 95, 97–9, 101–11
lingua franca 6, 21, 22, 155
lingua franca (LF) talk (House) 150, 154–5
    English (ELF) 150
    foreign language **155**
lingua general 26(n7)
lingua propia (own language) 180
linguicism 12
linguistic citizenship 154
linguistic codes and structures (LC) 56–7f, 58, 63, 64, 66f, 67, 70–3
    Hispanic community (USA) **71–2**
linguistic competence (in Catalan)
    reading 198–9, 205, 206, 207f, 209, 209f, 211f, 211, 212f, 213f, 213, 217
    speaking 198–9, 205–17
    understanding 198–9, 205–9, 210f, 212f, 212, 213f, 214, 214f
    writing 198–9, 205, 206, 207f, 209–13, 217
    see also proficiency
linguistic contact zones **143–54**, **156–7(n2–16)**
    genre as contact zone 143–9, 156–7(n2–10)
    transcribed speech as 'contact zone' 149–54, 157(n11–16)
    see also language contact
linguistic diversity 178–9
linguistic equality 154
linguistic human rights (LHR) 138
linguistic imperialism: forces of globalization in Spanish-speaking world **8–26**
linguistic inferiority 201
linguistic 'innovation' 118

linguistic insecurity 154
Linguistic Normalization Act (*Lei de Normalizión Lingüística*, 1983) 181
linguistic processes
    universal 118–19, 120
linguistic repression 199–200
linguistic rights xi, 73, 154
linguistic shift 179, 197, 199
    micro-intensive studies **4–5**
linguistic shift and community language (Valencian Region, Balearic Islands and Catalonia) **197–219**
    background (historical and political) 199–202
    changing abilities in Catalan 198–9, 205–17, 219(n5–7)
    demographic and political changes (1990s) 202–5, 219(n2–4)
    official sources 202, 219(n3)
linguistic structure
    general theory 119
linguistic surface structure 58
linguistic transfer 118
linguistic uniformity 178
linguistic variables
    Spanish–English interaction (US Hispanic heritage learners' writing) **80–3**, 93(n1–2)
literacy 15, 16, 55, 68, 75(n11), 180, 183
literature/literary texts 84, 118
Llei de Política Lingüística (Language Policy Law, Catalonia, 1998) 161, 218
loan words 80
local, the 3
loísmo (clitic phenomenon) 106
Los Angeles 82, 92

macro/global level 1
macro perspective 54
macro social sciences 52
macro societal factors and language shift 68, **70–2**, 75(n20)
Majorca 213, 214f, 215, 216f
'Majorcan' language 219(n5)

Mapa Sociolingüisico de Galicia (MSG)
182–4, 186, 194–5
maps 123, 198
marginality 37
marginalization 41, 43
markets 33
global 28, 135
international cultural 45
linguistic 41
strategic 45
USA 42
Marshall's informants: pseudonymous
177(n5)
media 9, 19, 33, 44, 181, 201
'agents of linguistic imperialism' 14
global 10, 14, 18, 187
Hispanic 39
press 23, 32, 40, 41, 162
Spanish 40, 41
written 179
see also radio; television
Mestizo people 142t, 155
Nicaragua 142
teachers 152
methodology
ethnographic 137
sociolinguistic study (Galicia)
185–7, 196(n1)
universal processes of language
acquisition 121–4
Mexican Indian languages 52
Mexican Spanish 16
Mexican-Americans 82, 93(n2)
Mexicans 16, 36
Mexico 4, 34, 73, 74(n5), 76, 84, 87,
87t, 101
census (1990) 75(n10)
ethnicity ideology 58
federal government 75(n17)
Mexico: central highlands 53
Mexico City xi, 53
Mezquital Valley (Mexico) 53, 54
modalities of language shift
57, 57f
micro-level findings
basis for (macro) language policy
72–4
micro–macro link
integrated approaches 74(n8)

language conflict in Spanish-
speaking world 47–75
sociolinguistics 52–3,
74–5(n8–9)
sociolinguistics of Spanish (USA)
71–2
migrant/non-migrant dichotomy
(Lima) 97, 98t, 109t
migrant work/workers 54, 64
migrants 78, 102, 102t, 104t, 110,
112, 161, 172, 179, 219(n4)
Andean 95–6
first-generation 98, 100t, 100, 101,
106, 108, 111
foreign 215, 219(n3)
illegal 202, 219(n3)
second-generation 111
socio-historical examination 100
migration 48, 50, 121–2, 171, 176,
202, 203f, 215
mountain-coast (Peru) 94, 95
international 96
mestizo features 112(n1)
rural–urban 4–5, 16, 53, 95, 182
Spanish-speaking Latin Americans
to Spain 159
migration paths 177(n2)
migration pattern 213
Minorca 213, 214f, 215, 216f
'Minorcan' language 219(n5)
minoritization 3
minority languages xii, 70, 153,
159, 160, 180, 189, 190–1,
193, 199
empowerment 181
Spain 2
minority rights 74(n3)
linguistic xi, 153, 176
social 176
Miskitu language 142, 142t, 144–9,
152, 155
Miskitu people 157(n12)
mixed codes
emerging 78
new 79, 80, 93
structural pattern 80
modernity 44, 49
modernization 7, 179, 180, 192
monoculturalism 180

monoglossia   3, 42–3
   'linguistic culture' (Schiffman)
      46(n5)
monolingualism   37, 38, 50, 53,
   82, 84, 91, 95, 123t, 145, 146,
   147, 150, 155, 159, 163, 169,
   187, 188
   Catalan   200
   Galician   179
   Spanish   202
   Spanish-speakers   201
morphemes   79, 130, 133
morphology   68, 99, 120, 132
   nominal and verbal   103
   verbal   131
morphosyntactic features   99
morphosyntactic information   131
morphosyntactic system   84
Mosquito Coast   141
Mosquito Coast Creole language   142t
mother tongue   15, 24, 50, 96, 98t,
   100, 101, 127, 134, 143, 146,
   147, 149, 189
multi-competence   150, 152
multiculturalism   49, 160
   differentiated from 'pluriculturalism'
      (Hamel)   74(n3)
multilingual regions   149
multilingualism   6, 28, 30, 36, 43,
   116, **120**
   oral testimony in 'contact zone'
      137–57
   shared problem   **152–3**
multivocality   147, 148, 157(n10)
mundo hispánico   30
Murcia (Autonomous Community)
   205

Nahuatl language   26(n7), 75(n10)
narratives   148, 152, 157(n11–12)
   autobiographical   145, 156(n4–5)
narrators' voices
   re-contextualized by
      researcher   149
nation-building   15, 26(n5), 27,
   139, 141
   Latin America   16
   linguistic ideology   138
   Spain   19

nation-state   14, 15, 19, 28, 29, 49,
   73, 191
   'utopian' ideal   48
nation-state paradigm   9–10, 25
national governments   25
national unity   74(n3), 201
nationalism   9, 26(n2), 32, 150,
   155, 163
   Catalan (middle-class)   200
   Catalan-speaking regions (Spain)
      205
   ethnic   **191**
   fanatical loyalties   31
   Galician   189–90, 195
   geographic   **190**
   linguistic   29
   US   37
Native Americans   94
native speakers   48, 152
   monolingual   152
   'potency of folk concept' (Rampton)
      157(n13)
native-speaker norms   153
Navarra   197, 198(map)
neighbourhoods   96–9, 112
   'shanty-towns'   98t
neo-grammarians   118
neocolonialism   139
neoliberalism   11
neologisms   93(n2)
New Hampshire   38
New Mexico State University   44
'new migrants'
   allochthonous   158, 176
new world order   12
Nicaragua   xi, 142
   independence (1838)   141
   'mythified' national language   141
   national government   21–2
Nicaragua: Atlantic Coast   6, 21
Nicaragua: Caribbean Coast
   'contact zone'   **141–3**
   'multiethnic, plurilingual'
      region   141
   oral testimony in multilingual
      'contact zone' (whose story is it
      anyway?)   **137–57**
Nicaraguan Spanish   153
non-assibilation   110

non-lateral palatal /y/ 99, 100t,
    112(n3)
non-lexical forms 79
non-standard language 21,
    106, 128, 128t, 130–2, 150,
    157(n11)
normalization (*normalización*) 181
    language policies/programmes
        7, 197
    linguistic 187, 202
normalization planning 180–1
normative procedures 160
normativization (*normativización*) 181
noun systems 117
NP referent 106
number and gender 83, 108

object
    animate 107t
    direct 106
    human 107t
    human direct 107
    inanimate 107t
    inanimate direct 107, 108
    third-person 106
occupations 98t, 102t, 104
    semi-skilled 97, 102t
    unskilled 96, 97
Oceania 219(n4)
Office of Censor (Spain) 200
Oliver, M. de 23
oral testimony 154
    'contact zones' with 'data'
        140–1
oral traditions 146
organizations (international) 50
orientalism 137
orthographic transfer 85
orthography 93(n3)
    Nicaraguan Kriol 156(n3)
    non-standard 149
other, the 115
outsiders 194
'own language' 161, 180

Padrón Municipal de Habitantes
    (Municipal Census) 203
Paerregaard, K. 95
Palma (Ciutat de Mallorca) 201, 213,
    214f, 215, 216f

pan-Hispanic brotherhood 30
pan-Hispanic community 20
pan-Hispanism 15
parents 147, 149, 151, 155, 209
Paris 112(n2)
partial restructuring 120
participant observation 123
particles 126
'passive bilingualism' (Pujolar) 158
patois 37
Pedernales (province) 116,
    117, 123, 123(map), 128,
    133–4
perception x, 171, 173, 187–8
person and number 130, 133
personal positive evaluation (Smolicz
    and Secombe) 189, 191
Peru x, xi, 4, 84, 87, 87t, 94, 95
Peruvians 16, 171
petite bourgeoisie 199
phonemes 100, 104
phonetic erosion 134
phonological variables 110
phonological system 110
phonology x, 81, 81f, 82, 99, 101,
    111, 133
pidgin languages 132, 134
pidginization 120, 121
plural
    neutralization 108
pluralism 180
pluriculturalism 49, 73, 74(n3)
    differentiated from
        'multiculturalism'
        (Hamel) 74(n3)
'polite' behaviour (Bourdieu) 194
    'courtesy' 175
Portugal 30, 179
Portuguese language 116,
    133, 197
    'super-central' language (de Swaan)
        74(n2)
power 6, 9, 12, 14, 15, 23, 38,
    46(n5), 150, 154, 180,
    191, 199
    administrative 178
    asymmetric relations 61, 64, 69
    institutionalized 19, 21
    linguistic 45

power – *continued*
  political   178, 194
  social   154
  sociopolitical   41
  symbolic   143
power relations   63
Pozuelos   59
pragmatics   55, 111
prepositions   83, 130
prestige   68, 98, 184, 199, 202
  linguistic   41
preverbal particles   125, 126, 133
Primary Linguistic Data (PLD)   119
principle of convergence   **42–3**
Principles and Parameters (P&P)   119
proficiency
  Galician language   183
  lexical, semantic, syntactic   131
  see also competence
pronouns   130, 132t
  clitic   105, 106
  clitic: full   109, 111
  clitic: hybrid   111
  clitic: partial   108, 111
  direct object   99, 106, 108, 111
  feminine direct-object   108
  indirect object   99
  possessive   137
  reduplicated direct object   112(n6)
  subject   132, 133
  used in subject position   134
proper nouns   85
Puebla (Mexico)   44
pueblos jóvenes   96
Puerto Rico   44, 116
Puerto Ricans   82, 131
Puneños   112(n3)
Pyrenees   175

quadrilingualism   142
Quechua language   4–5, 94, 95–6,
  98t, 100, 101, 112
  lingua general 26(n7)

/r/ (assibilation versus
    non-assibilation)   101, 101t
race   122
racial inequality   5
racism   137, 152, 174
  'ethnic discrimination'   127

Rama (ethnic group)   142, 142t
Rama Coast Creole language   142t
Ramón Llull Institute (IRL)   218,
  219(n8)
reading   183
reading aloud   152
Real Academia de la Lengua Española
  (RAE)   19, 22, 31, 34–5, 37, 38,
  40, 105
  sole authority on matters of
    language (1857-)   200
recordings
  conversational speech   123
reflexivity   154, 159, 160, 176
  reasons for conflicting
    constructions   **169–73**
  unsuccessful and negative   172
reflexivity and knowledgeability in
  constructions of Catalan
  (Spanish-speaking Latin
  Americans in Catalonia)
  158–77
reggaeton   44
Registro de Extranjeros   203
Representation in Ethnography (Van
  Maanen, 1995) 154
researchers   145, 156(n5)
  pre-constructions   167
  relationship with researched   137,
    138–9, 154
  role   167
retroflex /r/   102
'rhetoric of progress' (del Valle and
  Gabriel-Stheeman)   135
Rinkeby Swedish   46(n6)
Río Piedras   116
River Coco   149
Rivera Alamo   131
Roman script   26(n7)
Romance languages   129t, 198
  morphosyntactic patterns   124
Rosario   19
rural areas   179, 182, 183

/s/ (aspiration and elision)   99,
  103–5
Sahwang Project   137n
San Antonio   23, 89
Sao Paolo   112(n2)
Santo Domingo   116

Santurce 116
satellite 182
schooling 210, 217
  language of instruction 201
schools 16, 32, 53, 54, 146, 147,
    187, 200
  compulsory teaching of Catalan
    217–18
second language 22
  teaching/learning methodology 21
second language (L2) acquisition xi,
    xiii, 117–18
  theory **118–21**
self-consciousness 160
self-correction 163
self-reporting 26(n4), 177(n4)
semantic functions 121
semantic information 135(n5)
semantic reduction (Bybee *et al.*) 79
semantic-pragmatic constraints 92
semantics of verb 134
semiotic processes 42
sentence constituents (order) 99
settlement patterns 54
sex 97, 98t, 102t, 103, 104t, 123t
shared territories **48–51**
sibilants 99, 105
  reduced 103
  retained 103
skeptron (Bourdieu) 45
slave languages 134
slaves 116
social agents 176
  knowledgeable 172
  reflexive 172
social anthropology 112(n1)
social class 5, 29, 103, 158, 186
  landed oligarchy (Spain) 199
  lower 104, 105, 110, 112
  lower middle 97, 105
  middle 33, 97, 101, 105,
    112(n3), 183–5, 195,
    200, 202
  petite bourgeoisie 199
  upper 97, 200
  upper middle 20, 105, 110, 183
social exclusion 159, 162, 166
social integration 103, 105, 167
social mobility 28, 54, 186, 192–3,
    195, 201, 202

social mobilization 190–1
social networks 105, 112
social practice
  recursive 160, 176
  reflexive 172
society 74(n6)
  Galician 184
  mainstream 54
sociocultural change
  communicative repertoire **53–5**,
    75(n10–11)
sociocultural characteristics 95
socioeconomic change 53, 71
socioeconomic conditions 94
socioeconomic status 112(n3)
sociolinguistic agencies, 159
sociolinguistic behaviour
  prediction 54
sociolinguistic change 162
sociolinguistic context 22
sociolinguistic environment 176
  heteroglossic 171
sociolinguistic knowledge
    177(n2)
sociolinguistic network analysis 52
sociolinguistics x-xii, 28,
    49–50, 58, 70, 77, 83, 98,
    112(n2), 115, 141, 143, 158,
    159, 169
  Anglo-American mainstream
    51, 74(n6)
  Catalan 51, 54
  cultural conflict approach 51
  fragmentation tendency 68, 70,
    72, 75(n8)
  Galicia **182–5**, 186, 194–5
  Hispanic 48, 50, 73–4, 75(n8)
  Hispanic situations 51
  macro 3, 54
  macro–micro link **52–3**,
    74–5(n8–9)
  micro–macro research
    (integrated) 72
  multilingual societies 138, 142
  role of cultural models, discourse
    and language structure **68–72**,
    75(n17–20)
  societal bi- and multilingualism 68
  sociological critique 74(n6)
  Spanish (in USA) 71

sociolinguists   219(n6)
  Catalan   181
  methodology (Galicia)   **185–7,**
    196(n1)
sociology
  grand theory   75(n9)
sociology of language xii,   74(n6)
South America   50, 74(n5), 87, 99,
    142t, 198, 204f
  see also Central America
South Americans   219(n4)
Southwest (USA)   82
Spain   x, 2, 19–21, 24–5, 26(n4), 38,
    40–5, 47, 49–51, 74(n5), 76, 84,
    99, 134, 166, 201, 211, 212f, 213f,
    178, 193, 215
  autonomous regions   6
  demographic and political changes
    (1990s)   **202–5,** 219(n2–4)
  economic take-off   30
  'illegal' foreigners   161
  language policy   73
  language policy (LP) agents   27, 29,
    31, 32, 40, 41, 43, 45
  linguistic minorities   159
  minority language communities **6–7**
  national problem,   30
  official (and non-official)
    languages   197
  peripheries   179
  post-Franco constitution   6
  'provincial dialects'   200
  'vigour of everything Hispanic'
    32–4
Spain: Autonomous Communities
    (post-Franco)   x, 197, 198(map),
    199, 200, 202, 205, 213
Spain: Ministry of Education and
    Culture   22
Spain: Ministry of Foreign Affairs   34,
    219(n8)
Spain: southern   103
Spanglish   3–4, 24, 27, 29, 45(n2)
  language ideologies   **41–5,**
    46(n4–6)
  no man's 'land-gauge'   **36–41**
Spanglish dictionary   44
Spanish Constitution (1978)   6,
    180, 194

Spanish dictionaries   85
Spanish Empire   15, 29, 47, 141
Spanish as Foreign Language   21, 32
Spanish government   17–20, 22, 27,
    31, 42
  global promotion of Spanish
    language   3
  language-spread policies   25
  promotion of Spanish language in
    USA   3
Spanish invasion (Peru)   94
Spanish language   6, 23, 30, 36, 38,
    39–42, 44, 54, 67, 69, 95, 98t,
    114, 123t, 124, 126–7, 130,
    134–5, 135(n5), 142t, 145–8, 151,
    155, 157(n12, n14), 160, 165,
    171, 177(n3, n5), 198, 202
  approximate system   **127**
  colloquial, in-group,
    conversational   4
  contact with Galician language
    (young people's linguistic
    attitudes)   **178–96**
  'dominant, hegemonic
    language'   1
  economic resource   32
  'four boundaries'   50
  global status   45(n1)
  globalizing power   7
  hegemony contested   1
  hybrid   22
  historical spread   27
  inter-generational transmission
    (USA)   24
  international promotion   31
  Iberian variety   176(n1)
  language guardians   40
  language of power and social
    mobility (Galicia)   180
  language shift   **63–4**
  nationalistic possessiveness   155
  native-speaker norms   157(n16)
  native-speakers   50, 150
  new variety possible (Lima)   112
  new varieties   4–5
  non-standard   18, 133, 151, 150,
    156, 156(n7)
  number of speakers   15, 26(n4)
  public image   31–2

Spanish language – *continued*
  spread in globalized world **17–19,**
    26(n9)
  standard   3–4, 22, 24–5, 129, 131,
    133, 154
  'super-central' language (de Swaan)
    48, 74(n2)
  unity 41
  use 2
  varieties 72
  see also Castilian language
Spanish language courses 20–1
Spanish as *lingua franca* (SLF,
    Nicaragua) 139–42, 147–8, 150,
    152, 154, 156, 157(n16)
  norms 157(n15)
  translation issues 143
Spanish Royal Language Academy
    (RAE) 19, 22, 31, 34–5, 37, 38,
    40, 105, 200
Spanish as second language 96
Spanish as second language
    (Dominican/Haitian border):
    universal processes of acquisition
    114–36
  extra-linguistic factors 117, 124,
    134, 135
  infinitives 128–32, 136(n6–9)
  invariant third person 132–4,
    136(n10)
  lack of ethno-sociolinguistic
    studies 122
  linguistic variables 117, 124, 134
  system of Haitian Creole (HC)
    125–7
  verbal system of *creoles* 124–5
Spanish state 21, 158, 160, 176,
    189–91, 194, 199, 200
Spanish-speakers (allochthonous) 159
Spanish-speaking Latin Americans in
    Catalonia: reflexivity and
    knowledgeability in constructions
    of Catalan **158–77**
  conflicting constructions of being
    addressed in Catalan 162–6,
    177(n4–7)
  globalization: '*ensaladilla rusa
    en el barrio chino*' 160–2,
    177(n3)

'new-Catalan' perspective of
    constructing Catalan 173–5
reasons for conflicting
    constructions: knowledgeability
    and reflexivity 169–73
tu ets mestre: Catalan-speakers
    maintaining Catalan with
    unknown immigrants 166–9
Spanish-speaking world 28–30,
    76, 84, 87, 88f, 88, 91,
    105, 213
language conflict and micro–macro
    link **47–75**
contact, shift, competition **14–17,**
    26(n3–8)
forces of globalization **8–26**
historical background 14–15
speech
  linguistic contact zone with
    'writing' 141, 143
  meta-discursive 70
  non-standard 149
speech events 54, 55, 64, 72,
    75(n14, n19)
speech forms 159
'sphere of intercultural activity'
    (Kramsch) 153
Spolsky, B. 12
standard deviation 88t
standard language 18–20, 24–5,
    40–1, 43, 77, 111, 115, 128t,
    132, 150, 181
standardization 43
statistical analysis xii–xiii, 102
  Pearson, 2-tailed 87
statistical tests 99
statistics 26(n4)
status 69, 71, 97, 112(n3)
status planning (concept) 181,
    182, 187
status symbols 184
stigmatization 63, 77, 95, 101, 102,
    104, 111, 149, 153, 193
  Andean Spanish 5
  'denial of legitimacy' 38
  'negative attitudes' 112
  'negative evaluation' 110
structuralists 118
structuration (Giddens) 160

structure and agency (Giddens) 159, 176
students 7, 84, 91, 93(n3), 114, 137n, 143–7, 150–2, 155, 156(n5), 167, 173, 175
  analysis of variance (ANOVA) 196(n3–4)
  bilingual Hispanic 80
  country of origin 87, 87t, 88f, 88, 93(n4)
  linguistic attitudes (influencing factors, Vigo) **188–94**, 195, 196(n3–6)
  linguistic attitudes (Vigo) **186–8**, 196(n1–2)
  undergraduate 185
subject noun phrase 132
subjunctive mood 125, 126
  replaced by infinitive 129, 131, 132, 134
subordinate clauses 131
subsistence farming 53
substrate languages 124
Summer Institute of Linguists 26(n4)
Sumu language 142t
Sumu-Mayangna (ethnic group) xi, 142, 142t, 155
Sumu-Mayangna language 142
SV (subject-verb) 125
Swahili 78
Switzerland 78
synchronic, the
  'clear link with the diachronic' 177(n2)
syntactic constraints 82
syntactic expressions 121
syntactic structure 130
syntactical errors 157(n16)
syntax 111

target language 119, 120, 130
teacher training, 154
teachers 65, 142, 144–5, 151, 153, 155
  indigenous **59–64**, 157(n14)
  monolingual Mestizo 152
técnicos 142
television 18, 21, 24, 54, 162, 166, 168, 201

Televisión Galega (TVG) 181
television networks 23
television programmes 182
Telugu (Dravidian language) 78
tense
  future (definite, indefinite) 125
  imperfect 125, 126
  past/perfectivity 125
  perfect 126
  preterite 126
tense, mood, aspect (TMA) 83, 126, 127, 130t, **130**, 132
  TMA inflection 121, 131
  TMA information 125
  TMA system 124
territory/territories 28
  social and geographic 2
Tex-Mex 45(n2)
theory
  'third cultures' 13
Thomason, S. 127
time 43, 51, 55, 57, 63, 92, 116, 127, 145, 147, 170, 192, 205
  'apparent' 69–70
  apparent **97**
  real xiii, **97**
TMA *see* tense; mood; aspect
tolerability (Grin) 193
tolerance of imperfection 154, 155
totalitarian concept 201
tourism/tourists 10, 15, 18, 23, 198, 201
trade unions 219(n3)
transcription 177(n5)
  'authenticity' 149, 153
  'contact zone' **149–54**, 157(n11–16)
transcription conventions 144, **155–6**, 156(n3)
transitional bilinguals (Lipski) 77
Tu ets mestre campaign (You're the teacher, Catalonia, 2003–) 162
  Catalan-speakers maintaining Catalan with unknown immigrants **166–9**

Ulwa (sub-group of Sumu people) 142, 142t, 155
UN 74(n3)

unemployment 97, 98t, 102t, 103
UNESCO 74(n3)
unified linguistic market (Bourdieu)
30
United States of America 36, 42,
48–50, 53, 74(n3–5), 114,
135, 141
gubernatorial debate in Spanish 33
Hispanic population (1990–2000)
76
Hispanization (Huntington) 36
social polarization 49
universal grammar (UG) 119–20
unreality 125, 126
urban areas 179, 182, 183, 200
urbanization 7, 16, 180, 201
Uruguayans 16
US English Foundation 29, 36, 37
US Latinos/Hispanic community
16–17, 26(n8)
census (2000) 24, 26(n11)
countries of origin 22–3
globalization from below 22–5,
26(n11)
language ideologies of high
modernity 27–46
Spanish-speaking 3, 4
US Latinos, *la hispanofonía* and
language ideologies of high
modernity 27–46
foreign policy, language policy
34–5
la hispanofonía 29–32, 45(n3)
language ideologies (local, national,
global) 27–9, 45(n1–2)
Spain and 'vigour of everything
Hispanic' 32–4
Spanglish: language ideologies
41–5, 46(n4–6)
Spanglish: no man's 'land-gauge'
36–41
US Spanish 42, 77, 83, 92, 93,
93(n2)

Valencian language 178, 180,
219(n5)
Valencian Region 7, **197–219**
Catalan Renaissance 'did not make
much headway' 200

foreign population (1996–2003)
204f, 205
linguistic shift and community
language (effect of demographic
factors) **197–219**
Valencian Region: Parliament 218
values (cultural) 190, 191
VARBRUL analysis 99, 102–4, 112(n5)
Venezuela xii, 84, 87, 87t
Venezuelans 47, 167, 170–1
verb forms 83, 124
verb types
dynamic **126**, 130t
resultative **126**
stative **126**, 127, 130t, 132t, 132
verbal hygiene 43
verbal inflection 134–5
verbal interaction pattern (VIP) 62
verbal morphology 130
verbal semantics 132
verbal system 117, 127–8
creole **124–5**
verbal system variation 99
verbs
atelic 129
canonical form 129
invariant 125
dynamic 129, 131
inflection 130–1
invariant 129t, 131, **132–4**,
136(n10)
second person 130, 133
semantic class 121, 126, 131
singular 128
third person 118, 128, 129t, 130,
131, **132–4**, 136(n10)
verbs of activity 129, 131, 132t, 132
verbs of development 129, 131
vernacular reorganization **97–8**
vibrants
assibilation **101–3**
viejo (long-established immigrants,
DR) 5, 122, 135
Vigo 185
linguistic attitudes (influencing
factors) **188–94**, 196(n3–6)
linguistic attitudes (students)
186–8, 196(n1–2)
visible minorities 162, 173

Wales   189
Wall Street Journal   34
websites   221–4, 230–1, 238, 240
  Instituto Cervantes   20
  Ramōn Llull Institute (IRL)   219(n8)
  US English, Inc.   36
West African substrate languages   124
'White Nativism'   49
word order   95
  SVO (subject-verb-object)   135
World Englishes   150
  'global English'   20, 45(n1)
  'international English'   22
world languages   47, **139**, 155, 195
  definition and role   8
writing   26(n7), 151, 152, 153, 183
  linguistic contact zone with 'speech'
    141, 143

writing ability   87
written communication   16, 84
written texts   82

Xunta de Galicia (Galician
    autonomous government)   181

yeístas   100, 101, 112(n3)
young people/youth   99, 158,
    201, 209
  language contact between
    Galician and Spanish
    178–96

Zacatecas   19
Zaire   78
Zapatista Army of National Liberation
    (EZLN)   73, 75(n17)

Lightning Source UK Ltd.
Milton Keynes UK
UKOW06n1540240415

250293UK00005B/67/P